W9-AVB-980

HOLT

HIGH SCHOOL HANDBOOK

1

John E. Warriner

HOLT, RINEHART AND WINSTON
Harcourt Brace & Company

Austin • New York • Orlando • Chicago • Atlanta
San Francisco • Boston • Dallas • Toronto • London

Author

John E. Warriner developed the organizational structure upon which *Holt High School Handbook 1* is based. He was the author of *English Composition and Grammar* and coauthor of *Elements of Writing*. He coauthored the *English Workshop* series, was general editor of the *Composition: Models and Exercises* series, and was editor of *Short Stories: Characters in Conflict*. He taught English for thirty-two years in junior and senior high school and college.

Critical Readers

Grateful acknowledgment is made to the following critical readers, who reviewed pre-publication materials for this book:

Charlotte H. Geyer
Former Language Arts
    Director
Seminole County, Florida

Nancy Light
Clarence High School
Clarence, New York

Belinda Manard
McKinley High School
Canton, Ohio

Faye Nelson
Northeast High School
Greensboro, North Carolina

Mark Sweeney
Marblehead High School
Marblehead, Massachusetts

Copyright © 1995 by Holt, Rinehart and Winston.

All rights reserved. No part of this publication may be reproduced or transmitted in any form or by any means, electronic or mechanical, including photocopy, recording, or any information storage and retrieval system, without permission in writing from the publisher.

Requests for permission to make copies of any part of the work should be mailed to: Permissions Department, Holt, Rinehart and Winston, 6277 Sea Harbor Drive, Orlando, Florida 32887-6777.

Some material in this work was previously published in ELEMENTS OF WRITING, Pupil's Edition, Third Course, copyright © 1993 by Holt, Rinehart and Winston. All rights reserved.

Acknowledgments: See pages 518–520, which are an extension of the copyright page.

Printed in the United States of America

ISBN 0-03-094638-7

6   039   98

Contents in Brief

Table of Contents

CHAPTER 8 SENTENCE STRUCTURE 190

Subject, Predicate, Complement

▶ **CHAPTER 9 WRITING COMPLETE SENTENCES** 213

CHAPTER 10 WRITING EFFECTIVE SENTENCES 225

■■■■*Part Four*

MECHANICS 244

CHAPTER 11 CAPITALIZATION 246

The Rules for Capitalization

CHAPTER *12* PUNCTUATION   266

End Marks, Commas, Semicolons, and Colons

CHAPTER *13* PUNCTUATION   293

Italics and Quotation Marks

▶ CHAPTER **14** **PUNCTUATION** 307

Apostrophes, Hyphens, Dashes, Parentheses

▶ CHAPTER **15** **SPELLING AND VOCABULARY** 325

Improving Your Spelling and
Building Your Vocabulary

■ ■ ■ ■ ■ *Part Five*

COMPOSITION 350

CHAPTER 16 THE WRITING PROCESS 352

CHAPTER 17 PARAGRAPH AND COMPOSITION STRUCTURE 376

■ ■ ■ ■ ■ ■ *Part Six*

RESOURCES 434

Exploring the Library; Using Dictionaries;
Preparing Letters, Forms, and Manuscripts

PART ONE

WRITER'S QUICK REFERENCE

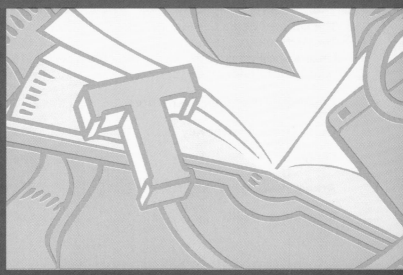

The **Writer's Quick Reference** is an alphabetical list of words, expressions, and special terms with definitions, explanations, and examples. When you run into a grammar or usage problem in the process of writing, turn to this handy section for a brief explanation. Each entry in this section will also tell you where in the handbook to turn for more information. If you don't find what you are looking for in the **Writer's Quick Reference**, look in the index on page 494.

As you'll notice, some of the examples have the following labels:

Standard or *Formal* These usages are appropriate in serious writing and speaking, such as compositions and speeches.

Informal Words and expressions with this label are standard English usages. Standard English usage is generally appropriate in conversation and in everyday writing such as personal letters.

Nonstandard These usages do not follow the guidelines of standard English.

WRITER'S QUICK REFERENCE

A

a, an   These indefinite articles refer to one member of a general group. Use *a* before words that begin with consonant sounds. Use *an* before words that begin with vowel sounds. Before numerals, letters, and abbreviations, use *a* or *an* according to the way the item is pronounced.

EXAMPLES
- **A** hawk flew over about **an** hour ago. [The *h* in *hawk* is pronounced, but the *h* in *hour* isn't.]
- Isn't this **a** one-way street?
- In "The Pear Tree," Edna St. Vincent Millay compares **an** "incredible" pear tree to **a** young girl in **a** white dress.
- **A** 1992 survey by the Motion Picture Association of America revealed that **a** movie ticket costs **an** average of $5.05 nationally.
- We went to **an** eightieth-birthday party for **a** neighbor on Saturday.
- Have you ever been to **an** NFL game?
- I got **an** A in English but **a** C in math.

abbreviation   An abbreviation is a shortened form of a word or phrase. See pages 270–271.

EXAMPLE
- **Ms**. Earline Hodges, **M.A.,** will be the speaker at the 10:00 **A.M.** meeting.

B.C. by Johnny Hart. By permission of Jonny Hart and Creators Syndicate.

abstract noun An abstract noun names an idea, a feeling, a quality, or a characteristic. See page 52.

EXAMPLES ■ Strong **emotions** such as **fear, joy,** and **sorrow** may bring about physical **changes.**
■ Many doctors are trying to learn more about the **relationship** between **emotions** and physical **health.**

accept, except *Accept* is a verb that means "to receive." *Except* may be either a verb or a preposition. As a verb, *except* means "to leave out." As a preposition, *except* means "excluding" or "other than."

EXAMPLES ■ We **accept** your apology.
■ Senior citizens will be **excepted** from the fee. [verb]
■ Everyone **except** me has seen the exhibit. [preposition]

acronym An acronym is a word formed from the first (or first few) letters of a series of words. Acronyms are written without periods. If you're not sure that your readers will know what an acronym stands for, add the complete term in parentheses the first time you use the acronym.

EXAMPLES ■ On Halloween we collected money for **UNICEF.**
■ The **laser** has many medical applications.
■ My cousin Max wants to join the **VISTA** (**V**olunteers **i**n **S**ervice **t**o **A**merica) program.

action verb An action verb is a verb that expresses physical or mental activity. See pages 61–62.

EXAMPLE ■ Last night I **dreamed** that **I had won** a marathon.

active voice A verb in the active voice expresses an action done *by* its subject. See **passive voice** and pages 108–109.

EXAMPLE ■ Every winter morning, the **father** in Robert Hayden's poem "Those Winter Sundays" **warmed** the cold house. [The action expressed by the verb *warm* is done by the subject, *father.*]

A.D., B.C. The abbreviation for the Latin phrase *anno domini,* meaning "in the year of the Lord," used with dates in the

WRITER'S QUICK REFERENCE

Christian era, is A.D. The abbreviation for "before Christ," used for dates before the Christian era, is B.C. See also **abbreviations** and page 459.

EXAMPLES ■ According to legend, Rome was founded by Romulus in 753 B.C.
■ Much of the Great Wall of China dates from the Ming dynasty (A.D. 1368–1644).

adjective An adjective is a word used to modify a noun or a pronoun. See pages 57–60.

EXAMPLE ■ Do you prefer pizza with a **thin, crisp** crust or with a **thick, doughy** crust?

adjective clause An adjective clause is a subordinate clause that modifies a noun or a pronoun. See pages 179–182.

EXAMPLE ■ The poem **that I liked best** was Leslie Marmon Silko's "In Cold Storm Light."

adjective phrase An adjective phrase is a prepositional phrase that modifies a noun or a pronoun. See pages 157–159.

EXAMPLE ■ Lightbulbs **in closets** don't need to be as bright as the ones **in reading lamps.**

adverb An adverb is a word used to modify a verb, an adjective, or another adverb. See pages 65–67.

EXAMPLE ■ **Yesterday,** the **nearly** equal opponents' tennis match lasted **much longer** than usual.

adverb clause An adverb clause is a subordinate clause that modifies a verb, an adjective, or an adverb. See pages 182–184.

EXAMPLE ■ **Until he meets Juliet,** Romeo is madly in love with Rosaline.

adverb phrase An adverb phrase is a prepositional phrase that modifies a verb, an adjective, or an adverb. See pages 159–160.

EXAMPLE ■ **At the last minute,** we changed our plans and went **to the beach for the afternoon.**

advice, advise *Advice* is a noun meaning "suggestion about what to do." *Advise* is a verb meaning "to offer a suggestion, to recommend."

EXAMPLES ▪ He gave me some excellent **advice**.
▪ She **advised** me to finish high school.

affect, effect *Affect* is a verb meaning "to influence." As a verb, *effect* means "to accomplish." As a noun, *effect* means "the result [of an action]."

EXAMPLES ▪ What he said did not **affect** my decision.
▪ The mayor has **effected** many changes during her administration. [verb]
▪ What **effect** will the new factory have on the environment? [noun]

agreement Agreement is the correspondence, or match, between grammatical forms: a verb and its subject or a pronoun and its antecedents. See **Chapter 2: Agreement.**

EXAMPLES ▪ Soledad **is working** in the computer lab; Mark and Toshio **are building** a model of the Globe Theatre.
▪ **We** have memorized **our** lines, and **all** of us **are** well prepared for **our** roles.

ain't Avoid this word in formal speaking and in all writing other than dialogue; it is nonstandard English.

all ready, already *All ready* means "all prepared." Use it if you can substitute *ready* alone without changing the meaning of the sentence. *Already* is an adverb meaning "previously."

EXAMPLES ▪ We were **all ready** to go.
▪ Sharon has **already** gone.

all right *All right* means "satisfactory," "unhurt; safe," "correct," or, in reply to a question or to introduce a remark, "yes." Although some dictionaries include *alright* as an optional spelling, it has not become standard usage.

EXAMPLES ▪ The title character in Paddy Chayefsky's play *The Mother* believes that she will be **all right** once she finds a job.
▪ **All right,** I'll be there in a minute.

all the farther, all the faster These expressions are used informally in some parts of the United States to mean "as far as" or "as fast as." Avoid them in formal situations.

| INFORMAL | This is all the faster I can go. |
| FORMAL | This is **as fast as** I can go. |

all together, altogether *All together* means "everyone in the same place." Use it if you can substitute *together* alone without changing the meaning of the sentence. *Altogether* is an adverb meaning "entirely."

EXAMPLES ▪ When we were **all together,** we voted.
▪ He was **altogether** wrong.

allusion, illusion   An allusion is an indirect reference to something. An illusion is a mistaken idea or a misleading appearance.

EXAMPLES ▪ The title of Robert Frost's poem "Out, Out—" is an **allusion** to a speech in Shakespeare's play *Macbeth.*
▪ Do you think that the snake in Roald Dahl's short story "Poison" is just an **illusion** on Harry's part?
▪ The magician's **illusions** thrilled the audience.

a lot   Always write the expression *a lot* as two words. *A lot* may be used as a noun meaning "a large number or amount" or as an adverb meaning "a great deal; very much." Avoid using *a lot* in formal writing.

EXAMPLES ▪ I have **a lot** of homework tonight. [noun]
▪ You seem **a lot** happier today. [adverb]

already   See **all ready, already.**

altogether   See **all together, altogether.**

ambiguous reference   An error involving ambiguous reference occurs when a pronoun can refer to either of two antecedents. See pages 130–131.

AMBIGUOUS	Beverly told LaShonda that Bob had called her.
CLEAR	"Bob called me," Beverly told LaShonda.
CLEAR	"Bob called you," Beverly told LaShonda.

among   See **between, among.**

A.M., P.M.   The abbreviation for the Latin phrase *ante meridiem,* meaning "before noon," used with times from midnight to noon, is A.M. The abbreviation for the Latin phrase *post meridiem,* meaning "after noon," used with times from noon to midnight, is *P.M.* See also **abbreviations** and pages 460–461.

EXAMPLE   ■ Mrs. Alma Jefferson will pick us up at exactly 7:30 A.M.

an See **a, an.**

and etc.   The abbreviation for the Latin phrase *et cetera,* meaning "and other things" is *etc.* Do not use *and* with *etc.*

EXAMPLE   ■ My younger sister collects string, bottle caps, stickers, **etc.** [*not* and etc.]

antecedent   An antecedent is the word a pronoun stands for. See pages 54–55 and 88–90.

EXAMPLE   ■ **Flo** gave **Jesse** and **Roberto** the souvenirs **she** had bought for **them.** [*Flo* is the antecedent of *she. Jesse* and *Roberto* are the antecedents of *them.*]

antonym   An antonym is a word that is opposite in meaning to another word.

EXAMPLES   ■ The **huge** Great Dane towers over the **tiny** Chihuahua.
    ■ **Long** books are better than **short** ones.

anyways, anywheres   Use these words (and others like them, such as *everywheres, nowheres,* and *somewheres*) without the final *s.*

EXAMPLES   ■ I have to baby-sit tonight **anyway** [*not* anyways].
    ■ I can't find my math book **anywhere** [*not* anywheres].

appositive   An appositive is a noun or a pronoun placed beside another noun or pronoun to identify or explain it. See page 170.

EXAMPLE   ■ Novelist **Pearl Buck** spent her early years in China. [*Pearl Buck* identifies the noun *novelist.*]

appositive phrase   An appositive phrase is made up of an appositive and its modifiers. See pages 170–171.

EXAMPLE   ■ Pearl Buck, **the daughter of American mis-
              sionaries,** translated the Chinese classic *Shui
              hu chuan* under the title *All Men Are
              Brothers.* [*The* and the prepositional phrase
              of American missionaries modify the apposi-
              tive *daughter.*]

article *A, an,* and *the,* the most frequently used adjectives,
are called articles. See pages 57–58.

as See **like, as.**

as if See **like, as if.**

at Do not use *at* after *where.*

NONSTANDARD   This is where I live at.
STANDARD   This is **where** I live.

B

---

bad, badly *Bad* is an adjective. *Badly* is an adverb. In standard English, only the adjective form, *bad,* should follow a
linking verb, such as *feel, see, hear, taste,* or *smell,* or forms of
the verb *be.*

NONSTANDARD   Does this leftover stew smell badly to
                you?
STANDARD   Does this leftover stew smell **bad** to
                you?

 NOTE The expression *feel badly* has become acceptable in
informal situations, but use *feel bad* in formal speaking and writing.

base word A base word is a word that is complete by itself
without prefixes or suffixes.

EXAMPLES ■ agree
          ■ hazard

Often, a prefix or suffix can be added to a base word.

EXAMPLES ■ **dis** + agree = **dis**agree
          ■ hazard + **ous** = hazard**ous**

See page 345.

B.C. See **A.D., B.C.**

being as, being that   Use *since* or *because* instead of these expressions.

EXAMPLE   ■ **Because** [*not* Being as] President Bill Clinton admires Maya Angelou's writing, he invited her to write a poem for his inauguration.

beside, besides   *Beside* is a preposition that means "by the side of" or "next to." As a preposition, *besides* means "in addition to" or "other than." As an adverb, *besides* means "moreover."

EXAMPLES   ■ Sit **beside** me on the couch. [preposition]
■ **Besides** songs and dances, the show featured several comedy sketches. [preposition]
■ Who **besides** you and Jerry volunteered? [preposition]
■ I don't want to go; **besides,** it's starting to snow. [adverb]

between, among   Use *between* when you are referring to two things at a time, even though they may be part of a group consisting of more than two.

EXAMPLES   ■ Take the seat **between** Alicia and me in the third row.
■ The manager could not decide which of the four players to select because there was not much difference **between** them. [Although there are more than two players, each one is being compared with the others separately.]

Use *among* when you are thinking of a group rather than of separate individuals.

EXAMPLES   ■ We were able to collect only ten dollars **among** the four of us.
■ There was some confusion **among** the jurors about one part of the defendant's testimony. [The jurors are thought of as a group.]

borrow, lend   The verb *borrow* means "to take [something] temporarily." The verb *lend* means "to give [something] temporarily." The principal parts of *lend* are *lend, (is) lending, lent, (have) lent.*

WRITER'S QUICK REFERENCE

EXAMPLE   ■ In Guy de Maupassant's short story "The Necklace," the Loisels **borrow** money to replace the missing jewelry that a wealthy friend had **lent** Mathilde Loisel.

Loan is sometimes used in place of *lend* in informal speech.

brake, break   As a verb, *brake* means "to slow down or stop." As a noun, it means "a device for slowing down or stopping." As a verb, *break* means "to cause to come apart; to shatter." As a noun, it means "a fracture" or "a short rest."

EXAMPLES   ■ The alert driver quickly **braked** the car. [verb]
■ The **brakes** on our car are good. [noun]
■ A high-pitched sound can **break** glass. [verb]
■ The doctor wants to check the **break** in my wrist in two weeks. [noun]
■ We'll take a **break** at 3 P.M. [noun]

bring, take   *Bring* means "to come carrying something." *Take* means "to go carrying something." Think of *bring* as related to *come;* think of *take* as related to *go.*

EXAMPLES   ■ **Bring** that box over here.
■ Now **take** it down to the basement.

bust, busted   Avoid using these words as verbs. Use a form of either *burst* or *break,* depending on the meaning.

EXAMPLES   ■ The balloon **burst** [*not* busted] loudly.
■ The firefighters **broke** [*not* busted] a window.

but, only   See **double negative.**

C

---

call number   A call number is the number and letter code that a library assigns to a book. The call number tells how the book has been classified and where it is shelved. See page 436.

can't hardly, can't scarcely   See **double negative.**

WRITER'S QUICK REFERENCE

capital, capitol As a noun, *capital* means "center of government" or "wealth." As an adjective, it means "punishable by death," "of major importance," or "uppercase." *Capitol* is a noun meaning "a building in which a legislature meets." It is capitalized when it refers to a building for a national legislature.

EXAMPLES
- Raleigh is the **capital** of North Carolina. [noun]
- Mrs. Ortiz needs more **capital** to modernize her factory. [noun]
- Killing a police officer is a **capital** crime. [adjective]
- I made a **capital** error in my report. [adjective]
- You need a **capital** letter here. [adjective]
- In Raleigh, the **capitol** is on Fayetteville Street.
- Last summer we visited the **Capitol** in Washington, D.C.

case Case is the form of a noun or pronoun that shows how it is used. The three cases are the nominative, the objective, and the possessive. See pages 119–125.

NOMINATIVE	**Thelma** promised that **she** would help.
OBJECTIVE	Will you sit with **Sam** and **me** at the **concert**?
POSSESSIVE	**My** skateboard needs **its** wheels oiled.

choose, chose *Choose* (pronounced *chooz*) is the present tense form; *chose* (pronounced *chōz*) is the past tense form.

EXAMPLES
- You may **choose** your own partner.
- The committee **chose** to postpone the meeting.

clause A clause is a word group that contains a subject and its predicate and is used as a sentence or part of a sentence. See also **independent clause, subordinate clause,** and **Chapter 7: Clauses.**

EXAMPLES
- S   V
- He saw a meteor shower last night. [one clause]
- S   V   S V
- Although the shower was late at night, it was worth seeing. [two clauses]

coarse, course   *Coarse* is an adjective meaning "rough" or "crude." *Course* is a noun meaning "a path of action," "a unit of study," "a track or way," or "one part of a meal." With *of, course* means "naturally" or "certainly."

EXAMPLES   ■ This **coarse** fabric is very durable.
■ He never uses **coarse** language.
■ The airplane strayed off its **course** in the storm.
■ I'm taking an algebra **course**.
■ The main **course** at the banquet was roasted turkey with dressing.
■ All cats, **of course,** are predators.
■ **Of course,** you're invited.

collective noun   A collective noun is singular in form but names a group of persons or things. See pages 53 and 83.

EXAMPLE   ■ A **crowd** gathered to watch the film crew.

comma splice   A comma splice is a run-on sentence in which only a comma separates independent clauses. See also **fused sentence, run-on sentence,** and pages 220–223.

COMMA SPLICE   My birthday fell on a Saturday this year, it fell on a Friday last year.

REVISED   My birthday fell on a Saturday this year, **but** it fell on a Friday last year.

REVISED   My birthday fell on a Saturday this year; it fell on a Friday last year.

REVISED   My birthday fell on a Saturday this year. **Last year, however,** it fell on a Friday.

common noun   A common noun is a general name for a person, place, thing, or idea. It is not capitalized. See pages 51–52 and 249.

EXAMPLE   ■ In George Orwell's **novel** *Animal Farm,* a **pig** uses **propaganda** to control the other **animals.**

comparative degree   The comparative degree is the form a modifier takes when it is used to compare two persons or things. See pages 140–145.

EXAMPLE   ■ Carlota's role was **larger** than Alma's, but Alma received **more** applause.

complement A complement is a word or group of words that completes the meaning of a verb. See also **direct object, indirect object, predicate adjective, predicate nominative, subject complement,** and pages 200–204.

complement, compliment As a noun, *complement* means "something that makes whole or complete." As a verb, it means "to make whole or complete." As a noun, *compliment* means "praise." As a verb, it means "to express praise."

EXAMPLES
- This book will serve as a **complement** to my set of mystery novels. [noun]
- The rug **complemented** the cozy room. [verb]
- Learning to accept **compliments** gracefully takes practice. [noun]
- Ms. García **complimented** us on our good behavior. [verb]

complex sentence A complex sentence has one independent clause and at least one subordinate clause. See page 208.

EXAMPLE
- Although she doesn't mind being alone, Audrey also enjoys getting together with friends. [subordinate clause/independent clause]

compliment See **complement, compliment.**

compound-complex sentence A compound-complex sentence has two or more independent clauses and at least one subordinate clause. See pages 208–209.

EXAMPLE
- Tomás hopes that he will be able to go with us, but he isn't sure whether his parents will let him. [independent clause/subordinate clause/independent clause/subordinate clause]

compound noun A compound noun consists of two or more words used together as a single noun. See page 53.

EXAMPLE
- The accident on the **freeway** during **rush hour** caused a massive **tie-up.**

compound sentence A compound sentence has two or more independent clauses but no subordinate clauses. See pages 207–208.

EXAMPLE ■ **Zora Neale Hurston studied African American folklore, and she drew on her findings in her fiction.** [two independent clauses]

compound subject A compound subject consists of two or more subjects that are joined by a conjunction and that have the same verb. See pages 81–82 and 198.

EXAMPLE ■ **Sally** and **Elvin** are designing posters for the play.

compound verb A compound verb consists of two or more verbs that are joined by a conjunction and that have the same subject. See page 199.

EXAMPLE ■ **Odysseus slays** Penelope's suitors and **reclaims** his kingdom.

concrete noun A concrete noun names an object that can be perceived by the senses. See page 52.

EXAMPLE ■ **The passengers** on board the **bus** complained about the heavy **fumes.**

conjugating Conjugating means listing all the forms of a verb in all its tenses. See pages 102–103 and 109–110.

conjunction A conjunction is a word used to join words or groups of words. See pages 69–70.

EXAMPLE ■ **Either** Kwam **or** Ben will sell the tickets **and** collect the money.

conjunctive adverb A conjunctive adverb is an adverb used as a connecting word between independent clauses in a compound sentence. See page 222.

EXAMPLE ■ Sherlock Holmes is a fictional character; **however**, many people are convinced that he actually existed.

connotation A word's connotations are the feelings associated with the word. See page 344. See also **denotation.**

consul, council, counsel *Consul* is a noun meaning "a representative of a foreign country." *Council* is a noun meaning "a group called together to accomplish a job." As a noun, *counsel* means "advice." As a verb, it means "to give advice."

EXAMPLES ■ The French **consul** was the guest of honor at the banquet.
■ The city **council** will debate the issue.
■ I'm grateful for your **counsel.** [noun]
■ Did the doctor **counsel** her to get more rest? [verb]

context The context of a word includes the surrounding words and the way the word is used. See pages 342–344.

contraction A contraction is a shortened form of a word, a figure, or a group of words. Apostrophes in contractions indicate where letters or numerals have been omitted. See pages 313–314.

EXAMPLE ■ Winsie said **she'd** meet us at the bus stop at seven **o'clock** unless her alarm **doesn't** go off.

coordinating conjunction A coordinating conjunction joins parallel words, phrases, or clauses. See page 69.

EXAMPLE ■ The TV in Colette Inez's poem "Slumnight" is like a person who keeps law **and** order, **for** the TV holds its viewers captive.

correlative conjunctions Correlative conjunctions are used in pairs to join parallel words, phrases, or clauses. See pages 69–70.

EXAMPLE ■ **Neither** Jack **nor** Brian has seen the movie yet.

could of See **of.**

council See **consul, council, counsel.**

councilor, counselor A councilor is a member of a council. A counselor is a person who gives advice.

EXAMPLES ■ My mother introduced Dr. Watkins, the new **councilor.**
■ Sir, I don't think I'm qualified to act as your **counselor.**

counsel See **consul, council, counsel.**

counselor See **councilor, counselor.**

course See **coarse, course.**

WRITER'S QUICK REFERENCE

D

dangling modifier   A dangling modifier is a modifying word, phrase, or clause that does not clearly and sensibly modify a word or a group of words in a sentence. See pages 145–147.

DANGLING   While eating lunch in the cafeteria, the fire alarm sounded. [Who was eating lunch in the cafeteria?]

REVISED   While eating lunch in the cafeteria, we heard the fire alarm sounding.

REVISED   While we were eating lunch in the cafeteria, the fire alarm sounded.

declarative sentence   A declarative sentence makes a statement and is followed by a period. See pages 205 and 268.

EXAMPLE   ■ Of all his novels, Charles Dickens liked the autobiographical *David Copperfield* best.

denotation   A word's denotation is its dictionary definition. See page 344. See also **connotation**.

dependent clause   See **subordinate clause**.

des'ert, desert', dessert'   *Des'ert* is a noun meaning "a dry region." *Desert'* is a verb meaning "to leave or abandon." *Dessert'* is a noun meaning "the final course of a meal."

The Far Side copyright 1985 FarWorks, Inc. Distributed by Universal Press Syndicate. Reprinted with permission. All rights reserved.

"Quick, Abdul! Desert! ... One 's' or two?"

EXAMPLES ▪ The Sahara, in Africa, is the world's largest **desert.** [noun]
▪ She would never **desert** her comrades. [verb]
▪ What would you like for **dessert** tonight?

direct object A direct object is a noun or pronoun that receives the action of the verb or shows the result of the action. It answers the question "Whom?" or "What?" after a transitive verb. See page 203.

EXAMPLE ▪ Have you ever tasted **sushi?**

direct quotation A direct quotation is a reproduction of a person's exact words, enclosed in quotation marks. See pages 298–302.

EXAMPLE ▪ What a relief it was to hear Mr. Clark say, **"This will be an open-book test"**!

See also **indirect quotation.**

discover, invent *Discover* means "to be the first to find, see, or learn about something that already exists." *Invent* means "to be the first to do or make something."

EXAMPLES ▪ Marguerite Perey **discovered** the element francium.
▪ The zipper was **invented** in 1893.

done *Done* is the past participle of *do.* Avoid using *done* for *did,* which is the past form of *do* and which does not require an auxiliary verb. When *done* is used as an adjective, it does not require an auxiliary verb.

NONSTANDARD   The hurricane done a lot of damage in our area.
STANDARD   The hurricane **has done** a lot of damage in our area.
STANDARD   The hurricane **did** a lot of damage in our area.
STANDARD   My science project is nearly **done.**

don't, doesn't *Don't* is the contraction of *do not. Doesn't* is the contraction of *does not.* Use *doesn't,* not *don't,* with *he, she, it, this,* and singular nouns.

EXAMPLES   ■ It **doesn't** [*not* don't] matter.
             ■ The bus **doesn't** [*not* don't] stop at this
               corner.

double comparison   Double comparison is the use of two comparative forms (usually *more* and *-er*) or two superlative forms (usually *most* and *-est*) to express comparison. In standard usage, the single comparative form is enough. See page 144.

NONSTANDARD   Tena is more better at math than I am.
   STANDARD   Tena is **better** at math than I am.

double negative   A double negative is the use of two negative words when one is enough.

Common Negative Words		
barely	never	not (-n't)
but (meaning	no	nothing
"only")	nobody	nowhere
hardly	none	only
neither	no one	scarcely

NONSTANDARD   That answer doesn't make no sense.
   STANDARD   That answer **doesn't make any** sense.
   STANDARD   That answer **makes no** sense.

NONSTANDARD   The field trip won't cost us nothing.
   STANDARD   The field trip **won't cost us anything.**
   STANDARD   The field trip **will cost us nothing.**

NONSTANDARD   We wanted grapes, but there weren't none.
   STANDARD   We wanted grapes, but there **weren't any.**
   STANDARD   We wanted grapes, but there **were none.**

NOTE   Avoid the common error of using *-n't,* the contraction of *not,* with another negative word, such as *barely, hardly,* or *scarcely.*

NONSTANDARD   I can't hardly turn the key in the
               lock.
   STANDARD   I can **hardly** turn the key in the lock.

NONSTANDARD   We haven't scarcely enough
               time.
   STANDARD   We have **scarcely** enough time.

WRITER'S QUICK REFERENCE

The words *but* and *only* are considered negative words when they are used as adverbs meaning "no more than." In such cases, using another negative word with *but* or *only* is considered informal usage.

INFORMAL   I don't need but two dollars.
FORMAL   I need but two dollars.

double subject   A double-subject error occurs when an unnecessary pronoun is used after the subject of a sentence. See **he, she, it, they.**

E

effect   See **affect, effect.**

emigrate, immigrate   *Emigrate* means "to leave a country or a region to settle elsewhere." *Immigrate* means "to come into a country or a region to settle there."

EXAMPLES   ■ In his autobiography, *Barrio Boy,* Ernesto Galarza recounts how he and his family **emigrated** from Mexico.
           ■ The Galarzas **immigrated** to the United States and eventually settled in Sacramento, California.

end marks   End marks are punctuation marks (periods, question marks, or exclamation points) used to indicate the purpose of a sentence. See pages 268–271.

essential clause, essential phrase   An essential (or **restrictive**) clause or phrase is one that is necessary to the meaning of a sentence. Commas are not used with essential clauses and phrases. See pages 275–276.

EXAMPLES   ■ All students **who have more than three unexcused absences in one grading period** will be suspended. [essential clause]
           ■ The girl **standing next to me in this picture** is my next-door neighbor. [essential phrase]

etc.   See **and etc.**

etymology The etymology of a word is its origin and history. See page 443.

everywheres See **anyways, anywheres.**

except See **accept, except.**

exclamatory sentence An exclamatory sentence expresses strong feeling and is followed by an exclamation point. See pages 206 and 269.

EXAMPLE   ■ What a great movie that was!

F

---

fewer, less *Fewer* tells "how many"; it is used with plural nouns. *Less* tells "how much"; it is used with singular nouns.

EXAMPLES   ■ There are **fewer** gypsy moths this year.
            ■ They have done **less** damage to the trees.

formally, formerly *Formally* means "properly; according to strict rules." *Formerly* means "previously; in the past."

EXAMPLES   ■ Should he be **formally** introduced?
            ■ The new consul was **formerly** a professor.

fragment See **sentence fragment.**

fused sentence A fused sentence is a run-on sentence in which there is no punctuation separating the run-together sentences. See also **comma splice, run-on sentence,** and pages 220–223.

FUSED   I enjoyed reading *Hisako's Mysteries* by Yoshiko Uchida it shows what everyday life in Japan is like.

REVISED   I enjoyed reading *Hisako's Mysteries* by Yoshiko Uchida. It shows what everyday life in Japan is like.

REVISED   I enjoyed reading *Hisako's Mysteries* by Yoshiko Uchida because it shows what everyday life in Japan is like.

G

general reference A general reference occurs when a pronoun refers to a general idea rather than to a specific word or group of words. See page 131.

GENERAL   The museum is being remodeled to meet the needs of people who have disabilities, and I support that.

REVISED   I support the fact that the museum is being remodeled to meet the needs of people who have disabilities.

REVISED   The museum is being remodeled to meet the needs of people who have disabilities, an action that I support.

gerund A gerund is a verb form ending in *-ing* that is used as a noun. See pages 164–165.

EXAMPLE   ■ **Shoplifting** costs store owners millions of dollars a year.

gerund phrase A gerund phrase consists of a gerund and its modifiers and complements. See pages 165–166.

EXAMPLE   ■ Often, you can make a complex process easier to understand by **using visuals such as charts, graphs, and diagrams.**

good, well *Good* is an adjective. *Well* may be used as an adjective or an adverb. Never use *good* to modify a verb; instead, use *well* as an adverb meaning "capably" or "satisfactorily."

NONSTANDARD   Juan Gonzáles played good.

STANDARD   Juan Gonzáles played **well**.

As an adjective, *well* means "healthy" or "satisfactory in appearance or condition."

EXAMPLES   ■ She does not feel **well**.
            ■ You look **well** in your new suit.
            ■ The teacher made sure Jani was **well**.

NOTE *Feel good* and *feel well* mean different things. *Feel good* means "to feel happy or pleased." *Feel well* simply means "to feel healthy."

WRITER'S QUICK REFERENCE

EXAMPLES   ■ The news made her feel **good.**
             ■ I didn't feel **well,** so I went home.

Good is often used as an adverb in conversation, but it should not be used that way in writing.

H

---

had of See **of.**

had ought, hadn't ought Unlike other verbs, *ought* is not used with *had.*

NONSTANDARD   Lee had ought to plan better; he hadn't ought to leave his packing until the last minute.
STANDARD   Lee **ought** to plan better; he **ought not** to leave his packing until the last minute.
STANDARD   Lee **should** plan better; he **shouldn't** leave his packing until the last minute.

hardly See **double negative.**

hear, here   *Hear* means "to receive sounds through the ears." *Here* means "at this place."

EXAMPLES   ■ Did you **hear** the president's speech?
             ■ The bus will be **here** soon.

helping verb A helping verb works together with a main verb to form a verb phrase. Helping verbs include all forms of the verbs *be* and *have,* among others. (For a list of helping verbs, see page 64.)

EXAMPLES   ■ Liz **has been** working all weekend!
             ■ How **does** she do it?
             ■ She **must have** been tired this evening.

he, she, it, they   Do not use an unnecessary pronoun after the subject of a clause or a sentence. This error is called the *double subject.*

NONSTANDARD   My mother she grows all her own herbs.
    STANDARD   My mother grows all her own herbs.

hisself, theirselves In formal situations, do not use these words for *himself* and *themselves.*

EXAMPLE ■ Ken hurt **himself** [*not* hisself] skiing.

I

---

illusion See **allusion, illusion.**

immigrate See **emigrate, immigrate.**

imperative sentence An imperative sentence gives a command or makes a request. It is followed by either a period or an exclamation point. See pages 205–206 and 270.

EXAMPLES ■ Don't slam the door! [command]
■ Please be seated. [request]

imply, infer *Imply* means "to suggest indirectly." *Infer* means "to interpret" or "to draw a conclusion" [from a remark or an action].

EXAMPLES ■ Doug **implied** that he will vote for me.
■ From Doug's remark, I **inferred** that he will vote for me.

indefinite pronoun An indefinite pronoun does not refer to a specific person or thing. See pages 56–57.

EXAMPLE ■ **Nobody** got the answer to the last **one** right.

indefinite reference An indefinite reference occurs when the pronoun *you, it,* or *they* refers to no particular person or thing. See page 132.

INDEFINITE On the school calendar **it** lists Friday as a teacher planning day.
REVISED The school calendar lists Friday as a teacher planning day.

independent clause An independent (or main) clause is a group of words that contains a verb and its subject and that expresses a complete thought. An independent clause can stand by itself. See pages 177–178.

EXAMPLE ■ While you were out, **Eli called you.**

indirect object An indirect object is a noun or pronoun that precedes a direct object and that usually tells *to whom* or *for whom* (or *to what* or *for what*) the action of the verb is done. See page 204.

EXAMPLE   ■ Don't forget to send **Grandpa** a thank-you note.

indirect quotation An indirect quotation is a rewording, or paraphrasing, of something a person has said. See page 298.

EXAMPLE   ■ Ms. Velarde said **that her hobby is playing chess.**

See also **direct quotation.**

infinitive An infinitive is a verb form, usually preceded by *to,* that can be used as a noun, an adjective, or an adverb. See pages 166–167.

EXAMPLE   ■ Are you ready **to go**?

infinitive phrase An infinitive phrase consists of an infinitive together with its modifiers and complements. See pages 167–168.

EXAMPLE   ■ I didn't mean **to hurt your feelings.**

interjection An interjection is a word used to express emotion. It has no grammatical relation to the rest of the sentence. See pages 70–71.

EXAMPLE   ■ **Ouch!** These mosquitoes are ferocious!

interrogative sentence An interrogative sentence asks a question and is followed by a question mark. See pages 206 and 268–269.

EXAMPLE   ■ Have you read John Steinbeck's *Travels with Charley* ?

intransitive verb An intransitive verb expresses action (or tells something about the subject) without passing the action from a doer to a receiver. See pages 61–62.

EXAMPLE   ■ The children **squirmed** and **fidgeted** until the movie **began.**

invent See **discover, invent.**

irregular verb   An irregular verb is a verb that forms its past and past participle in some way other than by adding *-d* or *-ed* to the base form. See pages 97–100.

EXAMPLE   ■ You should have **seen** the look on his face when we **threw** open the door and **sang** "Happy Birthday" to him!

it   See **he, she, it, they.**

its, it's   *Its* is the possessive form of *it. It's* is the contraction of *it is* or *it has.*

EXAMPLES   ■ The bird stopped **its** singing.
■ **It's** [It is] an easy problem.
■ **It's** [It has] been raining since noon.

K

kind of a, sort of a   In formal situations, omit the *a.*

INFORMAL   What kind of a snake was it?
  FORMAL   What **kind of** snake was it?

kind of, sort of   Avoid using these terms in formal situations. Instead, use *somewhat* or *rather.*

INFORMAL   We were kind of surprised to see him there.
  FORMAL   We were **somewhat** [*or* **rather**] surprised to see him there.

kind(s), sort(s), type(s)   Use *this* or *that* with the singular form of each of these nouns. Use *these* or *those* with the plural form.

EXAMPLE   ■ I like **this kind** of jeans better than any of **those** other **kinds.**

L

lay   See **lie, lay.**

lead, led, lead   *Lead* (pronounced "lĕd") is a verb meaning "to go first" or "to guide." *Led* is the past tense of *lead. Lead* (pronounced "led") is a noun meaning "a heavy metal" or "graphite in a pencil."

EXAMPLES ■ I'll **lead** the way. [verb]
■ Last week Marisa **led** us to victory. [verb]
■ We made fishing sinkers out of **lead.** [noun]
■ To draw fine lines, use a sharp **lead.** [noun]

learn, teach   *Learn* means "to acquire knowledge." *Teach* means "to instruct" or "to show how."

EXAMPLE ■ Some of our coaches **teach** classes in gymnastics, where young gymnasts can **learn** many techniques.

leave, let   *Leave* means "to go away" or "to depart from." *Let* means "to allow" or "to permit." Avoid using *leave* for *let.*

NONSTANDARD Leave her speak if she insists.
STANDARD **Let** her speak if she insists.
STANDARD Today we'll **leave** on time for a change.
STANDARD Mom **let** [*not* left] Jaime out at the corner.

led See **lead, led, lead.**

lend See **borrow, lend.**

less See **fewer, less.**

let See **leave, let.**

lie, lay   The verb *lie* means "to rest" or "to stay, recline, or remain in a certain position." *Lie* never takes an object. The verb *lay* means "to put [something] in a place." *Lay* usually takes an object. See pages 113–114.

EXAMPLES ■ Our town **lies** between Dallas and San Antonio. [no object]
■ **Lay** your paper about Kwanzaa on Mr. Palmer's desk. [*Paper* is the object of *lay.*]

like, as   In informal English, the preposition *like* is often used as a conjunction meaning "as." In formal English, use *like* to introduce a prepositional phrase, and use *as* to introduce a subordinate clause.

NONSTANDARD ■ We should do like our coach recommends.

STANDARD ■ We should do **as** our coach recommends. [*Our coach recommends* is a clause and needs the subordinating conjunction *as* to introduce it.]

■ She looks **like** her sister. [The preposition *like* introduces the phrase *like her sister.*]

like, as if In formal situations, *like* should not be used for the compound conjunction *as if* or *as though.*

EXAMPLE ■ Scamp looks **as though** [*not* like] he has been in the swamp again.

linking verb A linking verb connects the subject of a sentence with a word that identifies or describes the subject. See pages 62–63.

EXAMPLES ■ Sensing the approaching storm, the dog **grew** restless.

■ Jason **is** my mother's cousin.

loose, lose, loss As an adjective, *loose* (pronounced "loos") means "free, unbound;" "not tight;" or "not firmly fastened." As an adverb, it means "in a loose manner." As a verb, it means "to let go." *Lose* (pronounced "looz") is a verb meaning "to misplace," "to suffer a loss," or "to fail to win or gain." *Loss* is a noun meaning "an instance of misplacing or of failing to win or gain" or "the person, thing, or amount lost."

EXAMPLES ■ We reported the **loose** dog to the animal shelter. [adjective]

■ **Loose** clothing is comfortable in hot weather. [adjective]

■ The string on the package is too **loose**. [adjective]

■ The unlatched gate swung **loose** in the wind. [adverb]

■ The veterinarian **loosed** the owl once its wing had healed. [verb]

■ Don't **lose** your ticket.

■ The team members all felt bad about the **loss**.

■ The airline promised to pay us for the **loss** of our luggage.

lot   See **a lot.**

M

main clause   See **independent clause.**

might of, must of   See **of.**

miner, minor   *Miner* is a noun meaning "a worker in a mine." As a noun, *minor* means "a person under legal age." As an adjective, it means "less important."

EXAMPLES
- The American folk song "Clementine" recounts the death of a **miner's** daughter.
- Child-welfare laws are intended to protect **minors.** [noun]
- When I proofread my paper, I discovered a few **minor** errors. [adjective]

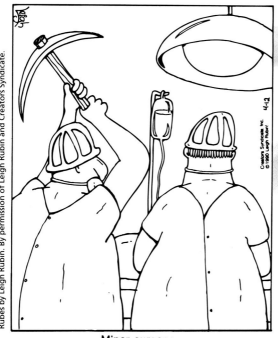

Miner surgery.

Rubes by Leigh Rubin. By permission of Leigh Rubin and Creators Syndicate.

WRITER'S QUICK REFERENCE

misplaced modifier A misplaced modifier is a word, phrase, or clause that makes a sentence awkward or unclear because it seems to modify the wrong word or group of words. See page 148.

MISPLACED   I found a great old photo of my grandmother in a photo album.

CORRECTED   In a photo album, I found a great old photo of my grandmother.

modifier A modifier is a word, a phrase, or a clause that describes or limits the meaning of another word. See **Chapter 5: Using Modifiers.**

EXAMPLE   ■ Langston Hughes, a **key** figure **in the Harlem Renaissance, often** used the rhythms and diction **of jazz and blues in his poetry.**

moral, morale As an adjective, *moral* means "good; virtuous." As a noun, it means "a lesson of conduct." *Morale* is a noun meaning "spirit; mental condition."

EXAMPLES   ■ In Pearl Buck's short story "The Old Demon," Mrs. Wang's **moral** values compel her to help the Japanese pilot. [adjective]
■ James Thurber's fables end with **morals** quite unlike the ones in traditional fairy tales. [noun]
■ The employees' **morale** is high.

N

nominative case The nominative case is the case a noun or pronoun takes when it is used as the subject or predicate nominative of a sentence. See pages 121–122.

EXAMPLE   ■ **We** hope that the other members of our brainstorming group will be **she** and **he.**

nonessential clause, nonessential phrase A nonessential (or **nonrestrictive**) clause or phrase adds information that is not needed to understand the main idea of a sentence. A nonessential clause or phrase is set off by commas. See pages 275–276.

EXAMPLES ■ My mother, **who is a Celtics fan,** has season
tickets to all the home games. [nonessential
clause]

■ Hanukkah, **also called the Festival of Lights,**
is a major Jewish celebration. [nonessential
phrase]

no, none, no one, nobody, not, nothing, nowhere   See
double negative.

noun   A noun is a word used to name a person, place,
thing, or idea. See pages 51–53.

EXAMPLE ■ **Collecting postcards** that feature **Native
Americans** of the **Southwest** has helped
Narciso learn a great **deal** about his
heritage.

noun clause   A noun clause is a subordinate clause used as
a noun. See pages 185–186.

EXAMPLE ■ **How we can raise money for the class picnic**
was **what we discussed at the meeting.**

noun of direct address   A noun of direct address identifies
the person spoken to, or addressed, in a sentence. See page
280.

EXAMPLE ■ What is your composition about, **Julie?**

nowheres See **anyways, anywheres.**

number   Number is the form of a word that indicates
whether the word is singular or plural. See page 77.

SINGULAR **Alonzo lives** with **his aunt** and **uncle.**
PLURAL **Our neighbors grow tomatoes** and **onions** in
containers on **their** front-porch **steps.**

O

object   An object is a complement that does not refer to the
subject of a clause. See **direct object, indirect object,** and
pages 202–205.

EXAMPLE ■ My sister gave **me** a **copy** of Toni Cade Bambara's first collection of stories, *Gorilla, My Love.* [*Me* is an indirect object; *copy* is a direct object.]

objective case Objective case is the form a noun or pronoun takes when it is used as a direct object, an indirect object, or the object of a preposition. See pages 123–124.

EXAMPLE ■ Kim told **us** to meet **her** at the **mall.**

object of a preposition The object of a preposition is the noun or pronoun that follows a preposition in a prepositional phrase. See pages 67– 68.

EXAMPLE ■ I found the material for my **report** in the **media center.** [*Report* is the object of the preposition *for*. *Media center* is the object of the preposition *in*.]

of *Of* is a preposition. Do not use *of* in place of *have* after verbs such as *could, should, would, might, must,* and *ought [to].* Also, do not use *had of* for *had*.

NONSTANDARD You would of enjoyed the picnic.
STANDARD You **would have** [*or* **would've**] enjoyed the picnic.

NONSTANDARD We ought to of left earlier.
STANDARD We **ought to have** left earlier.

NONSTANDARD If I had of known it was your birthday, I would of given you a card.
STANDARD If I **had** known it was your birthday, I **would have** given you a card.

Also, do not use *of* after other prepositions such as *inside, off,* or *outside*.

EXAMPLES ■ He fell **off** [*not* off of] the ladder **outside** [*not* outside of] the garage.
■ What's **inside** [*not* inside of] that box?

off of See **of.**

ought See **had ought, hadn't ought.**

ought to of See **of.**

P

WRITER'S QUICK REFERENCE

parallel structure   Parallel structure is the use of the same forms or structures to express equal ideas in a sentence. See page 235.

NONSTANDARD   Miki likes bowling, ice-skating, dancing, and to draw. [*Bowling, ice-skating,* and *dancing* are all gerunds, but *to draw* is an infinitive.]

STANDARD   Miki likes bowling, ice-skating, dancing, and drawing. [All four activities–*bowling, ice-skating, dancing* and *drawing*–are expressed in the same form.]

parenthetical expression   A parenthetical expression is a side remark that adds information. A parenthetical expression is set off by commas, parentheses, or dashes. See pages 280–281.

EXAMPLE   ▪ Your reasoning, **I believe,** is circular.

participial phrase   A participial phrase consists of a participle and its complements and modifiers. See pages 247–248.

EXAMPLES   ▪ **Known for their independence,** cats are supposedly hard to train.
▪ The toddler, **rubbing his eyes,** looked ready for a nap.

participle   A participle is one of the principal parts of a verb (see page 95) or a verb form that can be used as an adjective (see pages 246–247).

EXAMPLES   ▪ **Delighted,** our father thanked all of us for his birthday gift.
▪ Lynne Alvarez's poem "She loved him all her life" describes an **enduring** love.

passed, past   *Passed,* the past tense of the verb *pass,* means "went beyond." As a noun, *past* means "time gone by." As an adjective, it means "of a former time." As a preposition, it means "beyond."

EXAMPLES   ▪ He **passed** us in the corridor.

- I didn't ask him about his **past.** [noun]
- Her **past** employer recommended her for the job. [adjective]
- I walked right **past** your house without realizing you lived there. [preposition]

passive voice A verb in the passive voice expresses an action done *to* its subject. See pages 108–112.

EXAMPLE
- Ten of John Steinbeck's novels **have been made** into movies.

See also **active voice.**

peace, piece *Peace* means "calmness; the absence of war or strife." *Piece* means "a part of something."

EXAMPLES
- After the long war, **peace** was welcome.
- Do you have a **piece** of paper I can borrow?

personal, personnel *Personal* is an adjective meaning "individual; private." *Personnel* is a noun meaning "a group of people employed in the same work or service."

EXAMPLES
- Don't forget to take your **personal** belongings out of your locker at the end of the school year.
- The company will try to find other positions for all laid-off **personnel.**

phrase A phrase is a group of related words that is used as a single part of speech and that does not contain both a verb and its subject. See **Chapter 6: Phrases.**

EXAMPLE
- Darla and John, **two of our school's best poets, will represent** our class **in the poetry contest.** [*Two of our school's best poets* is an appositive phrase. *Will represent* is a verb phrase. *In the poetry contest* is an adverb phrase.]

piece See **peace, piece.**

plain, plane As an adjective, *plain* means "clear" or "not fancy." As a noun, it means "an area of flat land." *Plane* is a noun meaning "a flat surface," "a level of development, achievement, and so forth," or "a tool for smoothing a surface." It is also the clipped (shortened) form of the noun *air-plane.*

EXAMPLES
- She made her point of view **plain** to everyone in the room. [adjective]
- Steven wears very **plain** clothes. [adjective]
- The storm lashed the open **plain.** [noun]
- Each **plane** of the granite block was smooth. [noun]
- The debate was conducted on a high **plane.** [noun]
- Chris smoothed the wood with a **plane.** [noun]
- The **plane** arrived on time. [noun]

P.M.   See **A.M., P.M.**

possessive case   Possessive case is the form a noun or pronoun takes to show ownership or relationship. See pages 119–120.

EXAMPLE
- Listen to **Angela's** and **my** idea.

Drawing by Ziegler; © 1988 The New Yorker Magazine Inc.

predicate   The predicate is the part of a sentence that says something about the subject. See pages 193–195.

EXAMPLE
- **During the summer** she **works at her grandfather's shoe store.** [The predicate, *during the summer. . . works at her grandfather's shoe store* tells what the subject *she* does.]

WRITER'S QUICK REFERENCE

predicate adjective   A predicate adjective is an adjective in the predicate that modifies the subject of a sentence or a clause. See page 202.

EXAMPLE   ■ The band members seem **happy** and **excited** about their award.

predicate nominative   A predicate nominative is a noun or pronoun in the predicate that explains or identifies the subject of a sentence or a clause. See page 202.

EXAMPLE   ■ Mary Shelley's best-known work is *Frankenstein.*

prefix   A prefix is a word part that is added before a base word or root. See pages 330–331.

EXAMPLES   ■ **re** + ject = reject
■ **un** + known = unknown

preposition   A preposition shows the relationship of a noun or a pronoun to some other word. See pages 67–68.

EXAMPLE   ■ *A Fire **in** My Hands* is a collection **of** poems **by** Gary Soto.

prepositional phrase   A prepositional phrase is a group of words that contains a preposition, a noun or a pronoun called the *object of a preposition,* and any modifiers of that object. See pages 156–160.

EXAMPLE   ■ **After supper,** let's take the dogs **for a walk.**

principal parts of a verb   The principal parts of a verb are a verb's forms: the *base form* (also called the *infinitive*), the *present participle,* the *past,* and the *past participle.* The principal parts are used to form the verb tenses. See pages 95–100.

Base form	carry	swim
Present participle	(is) carrying	(is) swimming
Past	carried	swam
Past participle	(have) carried	(have) swum

principal, principle   As a noun, *principal* means "the head of a school." As an adjective, it means "main or most important." *Principle* is a noun meaning "a rule of conduct" or "a general truth."

EXAMPLES
- Ted had a long talk with the **principal.** [noun]
- Winning is not our **principal** goal. [adjective]
- My friends have high **principles.**
- I don't know the **principles** of physics.

progressive form of a verb In each tense of a verb, the progressive form is made up of a form of *be* and the verb's present participle. The progressive form is used to show continuing action. See pages 103–104.

Present progressive	am, are, is going
Past progressive	was, were going
Future progressive	will (shall) be going
Present perfect progressive	has, have been going
Past perfect progressive	had been going
Future perfect progressive	will (shall) have been going

pronoun A pronoun is a word used in place of a noun or more than one noun. See pages 53–57.

EXAMPLES
- Gwendolyn Brooks, **who** won the Pulitzer Prize for **her** poetry, often writes about Chicago, where **she** grew up. [*Who* is a relative pronoun; *her* and *she* are personal pronouns.]
- As **much** of society became politically active in the 1960s, Brooks **herself** began to write more political poetry. [*Much* is an indefinite pronoun. *Herself* is an intensive pronoun.]
- **Which** of **these** have you read? [*Which* is an interrogative pronoun. *These* is demonstrative.]

proper adjective A proper adjective is an adjective formed from a proper noun. See page 249.

EXAMPLES
- Appalachian
- Homeric
- Orwellian
- Mexican
- Shakespearean
- Jewish/Judaic

proper noun A proper noun names a particular person, place, or thing and is always capitalized. See pages 51–52 and 249–250.

EXAMPLES ▪ King Hussein ▪ North Carolina
▪ El Paso ▪ Gulf of Mexico
▪ Buddhism ▪ Golden Gate Bridge

Q

quiet, quit, quite *Quiet* is an adjective meaning "silent; still." *Quit* is a verb meaning "to stop." *Quite* is an adverb meaning "completely; rather; very."

EXAMPLES ▪ The library is usually fairly **quiet.**
▪ My little brother is **quite** clever for his age, and he won't **quit** teasing me.

R

raise See **rise, raise.**

regular verb A regular verb is a verb that forms its past and past participle by adding *-d* or *-ed* to the infinitive. See pages 95–96.

EXAMPLE ▪ After I **had washed** and **sliced** the tomatoes, I **added** them to the bowl and **tossed** the salad.

relative pronoun A relative pronoun (*who, whom, whose, which, that*) is a pronoun that relates an adjective clause to the word that the clause modifies. See page 56.

EXAMPLE ▪ The poster **that** I wanted was out of stock.

rise, raise The verb *rise* means "to go up" or "to get up." *Rise* almost never takes an object. The verb *raise* means "to cause [something] to rise" or "to lift up." *Raise* usually takes an object. See page 115.

EXAMPLES ▪ Everyone **rose** when the judge entered the room. [no object]
▪ We **raised** our hands to vote. [*Hands* is the object of *raised.*]

root   A root is the part of a word that carries the word's core meaning. See pages 328–329.

EXAMPLES   ■ mis + **spell** = misspell
■ pre + **dict** = predict
■ con + **fid** + ent = confident

run-on sentence   A run-on sentence is two or more complete sentences run together as one. See also **comma splice, fused sentence,** and pages 220–223.

RUN-ON   In Truman Capote's short story "A Christmas Memory," Buddy and his friend can't afford to buy each other Christmas presents his friend makes him a kite he makes her one, too.

REVISED   In Truman Capote's short story "A Christmas Memory," Buddy and his friend can't afford to buy each other Christmas presents. His friend makes him a kite; he makes her one, too.

REVISED   In Truman Capote's short story "A Christmas Memory," Buddy and his friend can't afford to buy each other Christmas presents. His friend makes him a kite, and he makes her one, too.

S

scarcely   See **double negative.**

sentence   A sentence is a group of words that contains a subject and a verb and that expresses a complete thought. See pages 192–240.

                                    S   V

EXAMPLE   ■ The space-shuttle launch has been delayed until further notice.

sentence fragment   A sentence fragment is a group of words that is punctuated as if it were a complete sentence but that does not express a complete thought. See pages 192 and 214–220.

SENTENCE FRAGMENT   As we walked along the beach.
SENTENCE   We looked for seashells as we walked along the beach.

set See **sit, set.**

she See **he, she, it, they.**

shone, shown *Shone* is the past tense of the verb *shine,* which means "to emit or reflect light" or "to exhibit [itself] clearly." *Shown* is the past participle of the verb *show,* which means "to exhibit."

EXAMPLES ▪ The sun **shone** brightly this morning.
           ▪ Joy **shone** from the new father's face.
           ▪ Li Hua has just **shown** me her scrapbook.

Other meanings of *shine* are "to direct the light of" and "to polish"; for these meanings, the preferred past-tense form is *shined,* not *shone.*

EXAMPLES ▪ Hank **shined** the flashlight into the attic.
           ▪ After I **shined** it, my old patent-leather purse looked almost new.

should of See **of.**

shown See **shone, shown.**

simple sentence A simple sentence has one independent clause and no subordinate clauses. It may have a compound subject, a compound verb, and any number of phrases. See page 207.

EXAMPLES ▪ I'm home!
           ▪ Deciding to try to reach the top of the peak, the mountain climbers and their guides pressed onward.

sit, set The verb *sit* means "to rest in an upright, seated position." *Sit* almost never takes an object. The verb *set* means "to put [something] in a place." *Set* usually takes an object. See pages 114–115.

EXAMPLES ▪ The campers were **sitting** around the fire. [no object]
           ▪ Michiko **set** the kettle on the stove. [*Kettle* is the object of *set.*]

slow, slowly *Slow* is an adjective. *Slowly* is an adverb. Although *slow* is also labeled as an adverb in many dictionaries, this usage applies only to informal situations and to such colloquial expressions as *drive slow* and *go slow*.

INFORMAL Perform the tai chi exercises slow.
FORMAL Perform the tai chi exercises **slowly.**

some, somewhat In formal situations, do not use *some* to mean "to some extent." Instead, use *somewhat*.

INFORMAL My grammar has improved some during the past year.
FORMAL My grammar has improved **somewhat** during the past year.

somewheres See **anyways, anywheres.**

sort of See **kind of, sort of.**

sort(s) See **kind(s), sort(s), type(s)** and **kind of a, sort of a.**

stationary, stationery *Stationary* is an adjective meaning "in a fixed position." *Stationery* is a noun meaning "writing paper."

EXAMPLES ■ These chairs are **stationary.**
■ Use white **stationery** for business letters.

stringy sentence A stringy sentence is a sentence that has too many independent clauses. Usually, the clauses are strung together with coordinating conjunctions like *and* or *but*. See pages 236–237.

STRINGY On our trip, the car broke down, and we had to call a tow truck, but the garage's only mechanic had left for the day, and we had to spend the night in a motel.
BETTER On our trip, the car broke down, and we had to call a tow truck. The garage's only mechanic had left for the day, however. As a result, we had to spend the night in a motel.
BETTER When our car broke down on our trip, we had to call a tow truck. The garage's only mechanic had left for the day, however; as a result, we had to spend the night in a motel.

subject The subject is the part of a sentence that names the person or thing spoken about in the rest of the sentence. See pages 193–198.

WRITER'S QUICK REFERENCE

EXAMPLE ■ August Wilson's ***The Piano Lesson*** won both the Pulitzer Prize for drama and the New York Drama Critics' Circle Award.

subject complement A subject complement is a noun, pronoun, or adjective that follows a linking verb. It describes or explains the subject. See **predicate adjective, predicate nominative,** and pages 201–202.

EXAMPLES ■ Sandra Cisneros is my favorite **writer.**
■ The breeze felt **refreshing.**

subordinate clause A subordinate (or **dependent**) clause is a group of words that contains a verb and its subject but does not express a complete thought and cannot stand alone. See pages 183–184.

EXAMPLE ■ I want to be an astronaut **when I grow up.**

subordinating conjunction A subordinating conjunction is a conjunction used to introduce an adverb clause. See pages 183–184.

EXAMPLE ■ Lani listened closely **as** I read my poem aloud.

suffix A suffix is a word part that is added after a base word or root. See pages 331–333.

EXAMPLES ■ excite + **ment** = excitement
■ critic + **ism** = criticism
■ loc + **ate** = locate

superlative degree The superlative degree is the form a modifier takes when used to compare more than two things. See pages 140–145.

EXAMPLE ■ Which of the three kittens is the **friskiest?**

syllable A syllable is a word part that can be pronounced by itself. See page 326.

EXAMPLE ■ chron • o • log • i • cal

synonym A synonym is a word that has a meaning similar to but not exactly the same as that of another word. See page 344.

EXAMPLE ■ The campers assembled their **equipment** and loaded the **gear** into the van.

WRITER'S QUICK REFERENCE

WRITER'S QUICK REFERENCE

take See **bring, take.**

teach See **learn, teach.**

tense Tense is the time expressed by a verb. Every verb has six tenses: **present, present perfect, past, past perfect, future,** and **future perfect.** See pages 101–107.

EXAMPLE   ■ Sarah **told** [past] me what time the concert **will begin** [future], but I **have forgotten** [present perfect].

than, then *Than* is a conjunction used in comparisons. *Then* is an adverb meaning "at that time" or "next."

EXAMPLES   ■ This box is heavier **than** that one.
■ Did you know Bianca **then?**
■ We went swimming; **then** we ate lunch.

that See **who, which, that** and **general reference.**

theirselves See **hisself, theirselves.**

theirs, there's *Theirs* is a possessive form of the pronoun *they. There's* is the contraction for *there is.*

EXAMPLES   ■ Our apartment is on the second floor; **theirs** is on the third floor.
■ **There's** some frozen yogurt in the freezer.

their, there, they're *Their* is a possessive form of *they.* As an adverb, *there* means "at that place." As an expletive, it is used to begin a sentence (see page 84). *They're* is the contraction of *they are.*

EXAMPLES   ■ The girls gave **their** opinions.
■ I'll be **there** on time. [adverb]
■ **There** isn't any milk left. [expletive]
■ **They're** at the station now.

them *Them* should not be used as an adjective. Use *those.*

EXAMPLE   ■ I like **those** [*not* them] jeans, don't you?

then See **than, then.**

there See **their, there, they're.**

there's See **theirs, there's.**

they See **he, she, it, they.**

they're See **their, there, they're.**

this here, that there The words *here* and *there* are unnecessary after *this* and *that*.

EXAMPLE ■ I'm buying **this** [*not* this here] cassette instead of **that** [*not* that there] one.

this, that, these, those See **kind(s), sort(s), type(s).**

threw, through *Threw,* the past tense of the verb *throw,* means "hurled." As a preposition, *through* means "in one side of and out the other side of." As an adverb, it means "from beginning to end." As an adjective, it means "extending from one place to another" or "finished."

EXAMPLES ■ Freddy **threw** three strikes.
■ The firetruck weaved **through** the heavy traffic. [preposition]
■ I think Holmes Boulevard is a **through** street. [adjective]
■ If you're **through** with the scissors, may I borrow them? [adjective]

to, too, two *To* is used as a preposition or as the sign of the infinitive form of a verb. *Too* is an adverb meaning "also" or "overly." As an adjective, *two* means "totaling one plus one." As a noun, it means "the number between one and three."

EXAMPLES ■ They've gone **to** the store. [preposition]
■ She told us **to** wash the windows. [sign of the infinitive]
■ I like soccer, and Ted does, **too.** [adverb]
■ He was **too** tired **to** think clearly. [adverb; sign of the infinitive]
■ I noticed **two** packages on the sofa. [adjective]
■ **Two** of my friends have moved away this year. [noun]

transitional expressions Transitional expressions connect ideas in a paragraph or composition and show how the ideas are related. See pages 284 and 386–387.

transitive verb A transitive verb is an action verb that expresses an action directed toward a person or thing named in a sentence. See page 61.

EXAMPLE ■ Luisa **removed** the faucet and **replaced** the washer that **was causing** the leak.

try and Use *try to,* not *try and.*

EXAMPLE ■ I **try to** [*not* try and] remember my friends' birthdays.

type(s) See **kind(s), sort(s), type(s).**

U

understood subject The understood subject is the unstated *you* in a request or a command. See pages 197–198.

EXAMPLE ■ [You] **Please help** me with this ladder.

unless See **without, unless.**

V

verb A verb is a word used to express an action or a state of being. See pages 61–64.

EXAMPLE ■ William Least Heat-Moon's book *Blue Highways* **records** his journey through the United States.

verbals Verbals (participles, gerunds, and infinitives) are formed from verbs. Like verbs, they may be modified by adverbs and adjectives and may have complements. However, verbals are used as other parts of speech. See pages 161–169.

EXAMPLES ■ **Weakened** and **exhausted,** the explorers began the homeward journey.
■ Their **demanding** but **exciting** trek was ended.

WRITER'S QUICK REFERENCE

verbal phrase A verbal phrase consists of a verbal and its modifiers and complements.

EXAMPLE ▪ **Scattered by the wind,** the litter spoiled the beauty of the picnic area.

verb phrase A verb phrase consists of a main verb preceded by at least one **helping verb** (also called an **auxiliary verb**). See pages 63–64.

EXAMPLE ▪ **Has** the mail **arrived** yet?

voice Voice is the form a transitive verb takes to indicate whether the subject of the verb performs or receives the action. See pages 108–112.

ACTIVE VOICE Wildlife officials **captured** the alligator.
PASSIVE VOICE The alligator **was captured** by wildlife officials.

W

waist, waste *Waist* is a noun meaning "the midsection of the body." As a noun, *waste* means "unused material." As a verb, it means "to squander."

EXAMPLES ▪ This skirt is too big in the **waist.**
▪ **Waste** is a major problem in the United States. [noun]
▪ Don't **waste** your money on that. [verb]

way, ways Use *way,* not *ways,* in referring to a distance.

INFORMAL We hiked a long ways.
FORMAL We hiked a long **way.**

weak reference A weak reference occurs when a pronoun refers to an antecedent that has not been expressed. See page 132.

WEAK Nori enjoys chemistry, and she hopes to be one someday.
CLEAR Nori enjoys chemistry, and she hopes to be a chemist someday.
WEAK I wanted to go for a bike ride, but it had a flat tire.

WRITER'S QUICK REFERENCE

CLEAR   I wanted to go for a bike ride, but my bike had a flat tire.

weak, week   *Weak* is an adjective meaning "feeble" or "lacking force; not strong." *Week* is a noun meaning "seven days."

EXAMPLES
- The fawn is still too **weak** to walk.
- We could hardly hear his **weak** voice.
- Carol has been gone a **week**.

weather, whether   *Weather* is a noun meaning "conditions outdoors." *Whether* is a conjunction used (with *or*) to introduce alternatives. *Whether* is also used (with or without *or*) in indirect questions and in expressions of doubt.

EXAMPLES
- The **weather** suddenly changed.
- I can't decide **whether** to order chili or pizza.
- Dwayne asked us **whether** we had seen the movie.
- She wondered **whether** to enter the contest.

well   See **good, well.**

what   Use *that*, not *what*, to introduce an adjective clause.

EXAMPLE
- The poem **that** [*not* what] I wrote about was William Stafford's "Fifteen."

when, where   Do not use *when* or *where* to begin a definition.

NONSTANDARD   A "bomb" in football is when a backfield player throws a long pass.

STANDARD   A "bomb" in football is a long pass thrown by a backfield player.

where . . . at   See **at.**

where, when   Do not use *where* or *when* for *that.*

EXAMPLES
- I read in this magazine **that** [*not* where] Carol Clay is a champion parachutist.
- Uncle Clarence told us about the time **that** [*not* when] he and Dad met Nelson Mandela.

whether   See **weather, whether.**

which   See **who, which, that.**

who's, whose *Who's* is the contraction of *who is* or *who has.* *Whose* is the possessive form of *who.*

EXAMPLES ■ I can't imagine **who's** at the door now.
  ■ **Who's** been marking in my book?
  ■ **Whose** bicycle is this?

who, which, that The relative pronoun *who* refers to persons only; *which* refers to things only; *that* may refer to either persons or things.

EXAMPLES ■ Here is the man **who** (*or* **that**) will install the new carpet. [person]
  ■ We decided to replace our old carpet, **which** we have had for nearly ten years. [thing]
  ■ It is the kind of carpet **that** will wear well. [thing]

who, whom See pages 125–127.

without, unless Do not use the preposition *without* in place of the conjunction *unless.*

EXAMPLE ■ I will not be able to sing **unless** [*not* without] my cold gets better.

wordiness Wordiness is the use of more words than necessary or of fancy words where simple ones will do.

WORDY   In my opinion we should make our plans to depart our abode no later than 7:30 in the early hours of the day.
BETTER   I think we should plan to leave home by 7:30 A.M.

would of See **of.**

Y

---

your, you're *Your* is a possessive form of *you.* *You're* is the contraction of *you are.*

EXAMPLES ■ What is **your** idea?
  ■ **You're** my best friend.

PART TWO

GRAMMAR
AND
USAGE

◇

1 PARTS OF SPEECH

The Work That Words Do

✓ Checking What You Know

Identifying Parts of Speech

Identify the part of speech of each italicized word in the following paragraph.

EXAMPLE   Everyone [1] *has* favorite summer [2] *places*.
           1. *verb*
           2. *noun*

For [1] *me*, no [2] *spot* is [3] *better* than the beach. On [4] *hot*, sunny days, when the sand [5] *burns* my feet, I am always [6] *careful* [7] *about* putting on [8] *sunscreen*. I like to run [9] *through* the foaming surf and later relax under a beach umbrella. Most of the time, I [10] *enjoy* being with friends, [11]*but* sometimes I prefer to be by [12]*myself*. With only [13] *strangers* around me, I [14] *feel* free to think my [15] *own* thoughts. I wander [16] *slowly* along the shore, poking through all the interesting things [17] *that* the sea has washed up. Once I accidentally stepped on a [18] *jelly-fish* and couldn't help but yell [19]*"Ouch!"* when it stung my foot. Since then, I've learned to be [20] *more* careful about where I step.   ✓

The Eight Parts of Speech		
noun	verb	conjunction
pronoun	adverb	interjection
adjective	preposition	

The Noun

1a. A *noun* is a word used to name a person, place, thing, or idea.

PERSONS	PLACES	THINGS	IDEAS
Sharon	Iowa	okra	peace
Captain Brown	district	Great Pyramid	truth
hair stylist	Mars	toothpicks	justice
swimmers	Antarctica	U.S.S. *Enterprise*	excellence
	library	merry-go-round	honesty

Common and Proper Nouns

A *common noun* is a general name for a person, place, thing, or idea. A common noun is not capitalized unless it begins a sentence or is part of a title. A *proper noun* names a particular person, place, thing, or idea and is always capitalized.

Born Loser reprinted by permission of NEA, Inc.

COMMON NOUNS	PROPER NOUNS
scientist	Marie Curie, Charles Drew
woman	Coretta Scott King, Rita Moreno, Maria Tallchief
city	Cairo, St. Louis, Paris
building	World Trade Center, Buckingham Palace
continent	North America, South America, Africa
mountain	Mount Everest, Kilimanjaro, Pikes Peak
day	Monday, Thursday, Labor Day
country	Mexico, Japan, Uruguay

 REFERENCE NOTE: For more information on capitalizing proper nouns, see pages 249–257.

Concrete Nouns and Abstract Nouns

A *concrete noun* names an object that can be perceived by the senses. An *abstract noun* names an idea, a feeling, a quality, or a characteristic.

CONCRETE NOUNS	cloud, tulip, thunder, silk, yogurt
ABSTRACT NOUNS	freedom, joy, beauty, kindness

 QUICK CHECK 1 **Classifying Nouns**

Identify each of the following nouns as a *common noun* or a *proper noun*. If the noun is proper, name a corresponding common noun.

1. Zora Neale Hurston
2. Vietnam
3. city
4. Mount Hood
5. cousin
6. month
7. singer
8. Boston Public Library
9. street
10. Christopher Columbus

GRAMMAR/USAGE

Collective Nouns

A *collective noun* names a group of persons or things.

| COLLECTIVE NOUNS | audience, class, committee, family, group, team |

 REFERENCE NOTE: For information on using verbs with collective nouns, see page 83.

Compound Nouns

A *compound noun* consists of two or more words used together as a single noun. A compound noun may be written as one word, as two or more words, or as a hyphenated word.

ONE WORD	firefighter, Iceland, newspaper
TWO OR MORE WORDS	prime minister, Red River Dam, fire drill
HYPHENATED WORD	sister-in-law, Stratford-on-Avon, push-up

 NOTE If you are not sure how to write a compound noun, look in a dictionary. Some dictionaries may give two correct forms for a word. For example, you may find the word *vice-president* written both with and without the hyphen. As a rule, use the form the dictionary lists first.

 REFERENCE NOTE: For information on capitalizing the parts of a compound word, see pages 250–256.

The Pronoun

1b. A *pronoun* is a word used in place of one or more nouns.

EXAMPLES **Gloria stepped back from the picture and looked at it carefully.** [The pronoun *it* takes the place of the noun *picture*.]

Where is Lian? **She** said **she** would be here on time. [The pronoun *she* takes the place of *Lian* twice.]

Our teacher and Mr. Barnes said **they** would go to the meeting. [The pronoun *they* takes the place of two nouns: *teacher* and *Mr. Barnes*.]

Antecedents

Usually, a pronoun takes the place of a noun used earlier. This noun is called the *antecedent* of the pronoun. In the following examples, the arrows point from the pronouns to their antecedents.

EXAMPLES   **Tomás** closed **his book** and put **it** down.

The coach showed the **players** how **they** should throw the ball.

Why did **Janet** take **her** dog to the veterinarian?

Have the **birds** flown south yet? **They** should start migrating soon.

Lee hit a **home run**. **It** was **his** first of the season.

STYLE NOTE

To keep your readers from getting confused, place pronouns near their antecedents—within the same sentence or in the very next sentence.

CONFUSING   My new in-line **skates** were a present from Aunt Rachel. I also got a subscription to *Seventeen*. **They** were on sale at the discount store.

CLEAR   My new in-line **skates** were a present from Aunt Rachel. **They** were on sale at the discount store. I also got a subscription to *Seventeen*.

The second example makes clear that the skates, not the skates *and* the subscription, were on sale at the discount store.

👉 REFERENCE NOTE: See pages 88–90 for information on choosing pronouns that agree with their antecedents. For information on clear pronoun reference, see pages 130–132.

Personal Pronouns

	SINGULAR	**PLURAL**
FIRST PERSON	I, my, mine, me	we, our, ours, us
SECOND PERSON	you, your, yours	you, your, yours
THIRD PERSON	he, his, him she, her, hers it, its	they, their, theirs, them

NOTE Possessive forms such as *my, your,* and *her* may also be classified as adjectives. See pages 58–59.

Reflexive and Intensive Pronouns

A *reflexive* pronoun refers to the subject and directs the action of the verb back to the subject. An *intensive* pronoun emphasizes a noun or another pronoun.

myself	ourselves
yourself	yourselves
himself, herself, itself	themselves

REFLEXIVE   Manuel bought **himself** a bicycle helmet.

INTENSIVE   Manuel **himself** organized bicycle-safety awareness week.

Relative Pronouns

A *relative pronoun* introduces a subordinate clause.

who	whom	whose	which	that

EXAMPLES   The family **whose** apartment is next door to
ours stopped by to visit.
The book **that** fell off the shelf is mine.

Interrogative Pronouns

An *interrogative pronoun* introduces a question.

Who . . . ?	Whose . . . ?	What . . . ?
Whom . . . ?	Which . . . ?	

EXAMPLES   **Who** may I say is calling?
Which science class are you taking next year?

Demonstrative Pronouns

A *demonstrative pronoun* points out a person, a place, a
thing, or an idea.

this	that	these	those

EXAMPLES   Teresa, **this** is my cousin Vincent.
Are **these** your books?

Indefinite Pronouns

An *indefinite pronoun* refers to a person, a place, or a thing
that is not specifically named.

all	each	more	nothing
another	either	most	one
any	everybody	much	other
anybody	everyone	neither	several
anyone	everything	nobody	some
anything	few	none	somebody
both	many	no one	someone

EXAMPLES   **Something** or **somebody** has frightened my dog.
Sanjay says **either** of these two movies is worth seeing.

✓ *QUICK CHECK 2*   **Identifying Pronouns**

Identify all the pronouns in each sentence below. Label each one as *personal, reflexive, intensive, relative, indefinite, interrogative,* or *demonstrative.*

1. I'll answer the phone myself.
2. Few of the club members know much about parliamentary procedure.
3. What do you call that?
4. The council member whom she wants to interview is out of town today.
5. We found ourselves in an embarrassing situation.

The Adjective

1c. An *adjective* is a word used to modify a noun or a pronoun.

To *modify* a word means to describe it or to make its meaning more definite. An adjective modifies a noun or a pronoun by telling *what kind, which one,* or *how many (how much).*

WHAT KIND?	WHICH ONE?	HOW MANY?	HOW MUCH?
gray sky	**that** girl	**five** fingers	**enough** space
old shoes	**next** day	**many** rivers	**more** water
clever dog	**either** way	**fewer** hours	**less** time
low price	**last** chance	**some** problems	**some** trouble

Articles

The most frequently used adjectives are *a, an,* and *the.* These words are called *articles.*

A and *an* are ***indefinite articles***. They refer to a noun that names one member of a general group. *A* is used before words beginning with a consonant sound. *An* is used before words beginning with a vowel sound. *An* is also used before a word beginning with the consonant *h* when the *h* is not pronounced.

EXAMPLES **A** girl won.
An elephant escaped.
This is **an** honor.

The is the ***definite article***. It refers to a noun that names a particular person, place, thing, or idea.

EXAMPLES **The** girl won.
The elephant escaped.
The honor goes to him.

Pronoun or Adjective?

The way a word is used in a sentence determines its part of speech. For example, the following words may be used as pronouns or adjectives.

all	each	more	one	that	what
another	either	most	other	these	which
any	few	much	several	this	whose
both	many	neither	some	those	

When these words take the place of nouns, they are pronouns. When they modify nouns, they are adjectives.

PRONOUN	ADJECTIVE
I like **that**.	I like **that** shirt.
Either will do.	**Either** car will do.
Sheila bought **some**.	Sheila bought **some** books.

NOTE The words *my, your, his, her, its, our,* and *their* are called pronouns throughout this book. They are the ***possessive*** *forms* of personal pronouns, showing ownership or relationship. Some teachers, however, prefer to call these words adjectives because they tell *which one* about nouns: *my* sister, *your* book, *our* team, *their* tents.

Nouns Used as Adjectives

Sometimes nouns are used as adjectives.

COMMON NOUNS	COMMON NOUNS USED AS ADJECTIVES
cheese	**cheese** sandwich
snow	**snow** sculpture
winter	**winter** sale
PROPER NOUNS	**PROPER NOUNS USED AS ADJECTIVES**
Sioux	**Sioux** tradition
Texas	**Texas** coast
Picasso	**Picasso** painting

When a noun is used as an adjective, your teacher may prefer that you call it an adjective. Proper nouns used as adjectives are called *proper adjectives*.

☞ REFERENCE NOTE: Sometimes a proper adjective and a noun are used together so frequently that they become a compound noun: *Brazil nut, French bread, India ink.* See page 53 for more on compound nouns. For information on capitalizing proper adjectives, see page 249.

Adjectives in Sentences

An adjective usually comes before the noun or pronoun it modifies.

EXAMPLES   Ms. Farrell tells **all** students that **good** workers

will be given **special** privileges.

GRAMMAR/USAGE

A **sweating, exhausted** runner crossed the line.

In some cases, adjectives follow the words they modify.

EXAMPLE   A **dog, old** and **flea-bitten**, snored in the sun.

Other words may separate an adjective from the noun or pronoun it modifies.

EXAMPLES   **Beverly** was **worried. She** felt **nervous** about the play.

Cheered by the crowd, the **band** played an encore.

COMPUTER NOTE

Using a software program's thesaurus can help you choose appropriate adjectives. To make sure that an adjective has exactly the connotation you intend, check the word in a dictionary.

 QUICK CHECK 3   **Identifying Adjectives and the Words They Modify**

Identify the adjectives and the words they modify in each of the following sentences. [Note: Do not include the articles *a, an,* and *the*.]

1. The marble towers of the castle reached high into the autumn sky.
2. Most public libraries will lend classic videotapes to anyone who has a library card.
3. That store sells those basketball shoes.
4. In the late seventies, the Dorothy Hamill haircut was a popular hairstyle.
5. That Siamese cat is giving me a peculiar look.

The Verb

1d. A *verb* is a word used to express an action or a state of being.

Action Verbs

An *action verb* expresses activity, whether physical or mental.

PHYSICAL	come	do	paint
	run	write	
MENTAL	believe	know	remember
	think	understand	

An action verb can be *transitive* or *intransitive*.

(1) A *transitive verb* expresses an action that is directed toward a person or a thing named in the sentence. Words that receive the action of a transitive verb are called *objects*.

EXAMPLES   Neil **rang** the bell. [The action of the verb *rang* is directed toward *bell*.]

Juanita **mailed** the package. [The action of *mailed* is directed toward *package*.]

☞ REFERENCE NOTE: For more information about objects of verbs and their uses in sentences, see pages 202–204.

(2) An *intransitive verb* expresses an action (or tells something about the subject) without reference to an object.

EXAMPLES   Last Saturday we **stayed** inside.
The children **laughed**.

Some verbs can be transitive in one sentence and intransitive in another.

EXAMPLES   Marcie **studied** her notes. [transitive]
Marcie **studied** very late. [intransitive]

GRAMMAR/USAGE

The poet **wrote** a sonnet. [transitive]
The poet **wrote** carefully. [intransitive]

"I MISS THE GOOD OLD DAYS WHEN ALL WE HAD TO WORRY ABOUT WAS NOUNS AND VERBS."

© 1984 by Sidney Harris—"Punch."

Linking Verbs

A *linking verb* links the subject with a noun, a pronoun, or an adjective.

EXAMPLES   The answer **is** three. [answer = three]
The winner **could be** you. [winner = you]
The answer **is** correct. [answer = correct]
The casserole **tasted** strange. [casserole = strange]

The most commonly used linking verbs are forms of the verb *be*.

COMMONLY USED LINKING VERBS		
FORMS OF *BE*		
be	shall be	should be
being	will be	would be
am	has been	can be
is	have been	could be
are	had been	should have been

(continued)

GRAMMAR/USAGE

COMMONLY USED LINKING VERBS *(continued)*		
FORMS OF *BE*		
was	shall have been	would have been
were	will have been	could have been
OTHERS		
appear	grow	seem	stay
become	look	smell	taste
feel	remain	sound	turn

Some verbs can be linking verbs in one sentence and action verbs in another.

EXAMPLES The wet dog **smelled** horrible. [linking verb—dog = horrible]
The dog **smelled** the cat. [action verb]
The motor **sounded** good. [linking verb—motor = good]
The horn **sounded** at noon. [action verb]

The verb *be* does not always link the subject with a noun, pronoun, or adjective in the predicate. *Be* can express a state of being without having a complement. For example, in the sentence below, a form of *be* is followed by an adverb that tells *where*.

EXAMPLE I **was** there. [*There* tells *where*.]

 REFERENCE NOTE: See pages 65–67 for a discussion of adverbs.

To be a linking verb, the verb must be followed by a *complement*—a noun or a pronoun that names the subject or an adjective that describes it.

 REFERENCE NOTE: For more on complements, see pages 200–204.

The Verb Phrase

A *verb phrase* consists of a main verb preceded by at least one *helping verb* (also called an *auxiliary verb*).

COMMONLY USED HELPING VERBS				
Forms of *be*	am	is	are	was
	were	be	being	been
Forms of *have*	has	have	having	had
Forms of *do*	do	does	doing	did
Others	may	can	could	
	might	shall	should	
	must	will	would	

Notice how helping verbs work together with main verbs to make complete verb phrases.

EXAMPLES   **is** leaving   **may** become
                 could jump   **does** sing
                 might have remained   **should** move
                 must have thought   **had** seemed

Sometimes the parts of a verb phrase are interrupted by other parts of speech.

EXAMPLES   She **had** always **been thinking** of her future.
                 We **could** never **have moved** the car alone.
                 Didn't you **hear** Jesse Jackson's speech?
                 Has my sister **played** her new CD for you?

NOTE   The word *not* and its contraction, *–n't*, are never part of a verb phrase. They are adverbs. See pages 65–67 for more information on adverbs.

 QUICK CHECK 4   **Identifying and Classifying Verbs and Verb Phrases**

Identify all of the verbs and verb phrases in the following sentences. Label each verb or verb phrase as *transitive, intransitive,* or *linking.*

1. She felt better when the tow truck arrived.
2. If I study biology every night, I will be ready for my test on Friday.
3. Jacob could have danced until midnight, but his curfew was 11 o'clock.

4. Should museums charge admission?
5. Marie made fresh pasta with basil sauce for dinner, and we ate luxuriously.

The Adverb

1e. An *adverb* is a word used to modify a verb, an adjective, or another adverb.

Adverbs modify other words by telling *where, when, how,* or *to what extent* (*how often* or *how much*).

Adverbs Modifying Verbs

Adverbs most commonly modify verbs or verb phrases.

WHERE?	WHEN?
We lived **there**.	May we go **tomorrow**?
Please step **up**.	Water the plant **now**.
I have the ticket **here**.	We'll see you **later**.
I'm **home**!	Our flight lands **soon**.

HOW?	TO WHAT EXTENT?
She **quickly** agreed.	I trust you **completely**.
The rain fell **softly**.	He **hardly** moved.
Drive **carefully**.	Did she hesitate **slightly**?
Dave laughed **loudly**.	I **fully** support you.

Adverbs may come before or after the verbs they modify. Sometimes adverbs interrupt the parts of a verb phrase. Adverbs may also introduce questions.

EXAMPLE **Where** in the world did you **ever** find that pink and purple necktie? [The adverb *where* introduces the question and modifies the verb phrase *did find*. The adverb *ever*, which interrupts the verb phrase, also modifies it.]

REFERENCE NOTE: See page 239 for information on beginning sentences with adverbs to create variety.

GRAMMAR/USAGE

Adverbs Modifying Adjectives

EXAMPLES   Beth did an **exceptionally** fine job. [The adverb *exceptionally* modifies the adjective *fine*, telling *how fine*.]

Slightly cooler temperatures are forecast for this Sunday. [The adverb *slightly* modifies the adjective *cooler*, telling *how cool*.]

STYLE NOTE   The adverbs *quite, really, too, so,* and *very* are often overused. To keep your writing lively, replace these inexact, overused words with adverbs such as those in the following list.

Adverbs That Frequently Modify Adjectives		
completely	especially	particularly
dangerously	generally	rather
definitely	largely	surprisingly
dreadfully	mainly	terribly
entirely	mostly	unusually

Adverbs Modifying Other Adverbs

EXAMPLES   Calvin was **almost** never late. [The adverb *almost* modifies the adverb *never*, telling *to what extent*.]

We'll meet **shortly** afterward. [The adverb *shortly* modifies the adverb *afterward*, telling *to what extent*.]

She slept **too** late. [The adverb *too* modifies the adverb *late*, telling *to what extent*.]

NOTE   Although many adverbs end in *-ly*, the *-ly* ending does not always signal that a word is an adverb. Some adjectives also end in *-ly*: the *daily* newspaper, an *early* train, an *only* child, a *friendly* person. And some words that do not end in *-ly*, such as *now, then, far, already, somewhat, not,* and *right* are often used as adverbs. To tell whether a word is an adverb, ask yourself these questions:

- Does the word modify a verb, an adjective, or an adverb?
- Does it tell *when, where, how,* or *to what extent*?

 QUICK CHECK 5 **Identify Adverbs and the Words They Modify**

Identify the adverbs in the sentences below. For each adverb, name the word it modifies.

1. Your parents are waiting downstairs.
2. Latrice's instincts are almost always right.
3. I visited San Antonio quite recently.
4. We heard the alarm and immediately exited the building.
5. When are you seeing *Dances with Wolves,* tonight or tomorrow?

The Preposition

1f. A *preposition* is a word used to show the relationship of a noun or a pronoun to some other word.

Notice in the following examples how changing the preposition changes the relationship of *Saint Bernard* to *bed* and *everything* to *beach*.

The Saint Bernard slept **near** my bed.

The Saint Bernard slept **under** my bed.

The Saint Bernard slept **on** my bed.

Everything **about** the beach was wonderful.

Everything **except** the beach was wonderful.

Everything **from** the beach was wonderful.

A preposition always introduces a *prepositional phrase.* The noun or pronoun that ends the phrase is the **object** of the preposition. In the examples above, *bed* and *beach* are the objects of the prepositions.

GRAMMAR/USAGE

👉 **REFERENCE NOTE:** For more about prepositional phrases, see pages 156–160.

Commonly Used Prepositions

aboard	below	from	since
about	beneath	in	through
above	beside	inside	throughout
across	besides	into	till
after	between	like	to
against	beyond	near	toward
along	but (meaning	of	under
amid	*except*)	off	underneath
among	by	on	until
around	concerning	onto	up
as	down	out	upon
at	during	outside	with
before	except	over	within
behind	for	past	without

NOTE Many of these words can be either adverbs or prepositions, depending on how they are used in a sentence.

EXAMPLES   Welcome **aboard**. [adverb]
Welcome **aboard** our boat. [preposition]

Let's wait **inside**. [adverb]
Let's wait **inside** the movie theater.
[preposition]

Prepositions that consist of more than one word are called *compound prepositions*.

Commonly Used Compound Prepositions

according to	in addition to	next to
as of	in front of	on account of
aside from	in place of	out of
because of	in spite of	up to
by means of	instead of	prior to

✓ *QUICK CHECK 6* **Identifying Prepositions**

Identify the prepositions (including compound prepositions) in the sentences below.

1. The passengers went aboard the cruise ship at noon.
2. No one besides me went to the meeting.
3. Without vegetation, the earth would perish.
4. Prior to the performance, the dancers stretched their
   muscles.
5. Horses first came to North America by means of a land
   bridge between Asia and Alaska, but these early horses
   became extinct.

The Conjunction

1g. A *conjunction* is a word used to join words or
groups of words.

Coordinating Conjunctions

A *coordinating conjunction* connects words or groups of
words that are used in the same way.

Coordinating Conjunctions			
and	but	or	nor
for	yet	so	

EXAMPLES   Paths **and** streets [two nouns] are shown on
the park map.
You might see a seagull on land **or** at sea.
[two prepositional phrases]
Judy wrote down the number, **but** she lost it.
[two complete thoughts]

Correlative Conjunctions

Correlative conjunctions are pairs of conjunctions that connect sentence parts used in the same way.

Correlative Conjunctions

both . . . and	not only . . . but also
either . . . or	neither . . . nor
whether . . . or	

EXAMPLES   **Both** Jim Thorpe **and** Roberto Clemente were outstanding athletes. [two proper nouns]
We want to go **not only** to Ontario **but also** to Quebec. [two prepositional phrases]
Either we will buy it now, **or** we will wait for the next sale. [two complete thoughts]

 REFERENCE NOTE: A third kind of conjunction—the *subordinating conjunction*—is discussed on pages 183–184.

✓ *QUICK CHECK 7*   **Identifying Coordinating and Correlative Conjunctions**

Identify all the conjunctions in the following sentences. Be prepared to tell whether they are *correlative* or *coordinating* conjunctions.

1. Diego and I are doing our research report on Jesse Jackson.
2. We admire both his courage and his skill as a public speaker.
3. Whether it rains or not, the soccer game will take place.
4. Janice wants to be an actor, so she is trying out for the lead role.
5. Not only my sister and my cousin but also my mother and my grandmother are named Irene.

The Interjection

1h.   An *interjection* is a word used to express emotion. It has no grammatical relation to the other words in the sentence.

EXAMPLES   hey   ouch   wow
            oops   well   yikes

An interjection is set off from the rest of the sentence by an exclamation point or by a comma.

STYLE NOTE

Interjections are common in casual conversation. In writing, however, they're usually used only in dialogue meant to represent such conversation. When you use interjections in dialogue, use an exclamation point to indicate strong emotion and a comma or a period to indicate mild emotion.

EXAMPLES   **Hey!** Be careful of that wire!
There's a skunk somewhere, **ugh!**
I like that outfit, but, **wow**, it's really
   expensive.
Well, I guess that's that.

Notice in the third example above that commas are used both before and after an interjection that interrupts a sentence.

Determining Parts of Speech

1i.   The way a word is used in a sentence determines the word's part of speech.

Many words can be used as different parts of speech. As you read each of the following sentences, notice how the *context*—the way *down* relates to the rest of the sentence— helps you identify what part of speech *down* is in that sentence.

EXAMPLES   The fine feathers of young birds are called
down. [noun]
She wore a **down** vest. [adjective]
Did the tackle **down** the ball in the end zone?
   [verb]
Her poster fell **down**. [adverb]
My cousin lives **down** the street. [preposition]

GRAMMAR/USAGE

☞ **REFERENCE NOTE:** See pages 342–344 for more information on using context clues when you read.

Beginning duck

The Far Side copyright 1986 FarWorks, Inc. Distributed by Universal Press Syndicate. Reprinted with permission. All rights reserved.

© 1986 Universal Press Syndicate

 QUICK CHECK 8   **Identifying Words as Different Parts of Speech**

Read each of the following sentences. Then, identify the part of speech of the italicized word. Be ready to justify your answer by telling how the word is used in the sentence.

1. Did the pond *ice* over?
2. An *ice* storm struck.
3. *Ice* covered the walk.

4. The light flashed *on*.
5. We rode *on* the subway.

6. They went to the *park*.
7. We can *park* the car here.
8. They waited by the *park* entrance.
9. We are all here *but* Jo.
10. I slipped, *but* I didn't fall.

Chapter Review 1

Identifying Parts of Speech

Write the part of speech of each italicized word in the following paragraph. Be ready to explain the use of the word in the sentence.

EXAMPLE   Pioneers [1] *learned* how to recognize
              [2] *danger.*
           1. *verb*
           2. *noun*

The [1] *first* pioneers on the Great Plains [2] *encountered* many kinds [3] *of* dangerous animals. Grizzly bears and [4] *huge* herds of bison were menaces to [5] *early* settlers. One of the [6] *most* ferocious beasts of the plains [7] *was* a [8] *grizzly* protecting her cubs. However, [9] *neither* the bison *nor* the grizzly was the most feared animal [10] *on* the frontier. [11] *None* of the other prairie creatures—not even the deadly [12] *rattlesnake*—were dreaded so much as the skunk. You may think, [13] *"Oh,* that is [14] *ridiculous,"* [15] *yet* it is true. Skunks were not feared because they [16] *smelled* bad but, instead, because they [17] *often* carried [18] *rabies.* Since there was no vaccine for rabies in [19] *those* days, the bite of a rabid skunk spelled certain [20] *doom* for the unlucky victim.

Chapter Review 2

Writing Sentences Using the Same Words as Different Parts of Speech

Use each of the following words as two different parts of speech in a sentence to make a total of 20 sentences. Underline the word and give its part of speech in parentheses after each sentence.

EXAMPLE   **1.** up
           1. *We looked <u>up</u>. (adverb)*
              We ran <u>up</u> the stairs. (preposition)

1. light   3. over
2. run   4. line

5. cook
6. ride
7. in

8. love
9. below
10. picture

SUMMARY OF PARTS OF SPEECH

Rule	Part of Speech	Use	Examples
1a.	noun	names	**Lydia** reads **novels.**
1b.	pronoun	takes the place of a noun	**You** and **they** saw **it.**
1c.	adjective	modifies a noun or a pronoun	I got a **new** bike. We were **hungry.**
1d.	verb	shows action or a state of being	We **swam** and **surfed.** She **was** a candidate.
1e.	adverb	modifies a verb, an adjective, or another adverb	They are **here.** We were **quite** surprised. You worked **very** quickly.
1f.	preposition	relates a noun or a pronoun to another word in the sentence	Some **of** the kittens **in** the pet-store window had bows **on** their necks.
1g.	conjunction	joins words or groups of words	Whitney **or** Jan will sing. We plan to hike **and** to camp.
1h.	interjection	expresses emotion	**Hey! Hooray! Well**, here we are.

2 **AGREEMENT**

Subject and Verb, Pronoun and Antecedent

 **Checking What You Know**

A. Correcting Errors in Subject-Verb and Pronoun-Antecedent Agreement

Most of the following sentences contain an agreement error. For each sentence, identify the incorrect verb or pronoun, and supply the correct form. If the sentence is correct, write C.

EXAMPLE   **1.** Peter and Mark likes to play baseball.
       1. *likes—like*

1. Computer science, in addition to foreign languages, are offered at our junior high school.
2. Since either Janet or Brian always bring a camera, we are sure to have plenty of good pictures of the school carnival.
3. The faculty at our school want to give the student body more privileges.
4. William Shakespeare's *Romeo and Juliet* are required reading in our class.

5. Neither Heather nor Rosa usually forgets to bring their running shoes.
6. Promises is all I have ever gotten from your company, and I want my money back.
7. There is some slices of bread left, but some of them are hard and stale.
8. She said that two gallons of milk was all the bucket would hold.
9. Either Alexis or the other girls are going to bring decorations for the party.
10. Each of the children completed their own project, which was to make a collage showing life at school.

B. Identifying and Correcting Errors in Subject-Verb and Pronoun-Antecedent Agreement

Each sentence in the following paragraph contains an error in agreement. Identify each incorrect verb or pronoun, and supply the correct form.

EXAMPLE   [1] Tapes and CDs of popular music is getting very expensive.
          1. *is—are*

[11] The economics of this situation hit young people right in the wallet! [12] Every one of my friends like music. [13] However, nobody ever have enough money to buy all the best new songs. [14] Teenagers have to use his or her intelligence to save money in the music store. [15] Several of my friends buys a single instead of an album if they want only one song from the album. [16] Danny, one of my best friends, take another approach. [17] The Caterpillars are his favorite group, and Danny tapes every new Caterpillars' song straight from the radio. [18] He don't have to pay for anything but the blank tape. [19] It is perfectly legal to copy music from a broadcast if all of the music that you tape are just for your own use. [20] Two of my other friends, Carla and Stephanie, save as much as four or five dollars per tape by buying her tapes on sale.

Number

Number is the form of a word that indicates whether the word is singular or plural.

2a. When a word refers to one person or thing, it is *singular* in number. When a word refers to more than one, it is *plural* in number.

SINGULAR	student	child	it	berry
PLURAL	students	children	they	berries

👉 REFERENCE NOTE: For more on forming the plurals of nouns, see pages 338–341. For a list of the singular and plural forms of personal pronouns, see page 55.

Agreement of Subject and Verb

2b. A verb should always agree with its subject in number.

(1) Singular subjects take singular verbs.

EXAMPLES **He washes** the dishes. [The singular verb *washes* agrees with the singular subject *he*.]
A **girl** in my neighborhood **plays** in the school band. [The singular subject *girl* takes the singular verb *plays*.]

(2) Plural subjects take plural verbs.

EXAMPLES **They wash** the dishes.
Three of my friends **play** in a band.

Like the single-word verbs in the examples above, verb phrases also agree with their subjects. In a verb phrase, only the first helping (auxiliary) verb changes its form to agree with the subject.

EXAMPLES A **girl** in my neighborhood **was playing** in the school band.
Several **girls** in my neighborhood **were playing** in the school band.

He has been washing the dishes.
They have been washing the dishes.

NOTE *Were* is plural except when it is used with the singular pronoun *you* and in statements that are contrary to fact.

EXAMPLES **They were** laughing about last night's movie. [The plural *they* is the subject of *were*.]
You were in my math class last year. [*You*, meaning one person, is used as subject.]
If I were free tonight, I'd go with you. [The statement containing *were* is contrary to fact.]

COMPUTER NOTE Some word-processing programs can find problems in subject-verb agreement. You can use such programs to search for errors when you proofread your writing. If you are not sure that an error found by the word processor is truly an error, check your handbook.

Intervening Phrases

2c. The number of the subject is not changed by a phrase following the subject.

Remember that a verb agrees in number with its subject. The subject is never part of a prepositional phrase.

EXAMPLES The **sign** near the glass doors **explains** the theme of the exhibit.
Several **paintings** by Emilio Sánchez **were hanging** in the gallery.

 REFERENCE NOTE: For information on prepositional phrases, see page 156–160.

Remember that some prepositions, such as *together with, in addition to, as well as,* and *along with,* are compound.

EXAMPLES   **Anne**, together with her cousins, **is backpacking** in Nevada this summer.

Robert, along with Kimberly and Elvin, **has been nominated** for class president.

The number of the subject is not changed by a negative construction following the subject.

EXAMPLE   **Ben**, not Rochelle and I, **is** in charge of the decorations.

Indefinite Pronouns

2d. The following indefinite pronouns are singular: *each, either, neither, one, everyone, everybody, everything, no one, nobody, nothing, anyone, anybody, anything, someone, somebody, something.*

EXAMPLES   **Each** of the athletes **runs** effortlessly. [Each one runs.]

Neither of the women **is** ready to start. [Neither one is ready.]

Someone was waving a large flag.

Does everyone in your family **enjoy** playing tennis?

2e. The following indefinite pronouns are plural: *several, few, both, many.*

EXAMPLES   **Several** of the runners **are exercising.**

Few of the athletes **have qualified.**

Were both of the games **postponed**?

Many on the team **practice** daily.

2f. The following indefinite pronouns may be either singular or plural: *some, all, most, any, none.*

These pronouns are singular when they refer to a singular word and plural when they refer to a plural word.

GRAMMAR/USAGE

EXAMPLES   **Some** of the show **is** funny. [*Some* refers to the singular noun *show*.]
Some of the entertainers **are** funny. [*Some* refers to the plural noun *entertainers*.]

All of the cast **looks** young.
All of the performers **look** young.

Most of his routine **sounds** familiar.
Most of his jokes **sound** familiar.

Was any of the criticism positive?
Were any of the reviews positive?

None of the music **is** catchy.
None of the tunes **are** catchy.

STYLE NOTE

The words *any* and *none* may be singular even when they refer to a plural word if you think of each item individually. *Any* and *none* are plural only if you think of several items as a group.

EXAMPLES   **Any** of these books **is** worth reading. [Any one book is worth reading.]
None of the books **was** overdue. [Not one book was overdue.]

Any of these books **are** worth reading. [All the books are worth reading.]
None of the books **were** overdue. [No books were overdue.]

✓ *QUICK CHECK 1*   **Identifying Verbs That Agree in Number with Their Subjects**

For each sentence in the following paragraph, choose the verb in parentheses that agrees with the subject.

[1] People in Japan often (*eat, eats*) noodles. [2] Some of the noodles (*is, are*) made from wheat flour, called *udon,* and

some from buckwheat flour, called *soba*. [3] A bowl of cooked noodles, together with sauce, broth, vegetables, or fish, (*makes, make*) a popular lunch. [4] Each of the thousands of noodle shops in Japan (*serves, serve*) a variety of noodle dishes. [5] Customers in search of a quick lunch or a snack (*order, orders*) noodles with their favorite toppings.

Compound Subjects

A *compound subject* consists of two or more nouns or pronouns that have the same verb.

2g. Subjects joined by *and* usually take a plural verb.

EXAMPLES　**Leslie Marmon Silko** and **Mari Evans are poets.** [Two persons are poets.]
Rhyme, rhythm, and **figurative language help** poets express their feelings. [Three things help.]

NOTE　Compound subjects that name only one person or thing take a singular verb.

EXAMPLES　**My pen pal and best friend is** my cousin. [One person is both your friend and your pen pal.]
Pumpkin seeds and raisins makes a tasty snack. [The one combination makes a tasty snack.]

2h. Singular subjects joined by *or* or *nor* take a singular verb.

EXAMPLES　After dinner, either **Anne** or **Tony loads** the **dishwasher.** [Either Anne or Tony loads the dishwasher, not both.]
Neither the **coach** nor the **principal is** happy with the team's performance. [Neither one is happy.]

2i. When a singular subject and a plural subject are joined by *or* or *nor*, the verb agrees with the subject nearer the verb.

GRAMMAR/USAGE

EXAMPLES   Neither the losers nor the **winner was** happy
with the outcome of the match.
Neither the winner nor the **losers were** happy
with the outcome of the match.

STYLE
NOTE

If such a construction sounds awkward to
you, revise the sentence to give each part of
the subject its own verb.

EXAMPLES   The **losers were** not happy with the outcome
of the match, and neither **was** the **winner**.

or

The **winner was** not happy with the outcome
of the match, and neither **were** the **losers**.

☑ *QUICK CHECK 2*   **Choosing Verbs That Agree in
Number with Their Subjects**

For each of the following sentences, choose the correct form
of the verb in parentheses.

1. In August, eager players and their fans (*looks, look*) forward to the start of the football season.
2. Neither the players nor the coach (*was, were*) surprised
by the referee's call.
3. The quarterback and star player (*is, are*) Virgil.
4. Neither the quarterback nor the wide receivers (*hear,
hears*) the whistle.
5. Either the marching band or the pep squad (*has, have*) already performed.

Other Problems in Agreement

2j.   *Don't* and *doesn't* must agree with their subjects.

Contractions are two words combined into one, with one
or more letters omitted. *Don't* is the contraction for *do not.*
Doesn't is the contraction for *does not.*

With the subjects *I* and *you* and with plural subjects, use *don't (do not)*.

EXAMPLES   I **don't** know.   They **don't** give up.
                   You **don't** say.   These **don't** shrink.
                   We **don't** want to.   Some people **don't** care.

With other subjects, use the singular *doesn't (does not)*.

EXAMPLES   He **doesn't** know.   One **doesn't** give up.
                   She **doesn't** say.   This **doesn't** shrink.
                   It **doesn't** want to.   Donna **doesn't** care.

2k.   Collective nouns may be either singular or plural.

Collective nouns are singular in form, but they name a group of persons or things.

Collective Nouns				
army	chorus	faculty	herd	squad
assembly	class	family	jury	staff
audience	club	fleet	majority	swarm
band	committee	flock	number	team
choir	crowd	group	public	troop

Use a plural verb with a collective noun to indicate that the individual parts or members of the group are acting separately. Use a singular verb to indicate that the group is acting as a unit.

EXAMPLES   The class **have** completed their projects. [The class is thought of as individuals.]
                   The class **has** elected its officers. [The class is thought of as a unit.]

☞ REFERENCE NOTE: Be sure that any pronoun referring to a collective noun also agrees with the noun in number. See pages 88–90 for more on pronoun-antecedent agreement.

2l.   A verb agrees with its subject, not with its predicate nominative.

                            S   PN
EXAMPLES   The marching **bands are** the main **attraction.**

GRAMMAR/USAGE

$$\overset{\text{S}}{} \qquad\qquad\qquad \overset{\text{PN}}{}$$
The main **attraction is** the marching **bands.**

$$\overset{\text{S}}{} \qquad\qquad \overset{\text{PN}}{}$$
My **favorite is** the trapeze **artists.**

$$\overset{\text{S}}{} \qquad\qquad \overset{\text{PN}}{}$$
The trapeze **artists are** my **favorite.**

 REFERENCE NOTE: For more information on predicate nominatives, see page 202.

STYLE
NOTE

If such a construction sounds awkward to you, revise the sentence so that it does not contain a predicate nominative.

EXAMPLE   The audience considers the marching bands the main attraction.

2m.   When the subject follows the verb, make sure that the verb agrees with it.

Most often, the subject follows the verb in sentences beginning with *here* and *there* and in questions.

EXAMPLES   Here **is** a **list** of addresses.
Here **are** two **lists** of addresses.

There **is** my **notebook.**
There **are** my **notebooks.**

Where **is Heather**? Where **is Chris**?
Where **are Heather** and **Chris**?

NOTE   Contractions such as *here's, where's, how's,* and *what's* include the singular verb *is.* Use one of those contractions only if a singular subject follows it.

NONSTANDARD   There's some facts on that topic in a chart at the back of the book.
STANDARD   There are some facts on that topic in a chart at the back of the book.
STANDARD   At the back of the book, there's a chart with some facts on that topic.

 REFERENCE NOTE: For more on finding the subject in a sentence, see pages 195–198. For more on contractions, see pages 313–314.

GRAMMAR/USAGE

2n. Words stating an amount are usually singular.

A weight, a measurement, or an amount of money or time is usually thought of as a unit. In that case, it takes a singular verb.

EXAMPLES   **Thirty dollars is** too much for a concert ticket.
Two hours is a long time to wait.
Three fourths of the show **is** over.

Sometimes, however, the amount is thought of as individual pieces or parts. If so, it takes a plural verb.

EXAMPLES   **Five** of the dollars **were** borrowed.
Two of the hours **were** spent in line.
Three fourths of the songs **are** new.

 NOTE   Use a singular verb when the expression *the number* comes before a prepositional phrase. Use a plural verb when the expression *a number* comes before a prepositional phrase.

EXAMPLES   **The number** of days in a leap year **is** 366.
A number of my friends **are taking** Spanish.

 QUICK CHECK 3   **Identifying Subjects and Verbs That Agree in Number**

Identify the subject of each verb in parentheses. Then choose the form of the verb that agrees with the subject.

1. The class (*has, have*) chosen their titles for their original plays.
2. First prize (*was, were*) two tickets to Hawaii.
3. Two thirds of the missing books (*was, were*) returned.
4. Where (*is, are*) the paragraphs you wrote?
5. Four weeks (*is, are*) enough time to rehearse the play.

2o. Even if it is plural in form, the title of a creative work (such as a book, song, film, or painting), the name of an organization, or the name of a country or city takes a singular verb.

EXAMPLES   ***Blue Lines* is** an early painting by Georgia O'Keeffe. [one painting]

GRAMMAR/USAGE

> **The Souls of Black Folk is** often **cited** as a classic of African American literature. [one book]
> **"Greensleeves" is** an old English folk song. [one song]
> **Friends of the Earth was founded** in 1969. [one organization]
> **Moira's Antiques is located** on Westview Drive. [one company]
> **The Netherlands has** thousands of canals. [one country]
> **New Orleans is** home to thirteen colleges and universities. [one city]

NOTE The names of some organizations may take singular or plural verbs. When the name refers to the organization as a unit, it takes a singular verb. When the name refers to the members of the organization as individuals, it takes a plural verb.

EXAMPLES   The **Talking Heads is** one of the most enduring musical groups of the New Wave. [*Talking Heads* as a unit]
The **Talking Heads are** former design school students. [*Talking Heads* as individuals]

2p. *Every* or *many a* before a subject calls for a singular verb.

EXAMPLES   **Every** homeowner and storekeeper **has** joined the cleanup drive.
Many a litterbug **was** surprised by the stiff fines.

2q. A few nouns, although plural in form, take singular verbs.

EXAMPLES   **Mumps is** a common childhood illness.
The **news** of the nominee for the Supreme Court **was** a surprise to many observers.
Rickets is a serious health problem in some countries.

Certain nouns that end in –*ic*s may be either singular or plural.

GRAMMAR/USAGE

EXAMPLES **Is politics** something you keep up with?
Their **politics are** quite different from ours.
Ethics is the study of standards of conduct.
The candidate's **ethics have raised** many
questions.

NOTE When you're not sure whether to use a singular verb
or a plural verb with a noun ending in -*ics*, check a
dictionary.

Some nouns that end in –*s* take a plural verb even though
they refer to a single item.

EXAMPLES The **scissors need** to be sharpened.
Were these **pants** on sale?
The **pliers are** next to the wrench.

Crock reprinted with special permission
of North America Syndicate, Inc.

 QUICK CHECK 4 **Identifying Subjects and
Verbs That Agree in Number**

Identify the subject of each verb in parentheses. Then
choose the form of the verb that agrees with the subject.

1. *Wild Swans* by Jung Chang (*tell, tells*) the story of three
generations of Chinese women.
2. (*Is, Are*) the Philippines your native country?
3. Every freshman and sophomore (*is, are*) eligible for the
award.
4. Women in Communication, Inc. (*host, hosts*) monthly
luncheon meetings in our area.
5. (*Is, Are*) economics taught at your high school?

GRAMMAR/USAGE

Agreement of Pronoun and Antecedent

Usually, a pronoun refers to a noun or another pronoun used earlier. The word that a pronoun refers to is called its *antecedent.*

 REFERENCE NOTE: For more information about antecedents, see pages 54–55 and 130–132.

2r. A pronoun should agree with its antecedent in number and gender.

A few singular personal pronouns have forms that indicate the gender of the antecedent. Masculine pronouns refer to males; feminine pronouns refer to females. Neuter pronouns refer to things and, often, to animals.

MASCULINE	he	him	his	himself
FEMININE	she	her	hers	herself
NEUTER	it	it	its	itself

EXAMPLES
Colette performs **her** solo today.
James makes **his** lunch every day.
The **cat** curled **itself** into a ball.

(1) Use a singular pronoun to refer to *each, either, neither, one, every, everyone, everybody, everything, no one, nobody, nothing, anyone, anybody, anything, someone, somebody,* or *something.*

EXAMPLES
Each of the clubs has **its** own service project.
One of the parakeets escaped from **its** cage.
Everyone on the softball team won **her** match.

When the antecedent of a personal pronoun is an indefinite pronoun, look in a phrase following the antecedent to determine the gender. A phrase after the antecedent does not change the number of the antecedent.

EXAMPLES
One of the **women** in the acting class designs **her** own costumes. [The antecedent *one*

GRAMMAR/USAGE

refers to a woman, so the personal pronoun is feminine.]
Each of the **boys** rode **his** bicycle to school.
[The antecedent *each* refers to a boy, so the personal pronoun is masculine.]

When the antecedent could be either masculine or feminine, use both the masculine and the feminine forms connected by *or.*

EXAMPLES   **Every one** of the students shouted **his or her** approval.
                 Everybody should always choose **his or her** friends carefully.

STYLE NOTE   When the antecedent could be either masculine or feminine, you can avoid the *his or her* construction. Revise the sentence and use the plural form of the pronoun instead.

EXAMPLES   **All** of the students shouted **their** approval.
                 People should always choose **their** friends carefully.

In conversation, plural personal pronouns are often used to refer to singular antecedents that can be either masculine or feminine. This form is becoming increasingly popular in writing, especially when the meaning of the antecedent is *clearly* plural.

EXAMPLES   **Everybody** has packed **their** lunch in insulated coolers.
                 Each member of the Senior Citizens Club received **their** tickets in advance.

(2) Use a singular pronoun to refer to two or more singular antecedents joined by *or* or *nor.*

EXAMPLES   Neither **Richard nor Bob** distinguished **himself** in the finals.
                 Paula or Janet will present **her** views on the subject.

If a sentence sounds awkward when the antecedents are of different genders, revise it.

AWKWARD   **Ben or Maya** will read to the class **his or her** report.

REVISED   **Ben** will read to the class **his** report, or **Maya** will read **hers**.

(3) Use a plural pronoun to refer to two or more antecedents joined by *and*.

EXAMPLES   **Mona and Janet** left early because **they** had to be home before ten o'clock.

           Mom and Dad celebrated **their** twentieth wedding anniversary yesterday.

NOTE The number of a relative pronoun (*who, whom, which,* or *that*) depends on the number of the word it refers to—its antecedent.

EXAMPLES   Aretha is one **friend who** always **keeps her** word. [*Who* refers to the singular noun *friend.* Therefore, the singular forms *keeps* and *her* are used to agree with *who.*]

           Many who volunteer find their experiences rewarding. [*Who* is plural because *many* is plural. Therefore, the plural forms *find* and *their* are used to agree with *who.*]

 REFERENCE NOTE: For more information on relative pronouns in adjective clauses, see pages 180–181.

 QUICK CHECK 5 **Proofreading Sentences for Pronoun-Antecedent Agreement**

Some of the following sentences contain errors in pronoun-antecedent agreement. If a sentence is correct, write *C*. If there is an error in agreement, identify the error and give the correct form of the pronoun.

1. By Friday, all of us will need to have chosen a topic for his or her reports.

2. Neither George nor Dominic will have difficulty finding material for their report.

3. Both Ming Chin and Sue offered their help with proof-reading to George and Dominic.
4. Will either George or Dominic forget to include anec-dotes about their subject?
5. Nobody likes to discover that they just read a list of dull facts about an interesting subject.

✓ *Chapter Review*

A. Proofreading Sentences for Subject-Verb and Pronoun-Antecedent Agreement

Each of the following sentences contains an error in agreement. Identify each incorrect verb or pronoun, and supply the correct form.

EXAMPLE   **1.** Rochelle Richardson, one of our city's for-mer mayors, live next door to me.
            1. *live—lives*

1. When the truck overturned, a herd of cattle were set free on the expressway.
2. The teacher reminded each student to sharpen their pencil before the test began.
3. Only one of our tomato plants are producing any fruit, but the green beans seem to be thriving.
4. Everybody have been talking about the class picnic ever since you thought of the idea.
5. I thought that either Carla or Tiffany hadn't gotten their grade on the test yet.
6. Many of their experiments in sleep disorder research have failed, but neither Dr. Jenkins nor her assistants ever gives up hope.
7. My entry in both flower shows were three specimens of a new strain of orchid.
8. There is a brush, a comb, and a mirror on the dresser top.
9. Many a sailor have perished when his or her ship ran aground on that reef.
10. Measles have been almost completely conquered in the United States by a vaccine.

B. Proofreading a Paragraph for Subject-Verb and Pronoun-Antecedent Agreement

Most of the sentences in the following paragraph contain at least one agreement error. For each error, identify the incorrect verb or pronoun and supply the correct form. If a sentence is correct, write *C*.

EXAMPLE [1] People who film an animal in its natural habitat faces many problems.

1. faces—face

[11] One problem is that the photographer, in most cases, have to get quite close to the animal. [12] Ten yards often make the difference between a good scene and no scene at all. [13] A zoom lens or a telephoto lens are generally used, but even then, getting good photographs can be very difficult. [14] Before filming, the crew usually watch the animal for weeks to learn its habits and find good vantage points for taking pictures. [15] In addition, the photographer and the crew uses every trick of the trade in filming wild animals. [16] For example, *Foxes at Night* were almost certainly not filmed at night! [17] "Nighttime" films are generally made during daylight hours, when there is plenty of natural light. [18] Later, all of the daytime footage are darkened using filters. [19] Also, many of the animals used in a nature film has been trained or partially tamed. [20] For example, if a photographer or a crew member take care of a bird from the moment it hatches, it will instinctively follow him or her everywhere. [21] The photographer can then easily take close-up pictures of the bird after it matures. [22] In many films, scenes of animals giving birth and raising their young is filmed in a studio, not in the wild. [23] A photographer shoots such a scene by building a den where they can film the baby animals through a window beside the nest. [24] This film, along with footage taken in the natural habitat, are then skillfully edited. [25] As a result, few of the viewers ever suspects that he or she is watching film that has been shot indoors.

3 USING VERBS

Principal Parts, Tense, Voice

✓ Checking What You Know

A. Using the Past and Past Participle Forms of Irregular Verbs

For each of the following sentences, give the correct form (past or past participle) of the verb in parentheses.

EXAMPLE   **1.** I have (*write*) a story about the big snow storm we had last winter.
          1. *written*

1. The wind (*blow*) all night long during the snowstorm.
2. When Latisha and I looked outside in the morning, at least a foot of snow had (*fall*).
3. Instead of a brown, lifeless yard, we (*see*) a glittering fantasy world.
4. Never in our lives had we (*eat*) cereal as fast as we did that morning!
5. We quickly put on our parkas and (*run*) out the door to build a snow fort.
6. To our surprise, Mom (*come*) outside, too, with a mischievous smile on her face.

7. We should have (*know*) she would start a snowball fight!
8. Before we could get our revenge, Mom (*go*) back into the house to warm up.
9. Pretty soon our feet felt as if they had (*freeze*) solid.
10. When we finally went inside, Mom (*bring*) us mugs of hot apple cider as a peace offering.

B. Revising Verb Tense or Voice

Some of the following sentences have verbs in the wrong tense, awkward use of the passive voice, or both. Revise each incorrect sentence to correct these errors. If a sentence is correct, write *C*.

EXAMPLE   [1]Some money was lost by someone at the beach.
            1. *Someone lost some money at the beach.*

[11] Ever since he was a boy, my grandfather loves to go beachcombing. [12] Last Saturday, two ten-dollar bills and two twenty-dollar bills were found by him among some dark green seaweed. [13] He ran right home and shouts to Grandma that he had found a bunch of money. [14]Of course, by the time Grandpa got back down to the ocean, the seaweed is being inspected by his neighbor Joe. [15] Between the two of them, Grandpa and Joe found over two hundred dollars that day.

C. Identifying Errors in the Use of *Lie* and *Lay, Sit* and *Set*, and *Rise* and *Raise*

For each of the following sentences, write *C* if the sentence is correct. If the sentence is incorrect, write the correct verb form.

EXAMPLE   1. We lay the boxes down and took a break.
            1. *laid*

16. Aunt Janet loves to set by the sunny window on winter afternoons.
17. I'll sit in a chair; the cat can lay in the hammock.

18. If you set the bread dough over a pan of warm water, the dough will rise faster.
19. The dogs are either laying under the porch or sitting by the gate.
20. The curtain rose just as we set down to watch the production of *Ain't Misbehavin'*. ✓

The Principal Parts of Verbs

Every verb has four basic forms. These forms are the verb's *principal parts.*

3a. The four principal parts of a verb are the *base form,* the *present participle,* the *past,* and the *past participle.*

The principal parts of the verb *ring,* for example, are *ring* (base form), *ringing* (present participle), *rang* (past), and *rung* (past participle). These principal parts are used to form different verb tenses.

EXAMPLES   The bells **ring** every day. [present tense]
The bells **are ringing** now. [present progressive tense]
The bells **rang** at noon. [past tense]
The bells **have rung** for the last time today. [present perfect tense]

Notice that the tenses made from the present participle and past participle contain helping verbs, such as *am, is, are, has,* and *have.*

 REFERENCE NOTE: For more about how participles and helping verbs work together, see pages 63–64. For more information on verb tenses, see pages 101–107.

Regular Verbs

3b. A *regular verb* is a verb that forms its past and past participle by adding *-d* or *-ed* to the base form.

GRAMMAR/USAGE

BASE FORM	PRESENT PARTICIPLE	PAST	PAST PARTICIPLE
use	(is) using	used	(have) used
suppose	(is) supposing	supposed	(have) supposed
risk	(is) risking	risked	(have) risked

☞ REFERENCE NOTE: The present participle of most regular verbs ending in *-e* drops the *-e* before adding *-ing*. See pages 335–337 for more on spelling words with verb endings or other suffixes.

One common error in the use of the past and the past participle forms is to leave off the *-d* or *-ed* ending.

NONSTANDARD We use to play soccer.
STANDARD We **used** to play soccer.

NONSTANDARD She was suppose to come early.
STANDARD She was **supposed** to come early.

☞ REFERENCE NOTE: For a discussion of standard and non-standard English, see page 1.

Another common error is to misspell or mispronounce verbs.

NONSTANDARD We were attackted by mosquitoes.
STANDARD We were **attacked** by mosquitoes.

NONSTANDARD Someone has drownded.
STANDARD Someone has **drowned**.

STYLE NOTE A few regular verbs have alternative past forms ending in *-t.* For example, the past form of *burn* is *burned* or *burnt.* Both forms are correct.

 QUICK CHECK 1 **Identifying Correct Forms of Regular Verbs**

For each of the following sentences, choose the correct form of the verb in parentheses.

GRAMMAR/USAGE

1. Aunt Rosie (*use, used*) to do needlepoint.
2. What has (*happen, happened*) to your bicycle?
3. Reggie (*frowned, frownded*) thoughtfully as he read the first question on the grammar test.
4. Aren't you (*suppose, supposed*) to sing?
5. Last night Aunt Catherine (*ask, asked*) me if I could come visit her in El Paso this summer.

Irregular Verbs

> **3c.** An *irregular verb* is a verb that forms its past and past participle in some other way than by adding -*d* or -*ed* to the base form.

Irregular verbs form the past and past participle by

- changing vowels *or* consonants
- changing vowels *and* consonants
- making no change

	BASE FORM	PAST	PAST PARTICIPLE
Vowel Change	begin	began	(have) begun
Consonant Change	send	sent	(have) sent
Vowel and Consonant Change	bring	brought	(have) brought
No Change	put	put	(have) put

NOTE Since most English verbs are regular, people sometimes try to make irregular verbs follow the same pattern. However, such words as *throwed, knowed, shrinked,* or *choosed* are considered nonstandard. If you are not sure whether a verb is regular or irregular, look in a dictionary. Entries for irregular verbs list the principal parts. If no principal parts are listed, the verb is a regular verb.

PRINCIPAL PARTS OF COMMON IRREGULAR VERBS			
BASE FORM	**PRESENT PARTICIPLE**	**PAST**	**PAST PARTICIPLE**
begin	(is) beginning	began	(have) begun
blow	(is) blowing	blew	(have) blown
break	(is) breaking	broke	(have) broken
bring	(is) bringing	brought	(have) brought
burst	(is) bursting	burst	(have) burst
choose	(is) choosing	chose	(have) chosen
come	(is) coming	came	(have) come
dive	(is) diving	dove	(have) dived
do	(is) doing	did	(have) done
draw	(is) drawing	drew	(have) drawn
drink	(is) drinking	drank	(have) drunk
drive	(is) driving	drove	(have) driven
eat	(is) eating	ate	(have) eaten
fall	(is) falling	fell	(have) fallen
freeze	(is) freezing	froze	(have) frozen
give	(is) giving	gave	(have) given
go	(is) going	went	(have) gone
grow	(is) growing	grew	(have) grown
hear	(is) hearing	heard	(have) heard
know	(is) knowing	knew	(have) known
leave	(is) leaving	left	(have) left
put	(is) putting	put	(have) put
ride	(is) riding	rode	(have) ridden
ring	(is) ringing	rang	(have) rung
run	(is) running	ran	(have) run
say	(is) saying	said	(have) said
see	(is) seeing	saw	(have) seen
send	(is) sending	sent	(have) sent
shake	(is) shaking	shook	(have) shaken

(continued)

	PRINCIPAL PARTS OF COMMON IRREGULAR VERBS *(continued)*		
BASE FORM	**PRESENT PARTICIPLE**	**PAST**	**PAST PARTICIPLE**
shrink	(is) shrinking	shrank	(have) shrunk
sing	(is) singing	sang	(have) sung
sink	(is) sinking	sank	(have) sunk
sleep	(is) sleeping	slept	(have) slept
speak	(is) speaking	spoke	(have) spoken
steal	(is) stealing	stole	(have) stolen
sting	(is) stinging	stung	(have) stung
strike	(is) striking	struck	(have) struck
swear	(is) swearing	swore	(have) sworn
swim	(is) swimming	swam	(have) swum
take	(is) taking	took	(have) taken
teach	(is) teaching	taught	(have) taught
tear	(is) tearing	tore	(have) torn
think	(is) thinking	thought	(have) thought
throw	(is) throwing	threw	(have) thrown
wear	(is) wearing	wore	(have) worn
write	(is) writing	wrote	(have) written

When the present participle and past participle forms are used as main verbs (simple predicates) in sentences, they always require helping verbs. Leaving out the helping verbs results in nonstandard usage.

PRESENT PARTICIPLE	+	HELPING VERB	=	MAIN VERB
taking		[*forms*		am taking
walking	+	*of*	=	was walking
going		**be**]		have been going

(continued)

PAST PARTICIPLE	+	HELPING VERB	=	MAIN VERB
taken		[*forms*		have taken
walked	+	*of*	=	has walked
gone		**have**]		had gone

NONSTANDARD   We already seen that program.
STANDARD   We **have** already **seen** that program.

☞ REFERENCE NOTE: Sometimes a past participle is used with a form of *be: was chosen, are known, is seen.* This usage is called the *passive voice*. See pages 108–112.

"WHEN I SAY 'RUNNED', YOU KNOW I MEAN 'RAN'. LET'S NOT QUIBBLE."

©1984 by Sidney Harris—"Phi Delta Kappan."

✓ *QUICK CHECK 2*   **Identifying Correct Forms of Irregular Verbs**

For each of the following sentences, choose the correct form of the verb in parentheses.

1. Mai's parents (*telled, told*) her about their journey from South Vietnam to Malaysia in a crowded boat.
2. They abandoned their home after the South Vietnamese capital, Saigon, had (*fell, fallen*) to North Vietnamese forces.

3. The refugees spent many days and nights on the ocean before they (*saw, seen*) land again.
4. After they had (*drank, drunk*) what little water was on board, they went thirsty.
5. It (*took, taken*) months for Mai's parents to be moved from Malaysian refugee camps to the United States.

Tense

3d. The *tense* of a verb indicates the time of the action or state of being expressed by the verb. Every English verb has six tenses: *present, past, future, present perfect, past perfect,* and *future perfect.* The tenses are formed from the verb's principal parts.

This time line shows how the six tenses are related to one another.

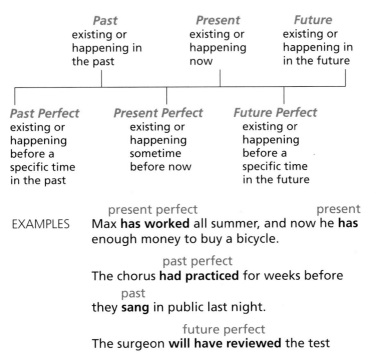

| | Past
existing or
happening in
the past | Present
existing or
happening
now | Future
existing or
happening in
in the future |

| *Past Perfect*
existing or
happening
before a
specific time
in the past | *Present Perfect*
existing or
happening
sometime
before now | *Future Perfect*
existing or
happening
before a
specific time
in the future |

EXAMPLES

       present perfect   present
Max **has worked** all summer, and now he **has** enough money to buy a bicycle.

       past perfect
The chorus **had practiced** for weeks before

    past
they **sang** in public last night.

       future perfect
The surgeon **will have reviewed** the test

GRAMMAR/USAGE

future

results by next Friday, and she **will decide** whether or not to operate then.

The following chart shows the six tense forms of *give* in the active voice. Listing all the forms of a verb in the six tenses is called *conjugating* a verb.

 REFERENCE NOTE: *Active voice* and *passive voice* are discussed on pages 108–112. See pages 109–110 for the conjugation of *give* in the passive voice.

CONJUGATION OF THE VERB *GIVE* IN THE ACTIVE VOICE			
PRINCIPAL PARTS			
BASE FORM	*PRESENT PARTICIPLE*	*PAST*	*PAST PARTICIPLE*
give	(is) giving	gave	(have) given
PRESENT TENSE			
SINGULAR		*PLURAL*	
I give		we give	
you give		you give	
he, she, it gives		they give	
PAST TENSE			
SINGULAR		*PLURAL*	
I gave		we gave	
you gave		you gave	
he, she, it gave		they gave	
FUTURE TENSE (*will* or *shall* + base form)			
SINGULAR		*PLURAL*	
I will (shall) give		we will (shall) give	
you will give		you will give	
he, she, it will give		they will give	

(continued)

CONJUGATION OF THE VERB *GIVE* IN THE ACTIVE VOICE *(continued)*	

PRESENT PERFECT TENSE
(*have* or *has* + past participle)

SINGULAR	*PLURAL*
I have given	we have given
you have given	you have given
he, she, it has given	they have given

PAST PERFECT TENSE
(*had* + past participle)

SINGULAR	*PLURAL*
I had given	we had given
you had given	you had given
he, she, it had given	they had given

FUTURE PERFECT TENSE
(*will have* or *shall have* + past participle)

SINGULAR	*PLURAL*
I will (shall) have given	we will (shall) have given
you will have given	you will have given
he, she, it will have given	they will have given

NOTE Traditionally, the helping verb *shall* was used in the second person (*you*) and third person (*he, she, it, they*) only to express a requirement or necessity. Now, however, *shall* can be used interchangeably with *will*.

Each of the six tenses has an additional form called the *progressive form*. The progressive form expresses a continuing action or state of being. It consists of the appropriate tense of *be* plus the verb's present participle. For the perfect tenses, the progressive form also includes one or more helping verbs.

GRAMMAR/USAGE

Present Progressive	am, are, is giving
Past Progressive	was, were giving
Future Progressive	will (shall) be giving
Present Perfect Progressive	has, have been giving
Past Perfect Progressive	had been giving
Future Perfect Progressive	will (shall) have been giving

3e. Each of the six tenses has its own special uses.

(1) The **present tense** is used mainly to express an action or a state of being that is occurring now.

EXAMPLES　　Melvin **has** a bad cold.
　　　　　　Leotie **belongs** to the Latin Club.
　　　　　　They **are decorating** the gym. [progressive form]

The present tense is also used
- to show a customary or habitual action or state of being
- to express a general truth—something that is always true
- to make historical events seem current (such use is called the historical present)
- to discuss a literary work (such use is called the literary present)
- to express future time

EXAMPLES　　We **recycle** newspapers, glass, and aluminum cans. [customary action]
　　　　　　The sun **sets** in the west. [general truth]
　　　　　　In 1905, Albert Einstein **makes** history when he **proposes** his theory of relativity. [historical present]
　　　　　　Maya Angelou's *I Know Why the Caged Bird Sings* **tells** the story of the author's childhood. [literary present]
　　　　　　Finals **begin** next week. [future time]

(2) The **past tense** is used to express an action or a state of being that occurred in the past but that is not occurring now.

EXAMPLES　　We **looked** for seashells.
　　　　　　We **were walking** along the beach. [progressive form]

NOTE A past action or state of being may also be shown with the verb *used to* followed by the base form.

EXAMPLE We **used to live** in Chicago.

(3) The *future tense* is used to express an action or a state of being that will occur. It is formed with *will* or *shall* and the verb's base form.

EXAMPLES Ben and Alexis **will arrive** soon. [future]
They **will be arriving** soon. [future progressive]

 NOTE A future action or state of being may also be shown in other ways.

EXAMPLES We **are going to make** our own Halloween costumes this year.
The president **holds** a press conference **next Monday**.

(4) The *present perfect tense* is used to express an action or a state of being that occurred at some indefinite time in the past. It always includes the helping verb *have* or *has*.

EXAMPLES Rachel **has missed** only one day of school this year.
The Mendozas **have invited** us over for a cookout.

 NOTE Avoid using the present perfect tense to express a *specific* time in the past. Instead, use the past tense.

NONSTANDARD We have seen that movie last Saturday. [Last Saturday indicates a specific time in the past.]
STANDARD We **saw** that movie last Saturday. [past tense]

The present perfect tense is also used to express an action or a state of being that began in the past and continues into the present.

EXAMPLES Li Hua **has taken** violin lessons for eight years.
We **have been living** in Amarillo since 1988. [progressive form]

(5) The **past perfect tense** is used to express an action or a state of being that was completed in the past before

some other past action or event. It always includes the helping verb *had*.

EXAMPLES   Once the judges **had viewed** the paintings, they **announced** the winners. [The viewing occurred before the announcing.]

When you called, I **had been studying** for three hours. [progressive form]

(6) The *future perfect tense* is used to express an action or a state of being that will be completed in the future before some other future occurrence. It always includes the helping verbs *will have* or *shall have*.

EXAMPLES   By the time Mom returns, I **will have done** my chores. [The doing will be completed before the returning.]

In August, I **will have been taking** Hebrew lessons for two years. [progressive form]

Frank & Ernest reprinted by permission of NEA, Inc.

✓ *QUICK CHECK 3*   **Explaining the Uses of Tenses in Sentences**

Explain the differences in meaning between the sentences in the following pairs. Both sentences in each pair are correct. Identify the tense of the verb in each sentence.

1. a. You will put down your pencils at 3:00.
   b. You will have put down your pencils at 3:00.
2. a. He worked at the gas station in summertime.
   b. He has worked at the gas station in summertime.

3. a. What caused the computer to crash?
   b. What has been causing the computer to crash?
4. a. Last year Morton held the record.
   b. Last year Morton had held the record.
5. a. Shelley was working on her bicycle.
   b. Shelley had been working on her bicycle.

Consistency of Tense

3f. Do not change needlessly from one tense to another.

NONSTANDARD   Cara fielded the ball and throws the runner out. [*Fielded* is past tense; *throws* is present tense.]

STANDARD   Cara **fielded** the ball and **threw** the runner out. [*Fielded* and *threw* are both past tense.]

NONSTANDARD   He stands on the mound and stared at the batter. [*Stands* is present tense; *stared* is past tense.]

STANDARD   He **stands** on the mound and **stares** at the batter. [*Stands* and *stares* are both present tense.]

NOTE Changing verb tenses is sometimes necessary to show the order of events that occur at different times.

NONSTANDARD   I regretted that I chose such a broad topic. [Since the action of choosing was completed before the action of regretting, the verb should be *had chosen*, not *chose*.]

STANDARD   I **regretted** that I **had chosen** such a broad topic.

✓ *QUICK CHECK 4*   **Proofreading a Paragraph to Make the Tenses of the Verbs Consistent**

Proofread the following paragraph for needless changes of verb tense. Decide whether the paragraph should be written in the present or past tense. Then change the verbs to make the tenses consistent.

[1] To my surprise, Nancy Chang has decided to drop by about five o'clock last Friday. [2] What she wanted is a fishing companion. She has been thinking about going fishing all week. [3] As I was getting my gear together, I have become excited and in my imagination see the fish on my line. [4] On our way out to the lake, clouds begin to form, and we knew we are in for trouble. [5] It rains all right, for the whole weekend; the fish were safe for another week.

Active and Passive Voice

3g. A verb in the ***active voice*** expresses an action done *by* its subject. A verb in the ***passive voice*** expresses an action done *to* its subject.

 REFERENCE NOTE: Only transitive verbs (action verbs that take objects) have voice. See page 61 for a discussion of transitive verbs.

ACTIVE VOICE   **The coach instructed us.** [The subject, *coach*, performs the action.]

PASSIVE VOICE   **I was instructed by the coach to bunt.** [The subject, *I*, receives the action.]

Compare the following related sentences:

	S	V	O
ACTIVE VOICE	**The author provides helpful diagrams.**		

	S	V
PASSIVE VOICE	**Helpful diagrams are provided** by the author.	

As you can see, the object of the active sentence becomes the subject of the passive one. The subject of the active sentence becomes the object of the prepositional phrase. In some sentences, such as this one, the phrase can even be omitted.

PASSIVE VOICE   **Helpful diagrams are provided.**

GRAMMAR/USAGE

The verb in a passive sentence is always a verb phrase made up of a form of *be* and the main verb's past participle. Depending on the tense, other helping verbs may also be included.

ACTIVE VOICE   Willa Cather **wrote** *My Ántonia*.

PASSIVE VOICE   *My Ántonia* **was written** by Willa Cather.

ACTIVE VOICE   Someone **has erased** the tapes.

PASSIVE VOICE   The tapes **have been erased**.

☞ REFERENCE NOTE: For more information on helping verbs, see pages 63–64.

The following chart shows the conjugation of the verb *give* in the passive voice.

☞ REFERENCE NOTE: The conjugation of *give* in the active voice is on pages 102–103.

CONJUGATION OF THE VERB *GIVE* IN THE PASSIVE VOICE			
PRINCIPAL PARTS			
BASE FORM	***PRESENT PARTICIPLE***	**PAST**	***PAST PARTICIPLE***
give	(is) giving	gave	(have) given
PRESENT TENSE			

SINGULAR   **PLURAL**

I am given   we are given

you are given   you are given

he, she, it is given   they are given

Present progressive: am, are, is being given

(continued)

CONJUGATION OF THE VERB *GIVE* IN THE PASSIVE VOICE *(continued)*

PAST TENSE

SINGULAR	PLURAL
I was given	we were given
you were given	you were given
he, she, it was given	they were given

Past progressive: was, were being given

FUTURE TENSE

SINGULAR	PLURAL
I will (shall) be given	we will (shall) be given
you will be given	you will be given
he, she, it will be given	they will be given

PRESENT PERFECT TENSE

SINGULAR	PLURAL
I have been given	we have been given
you have been given	you have been given
he, she, it has been given	they have been given

PAST PERFECT TENSE

SINGULAR	PLURAL
I had been given	we had been given
you had been given	you had been given
he, she, it had been given	they had been given

FUTURE PERFECT TENSE

SINGULAR	PLURAL
I will (shall) have been given	we will (shall) have been given
you will have been given	you will have been given
he, she, it will have been given	they will have been given

NOTE The progressive forms of the passive voice exist for the future, present perfect, past perfect, and future perfect tenses. However, the use of *be* or *been* with *being* is extremely awkward [*give*, for example, in the passive future perfect is *will (shall) have been being given*]. Consequently, the progressive form of the passive voice is usually used only in the present and past tenses.

Using the Passive Voice

3h. Use the passive voice sparingly.

The passive voice is not any less correct than the active voice, but it is less direct, less forceful, and less concise. You should avoid overusing the passive voice for two reasons. First, it generally requires more words to express a thought than the active voice does. Consequently, the passive voice can result in awkward writing. Second, the performer of the action in a passive voice construction is revealed indirectly or not at all. As a result, a sentence written in the passive voice can sound weak. Compare the following sentences.

AWKWARD PASSIVE	The ball was hit over the outfield fence by Jody.
ACTIVE	Jody hit the ball over the outfield fence.

The passive voice is useful in situations such as the following ones, however.

(1) when you do not know the performer of the action

EXAMPLES	The house **was built** of brick.
	A false alarm **had been telephoned** to the fire department.

(2) when you do not want to reveal the performer of the action

EXAMPLES	Unfounded accusations **were made** against the candidate.
	The suspects **are described** as a man and woman in their forties.

(3) when you want to emphasize the receiver of the action

EXAMPLES   Aung San Suu Kyi of Burma **was awarded** the
1991 Nobel Peace Prize.
The entire state **has been declared** a disaster
area.

COMPUTER NOTE   Some software programs can identify and
highlight passive voice verbs. If you use such
a program, keep in mind that it can't tell why
you used the passive voice. If you did so for one of the reasons just illustrated by the examples, you may want to leave the verb in the passive voice.

Shoe, by Jeff MacNelly, reprinted by permission: Tribune Media Services.

GRAMMAR/USAGE

QUICK CHECK 5 **Classifying Sentences by Voice**

Identify each of the following sentences as *active* or *passive*.

1. The album was reviewed unfavorably by most critics.
2. Your generous contribution to help the homeless is greatly appreciated.
3. This afternoon the baby stood up by himself.
4. Was Saul Bellow awarded the Nobel Prize?
5. I don't understand this math problem.

Six Troublesome Verbs

Lie and *Lay*

The verb *lie* means "to rest" or "to stay, recline, or remain in a certain position." *Lie* never takes an object. The verb *lay* means "to put (something) in a place." *Lay* usually takes an object.

PRINCIPAL PARTS OF *LIE* AND *LAY*			
BASE FORM	**PRESENT PARTICIPLE**	**PAST**	**PAST PARTICIPLE**
lie (to rest)	(is) lying	lay	(have) lain
lay (to put)	(is) laying	laid	(have) laid

These examples show how the verb *lie* is used. Notice that none of the examples contains an object.

EXAMPLES I sometimes **lie** on the floor.
The bills are **lying** on the table.
Yesterday Lambert **lay** on the grass.
How long **have** the bills **lain** there?

The following examples show how the verb *lay* is used. Notice that each example contains an object.

GRAMMAR/USAGE

EXAMPLES **Lay** those books down. [*Books* is the object of *Lay*.]

I **am laying** the clean sheets and towels on this chair. [*Sheets and towels* is the object of *am laying*.]

Yesterday Lambert **laid** the bricks for the new wall on the patio. [*Bricks* is the object of *laid*.]

Have you **laid** your report aside? [*Report* is the object of *Have laid*.]

When deciding whether to use *lie* or *lay,* ask yourself two questions:

QUESTION 1: What is my meaning? (Is the meaning "to be in a lying position," or is it "to put something down"?)

QUESTION 2: What time does the verb express, and which principal part correctly shows this time?

EXAMPLE: How long have you (*lain, laid*) there?

QUESTION 1: **Meaning?** The meaning here is "to be in a lying position." Therefore, the verb should be *lie.*

QUESTION 2: **Principal part?** The time is the past, and the sentence requires the past participle combined with *have.* The past participle of *lie* is *lain.*

ANSWER: How long **have** you **lain** there?

EXAMPLE: Calvin (*lay, laid*) the jacket on the bed.

QUESTION 1: **Meaning?** The meaning here is "to put." Therefore, the verb should be *lay.*

QUESTION 2: **Principal part?** The time is past. Therefore, the sentence requires the past form, which is *laid.*

ANSWER: Calvin **laid** the jacket on the bed.

Sit and *Set*

The verb *sit* means "to rest in an upright, seated position." *Sit* almost never takes an object. The verb *set* means "to put (something) in a place." *Set* usually takes an object.

PRINCIPAL PARTS OF *SIT* AND *SET*			
BASE FORM	**PRESENT PARTICIPLE**	**PAST**	**PAST PARTICIPLE**
sit (to rest)	(is) sitting	sat	(have) sat
set (to put)	(is) setting	set	(have) set

EXAMPLES   **Sit** down. [no object]
Set it down. [*It* is the object of *Set*.]
The cups **sat** on the tray. [no object]
I **set** the cups there. [*Cups* is the object of *set*.]
Have you ever **sat** on a porch swing? [no object]
Doug still hasn't **set** the table. [*Table* is the object of *has set*.]

Rise and *Raise*

The verb *rise* means "to go up" or "to get up." *Rise* almost never takes an object. The verb *raise* means "to cause (something) to rise" or "to lift up." *Raise* usually takes an object.

PRINCIPAL PARTS OF *RISE* AND *RAISE*			
BASE FORM	**PRESENT PARTICIPLE**	**PAST**	**PAST PARTICIPLE**
rise (to go up)	(is) rising	rose	(have) risen
raise (to lift up)	(is) raising	raised	(have) raised

EXAMPLES   I always **rise** early. [no object]
Someone **will raise** that question. [*Question* is the object of *will raise*.]
The price index **rose** sharply. [no object]
To the dismay of subscribers, the publisher **raised** the price of the paper. [*Price* is the object of *raised*.]

GRAMMAR/USAGE

 QUICK CHECK 6

Identifying the Correct Forms of *Lie* and *Lay*, *Sit* and *Set*, and *Rise* and *Raise*

For each of the following sentences, choose the correct verb in parentheses.

1. Please (*sit, set*) the won tons on this plate.
2. The cat is (*lying, laying*) in the sun.
3. Have you ever (*sat, set*) on the beach at sundown?
4. The children (*rose, raised*) their flag for Cinco de Mayo.
5. He (*lay, laid*) the report aside and called for order.

 **Chapter Review**

Proofreading Paragraphs for Correct Verb Forms

Read the following paragraphs. If a sentence contains an incorrect or awkward verb form, write the correct form or revise the sentence. If a sentence is correct, write *C*. Some sentences may have more than one incorrect verb.

EXAMPLES [1] I have always wanted a pet.
1. *C*

[2] As a child, I use to dream about having a dog or cat.
2. *used*

[1] Every time I ask my parents, they said, "No, not in an apartment." [2] One day last year, I was setting on the front steps reading the newspaper when I spot an ad for a female ferret. [3] Deciding to investigate, I fold the paper, hop on my bike, and rode to the pet shop that had placed the ad.

[4] When I walked into the store, I seen the ferret right away. [5] She was laying in a cardboard box on top of the counter. [6] I told the owner I wanted to hold her, and he reaches into the box. [7] When he withdrew his hand, the ferret was holding onto his finger with what looked like very sharp teeth.

[8] I cautiously reached out and takes the ferret's hindquarters in my cupped hands. [9] The rest of her long body poured slowly into my hands until she was sitting on her haunches. [10] She looked up at me and suddenly clamps her teeth on my thumb. [11] The ferret done that to show me who was boss. [12] I should have knowed then that my troubles had just began.

[13] I ran all the way home and persuaded my parents to let me keep the ferret on a trial basis. [14] I had already give her a name—Ferris the Ferret—and I lose no time rushing back to the pet shop. [15] When I come home with Ferris, I sit a dish of cat food in front of her. [16] She stuck her snout into the dish and ate greedily. [17] After she had went into each room in the apartment, she choosed the top of the TV as her special place. [18] When my parents objected, I made a cardboard house with two entry holes and set it in a corner of my bedroom. [19] Ferris sniffed around her new home; then she goes in and laid down for a nap.

[20] For the next few days, Ferris spent her time either napping or nipping. [21] She always attackted me when I least expected it. [22] Once, as she lies on my desk while I am studying, she suddenly locked her teeth onto my earlobe. [23] I was so startled that I jump up quickly, and Ferris wound up laying on the floor with a look that makes me feel guilty. [24] The next day the bad news was gave to me by my parents: Ferris had to go back to the pet shop. [25] I no longer want a pet ferret, but I have wrote to the local zookeeper to ask about snakes.

4 USING PRONOUNS

Nominative and Objective Uses; Special Problems; Clear Reference

✓ *Checking What You Know*

A. Identifying Correct Forms of Pronouns

For each of the following sentences, give the correct form of the pronoun in parentheses.

EXAMPLE   **1.** (*We, Us*) girls have built a picnic table.
            1. *We*

  1. Janell and (*I, me*) painted the room together.
  2. Alan, (*who, whom*) I did the typing for, said that he will pay me on Friday.
  3. The young Amish couple drove us and (*they, them*) into town in a horse-drawn wagon.
  4. Carolyn has been playing the guitar longer than (*she, her*).
  5. The last two people to arrive, Tranh and (*I, me*), had trouble finding the skating rink.
  6. Hector wrote this song for you and (*I, me*).

7. The winner is (*whoever, whomever*) finishes first.

8. Ellis was worried about his project, but Mrs. Asato gave (*he, him*) an A.

9. Was the winner of the race (*he, him*) or Aaron?

10. The pictures of the Grand Canyon impressed them more than (*we, us*), for we had seen the real thing.

B. Proofreading a Paragraph for Correct Pronoun Usage

Some of the following sentences contain an incorrect pronoun form or an inexact pronoun reference. If a sentence is incorrect, write the correct form of the pronoun or correct the unclear pronoun reference. If the sentence is correct, write C.

EXAMPLE   [1] Between you and I, I'd like to see a blue rose.

    1. *me*

[11] Are you as interested in plants as me? [12] Nowadays, scientists are hard at work trying to develop blue roses for the enjoyment of us plant enthusiasts. [13] That surprises Ms. Phillips, my science teacher. [14] Breeding a blue rose seems unlikely to her and I. [15] Us modern rose-lovers have never seen a blue rose. [16] But an Arab agriculturist in the thirteenth century said that he had grown such. [17] For centuries, rose breeders who have tried to produce the legendary blue rose have failed. [18] Some genetic engineers who I read about are working on this project now. [19] Scientists aren't sure whom would buy a blue rose. [20] But they can't resist a challenge.   ✓

Case

Case is the form of a noun or pronoun that shows how the word is used. In English, there are three cases: *nominative, objective,* and *possessive.*

 Choosing the correct case form for a noun is no problem, because the form is the same in the nominative and objective cases.

EXAMPLE   My **dentist** [nominative] has opened a new
              practice with another **dentist** [objective].

Only in the possessive case does a noun change its
form.

EXAMPLES   My **brother's** [singular possessive] baseball
              team won the division championship.
              The **farmers'** [plural possessive] fields lay un
              plowed.

☞ REFERENCE NOTE: For information about forming the
possessives of nouns, see pages 309–310.

Most personal pronouns, however, have a different
form for each case.

EXAMPLE   **I** [nominative] forgot to bring **my** [possessive]
              notebook with **me** [objective].

CASE FORMS OF PERSONAL PRONOUNS			
SINGULAR			
	NOMINATIVE CASE	**OBJECTIVE CASE**	**POSSESSIVE CASE**
FIRST PERSON	I	me	my, mine
SECOND PERSON	you	you	your, yours
THIRD PERSON	he, she, it	him, her, it	his, her, hers, its
PLURAL			
	NOMINATIVE CASE	**OBJECTIVE CASE**	**POSSESSIVE CASE**
FIRST PERSON	we	us	our, ours
SECOND PERSON	you	you	your, yours
THIRD PERSON	they	them	their, theirs

Notice that *you* and *it* are the only personal pronouns that
have the same form in the nominative case and in the objective case.

REFERENCE NOTE: For more information on possessive personal pronouns, see page 55 and pages 310–311.

GRAMMAR/USAGE

The Nominative Case

Pronouns used as *subjects* and *predicate nominatives* are in the *nominative case.*

4a. The subject of a verb is always in the nominative case.

EXAMPLES   **She** was glad that **they** were elected. [*She* is the subject of *was; they* is the subject of *were elected.*]

Did **Max** and **she** write the script? [*Max* and *she* is the compound subject of *did write.*]

REFERENCE NOTE: For information about subjects of verbs, see pages 193–198.

To choose the correct pronoun forms for a compound subject, try each pronoun separately with the verb.

EXAMPLES   (*She, Her*) and (*they, them*) answered the ad. [*She answered* or *Her answered*? *They answered* or *them answered*?]

She and **they** answered the ad.

Born Loser reprinted by permission of NEA, Inc.

STYLE NOTE

If using the pronouns *we* and *they* together as a compound subject sounds awkward to you, revise the sentence.

AWKWARD   We and they hope to sit together at the game.

BETTER   **We** hope to sit with **them** at the game.

4b. A *predicate nominative* is always in the nominative case.

A *predicate nominative* is a noun or pronoun that follows a linking verb and explains or identifies the subject of the sentence.

 REFERENCE NOTE: For more about predicate nominatives, see page 202.

A pronoun used as a predicate nominative always follows a form of the verb *be* or a verb phrase ending in *be* or *been*.

EXAMPLES   This is **he**.
It may be **she**.
It should have been **they**.

 REFERENCE NOTE: For a list of commonly used forms of *be*, see pages 62–63.

STYLE NOTE   Widespread usage has made such expressions as *It's me, That's him,* or *Could it have been her?* acceptable in informal conversation. Avoid using them in formal speaking, however, and use them in writing only in informal dialogue.

✓ QUICK CHECK 1   **Identifying Pronouns Used As Subjects and Predicate Nominatives**

For each of the following sentences, identify the correct pronoun in parentheses.

1. (*She, Her*) made the shrimp tempura that (*we, us*) liked so much.
2. (*We, Us*) heard that Tim and (*she, her*) were disappointed.
3. Where are my parents and (*they, them*)?
4. The caller may have been (*he, him*).
5. Are (*she, her*) and (*I, me*) going to be the only contestants in the three-legged race?

GRAMMAR/USAGE

GRAMMAR/USAGE

The Objective Case

Pronouns in the objective case are used as *direct objects, indirect objects,* and *objects of prepositions.*

 REFERENCE NOTE: For more information about the different types of objects, see pages 67 and 202–204.

4c. The *direct object* of a verb is always in the objective case.

A **direct object** is a noun or pronoun that follows an action verb. It tells *who* or *what* receives the action of the verb.

EXAMPLES   Clem called **her** last night. [*Her* tells *whom* Clem called.]

Calinda set **it** on the table. [*It* tells *what* Calinda set on the table.]

4d. The *indirect object* of a verb is always in the objective case.

An **indirect object** is a noun or a pronoun that tells *to whom* or *to what* or *for whom* or *for what* the action of a verb is done.

EXAMPLES   The librarian gave **her** a pass. [*Her* tells *to whom* the pass was given.]

Molly made **me** a tape. [*Me* tells *for whom* the tape was made.]

Ahmad worried about dust getting in his typewriter, so he made **it** a dustcover. [*It* tells *for what* a dustcover was made.]

To choose the correct pronoun forms when an object is compound, try each pronoun separately with the verb. All parts of the compound must be correct for the sentence to be correct.

NONSTANDARD   Clem's call surprised her and I. [*Clem's call surprised her* is correct, but *Clem's call surprised I* is incorrect. The second pronoun should be *me*.]

STANDARD   Clem's call surprised **her** and **me**.

NONSTANDARD   Lee gave him and she a ride. [*Lee gave him a ride* is correct, but *Lee gave she a*

GRAMMAR/USAGE

ride is incorrect. The second pronoun
should be *her*.]

STANDARD   Lee gave **him** and **her** a ride.

4e. The *object of a preposition* is always in the
objective case.

The noun or pronoun that follows a preposition is called
the *object of the preposition*.

EXAMPLES   with **me**   before **her**   next to **them**
            for **us**   behind **him**

 REFERENCE NOTE: For lists of commonly used prepositions, see page 68. For information on using prepositional phrases in sentences, see page 228.

To choose the correct pronoun forms when the object of
a preposition is compound, try each pronoun separately in
the prepositional phrase.

NONSTANDARD   The company sent an apologetic letter to
               her and I. [*The company sent a letter to
               her* is correct, but *The company sent a
               letter to I* is incorrect. The second pro-
               noun should be *me*.]

STANDARD   The company sent an apologetic letter to
               her and **me**.

 Avoid the common error of using incorrect pronoun
forms after the prepositions *between* and *for*.

NONSTANDARD   Just between you and I, I voted for
               Pilar.
STANDARD   Just between you and **me,** I voted
               for Pilar.

NONSTANDARD   The packages are for he and they.
STANDARD   The packages are for **him** and
               them.

✓ *QUICK CHECK 2*   **Identifying Pronouns Used as
                    Objects**

For each of the following sentences, choose the correct pronoun in parentheses.

1. Is that package for Mom or (*I, me*)?
2. My mother named my brother and (*me, I*) after her uncles.

3. The teacher gave Rosa and (*they, them*) extra math homework.
4. Between you and (*I, me*), I like your plan better.
5. Everyone in the class except (*she, her*) and (*him, he*) had read the selection from the *Mahabharata*.

Special Pronoun Problems

Who and *Whom*

NOMINATIVE	OBJECTIVE
who	whom
whoever	whomever

4f. The use of *who* or *whom* in a subordinate clause depends on how the pronoun functions in the clause.

NOTE In spoken English, the use of *whom* is becoming less common. In fact, when you are speaking, you may correctly begin any question with *who*. In written English, however, you should distinguish between *who* and *whom*.

> INFORMAL **Who** did you see at the mall?
> FORMAL **Whom** did you see at the mall?

> INFORMAL **Who** did you go to the party with?
> FORMAL With **whom** did you go to the party?

☞ REFERENCE NOTE: See pages 179–186 for information on subordinate clauses.

Who is used as a subject of a verb or as a predicate nominative. *Whom* is used as an object of a verb or as an object of a preposition. When you are choosing between *who* or *whom* in a subordinate clause, follow these steps:

> STEP 1: Find the subordinate clause.
> STEP 2: Decide how the pronoun is used *in the clause*—as subject, predicate nominative, ob-

ject of the verb, or object of a preposition. No words outside the subordinate clause affect the case of the pronoun.

STEP 3: Determine the correct case for this use of the pronoun.

STEP 4: Select the correct form of the pronoun.

EXAMPLE: Do you know *(who, whom)* she is?

STEP 1: The subordinate clause is *(who, whom) she is.*

STEP 2: In this clause, the pronoun *(who, whom)* is the predicate nominative.

STEP 3: A predicate nominative is in the nominative case.

STEP 4: The nominative form of the pronoun is *who.*

ANSWER: Do you know **who** she is?

In the example above, the entire clause *who she is* is used as the direct object of the verb *do know.* But the way the pronoun is used within the clause—as a predicate nominative—is what determines the correct case form.

EXAMPLE: Margaret Mead, *(who, whom)* I read about in several articles, wrote interesting books.

STEP 1: The subordinate clause is *(who, whom) I read about in several articles.*

STEP 2: In this clause, the pronoun *(who, whom)* is the object of the preposition *about.*

STEP 3: An object of a preposition is in the objective case.

STEP 4: The objective form of the pronoun is *whom.*

ANSWER: Margaret Mead, **whom** I read about in several articles, wrote interesting books.

STYLE NOTE

Frequently, *whom* is left out of subordinate clauses, but its use is understood.

EXAMPLES The woman (*whom*) I admire most is Dr. Mead. [*Whom* is understood to be the direct object of *admire.*]
The woman (*whom*) I read about is a well-known anthropologist. [*Whom* is understood to be the object of the preposition *about.*]

Leaving out *whom* in such cases tends to make your writing sound more informal. In formal situations, it is generally better to include *whom*.

Drabble reprinted by permission of UFS, Inc.

COMPUTER NOTE You can use the "Search" command of a word-processing program to find each use of *who* and *whom* in a document. Then you can double-check to make sure that you've used the correct form of the pronoun in each instance.

QUICK CHECK 3

Determining the Use of *Who* and *Whom* in Subordinate Clauses

For each of the following sentences, choose the correct pronoun in parentheses.

1. Is there anyone here (*who, whom*) needs a bus pass?
2. Eileen couldn't guess (*who, whom*) it was.
3. It was Octavio Paz (*who, whom*) won the 1990 Nobel Prize for literature.
4. Her grandmother, to (*who, whom*) she sent the flowers, won the over-fifty division of the marathon.

5. Shirley Chisholm, (*who, whom*) we are studying in history class, was the first black woman elected to Congress.

Appositives

4g. Pronouns used as *appositives* are in the same case as the words to which they refer.

An *appositive* is a noun or pronoun placed next to another noun or pronoun to identify or explain it.

EXAMPLES   The winners, **he, she**, and **I**, thanked the committee. [The pronouns are in the nominative case because they are used as appositives of the subject, *winners*.]
The candidates in the runoff will be the top two vote-getters, **she** and **I**. [The pronouns are in the nominative case because they are used as appositives of the predicate nominative, *vote-getters*.]
Every volunteer except two, **him** and **her**, received an award. [The pronouns are in the objective case because they are used as appositives of the object of the preposition, *two*.]
The teacher introduced the speakers, Laura and **me**. [The pronoun is in the objective case because it is used as an appositive of the direct object, *speakers*.]

Sometimes the pronouns *we* and *us* are used with noun appositives.

EXAMPLES   **We** cast members have a dress rehearsal tonight. [The pronoun is in the nominative case because it is the subject of the verb *have*.]
The principal thanked **us** members of the Ecology Club for our presentation to the school assembly. [The pronoun is in the objective case because it is the direct object of the verb *thanked*.]

GRAMMAR/USAGE

To choose the correct form of a pronoun used with an appositive, read the sentence with only the pronoun.

EXAMPLE   (*We, Us*) scouts offered to help. [Omit the appositive, *scouts*: **We** offered to help.]

To choose the correct form of a pronoun used as an appositive, read the sentence with only the pronoun.

EXAMPLE   Ms. Fernández asked two students, Stephanie and (*he, him*), to help the librarian. [Omit the direct object, *students*: Ms. Fernández asked Stephanie and **him** to help the librarian.]

☞ REFERENCE NOTE: For a further discussion of appositives, see pages 170–171.

Identifying the Correct Forms of Pronouns Used as Appositives and with Appositives

QUICK CHECK 4

For each of the following sentences, give the correct form of the pronoun in parentheses.

1. Our friends, (*she, her*) and Lucas, helped us make the refreshments.
2. All of the class saw the movie except three students, Floyd, Ada, and (*I, me*).
3. Mrs. López hired (*we, us*) boys for the summer.
4. (*We, Us*) girls are expert players.
5. The best singers may be the quartet, Ellen and (*they, them*).

Pronouns in Incomplete Constructions

4h. A pronoun following *than* or *as* in an incomplete construction is in the same case it would be if the construction were completed.

In a sentence with an incomplete construction, the case of the pronoun depends on how the omitted part of the sentence would be completed. Notice how changing the pronoun changes the meaning of such sentences.

EXAMPLES   I wrote you more often than **he** [wrote you].
I wrote you more often than [I wrote] **him**.
Did you help Jessica as much as **I** [helped Jessica]?
Did you help Jessica as much as [you helped] **me**?

✓ *QUICK CHECK 5*   **Using Pronouns to Complete Incomplete Constructions**

For each of the following sentences, choose the correct pronoun in parentheses and supply the omitted part of the sentence. If a sentence may be completed in two different ways, provide both alternatives.

1. Kim was as surprised as (*I, me*).
2. The story mystified him as well as (*we, us*).
3. Is your sister older than (*he, him*)?
4. We have known him longer than (*she, her*).
5. Did you read as much as (*we, us*)?

Inexact Pronoun Reference

4i.   A pronoun should always refer clearly to its antecedent.

(1) Make sure that a pronoun cannot refer to either of two antecedents.

Using a pronoun in such a way that it can refer to either of two antecedents produces an *ambiguous reference.*

AMBIGUOUS   Leotie saw Jewel while she was jogging.
[Who was jogging, Leotie or Jewel?]
CLEAR   While **Leotie** was jogging, **she** saw Jewel.
CLEAR   While **Jewel** was jogging, Leotie saw **her**.
AMBIGUOUS   When the car grazed the mailbox, it was dented. [What was dented, the car or the mailbox?]

| CLEAR | The **car** was dented when **it** grazed the mailbox. |
| CLEAR | The **mailbox** was dented when **it** was grazed by the car. |

(2) Make sure that you include a specific, stated antecedent for each pronoun you use.

Using a pronoun that refers to a general idea rather than to a specific noun produces a *general reference*. The pronouns commonly used in making general-reference errors are *it, that, this, such,* and *which.*

| GENERAL | Some of my friends go to private schools. That explains why I see them only on weekends. [*That* has no specific antecedent.] |
| CLEAR | The fact that some of my friends go to a private school explains why I see them only on weekends. |

or

| CLEAR | I see some of my friends only on weekends because they go to a private school. |

| GENERAL | The school board is considering requiring public school students to wear uniforms, which would be a big change. [*Which* has no specific antecedent.] |
| CLEAR | The school board is considering requiring public school students to wear uniforms. Such a requirement would be a big change. |

or

| CLEAR | Requiring public school students to wear uniforms would be a big change. |

Blondie reprinted with special permission of King Features Syndicate, Inc.

Suggesting a word or idea without actually stating it can produce *weak reference*.

WEAK   Ralph enjoys writing poetry, but he never shows them to anyone else. [*Them* most likely refers to the unstated noun *poems*, but the writer has used the singular noun *poetry* instead.]

CLEAR   Ralph enjoys writing poetry, but he never shows his poems to anyone else

CLEAR   Ralph enjoys writing poems, but he never shows them to anyone else.

WEAK   When I sit for the neighbors baby, I keep it amused by telling stories. [*It* most likely refers to the child, but the writer has not provided an antecedent for *it*.]

CLEAR   When I baby-sit, I keep the child amused by teling stories.

CLEAR   When I sit for the neighbor's baby, I keep him [*or* her] amused by telling stories.

In formal situations and in writing, avoid the indefinite use of the pronouns *it, they,* and *you.* An **indefinite reference** occurs when a pronoun refers to no particular person or thing.

INDEFINITE   In the owner's manual it explains how to program the VCR. [The pronoun *it* is not necessary to the meaning of the sentence.]

CLEAR   The owner's manual explains how to program the VCR.

INDEFINITE   On the evening news broadcast they announced the jury's decision. [The pronoun *they* is not necessary to the meaning of the sentence.]

CLEAR   The evening news broadcast announced the jury's decision.

NOTE   The indefinite use of *it* is acceptable in familiar expressions such as *It is snowing, It seems as though . . . ,* and *It's late.* In these expressions, *it* is understood to refer to the weather, the time, and so on.

✓ *QUICK CHECK* 6 | **Correcting Inexact Pronoun References**

Each numbered item below contains an inexact pronoun reference. Revise the item to correct the error.

1. Mavis has a bad cold. That is why she is absent today.
2. The Glee Club is presenting a concert next Friday, which should be enjoyable.
3. I became interested in stamp collecting when I got one from Fiji.
4. In this article, it discusses how teenagers spend their allowances.
5. My mother told my sister that she should be home early.

GRAMMAR/USAGE

✓ *Chapter Review*

A. Correcting Pronoun Forms

Most of the sentences below contain errors in pronoun usage. If a pronoun is used incorrectly, write the correct form of the pronoun. If a sentence is correct, write *C*.

EXAMPLE   1. This arrangement is strictly between Carl and I.
           1. *me*

1. The author spoke to us history students about the Slavic cultures of eastern Europe.
2. During the Olympic trials, every diver except she received a low score from the judges.
3. The instructor, who seemed nervous during the show, was proud of Lani's performance.
4. It couldn't have been her.
5. Van is more energetic than me.
6. Rick couldn't spot Maura and I in the crowd at the fair.
7. Tyrone and he are playing backgammon at Regina's house.
8. Laura gave he a beautiful poem about friendship.
9. Angie's neighbors, Mrs. Brandt and he, helped plant the tree.
10. Whomever do you think will take her place?

B. Proofreading a Paragraph for Correct Pronoun Usage

Some of the following sentences contain incorrect pronoun forms or inexact pronoun references. If a sentence is incorrect, write the correct form of the pronoun or correct the unclear pronoun reference. If a sentence is correct, write *C*.

EXAMPLE   [1] **To Velma and I, Dizzy Dean is one of the greatest baseball players of all time.**
              1. *me*

[11] There has never been another baseball player like him. [12] Fans still talk about he and his teammates. [13] Dean played for the Saint Louis Cardinals, to who his fastball was a great help, especially in the 1934 World Series. [14] Dean was such a character that his fans never knew what crazy notion might come to he during games. [15] He had a real confidence about him, too. [16] A boss once complained about Dean's bragging to Dean himself, whom glibly replied, "'Tain't braggin' if you kin really do it!" [17] When Dean became a sportscaster, him and his informal speech appealed to fans. [18] He liked watching baseball games and reporting on they. [19]Not surprisingly, Dean was elected to baseball's Hall of Fame; it was a big honor for him. [20]The Dizzy Dean Museum in Jackson, Mississippi, is a good place for we fans to find out more about Dean's career.

5 USING MODIFIERS

Forms and Uses of Adjectives and Adverbs; Comparison; Placement

✓ Checking What You Know

A. Correcting Forms of Modifiers

Revise each of the following sentences to correct the error in comparison. If the sentence is correct, write *C*.

EXAMPLE   **1.** His problem is more worse than yours.
           1. *His problem is worse than yours.*

1. Which did you like best, the book or the movie?
2. The sun is brighter than anything in our solar system.
3. The tomatoes from our garden taste sweeter than those from the store.
4. This is the most nicest surprise I've ever had in my entire life!
5. Raymond likes my brother more than you.
6. Did you know that the Nile is longer than any river in the world?
7. The price of apples is lower than grapes.
8. Don't you feel more better now that you've had a rest?

GRAMMAR/USAGE

9. Trees growing near the ocean are often much smaller than in more protected areas.
10. Which route do you think is better, upstream, downstream, or overland?

B. Correcting Dangling and Misplaced Modifiers

Each of the following sentences contains either a dangling modifier or a misplaced modifier. Rewrite each sentence so that it is clear and correct.

EXAMPLE   1. Every morning, that young girl walks her dog in a jogging outfit.
         1. *Every morning, that young girl in a jogging outfit walks her dog.*

11. Enjoying their lunch, the rain clouds loomed menacingly over the picnickers.
12. To paint miniatures, a steady hand is helpful.
13. Running the last lap of the race, my calf muscle cramped, and the other runners passed me.
14. In different parts of the world, we have read about unusual customs.
15. A tree was destroyed by a bulldozer that was almost two hundred years old.
16. Sharon relaxed in the sun and watched her fishing line happily whistling a tune.
17. The prisoners were caught by the police trying to escape from jail.
18. Rushing out, Ben's homework was left on the table.
19. Almost hidden under the pile of old books, Janelle saw the letter.
20. The mayor pledged that he would build more parks at the political rally. ✓

What Is a Modifier?

A *modifier* is a word or group of words that makes the meaning of another word more definite. The two kinds of modifiers are *adjectives* and *adverbs*.

☞ **REFERENCE NOTE:** For more information on adjectives, see pages 57–60. For more on adverbs, see pages 65–67. For more on phrases and clauses used as modifiers, see **Chapter 6: Phrases** and pages 179–184. For information on placement of modifiers, see pages 145–148.

One-Word Modifiers

Adjectives

5a. Use an *adjective* to limit the meaning of a noun or pronoun.

ADJECTIVE   Melanie gave a **broad** grin. [The adjective *broad* limits the meaning of the noun *grin.*]
Only he would think of that. [The adjective *Only* limits the meaning of the pronoun *he.*]

Adverbs

5b. Use an *adverb* to limit the meaning of a verb, an adjective, or another adverb.

ADVERBS   Melanie grinned **broadly**. [The adverb *broadly* limits the meaning of the verb *grinned.*]
The dog is **not** eager to swim. [The adverb *not* limits the meaning of the adjective *eager.*]

Fred Basset reprinted by permission:
Tribune Media Services.

The bell rang **surprisingly** loudly. [The adverb *surprisingly* limits the meaning of the adverb *loudly*.]

Adjective or Adverb?

Although many adverbs end in -*ly*, many do not. Furthermore, not all words with the -*ly* ending are adverbs. Some adjectives also end in -*ly*. Therefore, you can't tell whether a word is an adjective or an adverb simply by looking for the -*ly* ending.

ADVERBS NOT	arrive **soon**	sit **here**
ENDING IN –*LY*	**not** angry	run **loose**
	walk **home**	**very** hot
ADJECTIVES	**elderly** citizens	**holy** place
ENDING IN –*LY*	**curly** hair	**silly** joke

In addition, some words can be used as either adjectives or adverbs.

ADJECTIVES	ADVERBS
He is an **only** child.	She has **only** one sister.
Tina has a **fast** bicycle.	The baby is **fast** asleep.
We caught the **last** bus.	We left **last**.

Nor can you always tell whether a word is an adjective or an adverb by its position in a sentence. An adjective can appear in either the subject or the predicate of a sentence. To determine whether a word is an adjective or an adverb, figure out how it is used in the sentence.

5c. If a word in the predicate modifies the subject, use the adjective form. If it modifies the verb, use the adverb form.

| ADJECTIVE | The dancers were **graceful**. [what kind of dancers] |
| ADVERB | They danced **gracefully**. [how they danced] |

REFERENCE NOTE: For more information on subjects and predicates, see pages 193–199.

A linking verb is often followed by a *predicate adjective*—a word that modifies the subject.

Common Linking Verbs		
appear	grow	smell
be (am, is, are, etc.)	look	sound
become	remain	stay
feel	seem	taste

Most linking verbs can also be used as action verbs. You can tell whether a verb is a linking verb or an action verb by replacing the verb with a form of *seem*. If the substitution makes sense, the original verb is a linking verb. If the substitution does not make sense, it is an action verb.

LINKING   The grass **grew** tall. [*The grass seemed tall* makes sense.]

ACTION   The grass **grew** quickly. [*The grass seemed quickly* doesn't make sense.]

LINKING   The alarm **sounded** shrill. [*The alarm seemed shrill* makes sense.]

ACTION   The alarm **sounded** noisily. [*The alarm seemed noisily* doesn't make sense.]

 You may want to store the list of common linking verbs given above, along with your own sentences illustrating their use as either linking verbs or action verbs, in a computer file. Then you can access the file each time you need to decide whether to use an adjective or an adverb after one of these verbs.

 REFERENCE NOTE: Writers often have trouble with the following pairs of modifiers: *bad, badly; good, well;* and *slow, slowly.* For information on how to use these modifiers correctly, look up each pair in the **Writer's Quick Reference.** See pages 62–63 and 61–62 for more on linking verbs and action verbs.

✓ QUICK CHECK 1

Identifying Modifiers and the Words They Modify

Identify the italicized word in each of the following sentences as an *adjective* or an *adverb*. Then, identify the word the adjective or adverb modifies.

1. I *only* wanted to ask a question.
2. Moira was the *last* person to leave.
3. This chair is becoming *uncomfortable*.
4. That dress is *very* becoming.
5. The stew smells *lovely*.

Comparison of Modifiers

5d. The forms of modifiers change to show comparison.

Adjectives change form to show a comparison between one noun or pronoun with another noun or pronoun that has the same quality.

EXAMPLES   This beach is **sandier** than that one.
She is the **tallest** person in the class.

To make comparisons between verbs, adverbs are used.

EXAMPLES   I changed into my bathing suit **quickly,** but
Lois changed into hers even **more quickly.**

There are three degrees of comparison: *positive, comparative*, and *superlative*.

POSITIVE	COMPARATIVE	SUPERLATIVE
bad	worse	worst
fearful	more fearful	most fearful
good	better	best
innocent	more innocent	most innocent
rapidly	more rapidly	most rapidly
warm	warmer	warmest
young	younger	youngest

GRAMMAR/USAGE

Regular Comparison

(1) A one-syllable modifier regularly forms its comparative and superlative degrees by adding -er and -est.

POSITIVE	COMPARATIVE	SUPERLATIVE
deep	deeper	deepest
large	larger	largest
strong	stronger	strongest

 REFERENCE NOTE: See pages 335–337 for guidelines on spelling words with suffixes.

(2) Some two-syllable modifiers form their comparative and superlative degrees by adding -er and -est. Other two-syllable modifiers form their comparative and superlative degrees with *more* and *most*.

POSITIVE	COMPARATIVE	SUPERLATIVE
gentle	gentler	gentlest
lovely	lovelier	loveliest
careful	more careful	most careful
slowly	more slowly	most slowly

STYLE NOTE

Some two-syllable modifiers may take either *-er, -est* or *more, most.*

EXAMPLE   common, commoner, commonest

or

common, more common, most common

If you are not sure how a two-syllable modifier is compared, look in a dictionary. If a high school dictionary doesn't tell you, go to a college dictionary or an unabridged dictionary.

GRAMMAR/USAGE

(3) Modifiers that have more than two syllables form their comparative and superlative degrees with *more* and *most*.

POSITIVE	COMPARATIVE	SUPERLATIVE
energetic	more energetic	most energetic
significantly	more significantly	most significantly

(4) To indicate a decrease in a quality, modifiers use the word *less* or *least*.

POSITIVE	COMPARATIVE	SUPERLATIVE
helpful	less helpful	least helpful
frequently	less frequently	least frequently

Irregular Comparison

Some modifiers do not follow the regular methods of forming their comparative and superlative degrees.

POSITIVE	COMPARATIVE	SUPERLATIVE
bad	worse	worst
good/well	better	best
little	less	least
many/much	more	most

NOTE Do not add *-er, -est* or *more, most* to irregular comparative and superlative forms. Use *worse*, not *worser* or *more worse*, and *best*, not *bestest*.

QUICK CHECK 2 **Writing Comparative and Superlative Forms**

Give the comparative and superlative forms of the following modifiers. If you are unsure about the forms of a two-syllable modifier, look up the modifier in a dictionary.

1. bad
2. loose
3. well

4. noisy
5. patiently

Use of Comparative and Superlative Forms

5e. Use the comparative degree when comparing two things. Use the superlative degree when comparing more than two.

COMPARATIVE   Writing mysteries seems **more challenging** than writing nonfiction.

In my opinion, Dorothy L. Sayers is a **better** writer than Agatha Christie.

Which of the two assignments was **less difficult**?

SUPERLATIVE   This is the **best** Sherlock Holmes story that I have ever read.

Writing a mystery story is the **most challenging** assignment I've had so far.

Which of the three assignments was **least difficult**?

NOTE   In everyday conversation and in some standard expressions, people sometimes use the superlative degree to compare two things.

EXAMPLES   Put your **best** foot forward.

May the **best** person [of two] win.

Generally, however, always use the comparative degree when you are comparing two things in your writing.

Peanuts reprinted by permission of UFS, Inc.

5f.	Include the word *other* or *else* when comparing one thing with others in the same group.

NONSTANDARD	Ruth is more agile than any member of her gymnastics team. [Ruth is a member of her team, and she cannot be more agile than herself. The word *other* should be added.]
STANDARD	Ruth is more agile than any **other** member of her gymnastics team.
NONSTANDARD	Carlos ran faster than everyone. [The word *everyone* includes all people, and Carlos is a person. Since he cannot run faster than himself, the word *else* should be added.]
STANDARD	Carlos ran faster than everyone **else**.

5g.	Avoid double comparisons.

A *double comparison* is one that contains both *-er* and *more* (or *less*) or both *-est* and *most* (or *least*).

NONSTANDARD	She is more funnier than he.
STANDARD	She is **funnier** than he.
NONSTANDARD	This is the most cheapest bicycle in the store.
STANDARD	This is the **cheapest** bicycle in the store.

5h.	Be sure your comparisons are clear.

UNCLEAR	The average temperature in Dallas is higher than Spokane. [This sentence incorrectly compares a temperature to a city.]
CLEAR	The average temperature in Dallas is higher than **the average temperature in** Spokane.
UNCLEAR	The skin of the rhinoceros is harder than the alligator.
CLEAR	The skin of the rhinoceros is harder than the **alligator's**.

State both parts of an incomplete comparison if there is any chance of misunderstanding.

UNCLEAR   I visited her more than Elise.
   CLEAR   I visited her more than **I visited** Elise.
   CLEAR   I visited her more than Elise **visited her**.

UNCLEAR   Sheila likes movies more than Jaime.
   CLEAR   She likes movies more than Jaime **does**.
   CLEAR   Sheila likes movies more than **she likes** Jaime.

Using the Comparative and Superlative Forms of Modifiers Correctly in Sentences

Each of the following sentences contains an error in the use of a modifier. Find the errors and explain how you would correct them.

1. Nina's report on Native American legends was the more interesting of the several reports in the class.
2. Luís enjoys swimming more than any sport.
3. Today is more colder than usual for this time of year.
4. Our apartment is smaller than our next-door neighbor.
5. I call Brian more than Joe.

Placement of Modifiers

The placement of a modifier, especially a phrase or a clause, can affect a sentence's meaning.

 REFERENCE NOTE: For more information, see **Chapter 6: Phrases** and **Chapter 7: Clauses**.

Dangling Modifiers

5i. A modifying word, phrase, or clause that does not clearly and sensibly modify a word or group of words in the same sentence is a *dangling modifier*.

DANGLING   Together, most problems can be solved. [Who or what does the word *Together* modify?]

GRAMMAR/USAGE

CORRECTED **Working together**, people can solve most problems.

CORRECTED **People** can solve most problems **by working together**.

DANGLING Jogging in the park, it was a sunny day with a light breeze. [Who or what does the phrase *Jogging in the park* modify?]

CORRECTED Jogging in the park, **I** enjoyed the sunny day with a light breeze.

DANGLING When told of the potential threat, nothing was done. [Who or what does the elliptical clause *When told of the potential threat* modify?]

CORRECTED When told of the potential threat, **nobody** did a thing.

CORRECTED When **they were** told of the potential threat, **they did** nothing.

A verbal phrase at the beginning of a sentence should be followed by a comma. Immediately after that comma should come the word that the phrase modifies.

UNCLEAR To understand Countee Cullen's poetry, some knowledge of figurative language is necessary.

CLEAR To understand Countee Cullen's poetry, the **reader** needs some knowledge of figurative language.

UNCLEAR Equipped with even the best gear, the rock cliff was difficult to climb.

CLEAR Equipped with even the best gear, the **mountaineers** had difficulty climbing the rock cliff.

NOTE A sentence may appear to have a dangling modifier when *you* is the understood subject. In such cases, the modifier is not dangling; it is modifying the understood subject.

EXAMPLE To find the correct spelling, [you] look up the word in a dictionary.

REFERENCE NOTE: For more information on verbals and verbal phrases, see pages 161–169. For more information on incomplete constructions, see pages 129–130.

Shoe, by Jeff MacNelly, reprinted by permission: Tribune Media Services.

Correcting Dangling Modifiers

To correct a dangling modifier, rearrange the words in the sentence and add or change words to make the meaning logical and clear.

DANGLING   To become a physicist, years of study and research are required.

CORRECTED   To become a physicist, you [or a person] must spend years studying and doing research.

or

If you want to become a physicist, you must spend years studying and doing research.

DANGLING   While lighting the candles, my birthday cake started to crumble.

CORRECTED   While I was lighting the candles, my birthday cake started to crumble.

or

While lighting the candles, I saw my birthday cake start to crumble.

Misplaced Modifiers

5j. A *misplaced modifier* is a phrase or clause that makes a sentence awkward or unclear because it seems to modify the wrong word or group of words.

Modifying phrases and clauses should be placed as near as possible to the words they modify.

Misplaced Phrase Modifiers

MISPLACED	I read about the bank robbers who were captured in this morning's paper.
CORRECTED	I read in this morning's paper about the bank robbers who were captured.
MISPLACED	Born eight weeks ago, we adopted one of the beagle puppies.
CORRECTED	We adopted one of the beagle puppies born eight weeks ago.
MISPLACED	I found Enrique and Lada on my doorstep answering the door.
CORRECTED	Answering the door, I found Enrique and Lada on my doorstep.

Misplaced Clause Modifiers

MISPLACED	George made a vegetarian lasagna for the dinner party that had six layers.
CORRECTED	For the dinner party, George made a vegetarian lasagna that had six layers.
MISPLACED	There is a bicycle in the garage, which is a very efficient form of transportation.
CORRECTED	In the garage there is a bicycle, which is a very efficient form of transportation.
MISPLACED	The conductor complimented Lia's performance when the concert ended.
CORRECTED	When the concert ended, the conductor complimented Lia's performance.

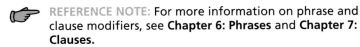

REFERENCE NOTE: For more information on phrase and clause modifiers, see **Chapter 6: Phrases** and **Chapter 7: Clauses.**

QUICK CHECK 4

Revising Sentences by Correcting Dangling Modifiers and Misplaced Modifiers

Revise each of the following sentences by placing the dangling modifier or misplaced modifier near the word it modifies or by rephrasing the sentence.

1. As a child, my grandfather taught me how to make corn tortillas.
2. Birds are kept away from crops by scarecrows, which like to eat seeds.
3. Standing on the beach, a school of dolphins suddenly appeared.
4. Chuck went outside to trim the hedge and weed the garden with our dog Snickers.
5. She crossed the river on a ferry, which was more than a mile wide.

✓ *Chapter Review*

A. Revising Sentences by Correcting Modifiers

Each of the following sentences contains at least one error in the use of modifiers: a faulty comparison or a dangling or misplaced modifier. Revise each sentence so that it is clear and correct.

EXAMPLE   1. When traveling through Scotland, I discovered that stories about monsters were more popular than any kind of story told there.

    1. *When traveling through Scotland, I discovered that stories about monsters were more popular than any other kind of story told there.*

1. Having received a great deal of publicity, I had already read several articles about the so-called Loch Ness monster.
2. One article described how a young veterinary student spotted the monster who was named Arthur Grant.
3. While cycling on a road near the shore of Loch Ness one day, Grant came upon the most strangest creature he had ever seen.
4. Cycling closer, the monster took two great leaps and plunged into the lake.
5. Numerous theories have been discussed about the origin and identity of the monster in the local newspapers.
6. Of all the proposed theories, the better and more fascinating one was that the monster must be a freshwater species of sea serpent.
7. Some people were more quick than others to say they thought the story was a hoax.
8. After finding a huge, dead creature on the shore of the lake in 1942, the mystery of the monster was thought to be solved finally.
9. However, sightings of the Loch Ness monster continue to be reported, perhaps more than any mysterious creature.
10. It is still one of the world's most famous and less understood monster legends.

B. Using Modifiers Correctly in a Paragraph

Most of the sentences in the following paragraph have mistakes in the use of modifiers. Revise each incorrect sentence to correct these errors. If a sentence is correct, write *C*.

[11] Kay has a better understanding of both solar and geothermal energy than anyone I know. [12] Yoko isn't sure she agrees, but I have talked with Kay more than Yoko. [13] Kay thinks that solar energy is the best of the two methods for generating power. [14] She claims that the energy from the sun will soon be more easy to harness than geothermal energy. [15] Arguing that the sun's energy could also be

least expensive to use, Kay says that more research into solar energy is needed. [16] Yoko disagrees and thinks that geothermal energy is more cheaper than solar energy. [17] She told me that for centuries people in other countries have been using geothermal energy, such as Iceland and Japan. [18] However, she added that geothermal energy is less well known than any source of power in our country. [19] Although often ignored in the United States, Yoko feels that geothermal energy has already proven itself to be safe and efficient. [20] According to her, it is one of the most promising of all energy sources.

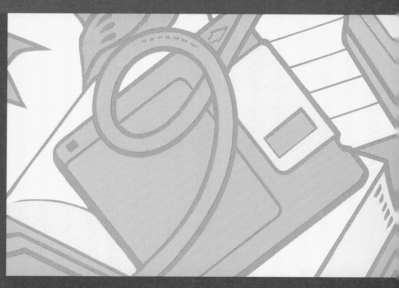

PART THREE

PHRASES, CLAUSES, SENTENCES

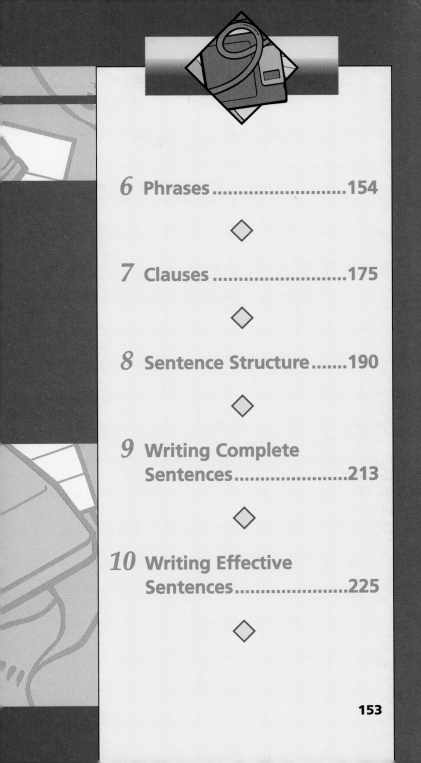

6 PHRASES

Prepositional, Verbal, and Appositive Phrases

✓ *Checking What You Know*

A. Identifying and Classifying Prepositional Phrases

Identify the ten prepositional phrases in the following sentences. Then give the word(s) modified by each phrase and the type of phrase (*adj.* for adjective phrase, *adv.* for adverb phrase).

EXAMPLE   [1] Our whole family reads the newspaper in the morning.
　　　　　 1. *in the morning—reads—adv.*

[1] A daily newspaper has something for almost everyone. [2] In addition to news, the paper offers recipes, entertainment, classified ads, and much more. [3] My family never argues over the sections of the paper. [4] Dad always begins with the sports pages; Mom prefers the national news. [5] My favorite part, the comics, appears in many newspapers. [6] My sister and I enjoy characters like Garfield and Snoopy. [7] I also find the editorial and opin-

ion pages interesting, especially when a debate between two sides develops. [8] Sometimes I can see the logic behind an argument, while other times I wonder why grown people argue about some trivial issue.

B. Identifying Verbals and Appositives

Identify each italicized word in the following sentences as a *participle,* a *gerund,* an *infinitive,* or an *appositive.*

EXAMPLE   [1] The young woman, an excellent *athlete,* wanted *to earn* a gold medal for her *swimming.*

    1. *athlete—appositive*
    to earn—infinitive
    swimming—gerund

[9] *Enjoyed* by people throughout history, amateur athletic competition involves more than [10] *winning* an event. When talented amateurs compete [11] *to test* their skills, they learn a great deal about their sports. In addition, the love of a sport, the best [12] *reason* for [13] *entering* into competition, usually grows as an athlete's performance improves. Furthermore, [14] *sharing* hard work with teammates leads a person [15] *to appreciate* cooperative effort. Competitions [16] *organized* on many levels give amateur athletes frequent opportunities [17] *to put* their abilities to the test. Many young people dream of participating in state, national, and international competitions, [18] *events* that draw the best athletes. ✓

6a. A *phrase* is a group of related words that is used as a single part of speech and does not contain both a verb and its subject.

EXAMPLES   **has been sitting** [verb phrase; no subject]
about you and me [prepositional phrase; no subject or verb]

A group of words that has *both* a subject *and* a verb is not a phrase.

EXAMPLES   **We found** your pen. [*We* is the subject of *found*.]
            if *she will go* [*She* is the subject of *will go*.]

☞ REFERENCE NOTE: If a group of words has both a subject and a verb, it is called a **clause.** For more information, see **Chapter 7: Clauses.**

Prepositional Phrases

6b.   A *prepositional phrase* is a group of words consisting of a preposition, a noun or a pronoun that serves as the *object of the preposition,* and any modifiers of that object.

EXAMPLES   Every weekend, Pedro works **in his parents' store.** [The noun *store* is the object of the preposition *in.*]
            Did you give the note **to them?** [The pronoun *them* is the object of the preposition *to.*]

The object of a preposition may be compound.

EXAMPLES   Kyoko called **to Nancy and me.** [Both *Nancy* and *me* are objects of the preposition *to.*]
            The marbles were scattered **under the table and chairs.** [The preposition *under* has a compound object, *table* and *chairs.*]

Some prepositions are made up of more than one word.

EXAMPLES   **instead of** them   **next to** her

☞ REFERENCE NOTE: For a list of commonly used prepositions, see page 68.

Modifiers of the object of the preposition can come either before or after the object.

EXAMPLES   We listened **to the shutters banging.** [The noun *shutters* is the object of the preposition *to.* The participle *banging* modifies the noun *shutters.*]
            We went **to the creek running out back.**

[The noun *creek* is the object of the preposition *to*. *Creek* is modified by the participial phrase *running out back*.]

She was **aboard the big ship that sailed this morning.** [The noun *ship* is the object of the preposition *aboard*. *Ship* is modified by the adjective *big* and by the subordinate clause *that sailed this morning*.]

A modifier following the object of the preposition is not necessarily part of the prepositional phrase.

EXAMPLE   Mom and Mrs. Braun worked **at the polls** today. [*At the polls* is the complete prepositional phrase. The adverb *today* tells when and modifies the verb *worked*.]

 NOTE   Be careful not to confuse the preposition *to* with the *to* that is the sign of a verb's infinitive form: *to swim, to know, to see.* For more information about infinitives, see pages 166–167.

A prepositional phrase can contain another prepositional phrase.

EXAMPLE   **According to the dictionary in our classroom, the meaning has changed.** [The noun *dictionary* is the object of the compound preposition *according to*. *Dictionary* is modified by the article *the* and by the prepositional phrase *in our classroom*.]

The Adjective Phrase

6c.   A prepositional phrase used as an adjective is called an *adjective phrase.*

EXAMPLES   The members **of the club** want sweatshirts **with the club emblem.** [The prepositional phrase *of the club* is used as an adjective to modify the noun *members*. *With the club emblem* is used as an adjective to modify the noun *sweatshirts*.]

All **of us** enjoyed the picnic. [*Of us* is used as an adjective to modify the pronoun *all*.]

An adjective phrase always follows the noun or pronoun it modifies.

EXAMPLE   Annie closed the cellar door.
           Annie closed the door **to the cellar.**

NOTE   If an adjective phrase is combined with a noun to form a compound noun, the entire group of words is considered one noun.

        EXAMPLES   **maid of honor   Cape of Good Hope
                     University of Texas at Austin**

More than one adjective phrase may modify the same noun or pronoun.

EXAMPLE   The bottle **of vitamins on the shelf** is mine.
           [The prepositional phrases *of vitamins* and *on the shelf* modify the noun *bottle.*]

An adjective phrase that is part of another prepositional phrase modifies the object of that other phrase.

EXAMPLE   The horse **in the trailer with the rusted latch** broke loose. [The phrase *in the trailer with the rusted latch* modifies the noun *horse. Trailer* is the object of the preposition *in.* The phrase *with a rusted latch* modifies *trailer.*]

STYLE NOTE   Often, you can convert the objects of adjective phrases into nouns used as adjectives. This makes your writing less wordy.

ADJECTIVE PHRASES	NOUNS USED AS ADJECTIVES
The light **in the kitchen** is on.	The **kitchen** light is on.
The airports **in Chicago and New York** are crowded.	The **Chicago** and **New York** airports are crowded.

However, not all adjective phrases can be changed into one-word modifiers that make sense. Sometimes changing an adjective phrase to a single adjective makes a sentence confusing.

CLEAR Please hand me the book **on the table.**

CONFUSING Please hand me the **table** book.

The Adverb Phrase

6d. A prepositional phrase used as an adverb is called an *adverb phrase.* Adverb phrases tell *when, where, how, why,* or *to what extent.*

EXAMPLES **By Wednesday** Christopher will be finished. [The adverb phrase *by Wednesday* tells *when* Christopher will be finished.]

They sailed **across the lake** yesterday. [*Across the lake* tells *where* they sailed.]

We traveled **by train.** [*By train* tells *how* we traveled.]

They stopped **for lunch.** [*For lunch* tells *why* they stopped.]

She answered **with a smile.** [*With a smile* tells *how* she answered.]

The calculations erred **by more than two inches.** [*By more than two inches* tells *to what extent* the calculations erred.]

In the previous examples, the adverb phrases all modify verbs. An adverb phrase may also modify an adjective or an adverb.

EXAMPLES Mom is good **at tennis** but better **at volleyball.** [*At tennis* modifies the adjective *good. At volleyball* modifies the adjective *better.*]

Is the water warm enough **for swimming?** [*For swimming* modifies the adverb *enough.*]

Adjective phrases always follow the words they modify, but an adverb phrase may appear at various places in a sentence.

EXAMPLES **Before noon** the race started.

The race started **before noon.**

STYLE NOTE

Be sure to place adverb phrases carefully. An adverb phrase's position in a sentence can affect the sentence's meaning.

EXAMPLES **In the park,** we waved to the children. [Both we and the children were in the park. The phrase *in the park* acts as an adverb and modifies the verb *waved.*]
We waved to the children **in the park.** [We were outside the park, and the children were in it. The phrase *in the park* acts as an adjective and modifies the noun *children.*]

More than one adverb phrase may modify the same word.

EXAMPLE **During summers,** my older sister works **at the museum.** [The adverb phrases *during summers* and *at the museum* both modify the verb *works.* The first phrase tells *when* my sister works; the second phrase tells *where* she works.]

 REFERENCE NOTE: For more information on the placement of modifiers, see **Chapter 5: Using Modifiers.**

 *QUICK CHECK* 1 **Identifying and Classifying Prepositional Phrases**

List all the prepositional phrases in each of the following sentences. After each phrase, write *adj.* if the phrase is used as an adjective or *adv.* if it is used as an adverb. Be prepared to identify the word each phrase modifies.

1. Theories about the universe have changed over the years.
2. In the 1920s, Edwin Hubble discovered the existence of galaxies outside the Milky Way.
3. Now we know that there are perhaps a million galaxies inside the bowl of the Big Dipper.

4. Astronomers believe that our galaxy is only one among billions throughout the universe.
5. Galileo, Copernicus, and other early scientists who were curious about outer space would probably be amazed at the extent of space exploration in the modern world.

Verbals and Verbal Phrases

Verbals are formed from verbs. Like verbs, they may be modified by adverbs, and they may have complements. However, verbals are used as other parts of speech—nouns, adjectives, or adverbs.

There are three kinds of verbals: *participles, gerunds,* and *infinitives.*

☞ REFERENCE NOTE: For a discussion of verbal phrases as sentence fragments, see page 217.

The Participle

6e. A *participle* is a verb form that can be used as an adjective.

EXAMPLES **Waxed** floors can be dangerously slippery. [The participle *waxed*, formed from the verb *wax*, modifies the noun *floors.*]
We saw the raccoon **escaping** through the back door. [The participle *escaping*, formed from the verb *escape*, modifies the noun *raccoon.*]

There are two kinds of participles: *present participles* and *past participles.*

(1) *Present participles* end in *-ing.*

EXAMPLES We ran inside to get out of the **pouring** rain. [*Pouring* is a present participle modifying the noun *rain.*]
Watching the clock, the coach became worried. [The present participle *watching* modifies the noun *coach—watching coach.*]

SENTENCES

Although participles are forms of verbs, they do not stand alone as verbs. However, a participle may be used with a helping verb to form a verb phrase. In that case, it is part of the verb, not an adjective.

EXAMPLES   The rain **was pouring.**
                The coach **had been watching** the clock.

(2) **Past participles** usually end in *-d* or *-ed.* Other past participles are irregularly formed.

EXAMPLES   A **peeled** and **sliced** cucumber can be added to a garden salad. [The past participles *peeled* and *sliced* modify the noun *cucumber.*]
                The speaker, **known** for her strong support of recycling, was loudly applauded. [The irregular past participle *known* modifies the noun *speaker—known speaker.*]

Like a present participle, a past participle can be part of a verb phrase. When a past participle is used in a verb phrase, it is part of the verb, not an adjective.

EXAMPLES   I **have peeled** and **sliced** the cucumber.
                The speaker **was known** for her strong support of recycling.

☞ REFERENCE NOTE: For more information on participle forms, see pages 95–96 and 101–106. For a discussion of irregular verbs, see pages 97–100.

The Participial Phrase

6f.   A *participial phrase* is a phrase containing a participle and any complements or modifiers the participle may have. The entire participial phrase acts as an adjective.

EXAMPLES   **Seeing the cat,** the dog barked loudly.
                The cat hissed at the dog **barking in the yard next door.**
                We hollered at the dog **noisily barking at the cat.**

SENTENCES

In each of the following sentences, an arrow points from the participial phrase to the noun or pronoun that the phrase modifies.

EXAMPLES **Switching its tail,** the panther paced back and forth in its cage. [participle with object *tail*]

She heard me **sighing loudly.** [participle with the adverb *loudly*]

Living within his budget, he never needs to borrow money. [participle with prepositional phrase modifier *within his budget*]

Quickly grabbing the keys, I dashed for the door. [participle with preceding adverb *quickly* and object *keys*]

STYLE NOTE A participial phrase should be placed very close to the word it modifies. Otherwise, the phrase may appear to modify another word, and the sentence may not make sense.

MISPLACED Ralph saw a moose riding his motorcycle through the woods. [The placement of the modifier calls up a silly picture. Ralph, not the moose, was riding the motorcycle.]

IMPROVED Riding his motorcycle through the woods, Ralph saw a moose.

REFERENCE NOTE: The punctuation of participial phrases is discussed on pages 275–276. The participle as a dangling or misplaced modifier is discussed on pages 145–148. Combining sentences by using participles is discussed on pages 228–229.

SENTENCES

☑ *QUICK CHECK 2* **Identifying Participles and Participial Phrases**

Identify the participles and participial phrases in the following paragraph and give the word each one modifies.

[1] How are skyscrapers created, and what keeps them standing? [2] Columns of steel or concrete reinforced with steel are sunk into bedrock beneath the building. [3] If a layer of rock isn't present, these columns are sunk into a thick concrete pad spread across the bottom of a deep basement. [4] From this foundation rises a steel skeleton supporting the walls and floors. [5] Covered with a "skin" of glass and metal, this skeleton becomes a safe working and living space for people.

The Gerund

6g. A *gerund* is a verb form ending in *-ing* that is used as a noun.

Like nouns, gerunds are used as subjects, predicate nominatives, direct objects, or objects of prepositions.

EXAMPLES **Singing** is fun. [subject]
Their favorite exercise is **running.** [predicate nominative]
Shelly likes **swimming.** [direct object]
Get specially designed shoes for **jogging.** [object of a preposition]

Like nouns, gerunds may be modified by adjectives and adjective phrases.

EXAMPLES We listened to **the beautiful singing of the famous soprano.** [The article *the*, the adjective *beautiful*, and the adjective phrase *of the famous soprano* modify the gerund *singing*. *Singing* is used as the object of the preposition *to*.]
The loud ringing of my alarm wakes me every morning. [The article *the*, the adjective *loud*, and the adjective phrase *of my alarm* modify

> the gerund *ringing,* which is the subject of
> the sentence.]

Like verbs, gerunds may also be modified by adverbs
and adverb phrases.

EXAMPLES   **Floating lazily in the pool** is my favorite summer pastime. [The gerund *floating* is used as
the subject of the sentence. It is modified by
the adverb *lazily* (telling *how*) and also by the
adverb phrase *in the pool* (telling *where*).]
Brandywine enjoys **galloping briskly on a cold
morning.** [The gerund *galloping* is the direct
object of the verb *enjoys.* The adverb *briskly*
(telling *how*) and the adverb phrase *on a
cold morning* (telling *when*) both modify
galloping.]

Gerunds, like present participles, end in *-ing.* To be a
gerund, a verbal must be used as a noun. In the following
sentence, three words end in *-ing,* but only one of them is a
gerund.

EXAMPLE   **Following** the coach's advice, she was **planning** to go on with her **training.** [*Following* is
a present participle modifying *she. Planning*
is part of the verb phrase *was planning.* Only
training, used as the object of the preposition
with, is a gerund.]

The Gerund Phrase

6h.   A **gerund phrase** contains a gerund and any
modifiers or complements it may have. The entire
gerund phrase acts as a noun.

EXAMPLES   **The gentle pattering of the rain** was a welcome sound. [The gerund phrase is the sub-
ject of the sentence. The gerund *pattering* is
modified by the article *the,* the adjective *gentle,* and the adjective phrase *of the rain.*
Notice that the modifiers preceding the
gerund are included in the gerund phrase.]

SENTENCES

I feared **skiing down the mountain alone.**
[The gerund phrase is used as the object of the verb *feared.* The gerund *skiing* is modified by the adverb phrase *down the mountain* and by the adverb *alone.*]
His job is **giving the customers their menus.**
[The gerund phrase is used as a predicate nominative. The gerund *giving* has a direct object, *menus,* and an indirect object, *customers.*]
Evelyn Ashford won a gold medal for **running the 100-meter dash.** [The gerund phrase is the object of the preposition *for.* The gerund *running* has a direct object, *dash.*]

 NOTE A noun or pronoun that comes before a gerund should be in the possessive form.

EXAMPLES **Pedro's** constant practicing improved his playing.
My playing the radio loudly is a bad habit.

 *QUICK CHECK 3* **Identifying and Classifying Gerund Phrases**

Find the gerund phrases in the following paragraph. Then identify how each phrase is used: as a *subject,* a *predicate nominative,* an *object of a preposition,* or a *direct object.*

[1] Exciting and challenging, wildlife photography is surprisingly similar to hunting with a gun. [2] In both activities, knowing the animals' habits and habitats is vital to success. [3] Other important skills are being quiet and keeping your aim steady. [4] In photography, you must also consider lighting the prey and choosing the correct film. [5] Your patience and skill are rewarded when you "capture" a wild creature without killing it.

The Infinitive

6i. An *infinitive* is a verb form, usually preceded by *to,* used as a noun, an adjective, or an adverb.

S E N T E N C E S

INFINITIVES	
USED AS	**EXAMPLES**
Nouns	**To love** is **to care.** [*To love* is the subject of the sentence; *to care* is the predicate nominative.]
	Cheryl wanted **to work** on the play in any way except **to act.** [*To work* is the object of the verb *wanted. To act* is the object of the preposition *except.*]
Adjectives	The place **to visit** is Williamsburg. [*To visit* modifies the noun *place.*]
	That was the record **to beat.** [*To beat* modifies the noun *record.*]
Adverbs	The basketball player jumped **to shoot.** [*To shoot* modifies the verb *jumped.*]
	Ready **to go,** we loaded the car. [*To go* modifies the adjective *Ready.*]

NOTE *To* plus a noun or a pronoun (*to school, to him, to the beach*) is a prepositional phrase, not an infinitive.

The Infinitive Phrase

6j. An **infinitive phrase** consists of an infinitive together with its modifiers and complements. The entire infinitive phrase can be used as a noun, an adjective, or an adverb.

EXAMPLES **To proofread your writing carefully** is important. [The infinitive phrase is used as a noun, as the subject of the sentence. The infinitive *to proofread* has a direct object, *writing,* and is modified by the adverb *carefully.*]
She is the player **to watch in the next game.** [The infinitive phrase is used as an adjective modifying the predicate nominative *player.* The infinitive *to watch* is modified by the adverb phrase *in the next game.*]

S E N T E N C E S

At ten o'clock, I went downstairs **to make my-self a sandwich.** [The infinitive phrase is used as an adverb modifying the verb *went*. The infinitive *to make* has an indirect object, *myself,* and a direct object, *sandwich.*]

We are eager **to finish this project.** [The infinitive phrase is used as an adverb modifying the predicate adjective *eager*. The infinitive *to finish* has a direct object, *project.*]

 NOTE An infinitive may have a subject, in which case it forms an **infinitive clause.** An infinitive clause consists of an infinitive with a subject, together with the modifiers and complements of the infinitive. The entire infinitive clause functions as the direct object of the main verb of the sentence.

EXAMPLE   I wanted **him to help me with my geometry.** [The entire infinitive clause is the direct object of the verb *wanted*. *Him* is the subject of the infinitive *to help*. The infinitive *to help* has a direct object, *me,* and is modified by the adverbial phrase *with my geometry.*]

Notice that a pronoun that functions as the subject of an infinitive clause takes the objective form.

STYLE NOTE   A *split infinitive* occurs when a word is placed between the sign of the infinitive, *to,* and the verb. Although split infinitives are common in informal speaking and writing, you should avoid them in formal situations.

SPLIT   It's wise to always have some money in savings.

REVISED   It's wise always **to have** some money in savings.

REVISED   It's wise **to have** some money in savings always.

REVISED   It's always wise **to have** some money in savings.

"*Before I begin, I should warn you that in my quest for truth and my relentless war against corruption I will now and then split an infinitive and end an occasional sentence with a preposition.*"

Drawing by Richter; © 1988 The New Yorker Magazine Inc.

SENTENCES

COMPUTER NOTE Some software programs can identify and highlight split infinitives in a document.
Using such a feature will help you eliminate split infinitives from your formal writing.

The Infinitive Without *To*

Sometimes the *to* of the infinitive is left out of a sentence.

EXAMPLES   This book can help [to] **make** life easier.
The archer let [to] **fly** an arrow.
I dare [to] **say** this invention will prove useful.

QUICK CHECK 4

Identifying and Classifying Infinitives and Infinitive Phrases

Identify the infinitives and infinitive phrases in the following sentences. After each one, give its use: *noun, adjective,* or *adverb.* A sentence may contain more than one infinitive or infinitive phrase.

1. To dance gracefully requires coordination.
2. Sandy needs to study.
3. I'm going to the pond to fish.
4. The best way to get there is to take the bus.
5. Don't you dare open that present before your birthday.

Appositives and Appositive Phrases

> **6k.** An **appositive** is a noun or a pronoun placed beside another noun or pronoun to identify or explain it.

EXAMPLES   The sculptor **Noguchi** has designed sculpture gardens. [The noun *Noguchi* identifies the noun *sculptor.*]
Eric, a talented **musician,** plans to study in Europe. [The noun *musician* explains the noun *Eric.*]

> **6l.** An **appositive phrase** is made up of an appositive and its modifiers.

EXAMPLES   My neighbor, **Dr. Jackson,** got her master's degree in entomology, the **scientific study of insects.**
Lucy Sánchez, **my longtime friend from my old neighborhood,** has a new Scottish terrier.

NOTE   An appositive phrase usually follows the noun or pronoun it refers to. Sometimes, however, it precedes the noun or pronoun.

EXAMPLE   **The terror of our block,** little Alisha was on the warpath.

Appositives and appositive phrases are usually set off by commas. However, if the appositive is a single word closely related to the preceding noun or pronoun, it should not be set off by commas.

SENTENCES

EXAMPLES   My brother **Richard** goes to college. [The
writer has more than one brother. The appositive is necessary to tell which brother is referred to. Because this information is essential to the meaning of the sentence, it is not
set off by commas.]

My brother, **Richard,** goes to college. [The
writer has only one brother. The appositive is
not necessary to identify the brother. Because
the information is nonessential, it is set off by
commas.]

Commas are always used with appositives that refer to
proper nouns.

EXAMPLE   Linda, **the editor,** assigned the Talmidge
Hospital story to Rastíl O'Brien and me.

☞ REFERENCE NOTE: For a discussion of essential and
nonessential phrases, see pages 275–276. For more information on how to punctuate appositives, see page
279. Using pronouns as appositives is discussed on pages
128–129.

 QUICK CHECK 5   **Identifying Appositives
and Appositive Phrases**

Identify the appositives and appositive phrases in the following sentences. Then give the word that each appositive
or appositive phrase identifies or explains.

1. Our community has a new organization, a writers' club
   called Writers, Inc.
2. The members of Writers, Inc., meet once a week to read
   their drafts, fiction or poetry, and to discuss suggestions
   for improvement.
3. People from all walks of life, the members have varied
   interests.
4. My friend Alnaba just had a short story about her culture, the Navajo, published in a national magazine.
5. I usually write haiku, a verse form invented by the
   Japanese.

SENTENCES

✓ *Chapter Review 1*

A. Identifying and Classifying Prepositional Phrases

Identify each prepositional phrase in the following sentences. Some sentences have more than one prepositional phrase. After each phrase, write the word or words it modifies. Then identify how the phrase functions as a part of speech (*adj.* for adjective phrase, *adv.* for adverb phrase).

EXAMPLE   [1] The museums of different cities throughout the world are endlessly fascinating to tourists.

1. *of different cities—museums—adj.*
throughout the world—cities—adj.
to tourists—fascinating—adv.

[1] Among its many other attractions, New York City offers tourists a number of museums. [2] Perhaps the best-known museum is the American Museum of Natural History. [3]This huge museum has exhibits concerning human history and culture and also shows animals, even dinosaurs, in natural-looking displays called dioramas. [4] Exhibits about earth and space interest young and old museum-goers alike. [5] In addition to these exhibits, the museum also houses the Hayden Planetarium, which features shows about outer space. [6]The entire complex is popular because it offers something for everyone. [7]New York City's other museums, which are also fascinating, attract visitors who are interested in specific subjects. [8]People who enjoy art can visit museums like the Metropolitan Museum of Art, the Museum of Modern Art, and the Guggenheim Museum. [9] New York City is also home to the Museum of Broadcasting, which is filled with old films and radio broadcasts. [10] One of the city's newest museums, Ellis Island Immigration Museum, opened during 1990, displays many artifacts that were once owned by immigrants who entered this country through Ellis Island.

B. Identifying Verbals and Appositives

Identify each italicized word or word group in the following paragraph as a *participle,* a *gerund,* an *infinitive,* or an *appositive.*

EXAMPLE [1] For some reason, *cleaning* a room, that *dreaded project,* always seems *to create* new projects.

1. *cleaning*—gerund; *dreaded*—participle; *project*—appositive; *to create*—infinitive

[11] John began with every intention of *cleaning* his entire room, the official disaster *area* of his home. [12] He first tackled the pile of CDs *lying* near his *unused* sound system. [13] *Sorting* through them, he found them mostly *outdated.* [14] John reasoned that his *broken* stereo system, a *gift* from his parents, was the culprit. [15] By *repairing* the stereo, he could give himself a reason *to update* his music collection. [16] *Trained* in electronics, John soon saw the problem and began *to work* on it. [17] Some hours later, John had a *working* stereo system but an *uncleaned* room. [18] He had a rude *awakening* when his sister announced, "Mom's coming *to see* how your room looks!" [19] A tough *taskmaster,* his mother expected him *to have* his room spotless. [20] She applauded his success in *fixing* his stereo but insisted that he clean the room before *doing* anything else.

✓ *Chapter Review 2*

Writing Sentences with Phrases

Write ten sentences according to the directions given below. Underline the specified phrase in each sentence.

EXAMPLE 1. Use an *adjective phrase* modifying the subject of a sentence.

1. *The store  on the corner sells video games.*

1. Use an *adjective phrase* modifying the object of a preposition.
2. Use an *adverb phrase* modifying an adjective.

3. Use an *adverb phrase* modifying a verb.
4. Use a *participial phrase* modifying a subject.
5. Use a *participial phrase* modifying a direct object.
6. Use a *gerund phrase* as a subject.
7. Use a *gerund phrase* as a predicate nominative.
8. Use an *infinitive phrase* as a noun.
9. Use an *infinitive phrase* as an adverb.
10. Use an *appositive phrase* that explains or identifies the subject of a sentence.

SENTENCES

7 CLAUSES

Independent and Subordinate Clauses

✓ *Checking What You Know*

A. Identifying and Classifying Clauses

Identify the italicized clauses in the following sentences as *independent* or *subordinate.* If a clause is subordinate, label it as an *adjective clause,* an *adverb clause,* or a *noun clause.*

EXAMPLES
1. *Emily Dickinson,* who was a great American poet, *was born in 1830.*
1. *independent*
2. I have noticed *that her poems do not have titles.*
2. *subordinate—noun clause*

1. Emily Dickinson appeared to have a fairly normal life *until she became a recluse in her family's home.*
2. *There she wrote poems* that critics now call "great American poetry."
3. *Only a few of Dickinson's poems were published* while she was alive.

4. *After she died in 1886,* her other poems were published.
5. My teacher, Mrs. Brooks, thinks *that everyone should read at least some of Dickinson's poetry.*
6. Emily Dickinson is a poet *whose work I read often.*
7. *The poems* I have just finished reading *are "A Narrow Fellow in the Grass" and "Apparently with No Surprise."*
8. Dickinson's imagery in "Apparently with No Surprise" is *what impresses me most.*
9. *I read her poems aloud* so that I can listen to their rhythms.
10. *Whatever I read* by Emily Dickinson inspires me.

B. Identifying and Classifying Subordinate Clauses

Identify each subordinate clause in the following sentences according to its use: as an adjective (*adj.*), an adverb (*adv.*), or a noun (*n.*). If the clause is used as an adjective or an adverb, write the word or phrase it modifies. If the clause is used as a noun, write *subj.* for subject, *d.o.* for direct object, *i.o.* for indirect object, *p.n.* for predicate nominative, or *o.p.* for object of a preposition.

EXAMPLES [1]Since my family has always wanted to see Alaska, we decided to drive there last summer.

1. *Since my family has always wanted to see Alaska—adv.—decided*

[2]After three long days on the road, I doubted that we would ever reach our destination.

2. *that we would ever reach our destination—n., d.o.*

[11] To get to Alaska, we drove along the Alaska Highway, which goes through the Yukon Territory in Canada. [12] Since this highway is 1,397 miles long, most tourists choose to fly to Alaska. [13] However, by driving, we were able to take pictures of whatever caught our attention along the way. [14] At a rest stop, I thought that I heard some small animals rustling in the brush, and I

grabbed my camera. [15] What I saw disappearing into the bushes certainly surprised me; it was an enormous moose and her calf. ✓

7a. A *clause* is a group of words that contains a verb and its subject and is used as part of a sentence.

Although every clause contains a subject and a verb, not every clause expresses a complete thought. Clauses that do are called *independent clauses.* Clauses that do not make sense by themselves are called *subordinate clauses.*

Kinds of Clauses

7b. An *independent* (or *main*) *clause* expresses a complete thought and can stand by itself as a sentence.

EXAMPLE   **Ms. Santana works in a law office in downtown Concord,** and **she has a successful practice.**

Each independent clause has its own subject and verb and expresses a complete thought. The two clauses can be joined in a single sentence because they express closely related ideas. In the example just given, the clauses are joined by a comma and the coordinating conjunction *and*. They could instead be joined by a semicolon.

EXAMPLE   Ms. Santana works in a law office in downtown Concord**;** she has a successful practice.

Two independent clauses can also be joined by a semicolon and a conjunctive adverb.

EXAMPLE   Ms. Santana works in a law office in downtown Concord**;** indeed**,** she has a successful practice.

Two independent clauses don't have to be joined at all. They can be written as separate sentences.

EXAMPLE   Ms. Santana works in a law office in down-
           town Concord. She has a successful practice.

☞ REFERENCE NOTE: For more information on using semicolons and conjunctive adverbs to join independent
clauses, see pages 231–232. For a list of coordinating
conjunctions, see page 69.

7c.   A *subordinate* (or *dependent*) *clause* does not
           express a complete thought and cannot stand
           alone.

Words such as *whom, because,* and *until* signal that the
clauses following them are subordinate. *Subordinate* means
"less important." To make a complete sentence, a subordinate clause must be joined to an independent clause.

SUBORDINATE   whom you know
   CLAUSES   because I told him the truth
               what the show is about

   SENTENCES   Will the player **whom you know** give us his
               autograph?
               Because I told him the truth, Dad wasn't
               too angry about the broken window.
               Amy wants to know **what the show is
               about.**

NOTE   The placement of a subordinate clause depends on
how it is used (as an adjective clause, an adverb
clause, or a noun clause). The various uses
of subordinate clauses are discussed on pages
179–186 of this chapter.

Complements and Modifiers in Subordinate Clauses

Many subordinate clauses contain complements (such as
predicate nominatives, direct objects, or indirect objects),
modifiers, or both.

EXAMPLES   **Although she gave us several clues** . . . [*Us* is
           the indirect object of *gave; clues* is the direct
           object of *gave.*]
           When you are late. . . [*Late* is a predicate ad-
           jective modifying *you.*]

After we had heard **from them** . . . [*From them* is an adverb phrase modifying *had heard.*]
The poster **that** he designed . . . [*That* is the direct object of *designed.*]
I don't know **who** he is . . . [*Who* is a predicate nominative: He is *who.*]

✓ *QUICK CHECK* 1   **Identifying Independent and Subordinate Clauses**

For each sentence in the following paragraph, identify the clause in italics as *independent* or *subordinate*.

[1] Beep baseball, invented by engineer Charley Fairbanks, enables people *who have visual impairments* to play the great American game. [2] *In this version of baseball, the ball beeps* and the bases buzz to let visually impaired players know when to swing and where to run. [3] Each team has a sighted pitcher and a sighted catcher, *who are not allowed to bat or to field the ball,* and six visually impaired fielders who wear blindfolds so that all players are equally impaired. [4] The pitcher shouts "Ready!" *before the ball is pitched* and "Pitch!" when the ball is released. [5] *Beep baseball is fun to play,* and it creates a bond between sighted and visually impaired players.

Uses of Subordinate Clauses

Like phrases, subordinate clauses can be used as adjectives, adverbs, or nouns.

The Adjective Clause

7d. An *adjective clause* is a subordinate clause used as an adjective to modify a noun or a pronoun.

An adjective clause follows the word it modifies. If a clause is necessary, or *essential,* to the meaning of a sentence, it is not set off with commas. If a clause only gives additional information and is *nonessential* to the meaning of a sentence, it is set off by commas.

EXAMPLES   This is the new music video **that I like best.**
[The clause *that I like best* modifies the compound noun *music video.* The clause is necessary to tell which video is being referred to. Because this information is *essential* to the meaning of the sentence, it is not set off by commas.]

Griffins, **which are seen on many coats of arms,** are mythological beasts. [The clause *which are seen on many coats of arms* modifies the noun *griffins.* The clause is not necessary to identify *griffins.* Because this information is *nonessential* to the meaning of the sentence, it is set off by commas.]

👉 REFERENCE NOTE: For help in deciding whether a clause is essential or nonessential, see pages 275–276, rule 12i.

Relative Pronouns

Adjective clauses are frequently introduced by *relative pronouns.*

RELATIVE PRONOUNS	who whom whose which that

These words are called *relative pronouns* because they *relate* a clause to the word that the clause modifies (the antecedent of the relative pronoun).

    A relative pronoun
■ introduces an adjective clause
■ relates the clause to another word in the sentence
■ has its own function in the clause

EXAMPLES   Luís, **who enjoys running,** has decided to enter the marathon. [The relative pronoun *who* relates the adjective clause to *Luís. Who* also serves as the subject of the adjective clause.]

Janice, **whom I have known for years,** is my lab partner this semester. [The relative pronoun *whom* relates the adjective clause to *Janice*. *Whom* also serves as the direct object of the verb *have known* in the adjective clause.]

The students questioned the data on which the theory was based. [The relative pronoun *which* relates the adjective clause to *data*. *Which* also serves as the object of the preposition *on*.]

We met the singer whose record was released this week. [The relative pronoun *whose* relates the adjective clause to *singer*. *Whose* also serves as a possessive pronoun in the adjective clause.]

REFERENCE NOTE: For more information on using *who* and *whom* correctly, see pages 125–127.

A relative pronoun is sometimes left out of an adjective clause, but the pronoun's meaning is understood. Though absent, the pronoun still has a function in the clause.

EXAMPLE   **Here is the salad [that] you ordered.** [The relative pronoun *that* is understood. The pronoun relates the adjective clause to *salad* and serves as the direct object of the verb *ordered* in the adjective clause.]

Occasionally an adjective clause is introduced by the relative adverb *where* or *when*.

EXAMPLES   **They showed us the stadium where the game would be held.**
Summer is the season when I feel happiest.

STYLE NOTE   Too much of anything is usually a bad idea. Although short, choppy sentences can be effective, it's a good idea to alternate between shorter sentences and more complex ones. To change choppy sentences into smoother writing, try placing ideas from shorter sentences into subordinate clauses. Also, avoid unnecessary repetition of subjects, verbs, and pronouns.

SENTENCES

CHOPPY   Mary Cassatt was an American painter. I enjoy her works. She was an impressionist.

SMOOTH   I enjoy the works of Mary Cassatt, who was an American impressionist painter.

In the example above, two of the short sentences are combined into a single subordinate clause.

 REFERENCE NOTE: For more information on complex sentences, see page 208. For more information on sentence combining, see pages 226–234.

✓ *QUICK CHECK 2*   **Identifying Adjective Clauses and the Words They Modify**

Identify the adjective clause in each of the following sentences, and give the noun or pronoun that it modifies. Then tell whether the relative pronoun is used as the *subject, direct object,* or *object of a preposition* in the adjective clause.

1. The citizens, who were furious about the recent tax increase, gathered in front of City Hall.
2. Edna Jackson easily won the first political campaign that she entered.
3. At the assembly, Ms. Leon made an announcement that surprised everyone in the audience.
4. The history books, which were yellow and tattered from many years of use, lay on the shelf.
5. The veterinarian to whom we took the injured cat performed emergency surgery on the animal.

The Adverb Clause

7e.   An *adverb clause* is a subordinate clause that modifies a verb, an adjective, or an adverb.

An adverb clause tells *how, when, where, why, to what extent (how much),* or *under what condition.* An adverb clause may modify the verb in the sentence's independent clause.

EXAMPLES   **After I proofread my paper,** I typed it. [The adverb clause *after I proofread my paper* tells *when* I typed it.]

Because manicotti takes so long to prepare, Joy makes it only on special occasions. [*Because manicotti takes so long to prepare* tells *why* Joy makes it only on special occasions.]

You can set down the flowers **wherever you want.** [*Wherever you want* tells *where* you can set down the flowers.]

Teresa looks **as if she knows a secret.** [*As if she knows a secret* tells *how* Teresa looks.]

You and your brother may come with us **if you want to.** [*If you want to* tells *under what condition* you and your brother may come with us.]

REFERENCE NOTE: Introductory adverb clauses are usually set off by commas. See page 278.

An adverb clause can also modify an adjective or an adverb in the sentence's independent clause.

EXAMPLES · His pitching arm is stronger today **than it ever was.** [The adverb clause modifies the adjective *stronger,* telling *to what extent* his arm is stronger.]

My cousin Adele reads faster **than I do.** [The adverb clause modifies the adverb *faster,* telling *how much* faster Adele reads.]

REFERENCE NOTE: When using adverb clauses to make comparisons, be sure your comparisons are complete. See pages 144–145.

Subordinating Conjunctions

Adverb clauses are introduced by *subordinating conjunctions.*

Common Subordinating Conjunctions		
after	before	unless
although	even though	until
as	if	when
as if	in order that	whenever
as long as	once	where
as soon as	since	wherever
as though	so that	whether
because	than	while

NOTE Some subordinating conjunctions, such as *after, as, before, since,* and *until,* may also be used as prepositions.

EXAMPLES Be sure to hand in your report **before the end** of class today. [prepositional phrase]
Be sure to hand in your report **before class ends today.** [adverb clause]

An adverb does not have a fixed location in a sentence, so you must choose where to put the clause. Although personal taste and style count, context often determines placement. If you use a computer, you can easily experiment with the placement of adverb clauses in sentences. Enter different versions of the sentence. Read each version aloud, along with the sentences just before and after, to see how the placement of the clause affects flow, rhythm, and overall meaning.

REFERENCE NOTE: For more information on placement of clauses, see pages 145–148.

  *QUICK CHECK 3* **Identifying and Classifying Adverb Clauses**

Identify each adverb clause in the following paragraph. Then write what the clause tells: *when, where, how, why, to what extent,* or *under what condition.*

[1] Although he used only nonviolent methods, Mohandas K. Gandhi (1869–1948) fought hard for India's independence from Great Britain. [2] Sometimes he led marches or fasted until the government met his requests. [3] As India's Congress and people increasingly supported Gandhi's nonviolent program, the British government was forced to listen. [4] After India's independence was assured, Gandhi turned his attention to helping the nation's many poor people. [5] Because he was loved throughout India and the world, Gandhi was called Mahatma, meaning "Great Soul."

The Noun Clause

7f. A *noun clause* is a subordinate clause used as a noun.

A noun clause may be used as a subject, a complement (predicate nominative, direct object, or indirect object), or the object of a preposition.

SUBJECT	**What Mary Anne did** was brave and earned her praise from everyone in the building.
PREDICATE NOMINATIVE	The winner will be **whoever runs fastest.**
DIRECT OBJECT	Did she finally discover **what the answer was?**
INDIRECT OBJECT	The clerk should tell **whoever calls** the sale prices.
OBJECT OF PREPOSITION	He checks the ID cards of **whoever visits.**

☞ REFERENCE NOTE: For more information on subjects, predicate nominatives, direct objects, and indirect objects, see **Chapter 8: Sentence Structure.** For more information on objects of prepositions, see pages 156–157.

Noun clauses are usually introduced by

that	when	who	whomever
what	where	whoever	whose
whatever	whether	whom	why

SENTENCES

REFERENCE NOTE: Some of the words in the list above may also be used to introduce adjective or adverb clauses. See pages 179–184.

The word that introduces a noun clause may or may not have a function within the noun clause.

EXAMPLES   They did not know **who the mystery caller could be.** [The introductory word *who* is the predicate nominative of the noun clause—*the mystery caller could be who.*]
Show us **what you bought.** [The introductory word *what* is the direct object of the noun clause—*you bought what.*]
She wished **that she were older.** [*That* has no function in the noun clause.]

Sometimes the word that introduces a noun clause is not stated, but its meaning is understood.

EXAMPLES   His mother said [that] **he could go get the milk himself.** [The introductory word *that* is understood.]
The Jeffersons are the ones [whom] **you should ask.** [The introductory word *whom* is understood.]

 QUICK CHECK 4   **Identifying and Classifying Noun Clauses**

Identify the noun clause in each of the following sentences. Then tell how the clause is used: as a *subject*, a *predicate nominative*, a *direct object*, an *indirect object*, or the *object of a preposition*.

1. Do you know what time it is?
2. Where I left my keys is a mystery to me.
3. The Civic Center is where the concert was held last year.
4. The sponsors will give whoever completes the race a T-shirt.
5. We took a vote on whether we should have a carwash or a bake sale.

✓ *Chapter Review 1*

A. Identifying and Classifying Clauses

Identify the italicized clauses in the following sentences as *independent* or *subordinate*. If a clause is subordinate, label it as an *adjective clause*, an *adverb clause*, or a *noun clause*.

1. *When my family went to New York last summer,* we visited the Theodore Roosevelt museum.
2. *The museum has been established in the house* where Roosevelt was born.
3. It is located on the basement floor of Roosevelt's birthplace, *which is on East Twentieth Street.*
4. *The museum contains books, letters, and documents* about Roosevelt's public life.
5. There are mounted heads of animals, a stuffed lion, and zebra skins from the days *when Roosevelt was big-game hunting in Africa.*
6. *Because Roosevelt was once a cowboy,* there are also branding irons and chaps.
7. Before Theodore Roosevelt became President, *he gained fame in the Spanish-American War.*
8. During that war he led the Rough Riders, *who made the famous charge up San Juan Hill.*
9. Trophies *that commemorate Roosevelt's war exploits* abound in the museum.
10. *The Roosevelt Memorial Association,* which established the museum, *charges a nominal admission fee to visitors.*

B. Identifying and Classifying Subordinate Clauses

Write the subordinate clause in each of the following sentences. Identify the clause as *adj.* (adjective), *adv.* (adverb), or *n.* (noun). If the clause is used as an adjective or an adverb, write the word or phrase it modifies. If the clause is used as a noun, write *subj.* for subject, *d.o.* for direct object, *i.o.* for indirect object, *p.n.* for predicate nominative, or *o.p.* for object of a preposition.

EXAMPLES
1. After our last class, Elena, Frieda, and I agreed that we would go bicycling in the park.
1. *that we would go bicycling in the park—n.—d.o.*

2. As we set out for the park, we had no idea of the difficulties ahead.
2. *As we set out for the park—adv.—had*

1. Since none of us own bicycles, we decided to rent them there.
2. The man who rented us the bikes was helpful.
3. The three of us had bicycled six miles when Frieda's bike got a flat tire.
4. How we would repair it became a topic of heated discussion.
5. We decided to take the bike to whatever bike shop was the nearest.
6. The woman at the bike shop told us that she could fix the tire quickly.
7. After we had paid for the repair, we rode back to the park and bicycled for an hour.
8. Our only worry was that the man at the rental shop might not pay us back for fixing the tire.
9. When we returned our bikes, we showed the man the receipt for the repaired tire.
10. He refunded us the money we had spent to fix the tire.

✓ *Chapter Review 2*

Writing Sentences with Subordinate Clauses

Write ten sentences of your own, using the following subordinate clauses. Identify the clauses as noun (*n.*), adjective (*adj.*), or adverb clauses (*adv.*). When you're done, label each noun clause as a subject, a complement, or the object of a preposition, depending on how you used it in the sentence.

1. that always breaks down just when I need it the most
2. in which the mail carrier leaves our letters

3. what to expect from someone like June
4. unless Charlayne mows the lawn this afternoon
5. who runs the video arcade in the mall
6. what Matt just did
7. although we left early to meet Aisha at the movie theater
8. whose piano I play in my free time
9. if you forget to return this book to the library
10. whatever we want for dessert

Subject, Predicate, Complement

✓ *Checking What You Know*

A. Identifying the Parts of Sentences

Identify the italicized words in the following passage. Use these abbreviations:

s. subject	*p.a.* predicate adjective
v. verb	*d.o.* direct object
p.n. predicate nominative	*i.o.* indirect object

EXAMPLE   Raising money is hard [1] *work.*
             1. *p.n.*

A carwash can be a good [1] *fund-raiser.* Knowing this, the freshman class [2] *planned* a carwash for last Saturday. On Saturday morning, the [3] *sky* did not look [4] *good.* In fact, the weather forecast predicted [5] *thunderstorms.* Did [6] *any* of this discourage [7] *us?* No, we had our carwash anyway. Our first customer, at 9:00 A.M., was a [8] *woman* in a pickup truck. Glancing at the sky, she paid [9] *us* a compliment. "You're really [10] *brave,*" she said. The rain [11] *began* as she was speaking, and our disappointment must have been [12] *obvious.* "Don't worry," she added, "there is [13] *nothing* like a rainwater rinse." We charged [14] *her* only one [15] *dollar* because she had cheered us up so much.

B. Identifying and Punctuating the Kinds of Sentences

Write the last word of each of the following sentences, and then give the correct end mark. Classify each sentence as *imperative, declarative, interrogative,* or *exclamatory.*

EXAMPLE   **1.** The zoo is a fascinating place
               1. *place.—declarative*

16. Why don't we go to the zoo tomorrow
17. What a good time we'll have
18. The big cats are awesome, especially at feeding time
19. Actually, I enjoy the entire wildlife park
20. Meet me at the front gate at nine o'clock

C. Classifying Sentences According to Structure

Classify each of the following sentences according to its structure: *simple, compound, complex,* or *compound-complex.*

EXAMPLE   [1] Before my history class visited the Senate chamber, we read about the United States Senate.
               1. *complex*

[21] Since the passage of the Seventeenth Amendment in 1913, senators have been chosen by popular elections in their states. [22] Unlike presidents, senators are elected to six-year terms, and they can be reelected any number of times. [23] To be eligible for the Senate, a person must have been a United States citizen for at least nine years and be at least thirty years old; a candidate must also live in the state that he or she would like to represent. [24] One important job that senators have is to introduce bills in the Senate. [25] Senators are also responsible for approving or rejecting certain presidential appointments, such as those of federal judges and ambassadors.

Sentence or Sentence Fragment?

In casual conversation, people often leave out parts of sentences. In writing, however, it is better to use complete sentences most of the time. They help to make your meaning clear to your readers.

> **8a.** A *sentence* is a group of words that contains a subject and a verb and expresses a complete thought.

If a group of words does not express a complete thought, it is a *fragment,* or a piece of a sentence. It is not a sentence.

FRAGMENT	the room with the high ceiling
SENTENCE	We looked into the room with the high ceiling.
FRAGMENT	waiting by the door
SENTENCE	The clerk was waiting by the door.
FRAGMENT	when you have time
SENTENCE	When you have time, will you read my story?

Notice that a sentence always begins with a capital letter and ends with a period, a question mark, or an exclamation point.

☞ REFERENCE NOTE: For information on how to correct fragments, see pages 214–220. For more information about punctuating sentences, see pages 205–206 in this chapter and pages 268–270.

COMPUTER NOTE

Many style-checking software programs can identify fragments. If you have access to such a program, use it to help you evaluate your writing. After you have identified each fragment, refer to **Chapter 9: Writing Complete Sentences** for information on revising fragments.

☑ *QUICK CHECK 1* **Identifying Sentences and Fragments**

Decide which of the following groups of words are *sentences* and which are *fragments.*

1. Will you be there tomorrow?
2. Four people in a small car.
3. It runs smoothly.
4. Leaning far over the railing.
5. While waiting in line at the theater.

Subject and Predicate

8b. A sentence consists of two parts: the subject and the predicate. The **subject** is the part that names the person, place, or thing spoken about in the rest of the sentence. The **predicate** is the part that says something about the subject.

In the following examples, blue vertical lines separate the subjects from the predicates. Subjects and predicates may be only one word each or more than one word each.

EXAMPLES

SUBJECT   PREDICATE
Coyotes | were howling in the distance.

SUBJECT   PREDICATE
The telephone in the lobby | rang.

SUBJECT   PREDICATE
The woman in the red blouse | is my aunt.

In these three examples, the words to the left of the vertical line make up the *complete subject.* The words to the right of the vertical line make up the *complete predicate.*

NOTE The subject may appear in the middle or at the end of a sentence.

EXAMPLES In the dim light, **the eager scientist** examined the cave walls.
Does **Brian's car** have a tape deck?
On the table stood **a silver vase.**

The Simple Subject

8c. The *simple subject* is the main word or group of words in the complete subject.

EXAMPLES
Their scientific *discoveries* made them famous. [The complete subject is *their scientific discoveries.* The simple subject is *discoveries.*]

The talented *Georgia O'Keeffe* is known for her paintings of huge flowers. [The complete subject is *the talented Georgia O'Keeffe.* The simple subject is *Georgia O'Keeffe.*]

 REFERENCE NOTE: Compound nouns such as *Georgia O'Keeffe* are considered one noun. For more information about compound nouns, see page 53.

 In this book, the term *subject* refers to the simple subject unless otherwise indicated.

The Simple Predicate

8d. The *simple predicate,* or *verb,* is the main word or group of words in the complete predicate.

EXAMPLES
The ambulance *raced* out of the hospital driveway and down the crowded street. [The complete predicate is *raced out of the hospital driveway and down the crowded street.* The simple predicate is *raced.*]

In 1986 Nigerian writer Wole Soyinke *became* the first black African to win the Nobel Prize for literature. [The complete predicate is *in 1986 became the first black African to win the Nobel Prize for literature.* The simple predicate is *became.*]

The simple predicate may be a single verb or a *verb phrase* (a verb with one or more helping verbs).

EXAMPLES   will sing   have been trying
              has been broken does seem

Commonly Used Helping Verbs

am	were	have	might	can
are	do	has	must	should
is	does	had	shall	would
was	did	may	will	could

When you are looking for the simple predicate in a sentence, be sure to include all parts of a verb phrase.

EXAMPLE   Diego **may have borrowed** my book. [The complete predicate is *may have borrowed my book.* The simple predicate is the verb phrase *may have borrowed.*]

NOTE   Throughout this book, the word *verb* refers to the simple predicate unless otherwise indicated.

☞   REFERENCE NOTE: For more information about verb phrases, see pages 63–64.

Shoe, by Jeff MacNelly, reprinted by permission: Tribune Media Services.

Finding the Subject of a Sentence

To find the subject of a sentence, find the verb first. Then ask "Who?" or "What?" before the verb.

EXAMPLES   Here you can swim year-round. [The verb is *can swim.* Who can swim? *You* can swim. *You* is the subject.]

The price of those tapes seemed too high to us. [The verb is *seemed.* What seemed? *Price* seemed. *Price* is the subject.]

8e. The subject of a verb is never in a prepositional phrase.

A *prepositional phrase* consists of a preposition, a noun or a pronoun called the object of the preposition, and any modifiers of that object.

EXAMPLES
to the bank	by the door	in the picture
of a book	on the floor	after class
at intermission	for them	except him

 REFERENCE NOTE: For more information about prepositional phrases, see pages 156–160.

The noun or pronoun that is the object of a preposition cannot be the subject of a verb.

EXAMPLE   Most **of the women** voted. [Who voted? *Most* voted, not *women*, which is part of the prepositional phrase *of the women*.]

Prepositional phrases can be especially confusing when the subject follows the verb.

EXAMPLE   **Around the corner from here** is a store. [What is? *Store* is, not *corner* or *here*, each of which is part of a prepositional phrase.]

In some sentences, you can find the subject and the verb just by crossing out the prepositional phrases.

EXAMPLE   Several ~~of our neighbors~~ will march ~~in the Cinco de Mayo parade.~~
   SUBJECT Several
    VERB will march

Sentences That Ask Questions

Questions often begin with a verb, a helping verb, or a word such as *what, when, where, how,* or *why.* The subject usually follows the verb or helping verb. In a question that begins with a helping verb, like the second example below, the subject always comes between the helping verb and the main verb.

EXAMPLES   Are **you** ready for the test?
    Does **she** have a ride home?
    How is the **movie** different from the book?

To find the subject of a sentence that asks a question, turn the question into a statement. Then find the verb and ask "Who?" or "What?" before it.

EXAMPLES   Was the train late? **becomes** The train was late. [What was late? *Train* was.]
Has she answered the letter? **becomes** She has answered the letter. [Who has answered? *She* has.]
How tall is your brother? **becomes** Your brother is how tall? [Who is tall? *Brother* is tall.]

Sentences Beginning with *There* or *Here*

Both *there* and *here* may be used as adverbs telling *where*. To find the subject, ask "Who?" or "What?" before the verb and the adverb. The word *there* or *here* is usually not the subject of a sentence.

EXAMPLES   There are your keys. [What are there? *Keys* are.]
Here is your pencil. [What is here? *Pencil* is.]

NOTE

There is sometimes used to begin a sentence in which the subject comes after the verb. In this use, *there* is not an adverb but an expletive. An **expletive** is a word that fills out the sentence's structure but doesn't add to its meaning.

           V   S
EXAMPLES   There is a drawbridge over the river.

           V   S
There are insects in our garden.

To find the subject in such a sentence, omit *there* or *here* and ask "Who?" or "What?" before the verb.

EXAMPLE   There was a clerk at the counter. [Who was? *Clerk* was.]

The Understood Subject

In a request or a command, the subject of a sentence is usually not stated. In such sentences, *you* is the **understood subject.**

SENTENCES

REQUEST **Please answer the phone.** [Who is to answer the phone? *You* are—that is, the person spoken to.]

COMMAND **Listen carefully to his question.** [Who is to listen? *You* are.]

Sometimes a request or a command includes a name.

EXAMPLES **Ellen, please answer the phone.**
Listen carefully to his question, class.

Ellen and *class* are not subjects in these sentences. These words are called **nouns of direct address.** They identify the person spoken to or addressed. *You* is still the understood subject of each sentence.

EXAMPLE **Ellen, (you) please answer the phone.**

Compound Subjects

SENTENCES

8f. A *compound subject* consists of two or more subjects that are joined by a conjunction and have the same verb.

The conjunctions most commonly used to connect the parts of a compound subject are *and* and *or.*

EXAMPLE **Antony and Mae baked the bread.** [Who baked the bread? *Antony* baked it. *Mae* baked it. Together, *Antony* and *Mae* form the compound subject.]

NOTE When more than two words are included in a compound subject, the conjunction is generally used only between the last two words. Also, the words are separated by commas.

EXAMPLE **Antony, Mae, and Pamela baked the bread.** [Compound subject: *Antony, Mae, Pamela*]

Correlative conjunctions may be used with compound subjects.

EXAMPLE **Either Antony or Mae baked the bread.** [Compound subject: *Antony, Mae*]

REFERENCE NOTE: See pages 69–70 for more about conjunctions. For more about using commas between
words in a series, see pages 272–274.

Compound Verbs

8g. A *compound verb* consists of two or more verbs
that are joined by a conjunction and have the
same subject.

EXAMPLES   Jim Thorpe **entered** and **won** several events
in the 1912 Olympics.
They **looked** but **saw** nothing.
The committee **met, voted** on the issue, and
adjourned.

STYLE
NOTE

The helping verb may or may not be
repeated before the second part of a
compound verb if the helper is the same for
both parts of the verb.

EXAMPLES   My sister **may buy** or **may lease** a car.
My sister **may buy** or **lease** a car.

Both the subject and the verb may be compound.

EXAMPLES   The **students** and **teachers wrote** the play
and **produced** it.
Either **Jan** or **Beverly will write** the story and
send it to the paper.

 QUICK CHECK 2   **Finding Subjects and Verbs**

Write each of the following five sentences. Then underline
all verbs twice and all subjects once. If the subject of a sentence is understood, write *you* in parentheses after the sentence.

1. Did you and your brother watch the Super Bowl?
2. A female vocalist with a throaty voice charmed the audience with her singing.

3. Down the street from our house, there are two bakeries.
4. Please clear the table and load the dishwasher.
5. On the bulletin board located outside the principal's office have been posted the winners' names.

Complements

8h. A *complement* is a word or group of words that completes the meaning of a verb.

Some groups of words need more than a subject and a verb to express a complete thought. Notice how the following sentences need the boldfaced words to complete their meaning. These boldfaced words are called *complements*.

EXAMPLES This stew tastes **strange.**
She always was a **leader.**
I told **them.**

A complement may be compound.

EXAMPLES Mr. García gave **me advice** and strong
encouragement.
Our new neighbors quickly befriended my
sister and **me.**

A complement may be a noun, a pronoun, or an adjective.

$$\begin{array}{ccc} & S & V & C \end{array}$$

EXAMPLES Marcella might become a **chemist.**

$$\begin{array}{ccc} S & V & C \end{array}$$

The cat watched **us.**

$$\begin{array}{ccc} S & V & C \end{array}$$

The clerks at that store are **helpful.**

An adverb that modifies a verb is not a complement.

EXAMPLES The bus turned **right.** [*Right* is an adverb, not
a complement.]
You may be **right.** [*Right,* an adjective, is a
complement.]

NOTE A complement is never part of a prepositional phrase.

EXAMPLES   She watched the cheering **crowd.** [*Crowd*
is the complement.]
She watched from the cheering **crowd.**
[*Crowd* is part of the prepositional
phrase *from the cheering crowd.*]

Both independent clauses and dependent clauses may
contain complements.

              S   V C   S   V
EXAMPLES   If you ask **me,** Toshiro should be our next
                           C
class **president.**

            S   V   C   S   V   C
Maggie is the **one** who raised the **issue.**

👉 REFERENCE NOTE: See **Chapter 7: Clauses** for a discussion of independent and dependent clauses.

The Subject Complement

8i.   A *subject complement* is a noun, pronoun, or
adjective that follows a linking verb. It describes
or identifies the subject.

EXAMPLES   Mark Twain's real name was **Samuel Clemens.**
[*Samuel Clemens* identifies *name.*]
The winner might be **you.** [*You* identifies
winner.]
The surface felt **sticky.** [*Sticky* describes *sur-
face.*]

👉 REFERENCE NOTE: Linking verbs are discussed on pages
62–63.

NOTE Keep in mind that both independent clauses and dependent clauses may contain subject complements.

EXAMPLE   Although Lars seems **shy,** I know that he
is a great **storyteller.** [*Shy* describes *Lars*
in the introductory adverb clause.
Storyteller identifies *he* in the noun
clause beginning with *that.*]

(1) A *predicate nominative* is a noun or pronoun in the predicate that explains or identifies the subject of a sentence or a clause.

EXAMPLES   A whale is a **mammal.**
The only people in line were **they.**
Angela has become a very talented **soloist.**

(2) A *predicate adjective* is an adjective in the predicate that modifies the subject of a sentence or a clause.

EXAMPLES   The soup is **hot.** [hot soup]
That soil seems awfully **dry.** [dry soil]

Subject complements may be compound.

EXAMPLES   The prizewinners are **Jennifer** and **Marcus.**
[compound predicate nominative]
The corn tastes **sweet** and **buttery.** [compound predicate adjective]

To find the subject complement in an interrogative sentence, rearrange the sentence to make a statement.

EXAMPLES   Is Darnell the treasurer?
Darnell is the **treasurer.** [predicate nominative]

To find the subject complement in an imperative sentence, insert the understood subject *you.*

EXAMPLE   Be a winner!
(You) Be a **winner!** [predicate nominative]

NOTE   The subject complement may precede the subject of a sentence or a clause.

EXAMPLES   How **clever** you are! [*Clever* is a predicate adjective describing *you.*]
I realize what a good **friend** you are.
[*Friend* is a predicate nominative identifying *you.*]

Objects

Objects are complements that do not refer to the subject. Objects follow transitive action verbs, not linking verbs.

EXAMPLE   Lee Trevino sank the **putt.** [*Putt* does not explain or describe the subject *Lee Trevino.*

Sank is a transitive action verb, not a linking verb.]

 REFERENCE NOTE: Action verbs are discussed on pages 61–62.

Both independent clauses and dependent clauses may contain objects.

EXAMPLE   If we win the **tournament,** the coach said that she will throw **us** a **party.**

8j.   A *direct object* is a noun or pronoun that receives the action of the verb or shows the result of the action. It answers the question "Whom?" or "What?" after a transitive action verb.

EXAMPLES   Dot asked **Ira** about the game.
Her poem won an **award.**

To find the object of an action verb, ask "Whom?" or "What?" after the verb.

                        S   V   DO
EXAMPLES   Lucy visited me. [Lucy visited *whom?* Lucy visited *me.*]

                        S   V   DO
            Germs cause illness. [Germs cause *what?* Germs cause *illness.*]

                        S   V   DO
            They were taking snapshots. [They were taking *what?* They were taking *snapshots.*]

 Transitive action verbs may express mental action (for example, *believe, imagine, remember*) as well as physical action (for example, *throw, press, announce*).

EXAMPLE   Now I understand the question.
[Understand *what?* Question.]

Do not confuse a direct object with an object of a preposition.

EXAMPLE   Josh was riding his **bicycle.** [*Bicycle* is the direct object.]
Josh was riding on his **bicycle.** [*Bicycle* is the object of the preposition *on.*]

8k. An *indirect object* is a noun or pronoun that precedes the direct object and usually tells *to whom* or *for whom* (or *to what* or *for what*) the action of the verb is done.

| INDIRECT OBJECTS | Sheila told the **children** a story. |
| | Ed gave the **American Red Cross** a donation. |

To find the indirect object of an action verb, ask "To whom?" or "For whom?" (or "To what?" or "For what?") something is done.

	S V IO DO
EXAMPLES	My little sister sang **me** a song. [Sang a song *to whom*? *To me.*]
	S V IO DO
	Natalie knitted her **friend** a sweater. [Knitted a sweater *for whom*? *For her friend.*]

If the word *to* or *for* is used, the noun or pronoun following it is part of a prepositional phrase instead of an indirect object.

PREPOSITIONAL PHRASES	Li showed the bird's nest **to the class.**
	I left some dessert **for you.**
INDIRECT OBJECTS	Li showed **the class** the bird's nest.
	I left **you** some dessert.

☞ REFERENCE NOTE: For more information about prepositional phrases and objects of prepositional phrases, see pages 156–160.

Both direct and indirect objects may be compound.

| EXAMPLES | Lydia sold **cookies** and **lemonade.** [compound direct object] |
| | Lydia sold **Freddy** and **me** lemonade. [compound indirect object] |

NOTE Don't mistake an adverb in the predicate for a complement.

| EXAMPLES | We went **outside.** [*Outside* is an adverb telling *where.*] |
| | We painted the **outside** of our house. [Here, *outside* is a noun used as a direct object.] |

☑ *QUICK CHECK 3*   **Identifying Complements**

Identify the complements in the following sentences. Then tell whether each complement is a *predicate nominative*, a *predicate adjective*, a *direct object,* or an *indirect object.* Some sentences have more than one complement.

1. Jesse, who is usually so eager to talk to us, seems quiet today.
2. Will the hall monitors for Wednesday be Charlene and LaReina?
3. The crowd grew quiet when Governor Markham walked to the podium, cleared his throat, and began his speech.
4. The director gave Todd and me careful instructions on how we should play our scene together.
5. Soft and cool was the grass under the grove of catalpa trees.

Classifying Sentences by Purpose

8l. Sentences may be classified as *declarative, imperative, interrogative,* or *exclamatory*.

(1) A **declarative** sentence makes a statement. All declarative sentences are followed by periods.

EXAMPLES   Dr. Rosalyn S. Yalow won a Nobel Prize in medicine in 1977.
Ray, the CD that you ordered has finally arrived.

(2) An **imperative** sentence gives a command or makes a request. Imperative sentences are usually followed by periods. A very strong command, however, may take an exclamation point.

EXAMPLES   Please open your books to page 3.
Be careful of the undertow.
Stop!

SENTENCES

NOTE In a command or a request, the understood subject is *you.*

(3) An *interrogative* sentence asks a question. Interrogative sentences are followed by question marks.

EXAMPLES   Can she finish in time?
            How did she find Yoshi and Sarah?

(4) An *exclamatory* sentence expresses strong feeling. Exclamatory sentences are always followed by exclamation points.

EXAMPLES   Oh, no! The battery is dead!
            I can't believe this is happening!
            What a mess we're in now!

 STYLE NOTE
In conversation, any sentence may be spoken with strong feeling so that it becomes exclamatory. When you are writing dialogue, use an exclamation point after any sentence in which you want to express strong feeling.

EXAMPLES   That can't be right! [Declarative becomes exclamatory.]
            Wait for me! [Imperative becomes exclamatory.]
            When will you ever learn! [Interrogative becomes exclamatory.]

Peanuts reprinted by permission of UFS, Inc.

 REFERENCE NOTE: For more information on using end marks, see pages 268–270.

 QUICK CHECK 4 | **Identifying the Four Kinds of Sentences**

Classify each sentence below as *imperative, declarative, interrogative,* or *exclamatory,* and choose the correct end mark.

EXAMPLE   **1.** There are many delicious foods from India
               1. declarative—period

1. Some Indian food is spicy, and some isn't
2. *Sambar* is a soup made with lentils and vegetables
3. Please save me some of those curried shrimp
4. What is that wonderful bread called
5. How delicious this yogurt drink called *lassi* is

Classifying Sentences According to Structure

Sentences may be classified according to *structure.* **Structure** refers to the number and types of clauses in a sentence.

 REFERENCE NOTE: See **Chapter 7: Clauses** for a discussion of dependent and independent clauses.

8m. Structure determines whether sentences are classified as *simple, compound, complex,* or *compound-complex.*

(1) A *simple sentence* has one independent clause and no subordinate clauses. It may have a compound subject, a compound verb, and any number of phrases.

EXAMPLE   After eating dinner and washing the dishes,
             S   S   V
             Rita and **Carlos decided** to see a movie.

(2) A *compound sentence* has two or more independent clauses but no subordinate clauses.

The independent clauses in a compound sentence may be joined by a comma and a coordinating conjunction, by a semicolon, or by a semicolon and a conjunctive adverb.

 SENTENCES

EXAMPLES

    S   V

Rita wanted to see an adventure film, but

    S   V

Carlos preferred a comedy.

               S   V

On the way to the theater, **they agreed** to

       S   V

toss a coin; **Rita won** the toss.

    S   V

Carlos tried to persuade Rita to see the

             S   V

comedy; however, **he was** unsuccessful.

 REFERENCE NOTE: For more information on punctuating compound sentences, see page 274 and pages 283–284.

NOTE Don't confuse a compound predicate in a simple sentence with the two subjects and two predicates of a compound sentence.

            S   V

COMPOUND **Rita considered** the coin toss final

PREDICATE   V

and **said** so.

          S   V

COMPOUND **Rita considered** the coin toss

SENTENCE   S   V

final, and **she said** so.

(3) A *complex sentence* has one independent clause and *at least* one subordinate clause.

         S   V   S   V

EXAMPLES **Carlos argued** that the coin **toss was** unfair.

          S   V

When **they reached** the theater where the

     S   V   S   V

movie was playing, Carlos apologized to Rita.

(4) A *compound-complex sentence* contains two or more independent clauses and at least one subordinate clause.

SENTENCES

EXAMPLES

S V   S   V
Rita knew that **Carlos was being** sincere,
   S   V
and **she accepted** his apology.

     S   V   S   V
Before the **feature started, Carlos offered** to
     S   V   S   V
buy popcorn; **Rita said** that **she would save**
his seat.

STYLE NOTE Paragraphs in which all of the sentences have the same structure can make for monotonous reading. To keep your readers interested in your ideas, evaluate your writing to see whether you've used a variety of sentence structures. Then use the four revising techniques—add, cut, replace, and re-order—to enliven your writing by varying the structure of your sentences.

✓ *QUICK CHECK 5* **Classifying Sentences According to Structure**

Classify each sentence in the following paragraph as *simple, compound, complex,* or *compound-complex.* Be sure that you can identify all subordinate and independent clauses.

[1] The Five Nations of the Iroquois—Mohawk, Oneida, Onondaga, Cayuga, and Seneca—have an ancient history of storytelling. [2] Most of what is known today about Iroquois folk tales comes from the Senecas, whose stories were written down by historians. [3] Some of the most popular stories are about Naked Bear, who was hairless except for one strip of fur up his back; he was so huge that his back could be seen above the trees, and he could not be killed in any ordinary way. [4] The tales about Naked Bear are even more frightening than the ones about Stone Coat, who had a skin like stone. [5] Other Iroquois stories tell about the adventures of the Whirlwinds, Elk, Partridge, Skunk, and Rattlesnake.

A word processor can help you check for varied sentence structure in your writing.

By inserting a carriage return or a page break after every period, you can examine the structure of each sentence in relation to the structure of the other sentences in a particular paragraph. Be sure to remove the carriage returns or page breaks before printing your draft.

✓ *Chapter Review 1*

A. Identifying the Parts of a Sentence

Identify each of the numbered italicized words in the following paragraphs. Use these abbreviations:

s. subject
v. verb
p.n. predicate nominative
p.a. predicate adjective
d.o. direct object
i.o. indirect object

EXAMPLE   Are you a mystery [1] *fan?*
           1. *fan—p.n.*

Sir Arthur Conan Doyle certainly gave [1] *readers* a wonderful [2] *gift* when he [3] *created* the character of Sherlock Holmes. [4] *Holmes* is a [5] *master* of the science of deduction. He [6] *observes* seemingly insignificant [7] *clues,* applies logical reasoning, and reaches simple yet astounding conclusions.

"The Hound of the Baskervilles" is an excellent [8] *example* of how Holmes solves a baffling [9] *mystery.* The [10] *residents* of a rural area are afraid of a supernatural dog that [11] *kills* people at night. Helpless against this beast, they seek the [12] *services* of Sherlock Holmes. Using logic, Holmes solves the mystery and relieves the people's [13] *fear.* This story is [14] *one* of Doyle's best because it is both [15] *eerie* and mystifying.

B. Identifying and Punctuating the Kinds of Sentences

Copy the last word of each of the following sentences, and then add the correct end mark. Classify each sentence as *imperative, declarative, interrogative,* or *exclamatory.*

EXAMPLE   **1.** Sherlock Holmes has many dedicated fans
             1. *fans.—declarative*

  16. How clever Sherlock Holmes is
  17. Sir Arthur Conan Doyle wrote four novels and fifty-six short stories about Holmes
  18. Have you read any of these stories
  19. I particularly like the stories in which Holmes confronts the evil Professor Moriarty
  20. Read just one of these stories and see why millions of mystery fans love Sherlock Holmes

C. Classifying Sentences According to Structure

Classify each of the following sentences as *simple, compound, complex,* or *compound-complex.*

EXAMPLE   **1.** Amanda now plays the violin because of a winter concert that she heard when she was in the third grade.
             1. *complex*

  21. Amanda loved the sound of the orchestra at her school's winter concert, and she decided that night to study the violin.
  22. Amanda did not always enjoy the many hours of practice, but they were necessary because the instrument is so complicated.
  23. Just playing the proper notes, without being too sharp or too flat, can be difficult on a violin.
  24. If the pitch of each note is not exactly correct, the tune can be barely recognizable.
  25. Once a student has mastered pitch to some extent, he or she still has a great deal to think about; posture, hand position, and bowing technique all require great concentration.

SENTENCES

✓ *Chapter Review 2*

Writing Sentences

Write your own sentences according to the following guidelines. Underline the specified part or parts.

EXAMPLE   **1.** a sentence beginning with *There* and containing a compound subject

         1. <u>There</u> *were* <u>games</u> *and* <u>contests</u> *for the children.*

  1. a declarative sentence with a compound verb
  2. an interrogative sentence with a compound subject
  3. an imperative sentence with a noun of direct address
  4. a compound-complex sentence with one subordinate clause
  5. a sentence with an indirect object
  6. a sentence with a predicate nominative
  7. a compound sentence with two independent clauses joined by the conjunction *or*
  8. a sentence with an adjective modifying a complement
  9. a sentence with a compound complement
 10. a compound sentence with two independent clauses joined by a semicolon and a conjunctive adverb

9 WRITING COMPLETE SENTENCES

 Checking What You Know

A. Identifying and Revising Sentence Fragments

Decide which of the following groups of words are complete sentences and which are fragments. If an item contains only a complete sentence, write *C*. If it contains a fragment, revise the item.

EXAMPLE   **1.** We went to the mall on Saturday. To look for a birthday present for Mom.

        1. *We went to the mall on Saturday to look for a birthday present for Mom.*

1. Thumbing through the first few pages of *The Way to Rainy Mountain* by N. Scott Momaday. I decided to read the book.

2. The fire completely destroyed the old house. Which was a historic landmark.

3. Singing is Martina Arroyo's profession.

4. My allowance doesn't last long. Only five dollars a week.

5. The annual athletic awards were presented. After the last game of the season.

B. Revising Run-on Sentences

Revise the following paragraph by correcting the run-on sentences.

EXAMPLE   **1.** Peppers come in many different shapes and sizes, they also vary in color and flavor.
           1. *Peppers come in many different shapes and sizes, and they also vary in color and flavor.*

or

1. *Peppers come in many different shapes and sizes; they also vary in color and flavor.*

or

1. *Peppers come in many different shapes and sizes; moreover, they also vary in color and flavor.*

[6] It is easy to grow ornamental peppers, with just one plant you can start a forest of them. [7] Each pod on the plant has scores of seeds, each seed is a potential plant. [8] In the spring, tiny white and purple blossoms appear on the plant the blossoms slowly transform themselves into green pods. [9] First the green turns to purple then it changes to yellow and orange and finally to a bright red. [10] Each pod is at a different stage of growth, the plant looks like a Christmas tree with multicolored lights.

Sentence Fragments

9a.   Avoid using sentence fragments.

A *sentence* is a word group that has a subject and a verb and expresses a complete thought. If you punctuate a part of a sentence as if it were a complete sentence, you create a *sentence fragment.* Unlike a sentence, a fragment does not express a complete thought. It is missing some important information.

To find out whether a word group is a complete sentence or a sentence fragment, use this simple three-part test:

1. Does the group of words have a subject?

2. Does it have a verb?

3. Does it express a complete thought?

If you answer no to any of these questions, the word group is a fragment.

FRAGMENT   Was the best sharpshooter in the United States. [The subject is missing. *Who* was the best sharpshooter in the United States?]

SENTENCE   **Annie Oakley** was the best sharpshooter in the United States.

FRAGMENT   Annie Oakley with "Buffalo" Bill Cody's Wild West show. [The verb is missing. *What* did she do with the Wild West show?]

SENTENCE   Annie Oakley **performed** with "Buffalo" Bill Cody's Wild West show.

FRAGMENT   As it fell through the air ninety feet away. [This group of words has a subject (*it*) and a verb (*fell*), but it doesn't express a complete thought. *What happened* as something fell through the air?]

SENTENCE   **Annie could shoot a playing card** as it fell through the air ninety feet away.

STYLE NOTE   By itself, a fragment doesn't express a complete thought. But fragments can make sense if the sentences that come before or after them help fill in the missing parts.

The following passage is from an essay that describes the cutting down of a great white oak. Notice how the first sentence, which is complete, helps you understand the fragments that follow.

> Then came the great moment. A few last, quick strokes. A slow, deliberate swaying. The crack of parting fibers. Then a long "swoo-sh!" that rose in pitch as the towering trunk arced downward at increasing speed.
>
> Edwin Way Teale, "The Death of a Tree"

S E N T E N C E S

Experienced writers like Teale sometimes use sentence fragments for effect. As a beginning writer, however, you need to practice writing complete sentences before you begin to experiment with fragments.

✓ *QUICK CHECK* 1   **Identifying Sentence Fragments**

Decide which of the following items are fragments and which are complete sentences. If an item is a complete sentence, write *C*. If the subject is missing, write *S*. If the verb is missing, write *V*. If the item has a subject and verb but doesn't express a complete thought, write *I*.

1. Truman Capote was an American author.
2. Was born in New Orleans in 1924.
3. When he moved to New York City.
4. His characters lively and eccentric.
5. Is one of his most moving stories.

"What was it like back in the days when people talked and wrote in complete sentences?"

Berry's World reprinted by permission of NEA, Inc.

Phrase Fragments

A *phrase* is a group of words that does not have a subject and a verb. Three kinds of phrases that are often mistaken for complete sentences are *verbal phrases, appositive phrases,* and *prepositional phrases.*

 REFERENCE NOTE: See **Chapter 6: Phrases** for explanations of these three types of phrases.

Verbal Phrases

Verbals are forms of verbs that are used as other parts of speech. They sometimes make a group of words seem as though it has a verb when it really doesn't. Some verbals typically end in *–ing, –d,* or *–ed* and don't have helping verbs (such as *is, were,* or *have*) in front of them. One type of verbal includes the word *to* with the base form of the verb (*to go, to play*).

A *verbal phrase* contains a verbal and other words related to the verbal. By itself, a verbal phrase is a fragment because it doesn't express a complete thought.

FRAGMENT   Seeing the movie *Glory.*
SENTENCE   I enjoyed **seeing the movie *Glory.***

FRAGMENT   To become good soldiers.
SENTENCE   Black volunteers in the Civil War trained hard **to become good soldiers.**

FRAGMENT   Gaining glory for itself and for black soldiers everywhere.
SENTENCE   **Gaining glory for itself and for black soldiers everywhere,** the 54th Massachusetts Regiment led the attack on Fort Wagner.

Appositive Phrases

An *appositive* is a noun or pronoun that identifies or explains another noun or pronoun in the same sentence. An *appositive phrase* is a phrase made up of an appositive and its modifiers. By itself, an appositive phrase is a fragment because it does not contain the basic parts of a sentence.

FRAGMENT   A twenty-five-year-old soldier.
SENTENCE   The 54th Massachusetts Regiment was commanded by Colonel Shaw, **a twenty-five-year-old soldier.**

Prepositional Phrases

A *prepositional phrase* is a group of words that includes a preposition, a noun or a pronoun called the *object of the preposition,* and any modifiers of that object. A prepositional phrase can't stand alone as a sentence because it doesn't express a complete thought.

FRAGMENT   With great courage on the battlefield.
SENTENCE   The 54th Massachusetts Regiment acted **with great courage on the battlefield.**

STYLE NOTE   Usually a phrase needs to stay as close as possible to the word it modifies. However, some phrases, such as the infinitive phrase *to become good soldiers* in the example on page 217, make sense either at the beginning or at the end of the sentence.

REFERENCE NOTE: To learn more about placing phrases in sentences, see pages 145–148.

✓ *QUICK CHECK 2*   **Revising Phrase Fragments**

Create sentences from the following phrases. You can either (1) attach the fragment to a complete sentence, or (2) develop the phrase into a complete sentence by adding a subject, a verb, or both.

1. setting foot on the planet
2. to explore the craters
3. without any signs of life
4. astronauts on their first mission
5. to return to Earth

Subordinate Clause Fragments

A *clause* is a group of words that has a subject and a verb. One kind of clause, an *independent clause,* expresses a complete thought and can stand on its own as a sentence.

EXAMPLE   I ate my lunch.

SENTENCES

However, the other kind of clause, a ***subordinate clause,*** does not express a complete thought. It is a fragment and can't stand by itself as a sentence.

FRAGMENT	When Paris stole the beautiful Helen. [*What happened* when Paris stole Helen?]
SENTENCE	**When Paris stole the beautiful Helen,** he started the Trojan War.
FRAGMENT	Who was a great hero of the Greeks. [This would be a complete sentence if it ended with a question mark.]
SENTENCE	Odysseus, **who was a great hero of the Greeks,** took part in the Trojan War.
FRAGMENT	Because of the trick with the wooden horse. [*What* was the result of the trick?]
SENTENCE	**Because of the trick with the wooden horse,** the Greeks finally won the Trojan War.

👉 REFERENCE NOTE: See **Chapter 7: Clauses** for more information about independent and subordinate clauses.

STYLE NOTE

A subordinate clause telling *why, where, when,* or *how* is called an *adverb clause.* You can place an adverb clause either before or after the independent clause in a sentence.

EXAMPLE	**After he started home from the Trojan War,** the Greek hero Odysseus had many more adventures.

or

The Greek hero Odysseus had many more adventures **after he started home from the Trojan War.**

To decide where to place the adverb clause, read both versions aloud to see which one sounds better with the surrounding sentences. If you decide to put the adverb clause first, use a comma to separate it from the independent clause. The comma makes the sentence easier for the reader to understand.

S E N T E N C E S

QUICK CHECK 3 **Using Subordinate Clauses in Sentences**

Use each of the following subordinate clause fragments as part of a complete sentence. Add whatever words are necessary to make the meaning of the sentence complete. Add capitalization and punctuation as necessary.

1. as we watched the spaceship land
2. who approached the house in long leaps
3. which startled the dog
4. if we go outside the house
5. when they handed me a glowing sphere

Series Fragments

A series of items is another kind of fragment that is easily mistaken for a sentence. Notice that the series of items in dark type in the following example is not a complete sentence.

FRAGMENT   I ate several things for lunch. **A sandwich, an apple, celery, and some popcorn.**

To correct a series fragment, you can

- make it into a complete sentence

EXAMPLE   I ate several things for lunch. **I ate** a sandwich, an apple, celery, and some popcorn.

or

- link it to the previous sentence with a colon

EXAMPLE   I ate several things for lunch**:** a sandwich, an apple, celery, and some popcorn.

Run-on Sentences

9b.   Avoid run-on sentences.

A *run-on sentence* is two or more complete sentences run together as one. Because they don't show where one idea ends and another one begins, run-on sentences can confuse your reader.

There are two kinds of run-ons. In the first kind, called a *fused sentence,* the sentences have no punctuation at all between them.

RUN-ON   Schools in the Middle Ages were different from ours students usually did not have books.

CORRECT   Schools in the Middle Ages were different from ours. Students usually did not have books.

In the other kind of run-on, called a *comma splice,* only a comma separates the sentences from one another.

RUN-ON   Schools today usually have books for every student, many schools also have televisions and computers.

CORRECT   Schools today usually have books for every student. Many schools also have televisions and computers.

NOTE   One way to spot run-on sentences is to read your writing aloud. A natural, distinct pause in your speech usually means that you need to separate sentences in some way. You can also check for run-ons by identifying subjects and verbs. Checking for clauses will help you find where one complete thought ends and another one begins.

Revising Run-on Sentences

There are several ways you can revise run-on sentences. As shown in the examples above, you can always make two separate sentences. But if the two thoughts are closely related and equally important, you may want to make a *compound sentence.*

RUN-ON   Canada, our neighbor to the north, has ten provinces each province has its own government. [fused]
Canada, our neighbor to the north, has ten provinces, each province has its own government. [comma splice]

Here are three ways to make a compound sentence out of a run-on.

1. You can use a comma and a coordinating conjunction—*and, but, or, yet, for, so,* or *nor.*

> REVISED Canada, our neighbor to the north, has ten provinces, **and** each province has its own government.

2. You can use a semicolon.

> REVISED Canada, our neighbor to the north, has ten provinces; each province has its own government.

3. You can use a semicolon and a *conjunctive adverb*—a word such as *therefore, instead, meanwhile, still, furthermore, nevertheless,* or *however.* Follow a conjunctive adverb with a comma.

> REVISED Canada, our neighbor to the north, has ten provinces; **furthermore,** each province has its own government.

NOTE Before you join two sentences in a compound sentence, make sure that the ideas in the sentences are closely related to one another. If you link unrelated ideas, you may confuse your reader.

> UNRELATED Canada is almost four million square miles in size, and I hope to visit my relatives there someday.
>
> RELATED Canada is almost four million square miles in size, but most of its people live on a small strip of land along the southern border.

REFERENCE NOTE: For more information on compound sentences and how to form them, see pages 207–208 and 231–232.

Style-checking software programs can be a big help to you when you evaluate your writing for the use of clear, complete sentences. Many such programs can identify and highlight sentence fragments. You can also use the "search" command offered by computer programs to identify sentences in which you've used a comma and a coordinating conjunction—one search for each different conjunction and the comma in front of it. That feature lets you check to make sure that the ideas you've combined in a compound sentence are closely related and equally important.

✓ *QUICK CHECK 4* **Revising Run-on Sentences**

Revise the following items to form clear, complete sentences. To revise, use the method given in parentheses after each sentence.

1. The first movie theaters opened in the early 1900s they were called *nickelodeons.* (two sentences)
2. Thomas Edison was a pioneer in early movie making he invented the first commercial motion-picture machine. (semicolon)
3. Early movies were silent, sometimes offscreen actors would fill in the dialogue for the audience. (comma and coordinating conjunction)
4. The first sound films were shown in the late 1920s they marked a milestone in movie-making history. (semicolon)
5. Movies are great entertainment they are also an art form. (semicolon and conjunctive adverb)

✓ *Chapter Review*

Identifying and Revising Fragments and Run-on Sentences

Identify each *fragment* and *run-on* in the following paragraph. Then revise the paragraph by changing the punctuation and capitalization as necessary to make clear and complete sentences. If a sentence is correct, write *C;* you may use a correct sentence to complete a fragment.

EXAMPLE   [1] Nurses have played important roles in America's military history. [2] Since colonial times.

> [1] C; [2] fragment—*Nurses have played im-*
> *portant roles in America's military history*
> *since colonial times.*

[1] During the Civil War. [2] Women nurses showed re-markable heroism. [3] Took care of sick and wounded sol-diers, risked their lives carrying supplies to military hospitals. [4] Sally L. Tompkins one such woman. [5] She ran a military hospital in the South she was the only woman commissioned in the Confederate Army. [6] Clara Barton who worked tirelessly. [7] Another heroic Civil War nurse. [8] Caring for sick and wounded soldiers in the North. [9] In 1864, Barton received an important appoint-ment she became superintendent of nurses for the entire Union Army. [10] Who later founded the American Red Cross Society.

10 WRITING EFFECTIVE SENTENCES

 Checking What You Know

A. Sentence Combining

Revise the following paragraph by combining each numbered set of sentences into a single sentence. Don't change the meaning of the original paragraph.

EXAMPLE [1] Scientists are learning a lot. They are learning by studying the North Pole and the South Pole. They are learning about the history of the earth.

1. *Scientists are learning a lot about the history of the earth by studying the North and South Poles.*

[1] The North Pole is among the most remote areas on earth. The South Pole is too. They are different from each other. The difference is dramatic. [2] The North Pole is covered by an ocean. The South Pole is within a frozen land. [3] The polar region in the North is inhabited. It has been the home of the Inuit people for thousands of years. [4] The Antarctic is still largely uninhabited. It was an unknown region until two centuries ago. [5] The climate of Antarctica is harsh. The climate is many degrees colder than the climate in the Arctic.

B. Improving Sentence Style

Revise the following paragraph so that (1) problems with parallel structure are eliminated, (2) stringy and wordy sentences are corrected, and (3) sentences have varied beginnings and structures. You may add or delete details as necessary. Remember, some sentences may sound fine on their own, but to introduce a variety of sentence beginnings and sentence structures, you will need to revise some of these sentences.

EXAMPLE [1] In what manner of festivities do you and your friends engage during the holidays that occur from June through August?

1. *How do you and your friends celebrate the summer holidays?*

[6] My friend Isaac and I every year, without fail, celebrate the holiday that falls on the fourth day of the month of July together with each other. [7] We usually swim at the lake, or we take a picnic to the city park, but this year we decided on renting a boat and exploring the river. [8] An outboard motor was out of the question. [9] We didn't have much money, so as an alternative we rented a small boat. [10] It was made to be rowed, and it had two long, wooden poles with broad, thin blades at one end. [11] The totality of our experience proceeded without difficulty at first. [12] Then with suddenness the river grew both narrow and it became shallow, and rowing became a problem. [13] I decided to jump onto the bank in order to pull the boat with a rope, but I missed my footing, and I fell into the river. [14] It was apparent that Isaac could tell by my expression that only my feelings were hurt, and I climbed back into the boat, and we headed toward our dwelling places. [15] Isaac made an attempt to elevate my spirits, and he said "This is one Fourth of July we will always retain in the memory banks of our minds!" ✓

Sentence Combining

Short sentences can be effective, but a long, unbroken series of them can sound choppy. For example, notice how repetitive the following paragraph sounds.

I've seen a lot of earthling-meets-alien movies. I saw <u>The Last Starfighter</u>. I saw all the <u>Star Trek</u> movies. I have noticed something about these movies. I've noticed that there are good humans in these movies. There are bad humans. There are good aliens. There are bad aliens. The humans and aliens are actually not so different from each other.

Notice how much smoother the paragraph sounds when the short, choppy sentences are combined into longer sentences.

I've seen a lot of earthling-meets-alien movies, including <u>The Last Starfighter</u> and all the <u>Star Trek</u> movies. I have noticed that there are good and bad humans in these movies as well as good and bad aliens. The humans and aliens are actually not so different from each other.

Inserting Words

10a. Combine short sentences by inserting a key word from one sentence into another sentence.

Combining sentences by inserting a key word lets you eliminate extra words and repeated ideas. Sometimes you can insert the word just as it is. At other times you will need to change the form of the key word before you insert it.

USING THE SAME FORM	
ORIGINAL	Edgar Allan Poe led a short life. His life was tragic.
COMBINED	Edgar Allan Poe led a short, **tragic** life.
CHANGING THE FORM	
ORIGINAL	Edgar Allan Poe wrote strange stories. He wrote stories of suspense.
COMBINED	Edgar Allan Poe wrote strange, **suspenseful** stories.

S E N T E N C E S

NOTE When you change the form of a key word, you often add an ending that makes the word an adjective or an adverb. Usually this ending is *-ed, -ing,* or *-ly.*

Inserting Phrases

10b. Combine closely related sentences by taking a phrase from one sentence and inserting it into another sentence.

 REFERENCE NOTE: See **Chapter 6: Phrases** for information about the different kinds of phrases.

Prepositional Phrases

A *prepositional phrase,* a preposition with its object, can usually be inserted into another sentence without changing the phrase. All you have to do is leave out some of the words in one of the sentences.

ORIGINAL   Twelve million immigrants came to the shores of the United States. They came by way of Ellis Island.
COMBINED   Twelve million immigrants came to the shores of the United States **by way of Ellis Island.**

Participial Phrases

A *participial phrase* contains a participle and words related to the participle. The entire phrase acts as an adjective, modifying a noun or a pronoun.

Sometimes you can insert a participial phrase just as it is. At other times you can change the verb from one sentence into a participle by adding *-ing* or *-ed.* Then you can combine the two sentences.

USING THE SAME FORM	
ORIGINAL	Many immigrants faced long months of waiting at Ellis Island. They were weakened by their journeys.
COMBINED	Many immigrants, **weakened by their journeys,** faced long months of waiting at Ellis Island.

(continued)

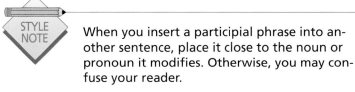

CHANGING THE FORM	
ORIGINAL	I can look at old photographs from Ellis Island. I can imagine the immigrants' hopes and dreams.
COMBINED	**Looking at old photographs from Ellis Island,** I can imagine the immigrants' hopes and dreams.

STYLE NOTE

When you insert a participial phrase into another sentence, place it close to the noun or pronoun it modifies. Otherwise, you may confuse your reader.

CONFUSING   Mowing the lawn, grass clippings got all over Jim.

CLEAR   Mowing the lawn, Jim got grass clippings all over himself.

☞ REFERENCE NOTE: For information on how to correct misplaced participial phrases, see pages 145–148.

Appositive Phrases

An *appositive phrase* is placed next to a noun or pronoun to identify or explain it. Sometimes you can combine sentences by changing one of the sentences to an appositive phrase.

ORIGINAL   My grandfather was an immigrant. My grandfather brought with him photographs that are now treasured souvenirs.

COMBINED   My grandfather, **an immigrant,** brought with him photographs that are now treasured souvenirs.

NOTE   Place the appositive phrase directly before or after the noun or pronoun it identifies or explains. Separate the phrase from the rest of the sentence by placing commas before and after it. (If the appositive phrase introduces the sentence, simply place a comma after it. If it ends the sentence, the appositive phrase should be followed by a period.)

QUICK CHECK 1 **Combining Sentences by Inserting Phrases**

Combine each of the following sets of sentences to create one sentence. (There may be more than one way to combine the sentences.) Change the forms of words where indicated in parentheses, and reorder words and add commas wherever you need to.

1. Auguste Piccard of Switzerland created an important invention. He invented an airtight gondola.
2. The gondola took Piccard ten miles into the air. The gondola was attached to a balloon.
3. Piccard then made numerous balloon trips. He studied electricity. (Change *studied* to *studying.*)
4. Piccard turned his interest to the ocean depths. He designed a deep-sea-diving ship. (Change *designed* to *designing.*)
5. Piccard and his son Jacques went two miles below the surface of the Adriatic Sea. They went in 1953.

Using Compound Subjects and Verbs

 10c. Combine sentences by making compound subjects and compound verbs.

To combine sentences with this technique, look for sentences that have the same subject or the same verb. Then make the subject, verb, or both compound by using a coordinating conjunction (*and, but, or, nor,* or *yet*).

ORIGINAL The Angles were fierce people. The Saxons were fierce people. [same verb with different subjects]

COMBINED **The Angles and the Saxons** were fierce people. [compound subject]

ORIGINAL The Angles and the Saxons invaded Britain. The Angles and the Saxons conquered Britain. [same subject with different verbs]

COMBINED The Angles and the Saxons **invaded and conquered** Britain. [compound verb]

ORIGINAL The Angles conquered Britain. The Saxons conquered Britain. They ran off the native Celts. [different subjects and different verbs]

COMBINED **The Angles and the Saxons conquered** Britain and **ran off** the native Celts. [compound subject and compound verb]

NOTE When you combine sentences by making compound subjects and compound verbs, make sure that your new subjects and verbs agree in number.

ORIGINAL The dialect of the Angles is an ancestor of Modern English. The dialect of the Saxons is an ancestor of Modern English.

COMBINED The **dialects** of the Angles and the Saxons **are** ancestors of Modern English. [The plural subject *dialects* takes the plural verb *are.*]

REFERENCE NOTE: For more information on agreement of subjects and verbs, see pages 77–87.

Creating a Compound Sentence

10d. Combine sentences by creating a *compound sentence.*

A compound sentence is really two or more simple sentences linked by

■ a comma and a coordinating conjunction

  or

■ a semicolon

  or

■ a semicolon and a conjunctive adverb

ORIGINAL The cat knocked over a lamp. The dog chewed up my shoe.

COMBINED The cat knocked over a lamp**, and** the dog chewed up my shoe. [comma and coordinating conjunction]
The cat knocked over a lamp**;** the dog chewed up my shoe. [semicolon]

The cat knocked over a lamp; **meanwhile,** the dog chewed up my shoe. [semicolon and conjunctive adverb]

NOTE Before linking two thoughts in a compound sentence, make sure that the thoughts are closely related to one another and are equally important. Otherwise, you may confuse your readers.

UNRELATED IDEAS The cat is just a kitten, but the dog is a beagle.

CLOSELY RELATED IDEAS The cat is just a kitten, but the dog is fully grown.

REFERENCE NOTE: For more information about how to create compound sentences, see pages 221–222.

STYLE NOTE You can use the coordinating conjunctions *and, but, nor, for, yet,* and *so* to form compound sentences. However, because *so* is often overworked in writing, you should think twice about using it.

When you join two sentences with a coordinating conjunction, remember to use a comma before the conjunction.

QUICK CHECK 2 **Combining Sentences by Using Compound Elements**

Combine each of the following pairs by using compound subjects and verbs or by creating a compound sentence. Remember to add commas and other marks of punctuation where they are needed.

1. The Hopi people live in Arizona. They occupy villages called pueblos.
2. Some Hopi carve wooden dolls. They dress the dolls in elaborate costumes.
3. The dolls are called kachina dolls. They have a special meaning for the Hopi.
4. Kachina dolls represent spirits. The dolls play an important part in Hopi religious ceremonies.

5. Peace is important to the Hopi people. Religion is important to the Hopi people.

Creating a Complex Sentence

`10e.` Combine sentences by creating a *complex sentence.*

A complex sentence includes one independent clause—a clause that can stand alone as a sentence. It also has one or more subordinate clauses—clauses that cannot stand alone as sentences.

 REFERENCE NOTE: See **Chapter 7: Clauses** for information about independent and subordinate clauses.

Adjective Clauses

You can make a sentence into an *adjective clause* by inserting *who, which,* or *that* in place of the subject. Then you can use the adjective clause to give information about a noun or a pronoun in another sentence.

ORIGINAL   Many people are afraid of bats. Bats are usually harmless creatures.
COMBINED   Many people are afraid of bats, **which are usually harmless creatures.**

 REFERENCE NOTE: See pages 46–47 for information on when to use *who, that,* or *which.*

Adverb Clauses

You can turn a sentence into an *adverb clause* by placing a subordinating conjunction (such as *after, although, because, if, when,* or *where*) at the beginning of the sentence. Then you can use the clause to modify a verb, an adjective, or an adverb in another sentence.

ORIGINAL   Bats are considered dangerous. They rarely attack humans.
COMBINED   **Although bats are considered dangerous,** they rarely attack humans.

SENTENCES

STYLE NOTE An adverb clause may be placed either before or after an independent clause. Try both versions to see which sounds better with the surrounding sentences. If you place the clause at the beginning of the sentence, separate it from the independent clause with a comma.

NOTE When you create an adverb clause, choose the conjunction carefully. It shows the relationship between the ideas in the adverb clause and those in the independent clause. For example, *when* shows that the ideas are related in time, and *where* shows that the ideas are related in space.

Noun Clauses

You can make a sentence into a ***noun clause*** and insert it into another sentence, using it just as you would use a noun. You can create a noun clause by inserting a word like *that, how, what,* or *who* at the beginning of a sentence. When you place the noun clause in the other sentence, you may have to change or remove some words.

ORIGINAL   Dracula is such a frightening character. This doesn't help the vampire bat's already bad reputation.

COMBINED   **That Dracula is such a frightening character** doesn't help the vampire bat's already bad reputation. [The word *that* introduces the noun clause, which becomes the subject of the verb *does help.*]

QUICK CHECK 3   **Combining Sentences by Creating Complex Sentences**

Use subordinate clauses to combine each of the following sets of sentences into one complex sentence. You may need to change or delete some words.

1. The shark is a member of a fish family. The family includes the largest and fiercest fish.

2. Sharks have long bodies, wedge-shaped heads, and pointed back fins. The back fins sometimes stick out of the water.
3. Sharks live mostly in warm seas. Some sharks have been found in bodies of cold water.
4. The whale shark is harmless to people. It feeds on plankton.
5. However, many sharks are ruthless killers. They feed on flesh.

Improving Sentence Style

Using Parallel Structure

10f. Use the same form to express equal ideas.

Using the same form for equal ideas creates balance in a sentence. For example, you balance a noun with a noun, a phrase with a phrase, and a clause with a clause. This balance is called *parallel structure.*

NOT PARALLEL	I'm not much of an athlete, but I like softball, soccer, and to play hockey. [two nouns and a phrase]
PARALLEL	I'm not much of an athlete, but I like **softball, soccer,** and **hockey.** [three nouns]
NOT PARALLEL	Dominic doesn't have enough time to play soccer, join the debating team, and band. [two phrases and a noun]
PARALLEL	Dominic doesn't have enough time **to play soccer, join the debating team,** and **participate in band.** [three phrases]
NOT PARALLEL	I knew that soccer was popular in Europe and its popularity in Latin America, too. [a clause and a phrase]
PARALLEL	I knew **that soccer was popular in Europe** and **that it was popular in Latin America, too.** [two clauses]

SENTENCES

✓ *QUICK CHECK 4*   **Revising Sentences to Create Parallel Structure**

Revise the following sentences by putting the ideas in parallel form. You may need to add or delete some words. If a sentence is correct, write *C*.

1. Paris, the capital of France, is famous for its history, its culture, and to eat in its excellent restaurants.
2. The Seine River runs through the city and supplies water to all Parisians.
3. Visiting the Cathedral of Notre Dame, walking through the Louvre museum, and the Eiffel Tower are all favorite pastimes of tourists.
4. It is interesting that Paris has always both attracted artists and refugees have always been welcome.
5. Many famous Americans, including Ernest Hemingway, lived and writing in Paris during the 1920s.

Revising Stringy Sentences

10g. Avoid using stringy sentences.

A *stringy sentence* usually has too many independent clauses strung together with coordinating conjunctions like *and* or *but*. Since all the ideas are treated equally, the reader has trouble seeing how they are related.

To fix a stringy sentence, you can

■ break the sentence into two or more sentences

or

■ turn some of the independent clauses into subordinate clauses or phrases

STRINGY   The fire alarm rang, and everyone started to file out of school, but then our principal came down the hall, and he said that the bell was a mistake, and we went back to our classes.

REVISED   The fire alarm bell rang, and everyone started to file out of school. Then our principal came down the hall to say that the bell was a mistake. We went back to our classes.

REVISED   When the fire alarm bell rang, everyone started to file out of school. Then our principal came down the hall. He said that the bell was a mistake, and we went back to our classes.

Revising Wordy Sentences

10h. Avoid using wordy sentences.

Extra words and unnecessarily difficult words clutter up your writing and make it hard to follow. Compare the following sentences.

WORDY   It would please me greatly if you would diminish the volume of your verbalizing during the time I am perusing this reading material.

IMPROVED   Please be more quiet while I'm reading.

Here are three tips for creating sentences that aren't too wordy.

- Don't use more words than you need to.
- Don't use complicated words where simple ones will do.
- Don't repeat yourself unless it's absolutely necessary.

WORDY   Ken is a talented drummer who plays the drums with great skill.

REVISED   Ken is a talented drummer.

WORDY   In the event that we are unable to go to the movie, we can play basketball at home.

REVISED   If we cannot go to the movie, we can play basketball at home.

© 1984, Washington Post Writers Group. Reprinted with permission.

SENTENCES

☑ *QUICK CHECK 5* **Revising Stringy and Wordy Sentences**

Revise the following items by correcting any sentences that are stringy, wordy, or both. If you find that a sentence doesn't need to be improved, write *C*.

1. Alexandre-Gustave Eiffel was a famous Frenchman, and he came into this world in France in the year 1832, and he departed from this life in the year 1923.
2. Eiffel was an engineer, and he designed the Eiffel Tower, and it was built for the World's Fair of 1889.
3. The chief focus of Eiffel's interest was structures constructed to provide a way over an obstacle such as a river, and the Eiffel Tower displays his bridge-designing skills, but so does another historical monument, and it's a monument that you're familiar with.
4. In 1885, Eiffel used his engineering knowledge to design part of a great American symbol, the Statue of Liberty in New York Harbor.
5. Toward the end of his life, Eiffel studied the effects of air on airplanes, and then in 1912, he built a wind tunnel and an aerodynamics laboratory, and later he conducted experiments from the Eiffel Tower, which is now a favorite tourist attraction.

Varying Sentence Beginnings

10i. Vary the beginnings of your sentences.

The basic structure of an English sentence is a subject followed by a verb. But following this pattern all the time can make your writing dull. Compare the two following paragraphs.

SUBJECT-VERB PATTERN   The theater was packed. Jan and I managed to find our seats. The musical began thirty minutes late. We were bored. We read the program four times. Jan wanted to find out the reason for the delay. She asked an usher. The usher was amused. The usher said that the star's costume had been damaged by her dog. We laughed because the musical was *Cats.*

VARIED
SENTENCE
BEGINNINGS

Although the theater was packed, Jan and I managed to find our seats. The musical began thirty minutes late. Bored, we read the program four times. To find out the reason for the delay, Jan asked an usher. Amused, the usher said that the star's costume had been damaged by her dog. We laughed because the musical was *Cats.*

You can use the following methods to vary sentence beginnings.

VARYING SENTENCE BEGINNINGS

SINGLE-WORD MODIFIERS

Excitedly, Marcia opened her presents. [adverb]

Hungry, the family stopped at the restaurant. [adjective]

Assembled, the bookcase is five feet high. [participle]

Grinning, the curious toddler reached for the red balloon. [participle]

PHRASES

With tears of joy, Greg received his prize. [prepositional phrase]

Smiling happily, Tanya told us the good news. [participial phrase]

To make good grades, you must study. [infinitive phrase]

A fast reader, Jerrold finished the novel in one sitting. [appositive phrase]

SUBORDINATE CLAUSES

Because the coach was angry, he made the team run ten laps. [adverb clause]

When Tom found the kitten on his doorstep, he decided to keep it. [adverb clause]

Varying Sentence Structures

10j. Vary the structure of your sentences.

You have already learned how you can combine sentences to create compound and complex sentences. When you use a variety of sentence-combining techniques, you will create a mix of sentence structures. Using a variety of sentence structures can make your writing livelier. Instead of using all simple sentences, you can use a mix of simple, compound, complex, and compound-complex sentences.

☞ REFERENCE NOTE: See pages 207–209 for an explanation of how sentences are classified according to their structure.

Compare the following paragraphs.

ALL SIMPLE SENTENCES   The music and the thump of the drums grew louder. The people lined up along the street. Finally, with a blast of brass, the high school band rounded the corner. First came the drum major. She set the tempo with her baton. She proudly raised her feet as high as possible. Behind her marched the musicians. They were wearing bright red jackets. The musicians were leading the parade of colorful floats. The crowd cheered and applauded. The children watched with shining eyes. They dreamed of being in the band someday.

VARIED SENTENCE STRUCTURES   As the music and the thump of the drums grew louder, the people lined up along the street. Finally, with a blast of brass, the high school band rounded the corner. First came the drum major; setting the tempo with her baton, she proudly raised her feet as high as possible. Behind her, leading the parade of colorful floats, the musicians marched in their bright red jackets. As the crowd cheered and applauded, the children watched with shining eyes and dreamed of being in the band someday.

S E N T E N C E S

When you revise your writing, use computer functions such as "Copy," "Cut," and "Move" to experiment with your sentences. Try different sentence beginnings and structures, and print them all. Then decide which ones work best with the other sentences in a particular paragraph.

 *QUICK CHECK* 6 — **Revising a Paragraph to Vary Sentence Beginnings and Structure**

Revise the following paragraph to vary sentence beginnings and structures. You may combine items to create varied sentence structures. (Consult the chart on page 239 for help.)

[1] Penguins are at risk in oceans of the Southern Hemisphere. [2] Many penguin species have problems today because of oil pollution and commercial fishing. [3] Turtles are endangered because they are slaughtered for food and for their shells. [4] Lobsters become threatened when people overfish. [5] Mediterranean monk seals also are threatened by increased land development and tourism.

S E N T E N C E S

 **Chapter Review**

A. Revising a Paragraph by Combining Sentences

Using sentence-combining techniques, revise the following paragraph. Don't change the meaning of the original paragraph.

EXAMPLE [1] Stonehenge was built about five thousand years ago. It was built on the Salisbury Plain. It was built in southwestern England.

  1. *Stonehenge was built about five thousand years ago on the Salisbury Plain in southwestern England.*

[1] Stonehenge is a series of stones. They are huge stones. They are carefully arranged. They weigh as much as fifty tons. [2] The stones were moved to their present site. They were moved by as many as one thousand people. [3] There are many myths about the origins of the stones. There are many theories about the purpose of the stones. [4] One popular theory is that the stones served as an observatory. The observatory was astrological. [5] Sometimes, the sun rises directly over one of the stones. This phenomenon occurs at one point in the summer.

B. Revising a Paragraph to Improve Sentence Style

Revise the following paragraphs so that (1) each sentence has parallel structure, (2) stringy and wordy sentences are corrected, and (3) sentences have varied beginnings and structures. You may add or delete details as necessary, and you may combine sentences. Remember, some sentences may sound fine on their own. However, to introduce a variety of sentence beginnings and structures, you will need to revise some of these sentences.

EXAMPLE [1] One time in the recent past, my family and I went on a picnic in the Big Bend National Park in west Texas.

1. *Recently, my family and I went on a picnic in the Big Bend National Park in west Texas.*

[6] It had rained heavily all night to the north of the park. [7] A friend of ours, Mrs. Brown, went with us. [8] She had lived in that part of Texas for a large number of years and knew all about what to expect if it rained. [9] She said that there could be a flash flood in the park. [10] The park could be a really dangerous place to be even if it didn't rain there because the water could run across the dry desert sand.

[11] Mrs. Brown made us turn our cars around to face in the other direction because she wanted us to be able to leave the low area fast if a flood came. [12] The sun was

shining with great brightness and hot, and my family and I thought Mrs. Brown was crazy, and we settled down to eat our picnic lunch.

[13] A very high wall of water four feet high came toward us suddenly. [14] We jumped into the cars and managed to get away from the fearsome deluge just at the last possible moment and not a moment too soon. [15] Our picnic floated away, but we were glad to be alive, and we thanked Mrs. Brown.

SENTENCES

PART FOUR

MECHANICS

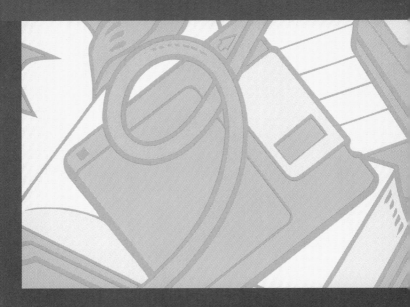

11 CAPITALIZATION

The Rules for Capitalization

✓ Checking What You Know

A. Correcting Sentences by Capitalizing Words

Identify the word or words that should be capitalized in each of the following sentences. If a sentence is correct, write C.

EXAMPLE   **1.** Aunt claire donated her hoover vacuum cleaner to the salvation army.
            1. Claire, Hoover, Salvation Army

1. The judges of the essay contest are miss helen fry and mr. c. m. gonzalez, jr.
2. Before fishing on sylvan lake in custer state park, we bought bait at a stand on highway 385.
3. The travel section of the *New York times* featured an excellent article on jewel cave national monument.
4. The Industrial Revolution drastically changed American life in the 1800s.
5. Gloria said, "during world war II, my grandmother was a volunteer for the international red cross."

6. The bomber the troops called *lady luck* is now on display in the park on Fifty-third Street, two blocks west of the methodist church.

7. Last August, grandpa Henry and aunt Frances took an amtrak express train from New York to chicago.

8. Students at Adams high school may take spanish, geometry, and chemistry I when they are sophomores.

9. In english class we compared the tones of Grant Wood's painting *American gothic* and Willa Cather's novel *One of ours.*

10. After hurricane allen struck, the governor declared the region a disaster area.

B. Proofreading a Paragraph for Correct Capitalization

In the following paragraph, capitalize the words that should begin with a capital letter. If a sentence is correct, write *C.*

EXAMPLE   [1] Yellowstone National Park, which lies in northwestern wyoming, has to be seen to be believed.
       1. *Wyoming*

[11] Early reports about this area arrived back east some two hundred years ago from explorers and trappers such as william Clark and Jim Bridger. [12] Their accounts of boiling mud cauldrons and water spewing hundreds of feet into the air seemed unbelievable. [13] Many people laughed at the stories that the area's native inhabitants, the shoshone, told about angry gods who turned trees to stone and caused tremors and thundering noises. [14] Yet settlers avoided the area until after the American civil war. [15] Then, adventurers and local leaders explored the area and persuaded dr. Ferdinand Hayden, director of the U.S. Geological Survey, to see the wonders for himself. [16] In 1871, Dr. Hayden surveyed the region with an artist and a photographer, who recorded the amazing sights they saw. [17] In march of 1872, congress voted to set aside 2.2 million acres as Yellowstone national park. [18] Since then, visi-

MECHANICS

tors have taken millions of snapshots of such features as the famous geyser old faithful. [19] When mom, dad, and i visited the park last summer, we were amazed at the geysers, mudpots, and other sights. [20] Next summer, I'm going to take a course in geology offered by the yellowstone institute. ✓

As you'll notice in your reading, publications vary somewhat in the way they use capital letters. In your own writing, however, using the rules presented in this chapter will help you communicate clearly with any audience.

11a. Capitalize the first word in every sentence.

EXAMPLES **T**he world of computers has its own language. **A** complete list of instructions for the computer is a *program*. **C**omputer equipment is called *hardware,* and the programs are called *software*.

(1) Capitalize the first word of a direct quotation.

EXAMPLE Maria asked me, "**H**ave you seen Jennifer this morning?"

(2) Traditionally, the first word of a line of poetry is capitalized.

EXAMPLES **S**torm, blow me from here
With your fiercest wind
Let me float across the sky
'**T**ill I can rest again.

Maya Angelou, "Woman Work"

 NOTE Some writers do not follow these practices. When you are quoting, use capital letters exactly as they are used in the source of the quotation.

 REFERENCE NOTE: For more about using capital letters in quotations, see page 299.

11b. Capitalize the first word both in the salutation and in the closing of a letter.

MECHANICS

EXAMPLES   **D**ear Ann,   **D**ear Sir:
              Sincerely,   **Y**ours truly,

 REFERENCE NOTE: For more information on writing letters, see pages 444–451.

11c. Capitalize the pronoun *I* and the interjection *O*.

The interjection *O* is always capitalized. Generally, it is reserved for invocations and is followed by the name of the person or thing being addressed. The common interjection *oh* is not capitalized unless it is the first word in a sentence.

EXAMPLES   "Exult **O** shores! and ring **O** bells!" is a line
             from Walt Whitman's poem "**O** Captain!
             My Captain!"
           The play was a hit, but **oh**, how nervous **I**
           was!

11d. Capitalize proper nouns and proper adjectives.

A *common noun* is a general name for a person, place, thing, or idea. A *proper noun* names a particular person, place, thing, or idea. *Proper adjectives* are formed from proper nouns.

 REFERENCE NOTE: For more about common and proper nouns, see pages 51–52. For a discussion of proper adjectives, see page 59.

Proper nouns are always capitalized. Common nouns are not capitalized unless they

■ begin a sentence
■ begin a direct quotation
■ are included in a title (see pages 257–260)

COMMON NOUNS	PROPER NOUNS	PROPER ADJECTIVES
a poet	Homer	Homeric simile
a country	Turkey	Turkish border
a queen	Queen Elizabeth	Elizabethan drama
a planet	Mars	Martian landscape

MECHANICS

In proper nouns with more than one word, do *not* capitalize

- articles (*a, an, the*)
- short prepositions (ones with fewer than five letters, such as *at* and *with*)
- coordinating conjunctions (*and, but, for, nor, or, so, yet*)
- the sign of the infinitive (*to*)

EXAMPLES   Tomb **of** the Unknown Soldier
American Society **for** the Prevention **of** Cruelty **to** Animals
Ivan **the** Terrible
National Campers **and** Hikers Association
"Writing **a** Paragraph **to** Inform"

NOTE   Words based on proper nouns and proper adjectives sometimes lose their capitals through frequent usage.

EXAMPLES   **w**att   **t**itanic   **s**andwich

To find out whether such a word should be capitalized, check a dictionary. It will tell you if the word should always be capitalized or if it should be capitalized only in certain uses.

(1) Capitalize the names of persons and animals.

GIVEN NAMES	Alana	Mark	Yoshi	Ezell
SURNAMES	Diaz	Collins	Nakamura	Williams
ANIMALS	Puff	Old Yeller	King Kong	Brer Rabbit

NOTE   For names with more than one word, capitalization may vary. Always check the spelling of such a name with the person, or look in a reference source.

EXAMPLES   **La** Croix   **de** Leon
McEwen   **O'Connor**
Young Bear   **Ben-Gurion**
Santa Ana   **Van Doren**

Abbreviations such as *Ms., Mr., Dr.,* and *Gen.* should always be capitalized.

EXAMPLES   **Mr.** Henry Cisneros   **Dr.** Mary McLeod Bethune
Ms. Richardson   **Gen.** Chiang Kai-shek

MECHANICS

👉 REFERENCE NOTE: For more about punctuating abbreviations, see pages 270–271.

Capitalize the abbreviations *Jr. (junior)* and *Sr. (senior)* after a name, and set them off with commas.

EXAMPLE   In 1975, Gen. Daniel James, Jr., became the first African-American four-star general in the U.S. Air Force.

(2) Capitalize geographical names.

TYPE OF NAME	EXAMPLES		
Towns and Cities	Portland Detroit	San Francisco Rio de Janeiro	St. Charles Little Rock
Counties, Townships, and Parishes	Kane County Hayes Township East Baton Rouge Parish		
States	Florida Missouri	Alaska North Carolina	Maine Ohio

👉 REFERENCE NOTE: Abbreviations of the names of states are always capitalized. See pages 270–271 for more about using and punctuating such abbreviations.

TYPE OF NAME	EXAMPLES	
Countries	Canada New Zealand	United States of America
Continents	Africa Australia	North America Asia
Islands	Long Island the West Indies	Isle of Palms Florida Keys
Mountains	Rocky Mountains Mesabi Range	the Alps Mount Whitney

NOTE   Words such as *north, west,* and *southeast* are not capitalized when they indicate direction.

EXAMPLES   north of town   traveling southeast

MECHANICS

TYPE OF NAME	EXAMPLES	
Other Land Forms and Features	Cape Hatteras Lodge Grass Valley Kenai Peninsula	Niagara Falls Mammoth Cave Kalahari Desert
Bodies of Water	Pacific Ocean Bay of Plenty Lake of the Woods	Red River of the North Adriatic Sea Gulf of Mexico
Parks	Yellowstone National Park Cleburne State Recreation Area Gates of the Arctic National Park	
Regions	the North Bermuda Triangle New England	the Middle West the Southeast the Great Plains
Roads, Streets, and Highways	Route 66 Interstate 787 Kirk Road	Pennsylvania Turnpike West First Street Gibbs Drive

 NOTE In a hyphenated number, the second word begins with a small letter.

EXAMPLE   Thirty-first Street

Words like *city, island, river, street,* and *park* are capitalized only when they are part of a name.

PROPER NOUNS	COMMON NOUNS
life in New York City	life in a big city
a trip to Liberty Island	a trip to a small island
crossing the Spokane River	crossing the river
on State Street	on a narrow street
jog through Central Park	picnic in the park

 QUICK CHECK 1   **Recognizing the Correct Use of Capital Letters**

Give the letter of the correctly capitalized sentence in each of the following pairs.

1. **a.** Mark Ozawa, jr., and I went canoeing on the Ohio river.
   b. Mark Ozawa, Jr., and I went canoeing on the Ohio River.
2. **a.** I read an article on south American rain forests.
   b. I read an article on South American rain forests.
3. **a.** Kim Lee's address is 1614 Forty-second Street.
   b. Kim lee's address is 1614 Forty-Second street.
4. **a.** Fred said, "oh, let's go bowling instead."
   b. Fred said, "Oh, let's go bowling instead."
5. **a.** The Hawaiian Islands are southwest of California.
   b. The Hawaiian islands are Southwest of California.

(3) Capitalize the names of organizations, teams, business firms, institutions, buildings and other structures, and government bodies.

TYPE OF NAME	EXAMPLES	
Organizations	United Nations National Basketball Association Boy Scouts of America B'nai B'rith League of Women Voters	
Teams	Tampa Bay Buccaneers Minnesota Twins Golden State Warriors River City All-Stars	
Business Firms	Quaker Oats Company Southern Bell Aluminum Company of America B. F. Goodrich	
Institutions	United States Naval Academy Stanford University Bethune-Cookman College North High School Bellevue Hospital Smithsonian Institution	
Buildings and Other Structures	Norwood Mall Apollo Theater Proviso High School the Alamo	First Baptist Church Taj Mahal Art Institute of Chicago Brooklyn Bridge

MECHANICS

Do not capitalize words like *hotel, theater, college, high school, post office,* and *courthouse* unless they are part of a proper name.

EXAMPLES   Copley Square Hotel
a hotel in Boston

Fox Theater
a theater in Dallas

Douglass College
a local community college

Jackson High School
an urban high school

Kearney Post Office
a post office nearby

Victoria County Courthouse
a rural courthouse

TYPE OF NAME	EXAMPLES
Government Bodies	Congress Environmental Protection Agency Federal Bureau of Investigation House of Representatives Supreme Court State Department

Capitalize words such as democratic or republican only when they refer to a specific political party.

EXAMPLES   The new leaders have promised democratic reforms.
The Democratic candidates for mayor held a press conference.

The word *party* in the name of a political party may be capitalized or not; either way is correct. Be consistent in the way you treat the word throughout a particular piece of writing.

EXAMPLES   Republican party *or* Party
Federalist party *or* Party

(4) Capitalize the names of historical events and periods, special events, holidays, and other calendar items.

MECHANICS

TYPE OF NAME	EXAMPLES	
Historical Events and Periods	French Revolution Boston Tea Party Reconstruction	World War II Middle Ages Stone Age
Special Events	Interscholastic Debate Tournament Gulf Coast Track-and-Field Championship Parents' Day Kansas State Fair	
Holidays and Other Calendar Items	Saturday December New Year's Day Yom Kippur	Labor Day Martin Luther King, Jr. Day Election Day

NOTE Do not capitalize the name of a season (summer, winter, spring, autumn, fall) unless it is being personified or used in the name of a special event.

EXAMPLES I'm on the committees for both the **W**inter Carnival and the **S**pring Jubilee.

"**W**inter slumbering in the open air, Wears on his smiling face a dream of **S**pring!"

Samuel Taylor Coleridge, "Work Without Hope"

(5) Capitalize the names of nationalities, races, and peoples.

EXAMPLES **C**anadian, **G**reek, **A**frican **A**merican, **C**aucasian, **A**sian, **H**ispanic, **Z**ulu, **C**herokee, **V**iking, **S**ioux, **I**talian, **K**orean

STYLE NOTE The words *black* and *white* may or may not be capitalized when they refer to races. However, within a particular piece of writing, be sure to be consistent in the way you capitalize these words.

MECHANICS

(6) Capitalize the brand names of business products.

EXAMPLES   **F**ormica, **C**hevrolet, **T**eflon, **K**enmore

NOTE Do not capitalize a common noun that follows a brand name: *Chevrolet van, Teflon pan.*

(7) Capitalize the names of ships, trains, aircraft, spacecraft, monuments, awards, planets, and other particular places, things, or events.

TYPE OF NAME	EXAMPLES	
Ships and Trains	*Mayflower* *City of Miami* *Silver Meteor*	*Yankee Clipper* *Discovery* USS *Saratoga*
Aircraft, Spacecraft, and Missiles	the *Spirit of St. Louis* *Columbia* *Apollo 11*	*Pioneer 10* *Skylab* *Sputnik 1*
Monuments and Memorials	Washington Monument Lincoln Memorial	Statue of Liberty Colorado National Monument
Awards	Purple Heart Academy Award Key Club Achievement Award Congressional Medal of Honor	
Planets, Stars, and Constellations	Mercury Betelgeuse Little Dipper	the Dog Star Jupiter Ursa Major

NOTE The word *earth* is not capitalized unless it is used along with the names of other heavenly bodies that are capitalized. The words *sun* and *moon* are not capitalized.

11e. Do *not* capitalize the names of school subjects, except for languages or course names followed by a number.

EXAMPLES   This year I am taking **a**lgebra, **E**nglish, **c**ivics, **T**yping **I**, and a **f**oreign **l**anguage. Next year I plan to take **A**merican **g**overnment, **E**nglish, **g**eometry, **B**iology **I**, and **S**panish.

NOTE Do not capitalize the name of a class (*freshman, sophomore, junior, senior*) unless it is used as part of a proper noun.

EXAMPLE All **f**reshmen should meet after school to discuss the **F**reshman-**S**ophomore Banquet.

QUICK CHECK 2

Correcting the Capitalization of Words and Phrases

Correct the following words and phrases, using capital letters as needed.

1. earth, mars, and jupiter
2. over the golden gate bridge
3. lafayette park in tallahassee, florida
4. some wheaties cereal
5. held the junior prom at the jefferson racquet club
6. studying history at harvard university
7. appointed to the supreme court last summer
8. a memorial day speech by a democratic candidate
9. an african american winner of the newbery medal
10. the sinking of the *lusitania* off the coast of ireland

11f. Capitalize titles.

(1) Capitalize the title of a person when it comes before the person's name.

EXAMPLES   **President K**ennedy   **M**r. **N**akamura
                 Dr. **D**ooley   **M**s. **A**costa
                 Professor Simmons   **Principal P**hillips

Do not capitalize a title that is used alone or following a person's name, especially if the title is preceded by *a* or *the*.

EXAMPLES   We saw the **r**everend at the park.
                 Daniel Inouye was first elected **s**enator from Hawaii in 1962.
                 Cleopatra ruled as the **q**ueen of Egypt from 51–30 B.C.

When a title is used alone in direct address, it is *usually* capitalized.

MECHANICS

EXAMPLES   Well, **D**octor, what is your diagnosis?
             I think, **S**enator, the issue is critical.
             May I speak now, **S**ir [*or* sir]?
             Good morning, **Ma**'am [*or* ma'am].

STYLE
NOTE

For special emphasis or clarity, writers sometimes capitalize a title used alone or following a person's name.

EXAMPLES   Many young people admire the **R**everend.
             How did the **S**enator vote on this issue?
             At the ceremony, the **Q**ueen knighted several
             men for their outstanding achievements.

(2) Capitalize words showing family relationship when
used with a person's name but *not* when preceded by a
possessive.

EXAMPLES   **A**unt **C**lara, **C**ousin Joshua, **G**randfather,
             my **m**other, your **f**ather, Harold's **g**rand-
             mother

(3) Capitalize the first and last words and all important
words in titles of books, periodicals, poems, stories,
essays, speeches, plays, historical documents, movies,
radio and television programs, works of art, musical
compositions, cartoons, and comic strips.

Unimportant words in a title are

■ articles: *a, an, the*
■ short prepositions (fewer than five letters): *of, to, for, from,
  in, over,* etc.
■ coordinating conjunctions: *and, but, so, nor, or, yet, for*

NOTE

The words *a, an,* and *the* written before a title are
capitalized only when they are part of the official
title.

EXAMPLES   *A Tale of Two Cities*
             The Autobiography of Malcolm X
                              but
             the *Austin American-Statesman*

MECHANICS

The official title of a book is found on the title page. The official title of a newspaper or periodical is found on the masthead, which usually appears on the editorial page.

TYPE OF NAME	EXAMPLES
Books	*The Sea Around Us* *Ordinary People* *I Know Why the Caged Bird Sings*
Periodicals	*Field and Stream* *The Atlantic Monthly*
Poems	"The Charge of the Light Brigade" "In Cold Storm Light" "Boy at the Window"
Stories	"The Pit and the Pendulum" "Raymond's Run"
Essays and Speeches	"The Death of a Tree" "Work and What It's Worth" "Woman's Right to the Suffrage"
Plays	*The Piano Lesson* *The Phantom of the Opera* *From Approximately Coast to Coast . . . It's the Bob & Ray Show*
Historical Documents	The Treaty of Paris Declaration of Independence Emancipation Proclamation
Movies	*Dances with Wolves* *It's a Wonderful Life* *Stand and Deliver*
Radio and Television Programs	*All Things Considered* *I'll Fly Away* *Meet the Press* *Home Improvement* *Sixty Minutes* *Roseanne*
Works of Art	*American Gothic* [painting] *The Thinker* [sculpture] *Young Woman Attended by a Maid* [wood-block print]
Musical Compositions	"The Tennessee Waltz" "The Flight of the Bumblebee" *The Surprise Symphony*
Cartoons and Comic Strips	*Calvin and Hobbes* *The Neighborhood*

MECHANICS

REFERENCE NOTE: See pages 296–297 and pages 303–304 for information on when to use italics for titles and when to use quotation marks.

(4) Capitalize the names of religions and their followers, holy days and celebrations, holy writings, and specific deities.

TYPE OF NAME	EXAMPLES		
Religions and Followers	Judaism Buddhism Catholicism	Mormonism Muslim Taoist	Baptist Quaker
Holy Days and Celebrations	Lent Ramadan	Passover Easter	Good Friday Purim

Holy Writings	Bible
	Dead Sea
	  Scrolls
		Upanishads
		Deuteronomy
			Koran
			Book of
			  Mormon

Specific Deities	Allah God	Brahma the Holy Spirit	

 NOTE The word *god* is not capitalized when it refers to the gods of ancient mythology. The names of such gods are capitalized, however.

EXAMPLE   The Greek poet paid tribute to the **g**od Zeus.

 STYLE NOTE   In some writings, you may notice that pronouns referring to deities are capitalized. In other cases, writers capitalize such pronouns only to prevent confusion.

EXAMPLE   The Lord called upon Moses to lead **H**is people out of Egypt. [*His* is capitalized to show that it refers to the Lord, not Moses.]

MECHANICS

COMPUTER NOTE Some software programs can identify and highlight errors in capitalization. However, even the most comprehensive programs may not include all the terms you've used in a particular paper. In addition, the program you're using may be based on rules that vary somewhat from the ones presented in this chapter. If your software allows it, modify the program by adding terms that you use frequently and have trouble capitalizing correctly.

 QUICK CHECK 3 **Correcting Capitalization Errors in Phrases**

If the capitalization in a phrase or sentence below is correct, write C. If the capitalization is incorrect, write the correct form.

1. mayor Feinstein
2. "Home on The Range"
3. the *Reader's Digest*
4. elected governor
5. president Clinton
6. was the Roman God mars
7. my mom and grandma Higgins
8. my Cousin's parents
9. the Pulitzer Prize won by N. Scott Momaday
10. *Why Dogs Are the Most Superior of All Creatures On Land, Sea and Sky and Maybe Space*

Peanuts reprinted by permission of UFS, Inc.

MECHANICS

✓ *Chapter Review*

A. Correcting Sentences That Contain Errors in Capitalization

Correct the errors in capitalization in the following sentences. If a sentence contains no errors, write *C*.

EXAMPLE **1.** My Aunt and I visited the White house in Washington, D.C.

1. *aunt, House*

1. Val's new schwinn bike had a flat tire.
2. My father is taking a course in public speaking.
3. The atmosphere on venus is one hundred times denser than the atmosphere on earth.
4. Ramón asked me, "did you watch Macy's Thanksgiving day parade on television?"
5. The opossum can be found as far south as Argentina and as far north as Canada.
6. Our Club raised money for the American heart association.
7. The mayan peoples of the Yucatán peninsula worshiped nature Gods such as chac, a god of rain, and Itzamná, a sky god.
8. My uncle Scott works as a waiter at the restaurant martha's place.
9. In drama 2, we staged a production of Denise Chávez's *The flying tortilla Man*.
10. The U.S. senate and house of representatives may pass a bill to become a law, but the president can veto it.
11. Mr. Ralph Williams, sr., is a Reporter for Associated press.
12. We went to Sea World over easter vacation and had a great time.
13. Both rabbi Frankel and reverend Stone organized aid for the victims of the fire.
14. The summer Games of the 1988 olympics were held in seoul, South Korea.
15. Michelangelo's *The creation of Adam* and *The Last Judgment* are famous paintings that depict biblical events.

MECHANICS

B. Correcting Capitalization Errors in a Paragraph

Correct the following sentences by adding or deleting capital letters as needed. If a sentence has no errors, write *C*.

EXAMPLE [1] A gentle elephant named jumbo was once the largest, most popular captive animal on Earth.
1. *Jumbo, earth*

[16] When p. t. barnum bought Jumbo in 1882, the elephant had already become a star with the London royal circus. [17] All of england protested the sale when the unhappy elephant refused to board the ship for New York city. [18] however, even queen Victoria and the prince of Wales could not prevent Jumbo's going, since the sale had been completed. [19] Jumbo's Trainer, Matthew Scott, kept the elephant content on the journey across the atlantic ocean. [20] In april, the ship arrived in New York, and the 13,500-pound Star marched up broadway to the cheers of a huge crowd. [21] Soon Jumbo's fame swept across the United States. [22] The elephant became so popular that his name was soon a common word in the english language—*jumbo*, meaning "extra large." [23] He died tragically on September 15, 1885, in the canadian town of St. Thomas, Ontario. [24] The big-hearted giant, seeing a train bearing down on a baby elephant, pushed the youngster to safety but could not save himself. [25] To keep Jumbo's memory alive, Barnum donated the skeleton of his beloved elephant to the American Museum of natural history.

SUMMARY STYLE REVIEW

Names of Persons

Malvina **H**offman	a **s**culptor
Mr. Jeff **R**osenwald	a **f**riend of the family
Dr. Marjorie **H**empel	our family **d**octor

Geographical Names

Mexico **C**ity	a **c**ity in Mexico
Shetland **C**ounty	a **c**ounty in North Carolina
the **C**anary **I**slands	some **i**slands in the Atlantic
Great **S**moky **M**ountains	climbing **m**ountains
Pacific **O**cean	across the **o**cean
Twenty-**s**econd **S**treet	a narrow **s**treet
Abilene **S**tate **P**ark	a state **p**ark
in the **E**ast, **N**orth, **M**idwest	traveling **e**ast, **n**orth, **w**est

Organizations, Teams, Business Firms, Institutions, Buildings, Government Bodies

Oakdale **G**arden **C**lub	a **c**lub for gardeners
Chicago **C**ubs	a baseball **t**eam
Your **M**ove **V**an **L**ines	a moving **c**ompany
Vernon **H**igh **S**chool	a small **h**igh **s**chool
the **T**ower of **L**ondon	a **f**ortress in England
Supreme **C**ourt	a traffic **c**ourt
Department of **C**ommerce	a **d**epartment of government

Historical Events and Periods, Special Events, Calendar Items

the **C**ivil **W**ar	a bitter **w**ar
Atomic **A**ge	an **a**ge of progress
Masters **T**ournament	a golf **t**ournament
Thanksgiving **D**ay	a national **h**oliday
in **A**pril or **J**anuary	in **s**pring or **w**inter

Nationalities, Races, Peoples

Japanese	a **n**ationality
Caucasian	a **r**ace
Bantu	a **p**eople of southern Africa

Brand Names

Ford **T**hunderbird	an **a**utomobile
Magnavox	a tape **p**layer

Other Particular Places, Things, Events, Awards

Great Republic	a clipper **s**hip
City of New Orleans	a **t**rain
Apollo	a **s**pacecraft
Nobel **P**rize	a **p**rize

(continued)

MECHANICS

SUMMARY STYLE REVIEW *(continued)*

Other Particular Places, Things, Events, Awards *(continued)*

North Star	a bright star
Earth, Neptune, Pluto	on the earth
Jefferson Memorial	a memorial to Jefferson
Washington Monument	a monument in Washington, D.C.
Senior Class Picnic	a senior in high school
Congressional Medal of Honor	a medal for bravery
Battle of Gettysburg	a war battle
Great Wall of China	a wall

Specific Courses, Languages

Chemistry I	my chemistry class
French	a foreign language
United States History II	the history book

Titles

Mayor Bradley	a mayor
Good morning, Mayor.	
the President of the United States	the president of the class
Senator Dole	a senator's decision
Queen Elizabeth II	a queen's duties
Uncle John	my uncle
The Color Purple	a novel
The New York Times	a daily newspaper
Holy Bible	a religious book
"On the Pulse of Morning"	a poem
"The Fall of the House of Usher"	a short story
the Constitution	a document
Out of Africa	a movie
Ghostwriter	a television program
Echoes of Harlem	a work of art
"Return to Sender"	a musical composition
For Better or Worse	a comic strip

Names of Religions, Their Followers, Holy Days, Celebrations, Holy Writings, Deities

Judaism	the religious faith of the Jews
Ramadan	the ninth month of the Muslim year
New Testament	part of a holy book
Ceres	a Greek goddess

MECHANICS

12 PUNCTUATION

End Marks, Commas, Semicolons, and Colons

✓ *Checking What You Know*

A. Correcting Sentences by Changing Punctuation

Rewrite the following sentences, and add, delete, or replace end marks, commas, semicolons, and colons as necessary. If a sentence is correct, write C.

EXAMPLE
1. After our hike in the woods can we go swimming in the lake
1. *After our hike in the woods, can we go swimming in the lake?*

1. Studying tae kwon do a Korean martial art has improved Christy's concentration, moreover it has increased her self-confidence

2. Well the Lord's Prayer I believe appears in Matthew 6 9–13

3. Is the card addressed to Robert Daniels Jr or to Robert Daniels Sr

4. The batter hoping to advance the runners laid down a perfect bunt

5. Use light colors by the way to make a small room seem larger use dark colors to achieve the opposite effect

6. Until the summer of 1993 we lived in Lansing but now our address is as follows 457 Cleveland Rd Huntsville Alabama

7. Did you ask Joe to bring the forks plates and cups to the picnic or shall I bring them

8. What an interesting enjoyable book this is

9. After we had complained to Mrs Finch about the assignment we had to write letters of apology

10. Reva look out for that pothole in the road

B. Proofreading a Paragraph for End Marks, Commas, Semicolons, and Colons

Add at least ten punctuation marks (end marks, commas, semicolons, and colons) that are needed in the following paragraph.

EXAMPLE   [1] By the way have you ever wondered who invented the instant camera

1. *By the way, have you ever wondered who invented the instant camera?*

[11] When Edwin Land's daughter asked him why a camera couldn't immediately produce pictures Land started thinking. [12] Land, who had taught himself physics quickly worked out the basic principles and design for the instant camera. [13] What a tremendous achievement that was [14] He became head of Polaroid Corp That company manufactured not only the Polaroid camera but also the following products sunglasses, headlights, and camera filters. [15] Did you know that Land later made important contributions to the study of color vision and lasers [16] Land died on March 1 1991 [17] He won the Presidential Medal of Freedom then not surprisingly, he won the National Medal of Science.

MECHANICS

STYLE
NOTE

In speaking, the tone and pitch of your voice, the pauses in your speech, and the gestures and expressions you use all help make your meaning clear. In writing, marks of punctuation tell readers where these verbal and nonverbal cues occur. Punctuation alone won't clarify the meaning of a confusing sentence, however. If you have trouble punctuating a sentence, check to see whether revising it would help express your meaning more clearly.

End Marks

Sentences

End marks—periods, question marks, and *exclamation points—* are used to indicate the purpose of a sentence.

 REFERENCE NOTE: For a discussion of how sentences are classified according to purpose, see pages 205–206. For information on using quotation marks with end marks, see pages 299–300.

12a. A statement (or declarative sentence) is followed by a period.

EXAMPLES   Nancy Lopez won the tournament.
What Vasco Núñez de Balboa saw was the Pacific Ocean.
Flora wondered who had already gone.

NOTE   As the third example above shows, a declarative sentence containing an indirect question is followed by a period. (An indirect question is one that does not use the speaker's exact words.)

12b. A question (or interrogative sentence) is followed by a question mark.

EXAMPLES   Can a cat see color?
Was the plane late?
Who wrote this note? Did you?

MECHANICS

A direct question may have the same word order as a declarative sentence. Since it *is* a question, however, it is followed by a question mark.

EXAMPLES   A cat can see color?
            The plane was late?

NOTE Be sure to distinguish between a declarative sentence that contains an indirect question and an interrogative sentence, which asks a direct question.

INDIRECT QUESTION   He asked me **what was worrying her.** [declarative]
DIRECT QUESTION   **What is worrying her?** [interrogative]

12c. An exclamation is followed by an exclamation point.

EXAMPLES   Hurrah! What a great play!
            Ouch!
            Look out!

Garfield reprinted by permission of UFS, Inc.

STYLE NOTE   Sometimes declarative and interrogative sentences show such strong feeling that they are more like exclamations than like statements or questions. In such cases, an exclamation point should be used instead of a period or a question mark.

EXAMPLES   Here comes the bus!
            Can't you speak up!

MECHANICS

12d. A command or request (or imperative sentence) is followed by either a period or an exclamation point.

When an imperative sentence makes a request, it is generally followed by a period. However, some imperative sentences, particularly commands, may also show strong feeling. In such cases, an exclamation point should be used.

EXAMPLES   Please be quiet.
Turn off your radio.
Be quiet!

Sometimes a command or request is stated in the form of a question. Because of its purpose, however, the sentence is really an imperative sentence and should be followed by a period or an exclamation point.

EXAMPLES   Could you please send me twenty-five copies.
Will you stop that!

Abbreviations

12e. An abbreviation is usually followed by a period.

TYPES OF ABBREVIATIONS	EXAMPLES		
Personal Names	A. E. Housman	Ida B. Wells	
	I. M. Pei	P.D.Q. Bach	
Organizations and Companies	Assn.	Co.	Inc.
	Corp.	Ltd.	
Titles Used with Names	Mr.	Ms.	Mrs.
	Jr.	Dr.	
Time of Day	A.M.	P.M.	
Years	B.C. (written after the date)		
	A.D. (written before the date)		
Addresses	Ave.	St.	Blvd.
	Pkwy.	Hwy.	
States	Calif.	Mass.	Tex.
	Nebr.	N. Dak.	

NOTE Two-letter state abbreviations without periods are used only when the ZIP Code is included.

EXAMPLE   Cincinnati, OH 45233

If a statement ends with an abbreviation, do not use an additional period as an end mark. However, do use a question mark or an exclamation point if one is needed.

EXAMPLES   Mrs. Tavares will be arriving at 3 P.M.
            Can you go to meet her at 3 P.M.?

Abbreviations for government agencies and international organizations and some other frequently used abbreviations are written without periods. Abbreviations for most units of measurement are usually written without periods, especially in science books.

EXAMPLES   CD, CPR, FM, GI, IQ, IRS,
            TV, UFO, UN, USAF
            cm, kg, km, lb, ml, rpm

Do use a period with the abbreviation for *inch* (*in.*), so that it will not be confused with *in,* the word.

 NOTE In most cases, an abbreviation is capitalized only if the words it stands for are capitalized. If you are unsure whether to capitalize an abbreviation or to use periods with it, look in a recent dictionary.

 QUICK CHECK 1   **Correcting Sentences by Adding End Marks**

Rewrite the following sentences, and add periods, question marks, or exclamation points as needed.

1. What a car
2. We asked who owns that car
3. Roman troops invaded Britain in 54 BC
4. Why do children enjoy using computers
5. Please explain why so many children enjoy computers
6. Did you know paper was invented in 105 BC
7. Watch out for sharks
8. I was surprised to hear the news
9. Tell me why you are so upset
10. Will you please say goodbye to your aunt

MECHANICS

Commas

Items in a Series

12f. Use commas to separate items in a series.

Notice in the following examples that the number of commas in a series is one less than the number of items in the series.

EXAMPLES All my cousins, aunts, and uncles came to our family reunion. [words]

The children played in the yard, at the playground, and by the pond. [phrases]

Those who had flown to the reunion, who had driven many miles, or who had even taken time off from their jobs were glad that they had made the effort to be there. [clauses]

When the last two items in a series are joined by *and,* you may omit the comma before the *and* if the comma is not necessary to make the meaning clear.

CLEAR WITH COMMA OMITTED The salad contained lettuce, tomatoes, cucumbers, carrots and radishes.

NOT CLEAR WITH COMMA OMITTED Our school newspaper has editors for news, sports, humor, features and art. [How many editors are there, four or five? Does one person serve as editor for both features and art, or is an editor needed for each job?]

CLEAR WITH COMMA INCLUDED Our school newspaper has editors for news, sports, humor, features, and art. [five editors]

Some writers prefer always to use the comma before the *and* in a series. Follow your teacher's instructions on this point.

NOTE Some words—such as *bread and butter, rod and reel,* and *table and chairs*—are used in pairs and may be considered one item in a series.

EXAMPLE   My favorite breakfast is milk, **biscuits
             and gravy,** and fruit.

(1) If all items in a series are joined by *and* or *or,* do not
use commas to separate them.

EXAMPLES   I need tacks **and** nails **and** a hammer.
             Sam **or** Carlos **or** Yolanda will be able to
             baby-sit tomorrow night.

(2) Independent clauses in a series are usually separated
by semicolons. Short independent clauses, however, may
be separated by commas.

EXAMPLES   As the day wore on, the sky grew dark; tree
             branches swayed in the wind; the bitter
             cold deepened; and the first snowflakes
             fell.
             The sky darkened, branches swayed, the cold
             deepened, and snow fell.

☞ REFERENCE NOTE: For more information about compound sentences, see pages 207–208.

12g. Use commas to separate two or more adjectives
          preceding a noun.

EXAMPLE   Are you going to that hot, crowded, noisy
             mall?

     When the last adjective in a series is thought of as part
of the noun, the comma before the adjective is omitted.

EXAMPLES   I study in our small dining room.
             I'll drink cool, refreshing orange juice.

Compound nouns like *orange juice, dining room,* and *post office* are considered single units—as though the two words
were one word.
     When two or more adjectives precede a noun, you can
use two tests to determine whether the last adjective and
the noun form a unit.

TEST 1:   Insert the word *and* between the adjectives.
               If *and* fits sensibly between the adjectives,
               use a comma. In the second example sen-
               tence, *and* cannot be logically inserted: *small*

and dining room. In the third sentence, *and* sounds logical between the first two adjectives (*cool and refreshing*) but not between the second and third (*refreshing and orange*).

TEST 2: Change the order of the adjectives. If the order of the adjectives can be reversed sensibly, use a comma. *Refreshing, cool orange juice* makes sense, but *orange cool, refreshing juice* and *dining small room* do not.

Independent Clauses

12h. Use commas before *and, but, or, nor, for, so,* and *yet* when they join independent clauses.

In the following correctly punctuated compound sentences, notice that independent clauses appear on both sides of the coordinating conjunctions.

EXAMPLES   Hector pressed the button**, and** the engine started up.

She would never argue**, nor** would she complain to anyone.

Do not be misled by compound verbs, which often make a sentence look as if it contains two independent clauses.

COMPOUND SENTENCE **Mara cleared the table, and Roland did the dishes.** [two independent clauses]

SIMPLE SENTENCE **Mara cleared** the table and **did** the dishes. [one subject with a compound verb]

 REFERENCE NOTE: For more on compound sentences, see pages 207–208. For a discussion of compound subjects and compound verbs, see pages 198–199.

 A comma is always used before *for, so,* or *yet* joining two independent clauses. The comma may be omitted, however, before *and, but, or,* or *nor* when the independent clauses are very short and when there is no possibility of misunderstanding.

EXAMPLE   I read that book and I liked it.

Nonessential Clauses and Phrases

12i. Use commas to set off nonessential clauses and nonessential participial phrases.

A *nonessential* (or *nonrestrictive*) clause or participial phrase adds information that is not needed to understand the main idea in the sentence.

NONESSENTIAL CLAUSES — Eileen Murray, **who is at the top of her class,** wants to go to medical school.
Texas, **which has the most farms in this country,** produces one fourth of our oil.

NONESSENTIAL PHRASES — Tim Ricardo, **hoping to make the swim team,** practiced every day.
The Lord of the Rings, **written by J.R.R. Tolkien,** has been translated into many languages.

Omitting each boldfaced clause or phrase above does not change the main idea of the sentence.

EXAMPLES — Eileen Murray wants to go to medical school.
Texas produces one fourth of our oil.
Tim Ricardo practiced every day.
The Lord of the Rings has been translated into many languages.

When a clause or phrase is necessary to the meaning of a sentence—that is, when it tells *which ones*—the clause or phrase is *essential* (or *restrictive*), and commas are *not* used.

Notice how the meaning of each of the sentences below changes when the essential clause or phrase is omitted.

ESSENTIAL CLAUSE — All students **whose names are on that list** must report to Mrs. Washington today.
All students must report to Mrs. Washington today.

ESSENTIAL PHRASE — Actors **missing more than two rehearsals** will be replaced.
Actors will be replaced.

NOTE An adjective clause that begins with *that* is usually essential.

MECHANICS

EXAMPLE   Is this the dog **that** dug up Grandmother Kanzerski's petunias?

Depending on the writer's meaning, a participial phrase or clause may be either essential or nonessential. Including or omitting commas tells the reader how the clause or phrase relates to the main idea of the sentence.

NONESSENTIAL CLAUSE	LaWanda's brother, who is a senior, works part time at the mall. [LaWanda has only one brother. He works at the mall.]
ESSENTIAL CLAUSE	LaWanda's brother who is a senior works part time at the mall. [LaWanda has more than one brother. The one who is a senior works at the mall.]
NONESSENTIAL PHRASE	My parents' record store, located at Twelfth and Main, is open every night until nine o'clock. [My parents have only one record store. It is open every night until nine o'clock.]
ESSENTIAL PHRASE	My parents' record store located at Twelfth and Main is open every night until nine o'clock. [My parents have more than one record store. The one at Twelfth and Main is open every night until nine o'clock.]

 REFERENCE NOTE: See **Chapter 7: Clauses** for more information on clauses. See pages 162–163 for more information on participial phrases.

✓ *QUICK CHECK 2*   **Correcting Sentences by Adding Commas**

For the following sentences, write each word that should be followed by a comma. Then write the comma. If a sentence is correct, write *C.*

1. The students sold crafts second-hand books and home-made baked goods at the bazaar.
2. *A Raisin in the Sun* written by Lorraine Hansberry will be performed by the Grantville Community Players and will run for three weeks.

3. We stayed in the airy spacious library all afternoon and looked at outdated geography books.
4. Members of the committee met for three hours but they still have not chosen a theme for the dance.
5. An eclipse that occurs when earth blocks the sun's light from the moon is called a lunar eclipse.

Introductory Elements

12j. Use commas after certain introductory elements.

(1) Use commas after words such as *next, yes,* and *no.* Introductory interjections such as *why, well,* and *oops* are also set off by commas when they express mild emotion.

EXAMPLES   **Yes,** she's going to the cafeteria.
Next, move the cursor to the word you want to replace.
Ah, there's nothing like cold water on a hot day!

☞ REFERENCE NOTE: For more information about interjections, see pages 70–71.

(2) Use a comma after an introductory participial phrase.

EXAMPLES   **Switching on a flashlight,** the ranger led the way down the path.
Disappointed by the high prices, we made up a new gift list.

(3) Use a comma after an introductory prepositional phrase that contains additional prepositional phrases.

EXAMPLES   **Inside the fence at the far end of her property,** she built a potting shed.
By the end of the train ride, the children were exhausted.

NOTE One introductory prepositional phrase does not require a comma unless the sentence is confusing without the comma.

EXAMPLES   **At our house** we share all the work.

MECHANICS

At our house, plants grow best in the sunny, bright kitchen. [The comma is needed to avoid reading *house plants.*]
Down below, the faucet was still dripping. [The comma is necessary to avoid reading *below the faucet.*]

(4) Use a comma after an introductory adverb clause.

An adverb clause may introduce any independent clause in the sentence.

EXAMPLES   **After Andrés Segovia had played his last guitar concert,** the audience applauded for more than fifteen minutes.
This will be an open-book test; **when you've finished,** you may use the rest of the period to study.

NOTE   Do not make the mistake of putting a comma before an adverb clause when the clause is in the middle or at the end of a sentence.

EXAMPLES   I gave in even though I didn't believe she was right. [No comma is necessary between *in* and *even.*]
We stayed a long time because all our friends were there and we were having fun. [No comma is necessary between *time* and *because.*]

✓ *QUICK CHECK* 3   **Correcting Sentences by Adding Commas**

For the following sentences, write each word or number that should be followed by a comma. Then write the comma.

1. Scuttling across the dirt road the large hairy spider a tarantula terrified Steve Alice and me.
2. Although German shepherds are most often trained as guide dogs other breeds used include Labrador retrievers golden retrievers and Doberman pinschers.
3. According to this copy of her birth certificate she was born July 7 1976 in Juneau Alaska.
4. Yes as a matter of fact most horses can run four miles without having to stop.
5. Up above the clock ticked away.

MECHANICS

Interrupters

12k. Use commas to set off elements that interrupt a sentence.

Two commas are used around an interrupting element— one before and one after.

EXAMPLES   That boy, in fact, worked very hard.
            Linda, my friend who moved to Ecuador, sent me a long letter.

Sometimes an "interrupter" comes at the beginning or at the end of a sentence. In these cases, only one comma is needed.

EXAMPLES   Nevertheless, you must go with me.
            I need the money, Josh.

(1) Appositives and appositive phrases are usually set off by commas.

EXAMPLES   My dog, **a collie,** is very gentle.
            My favorite actress, **Rita Moreno,** stars in the movie I rented.

NOTE In setting off an appositive, include the words that modify it.

EXAMPLE   Everyone, **even his parents,** thinks he is making a mistake.

Sometimes an appositive is so closely related to the word it identifies or explains that it should not be set off by commas. Such an appositive is called a *restrictive appositive;* it usually has no modifiers.

EXAMPLES   My friend **Tamisha** lost her favorite necklace. [The writer has more than one friend. The appositive *Tamisha* identifies which friend.]
            He recited the second stanza of "Childhood" by the poet **Margaret Walker.** [The appositive *Margaret Walker* identifies which poet.]
            We **freshmen** made the decorations for the dance. [The appositive *freshmen* explains who is meant by *we.*]

REFERENCE NOTE: For more information on appositives and appositive phrases, see pages 170–171.

(2) Words used in direct address are set off by commas.

EXAMPLES **Linda,** you know the rules.
I did that exercise last night, **Ms. Ryan.**
Your room, **Bernice,** needs cleaning.

(3) Parenthetical expressions are set off by commas.

Parenthetical expressions are side remarks that add minor
information or that relate ideas to each other.

Commonly Used Parenthetical Expressions		
after all	however	nevertheless
at any rate	I believe	of course
consequently	in fact	on the contrary
for example	in the first place	on the other hand
for instance	meanwhile	therefore
generally speaking	moreover	

EXAMPLES **On the contrary,** I am glad that you told me
about the error.
She is, **in fact,** an exchange student from
Argentina.
You should try out for quarterback, **in my
opinion.**

 REFERENCE NOTE: Sometimes parentheses and dashes
are used to set off parenthetical expressions. See pages
318–320.

Some expressions may be used either parenthetically
or not parenthetically. Don't set them off with commas unless they are truly parenthetical.

EXAMPLES Sandra will, **I think,** enjoy her trip to Belize.
[parenthetical]
I think Sandra will enjoy her trip to Belize.
[not parenthetical]
However, did you finish your report on
time? [parenthetical]

MECHANICS

However did you finish your report on time?
[not parenthetical—similar to "How did you
manage to finish on time?"]
To tell the truth, he tries. [parenthetical]
He tries **to tell the truth.** [not parenthetical]

NOTE   A contrasting expression introduced by *not* or *yet* is
parenthetical and is set off by commas.

EXAMPLES   It is the spirit of the giver, **not the cost of
the gift,** that counts.
The judge was firm, **yet fair.**

Conventional Uses

12l.   Use commas in certain conventional situations.

**(1) Use a comma to separate items in dates and
addresses.**

EXAMPLES   My family moved to Oakland, California, on
Wednesday, December 5, 1990.
On December 5, 1990, our address became 25
Peralta Road, Oakland, CA 94611.

Notice that no comma divides the month and day
(December 5) or the house number and the street name (25
Peralta Road) because each is considered one item. Also,
the ZIP Code is not separated from the abbreviation of the
state by a comma: Oakland, CA 94611.

NOTE   Commas are not needed if the day precedes the
month or if only the month and year are given.

EXAMPLES   President Bill Clinton took office on 20
January 1993.
Hurricane Andrew hit South Florida in
August 1992.

**(2) Use a comma after the salutation of a friendly letter
and after the closing of any letter.**

EXAMPLES   Dear Ms. Chen,   Sincerely yours,
My dear Anna,   Yours very truly,

NOTE   Use a colon after the salutation of a business letter.

EXAMPLE   Dear Mr. Sanchez:

MECHANICS

(3) Use a comma after a name followed by an abbreviation such as *Jr., Sr.,* or *M.D.* Follow such an abbreviation with a comma unless it ends the sentence.

EXAMPLES   Allen Davis, Sr.

             Ens. Tanya Jay, U.S.N.

             Carol Ferrara, M.D., announced the opening of her practice.

             The one who made that speech was Dr. Martin Luther King, Jr.

Unnecessary Commas

12m. Do not use unnecessary commas.

Too much punctuation is as confusing as not enough punctuation, especially where the use of commas is concerned.

CONFUSING   My friend, Jessica, said she would feed my cat and my dog while I'm away, but now, she tells me, she is too busy.

    CLEAR   My friend Jessica said she would feed my cat and my dog while I'm away, but now she tells me she is too busy.

STYLE NOTE   Have a reason for every comma or other mark of punctuation that you use. When there is no rule requiring punctuation and when the meaning of the sentence is clear without it, do not insert any punctuation mark.

 *QUICK CHECK 4*   **Correcting Sentences by Adding Commas**

For the following sentences, write each word that should be followed by a comma. Then write the comma. If no comma is necessary, write *C*.

1. Whitney not Don won first prize.
2. Angela and Jennifer are you both planning to write poems?

MECHANICS

3. All poetry entries should be submitted no later than Friday to Poetry Contest 716 North Cliff Drive Salt Lake City UT 84103.
4. The best time to plant flower seeds of course is just before a rainy season not in the middle of a hot dry summer.
5. Our neighbor Ms. Allen manages two apartment buildings downtown.

Semicolons

12n. Use a semicolon between independent clauses in a sentence if they are not joined by *and, but, or, nor, for, so,* or *yet*.

Notice in the following pairs of examples that the semicolon takes the place of the comma and the conjunction joining the independent clauses.

EXAMPLES First I had a sandwich and a glass of milk**, and** then I called you for the homework assignment.
First I had a sandwich and a glass of milk**;** then I called you for the homework assignment.

Patty likes to act**, but** her sister gets stage fright.
Patty likes to act**;** her sister gets stage fright.

Similarly, a semicolon can take the place of a period to join two sentences that are closely related.

EXAMPLES Manuel looked out at the downpour**.** Then he put on his raincoat and boots. [two simple sentences]
Manuel looked out at the downpour**;** then he put on his raincoat and boots. [one compound sentence]

As you can see in the following sentences, a complete thought appears on both sides of each semicolon, and the

MECHANICS

two independent clauses are not joined by *and, but, or, nor, for, so,* or *yet.*

EXAMPLES   Excellence does not remain alone; it is sure to attract neighbors.

> Confucius, *The Sayings of Confucius*

And so, my fellow Americans, ask not what your country can do for you; ask what you can do for your country.

> John F. Kennedy,
> 1961 Inaugural Address

The night was dark, gloomy; the wind moaned over the treetops, and the coyotes howled all around.

> Jovita González, *Among My People*

12o. Use a semicolon between independent clauses joined by a conjunctive adverb or a transitional expression.

EXAMPLES   Emma felt shy; **however,** she soon made some new friends.
My parents are strict; **for example,** I can watch TV only on weekends.

Notice in the preceding sentences that the conjunctive adverb and the transitional expression are preceded by semicolons and followed by commas.

Commonly Used Conjunctive Adverbs		
accordingly	indeed	next
also	instead	otherwise
besides	meanwhile	still
consequently	moreover	then
furthermore	nevertheless	therefore
however		

Commonly Used Transitional Expressions		
as a result	in addition	on the other hand
for example	in fact	that is
for instance	in other words	

MECHANICS

NOTE When a conjunctive adverb or a transitional expression appears *within* one of the clauses and not *between* the clauses, it is usually punctuated as an interrupter (set off by commas). The two clauses are still separated by a semicolon.

EXAMPLE   Our student council voted to have a Crazy Clothes Day; the principal**,** **however,** vetoed the idea.

12p. A semicolon (rather than a comma) may be needed to separate independent clauses joined by a coordinating conjunction when there are commas within the clauses.

CONFUSING   Alana, Eric, and Kim voted for Stephanie, and Scott, Robert, and Vanessa voted for Jay.
CLEAR   Alana, Eric, and Kim voted for Stephanie**;** and Scott, Robert, and Vanessa voted for Jay.

CONFUSING   Scanning the horizon for the source of the whirring sound, Pedro saw a huge, green cloud traveling in his direction, and suddenly, as he recognized what it was, he knew that the crops would soon be eaten by a horde of grasshoppers.
CLEAR   Scanning the horizon for the source of the whirring sound, Pedro saw a huge, green cloud traveling in his direction**;** and suddenly, as he recognized what it was, he knew that the crops would soon be eaten by a horde of grasshoppers.

12q. Use a semicolon between items in a series if the items contain commas.

EXAMPLES   My cousins have sent me postcards from Paris, France**;** Rome, Italy**;** Lisbon, Portugal**;** Amsterdam, the Netherlands**;** and London, England.
The Photography Club will meet on Wednesday, September 12**;** Wednesday, September 19**;** Tuesday, September 25**;** and Tuesday, October 2.

"SURE I GOT ALL THE PUNCTUATION: COMMA, COMMA, PERIOD, PERIOD, QUESTION MARK, COMMA, SEMI-COLON, COMMA, EXCLAMATION POINT, PERIOD..."

© 1993 by Sidney Harris

 QUICK CHECK 5 **Correcting Sentences by Adding Semicolons**

For the following sentences, write each word that should be followed by a semicolon. Then write the semicolon. If a sentence is correct, write *C*.

1. Whales, which are warmblooded marine mammals, are divided into two main families, these families are the toothed whales (the larger family) and the toothless whales.
2. The many species of whales include the gray whale, which is probably the best-known toothless whale, the Baird's beaked whale, which is also called the giant bottlenose whale, the bowhead whale, which is also known as the Arctic whale, and the killer whale, which eats almost anything.
3. Whales take very deep breaths consequently, they can dive almost a mile beneath the ocean moreover, they can remain there for more than an hour.
4. Several countries have banned the killing of certain whale species; but the blue whale, which is close to extinction, remains an endangered species.

MECHANICS

5. Whale-watching cruises originated with the public's growing concern over the survival of whales today whale-watching attracts as many as 350,000 people a year.

Colons

12r. Use a colon to mean "note what follows."

(1) In some cases a colon is used before a list of items, especially after the expressions *the following* and *as follows.*

EXAMPLES   You will need to bring **the following equip-ment:** a sleeping bag, a warm sweater, and extra socks.
Additional supplies are **as follows:** a tooth-brush, toothpaste, a change of clothes, and a pillow.

Sometimes, the items that follow the colon are used as appositives. If a word is followed by a list of appositives, the colon is used to make the sentence clear.

EXAMPLES   At the crossroads we saw three signs: To Barcelona, To Paris, and To Lisbon.
You need to shop for several items: brown shoelaces, a quart of milk, and five or six carrots.

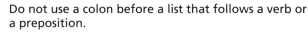 REFERENCE NOTE: For more information on appositives and appositive phrases, see pages 170–171.

 Do not use a colon before a list that follows a verb or a preposition.

INCORRECT   Additional supplies are: a toothbrush and toothpaste, a change of clothes, a towel, a pillow, and an air mattress.

CORRECT   Additional supplies are a toothbrush and toothpaste, a change of clothes, a towel, a pillow, and an air mattress.

INCORRECT   You need to shop for: brown shoelaces, a quart of milk, and five or six carrots.

MECHANICS

CORRECT   You need to shop for brown shoelaces, a quart of milk, and five or six carrots.

(2) Use a colon before a long, formal statement or a long quotation.

EXAMPLE   Horace Mann had this to say: "Do not think of knocking out another person's brains because he differs in opinion from you. It would be as rational to knock yourself on the head because you differ from yourself ten years ago."

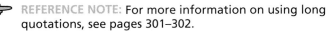 REFERENCE NOTE: For more information on using long quotations, see pages 301–302.

12s. Use a colon in certain conventional situations.

(1) Use a colon between the hour and the minute.

EXAMPLES   9:30 P.M.
8:00 A.M.

(2) Use a colon between chapter and verse in referring to passages from the Bible.

EXAMPLES   Esther 3:5
Exodus 1:6–14

(3) Use a colon after the salutation of a business letter.

EXAMPLES   Dear Ms. González:
Dear Sir or Madam:
Dear Dr. Fenton:
To Whom It May Concern:

 Use a comma after the salutation of a friendly letter.

EXAMPLES   Dear Kim,
Dear Uncle Remy,

Some software programs can evaluate your writing for common errors in the use of end marks, commas, semicolons, and colons. Such programs can help as you proofread your drafts.

QUICK CHECK 6 **Correcting Sentences by Adding Colons**

For the following sentences, write each word or number that should be followed by a colon. Then write the colon. If a sentence is correct, write *C*.

1. Last month I read the following novels *Julie of the Wolves,* by Jean George; *The Color Purple,* by Alice Walker; and *The Joy Luck Club,* by Amy Tan.

2. The desk was littered with papers, pencils, paperback books, food wrappers, and dirty socks.

3. Learn to spell the following words *aneurysm, fluoroscope, peregrination,* and *serendipity.*

4. An enduring statement of loyalty, found in Ruth 1 16, begins as follows "Entreat me not to leave thee or to return from following after thee, for whither thou goest, I will go."

5. From 8 00 A.M. until 6 00 P.M., Brooks Appliances will have a sale on vacuum cleaners, washing machines, and refrigerators.

✓ *Chapter Review*

A. Correcting Sentences by Changing Punctuation

Rewrite the following sentences, and add, delete, or replace end marks, commas, semicolons, and colons as necessary. If a sentence is correct, write *C*.

EXAMPLE   1. Someday, robots may do many simple household chores, in addition, robots may perform basic record-keeping tasks in offices

1. *Someday, robots may do many simple household chores; in addition, robots may perform basic record-keeping tasks in offices.*

1. Well, to tell the truth Al I didn't go to the game last night, instead I took care of my six-month-old, baby brother.

MECHANICS

2. Did you know that the band members will perform at the civic center on Tuesday January 15, at the Kiwanis Club on Saturday, January 19, and at the Oak Nursing Home on Friday January 25.

3. For the lesson on figures of speech we had to find examples of: simile metaphor, personification and hyperbole.

4. Dr. A. J Enríquez Jr. has traveled to rain forests in many parts of the world, Borneo Brazil Costa Rica and Sri Lanka

5. What a major influence the first Spaniards, who settled in the Southwest, had on American architecture.

6. The Tower of Babel which is described in Genesis 11 1–9 apparently closely resembled a ziggurat a terraced pyramid.

7. My friend Erica never misses a football game on TV, last Sunday, for example she watched football from noon to 7 00 PM

8. The Flashbacks touring to promote a new album of their greatest hits performed their most popular songs for the fans, and everywhere the group went they were greeted with cheers and applause.

9. Because he doesn't like violence my oldest brother Sam plays only nonviolent games like golf and badminton not contact sports.

10. Held in Hawaii the annual Ironman Triathlon, which is open to both women and men, consists of the following events, swimming 2.4 miles in the ocean bicycling 112 miles and running 26.2 miles.

B. Proofreading a Letter for the Correct Use of Punctuation Marks

Add, delete, or replace end marks, commas, semicolons, or colons to correct the following letter.

EXAMPLE   [1] Last summer we stayed home during summer vacation; but this summer we took a trip in the car.

1. *Last summer we stayed home during summer vacation, but this summer we took a trip in the car.*

290 Eureka Street
Dallas, TX, 76013

August 15, 1994

Director
California Department of Parks and Recreation
Box 2390
Sacramento, CA 95811

[11] Dear Sir or Madam,

[12] While we were on vacation this summer my parents and I visited the following states New Mexico, Arizona, Oregon, Utah, Idaho, Nevada, and California. [13] We wanted you to know that we especially enjoyed our stay in California; we learned a lot, and had a great time.

[14] What fun we had visiting the Spanish missions in the Los Angeles area [15] Do many other people, who visit them, comment on what a real sense of history the missions give. [16] My favorite places were Mission San Fernando Rey de España, located in Mission Hills, Mission San Gabriel Arcangel, located in San Gabriel, and El Pueblo de Los Angeles. [17] The Old Plaza Church, Nuestra Señora la Reina de Los Angeles which dates from 1822 was especially wonderful, unfortunately however we couldn't stay long, because it was nearly 12 30 P.M. and we had reservations for lunch.

[18] Our stay in California was really great, we hope to return again soon when we have more time. [19] I want to visit some of the missions around San Francisco therefore, I'd like you to send me some information on that area.

[20] Very truly yours

Angie Barnes

Angie Barnes

SUMMARY OF COMMA USES

12f Use commas to separate items in a series.

(1) If all items in a series are joined by *and* or *or,* do not use commas to separate them.

(2) Independent clauses in a series are usually separated by semicolons. Short independent clauses, however, may be separated by commas.

12g Use commas to separate two or more adjectives preceding a noun.

12h Use commas before *and, but, or, nor, for, so,* and *yet* when they join independent clauses.

12i Use commas to set off nonessential clauses and nonessential participial phrases.

12j Use commas after certain introductory elements.

(1) Use a comma after words such as *well, yes, no,* and *why* when they begin a sentence.

(2) Use a comma after an introductory participial phrase.

(3) Use a comma after two or more introductory prepositional phrases.

(4) Use a comma after an introductory adverb clause.

12k Use commas to set off sentence interrupters.

(1) Appositives and appositive phrases are usually set off by commas.

(2) Words used in direct address are set off by commas.

(3) Parenthetical expressions may be set off by commas.

12l Use commas in certain conventional situations.

(1) Use a comma to separate items in dates and addresses.

(2) Use a comma after the salutation of a friendly letter and after the closing of any letter.

(3) Use a comma after a name followed by an abbreviation such as *Jr., Sr.,* and *M.D.*

12m Do not use unnecessary commas.

13 PUNCTUATION

Italics and Quotation Marks

✓ Checking What You Know

A. Correcting Sentences by Adding Underlining (Italics) and Quotation Marks

Write each letter, word, or title that should be either underlined (italicized) or put in quotation marks. Then supply the underlining or quotation marks.

EXAMPLE   1. According to The Book of Word Histories, there is a close link between the words lettuce and galaxy.
            1. <u>The Book of Word Histories</u>, lettuce, galaxy

1. The concert ended with a stirring rendition of The Stars and Stripes Forever.
2. There's Still Gold in Them Thar Hills, an article in Discovery, describes attempts to mine low-grade gold deposits on Quartz Mountain in California.
3. The overture to Mozart's opera The Magic Flute is often played as a concert piece.
4. The fifth unit in African American Literature is titled The Harlem Renaissance.

5. I Am Joaquín is a long, epic poem that celebrates Mexican American culture.
6. As a baby sitter I have read the children's book The Pokey Little Puppy at least a dozen times.
7. Horace Greeley founded the Tribune, an influential New York newspaper; in it he published his antislavery essay The Prayer of Twenty Millions.
8. Although the poem When You Are Old has three stanzas, it contains only one sentence.
9. The word recommend has only one c.
10. Robert Fulton's steamboat, Clermont, was the first one that could be operated without losing money.

B. Punctuating Dialogue by Adding Quotation Marks

Insert quotation marks where they are needed in the following dialogue.

EXAMPLE   [1] Listen carefully! said Mrs. García. Every student who plans to go on the field trip must have a note from home.

    1. *"Listen carefully!" said Mrs. García. "Every student who plans to go on the field trip must have a note from home."*

[11] Before our field trip begins, continued Mrs. García, be sure that you have a notebook and a collection kit.

[12] Will we need binoculars? asked Melvin.

[13] Leave your binoculars at home, answered Mrs. García. Your ears will be more helpful than your eyes on this trip.

[14] What will we be able to hear so far out in the country? asked Arnold.

[15] What a question! exclaimed Felicia. This time of year, you can hear all sorts of sounds.

[16] I hope that we hear and see some birds, said Koko. Didn't someone once say, The birds warble sweetly in the springtime?

[17] When, asked James, do we eat lunch? My mom packed my favorite kinds of sandwiches.

MECHANICS

[18] Don't worry, said Mrs. García. Most birds are quiet at midday. We can have our lunch then.

[19] Ruth Ann said, Mrs. García, would you believe that I don't know one birdcall from another?

[20] That's all right, Ruth Ann, laughed Mrs. García. Some birds call out their own names. For example, the bobolink repeats its name: Bob-o-link! Bob-o-link!

Italics

When writing or typing, indicate italics by underlining. If your composition were to be printed, the typesetter would set the underlined words in italics. For example, if you typed the sentence

Alice Walker wrote The Color Purple.

it would be printed like this:

Alice Walker wrote *The Color Purple.*

If you use a personal computer, you can probably set words in italics yourself. Most word-processing software and many printers are capable of producing italic type.

Shoe, by Jeff MacNelly, reprinted by permission: Tribune Media Services.

13a. Use underlining (italics) for titles of books, plays, long poems, films, periodicals, works of art, recordings, long musical works, television series, trains, ships, aircraft, and spacecraft.

TYPE OF TITLE	EXAMPLES	
Books	*The Diary of Anne Frank* *Invisible Man*	
Plays	*The Piano Lesson*	*Romeo and Juliet*
Long Poems	*Evangeline*	*Beowulf*
Films	*Casablanca*	*Harvey*
Periodicals	*Seventeen*	*The New York Times*

NOTE The words *a, an,* and *the* written before a title are italicized only when they are part of the official title. The official title of a book appears on the title page. The official title of a newspaper or periodical appears on the masthead, which is usually found on the editorial page.

EXAMPLES   I am reading John Knowles's *A Separate Peace.*

My parents subscribe to *The Wall Street Journal* and the *Austin American-Statesman.*

TYPE OF TITLE	EXAMPLES	
Works of Art	*Death of Cleopatra*	*Birth of Venus*
Recordings	*Into the Light*	*Two Worlds, One Heart*
Long Musical Works	*Tremonisha* *Rhapsody in Blue*	*The Jupiter Symphony*
Television Series	*Sixty Minutes*	*In Living Color*
Trains and Ships	*Orient Express*	*Titanic*
Aircraft and Spacecraft	*Spirit of St. Louis*	*Apollo 1*

NOTE A long poem is one that is long enough to be published as a separate volume. Such poems are usually

MECHANICS

divided into titled or numbered sections, such as cantos, parts, or books. Long musical compositions include operas, symphonies, ballets, oratorios, and concertos.

EXAMPLES   In my report on Coleridge, I plan to quote from Part VII of *The Rime of the Ancient Mariner.*
At her recital, she will play a selection from Tchaikovsky's *Swan Lake.*
Mr. Kellen sang a popular song that came from the opera *Porgy and Bess.*

 REFERENCE NOTE: For examples of titles that should be placed in quotation marks rather than be italicized, see pages 303–304.

13b. Use underlining (italics) for words, letters, and figures referred to as such and for foreign words not yet a part of the English vocabulary.

EXAMPLES   The word *Mississippi* has four *s*'s and four *i*'s.
The *3* on that license plate looks like an *8.*
The *corrido,* a fast-paced ballad, evolved from a musical form brought to the New World by early Spanish explorers and colonizers.

 English has borrowed many words from other languages. Once such words are considered a part of the English vocabulary, they are no longer italicized.

EXAMPLES   amoeba (Greek)   canyon (Spanish)
okra (African)   judo (Japanese)
boss (Dutch)   chipmunk (Algonquian)

If you're not sure whether to italicize a word with a foreign origin, look in a recent dictionary.

✓ *QUICK CHECK 1*   **Correcting Sentences by Adding Underlining (Italics)**

Underline all the words and word groups that should be italicized in the following sentences.

1. Jason named his ship Argo because Argos had built it.
2. The Marine Corps' motto is semper fidelis, which is Latin for "always faithful."

MECHANICS

3. Have you read the novel Dragonsong by Anne McCaffrey?
4. When I spelled occurrence with only one *r*, I was eliminated from the spelling contest.
5. The Gilbert and Sullivan comic opera The Mikado and the Puccini opera Madame Butterfly are both set in Japan.

Quotation Marks

13c. Use quotation marks to enclose a ***direct quotation***—a person's exact words.

EXAMPLES   Melanie said, **"**This car is making a very strange noise.**"**

    "Maybe we should pull over,**"** suggested Lamont.

Do not use quotation marks for *indirect quotations.*

DIRECT QUOTATION   Stephanie said, **"**I'm going to wash the car.**"** [The speaker quotes Stephanie's exact words.]

INDIRECT QUOTATION   Stephanie said that she was going to wash the car. [The speaker does not quote Stephanie's exact words.]

 NOTE   Always be sure to place quotation marks at both the beginning and the end of a direct quotation.

    INCORRECT   He shouted, "We can win, team!
    CORRECT   He shouted, **"**We can win, team!**"**

An interrupting expression, such as "she said" or "he asked," is not a part of a quotation. Therefore, never place such an expression inside quotation marks.

INCORRECT   **"**Let's sit here, Jennifer whispered, not way down there in front.**"**
CORRECT   **"**Let's sit here,**"** Jennifer whispered, **"**not way down there in front.**"**

When two or more sentences by the same speaker are quoted together, use only one set of quotation marks.

MECHANICS

INCORRECT	Brennan said, "I like to sit close to the screen." "The sound is better there."
CORRECT	Brennan said, "I like to sit close to the screen. The sound is better there."

13d. A direct quotation begins with a capital letter.

EXAMPLES Explaining the lever, Archimedes said, "**G**ive me a place to stand, and I can move the world."

Miss Pérez answered, "**T**he rest of the chapter, of course." [Although this quotation is not a sentence, it is Miss Pérez's complete remark.]

NOTE If a direct quotation is obviously a fragment of the original quotation, it should begin with a small letter.

EXAMPLE Are our ideals, as Scott says, mere "statues of snow" that soon melt? [The quotation is obviously only a part of Scott's remark.]

13e. When a quoted sentence is divided into two parts by an interrupting expression, the second part begins with a small letter.

EXAMPLES "I wish," she said, "**t**hat we went to the same school."

"I know," I answered, "**b**ut at least we are friends."

If the second part of a quotation is a new sentence, a period (not a comma) follows the interrupting expression, and the second part begins with a capital letter.

EXAMPLE "I requested an interview," the reporter said**.** "**S**he told me she was too busy."

13f. A direct quotation is set off from the rest of the sentence by commas or by a question mark or an exclamation point.

EXAMPLES Delores explained**,** "You know how much I like chicken**,**" as she passed her plate for more.

"Have you seen Mel this morning?" Wanda asked.

The plumber shouted, "Turn off that faucet!" when the water started gushing out of the pipe.

13g. When used with quotation marks, other marks of punctuation are placed according to the following rules:

(1) Commas and periods are always placed inside the closing quotation marks.

EXAMPLES   "I haven't seen the movie," remarked Jeannette, "but I understand it's excellent."

He read aloud "Ode to the End of Summer," a poem by Phyllis McGinley.

(2) Semicolons and colons are always placed outside the closing quotation marks.

EXAMPLES   Socrates once said, "As for me, all I know is that I know nothing"; I wonder why everyone thinks he was such a wise man.

The following actresses were nominated for "best performer in a leading role": Sally Field, Meryl Streep, Cher, and Jodie Foster.

(3) Question marks and exclamation points are placed inside the closing quotation marks if the quotation is a question or an exclamation; otherwise, they are placed outside.

EXAMPLES   "Is it too cold in here?" the manager asked as I shivered.

"Yes!" I answered. "Please turn off the air conditioner!"

Can you explain the saying "Penny wise, pound foolish"?

It is *not* an insult to be called a "bookworm"!

13h. When you write dialogue (a conversation), begin a new paragraph every time the speaker changes.

MECHANICS

EXAMPLE   "What's that?" Sally demanded impa-
                  tiently.
                      Luisa seemed surprised. "What's what?"
                      "That thing, what you got in your hand."
                      "Oh this . . ." and she held it up for Sally to
                  inspect. "A present."
                      "A what?"
                      "A present I picked up."
                      "Oh." Sally moved her eyes to the house.
                  "Looks like his place burned down. What
                  d'you find inside?"
                      "Just this," Luisa said, gazing blankly at
                  the house.
                      "What d'you want that for?"

                              Ron Arias, "El Mago"

Notice that a paragraph may be only one line long. Also
notice that a paragraph of dialogue may consist of only a
word or two treated as a complete sentence, even though it
is not one.

13i. When a quoted passage consists of more than
one paragraph, put quotation marks at the
beginning of each paragraph and at the end of
the entire passage. Do not put quotation marks
after any paragraph but the last.

EXAMPLE   "At nine o'clock this morning," read the
                  news story, "someone entered the Mill Bank
                  by the back entrance, broke through two
                  thick steel doors guarding the bank's vault,
                  and escaped with sixteen bars of gold.
                      "No arrests have been made, but state po-
                  lice are confident the case will be solved
                  within a few days."

NOTE   A long passage (not dialogue) quoted from a book
or another printed source is usually set off from the
rest of the text. The entire passage is usually indented
and double-spaced. In some cases, it is also set in
smaller type. When a quoted passage has been set
off in one of these ways, no quotation marks are
necessary.

MECHANICS

EXAMPLE

In his autobiography <u>The Interesting Narrative of the Life of Olaudah Equiano or Gustavus Vassa, the African</u> , Olaudah Equiano describes encountering African languages other than his own:

> From the time I left my own nation I always found somebody that understood me till I came to the sea coast. The languages of different nations did not totally differ, nor were they so copious as those of the Europeans, particularly the English. They were therefore easily learned; and while I was journeying thus through Africa, I acquired two or three different tongues.

13j. Use single quotation marks to enclose a quotation within a quotation.

EXAMPLES   Becky snapped, "I know what I'm doing. Don't tell me, 'That's not the way to do it.'"

Mrs. Wright said, "In a letter to a schoolgirl, W.E.B. Du Bois wrote, 'Get the very best training possible, and the doors of opportunity will fly open before you.'"

Gregory shouted, "How dare you say 'Yuck'! You haven't even tasted it."

The choir director asked us, "How many of you know the words to 'Lift Every Voice and Sing'?"

NOTE The last example above contains a song title within a quotation. A title that normally appears within quotation marks is enclosed in single quotation marks when it is part of a quotation.

☞ REFERENCE NOTE: A chart showing the types of titles that appear in quotation marks appears on page 304.

MECHANICS

✓ *QUICK CHECK 2*   **Correcting Passages by
Adding Quotation Marks**

Rewrite each of the following passages, adding quotation marks where they are needed. Remember to begin a new paragraph each time the speaker changes. If a passage is correct, write *C*.

1

I told Mai that she could ride with us, but she said that she'd meet us at the theater.

2

Race-car driver Janet Guthrie, said Chet, reading from his notes, is a trained physicist who has spent many years working for an aircraft corporation.

3

Who shot that ball? Coach Larsen wanted to know. I did, came the reply from the small, frail-looking player. Good shot, observed the coach, but always remember to follow your shot to the basket. I tried, but I was screened, the player explained.

4

The *Brownsville Beacon,* the editorial began, will never support a candidate who tells the taxpayers, Vote for me, and I will cut taxes.

The reason is simple: Taxes, just like everything else in this inflationary society, must increase. Any candidate who claims otherwise is either a fool or a liar.

5

In the interview the candidate said, I am a very hospitable person. Yes, her husband agreed, Ralph Waldo Emerson must have been thinking of you when he said, Happy is the house that shelters a friend.

13k. Use quotation marks to enclose titles of articles, short stories, essays, poems, songs, individual episodes of TV shows, chapter titles, and other parts of books and periodicals.

TYPE OF TITLE	EXAMPLES
Short Stories	"The Man to Send Rain Clouds" "The Pit and the Pendulum"
Poems	"On Ageing" "The End of My "Incident" Journey"
Essays	"Charley in Yellowstone" "An Apartment in Moscow"
Articles	"What Teenagers Need to Know About Diets" "Satellites That Serve Us"
Songs	"The Ballad of Gregorio Cortez" "Peace Train"
TV Episodes	"The Sure Thing" "Monarch in Waiting"
Chapters and Parts of Books and Periodicals	"Life in the First Settlements" "The Talk of the Town" "Guide to the Dictionary"

 REFERENCE NOTE: Remember that the titles of long poems and long musical works are italicized, not enclosed in quotation marks. See the examples on page 296.

13l. Use quotation marks to enclose slang words, technical terms, and other special uses of words.

EXAMPLES   The impatient customer did a "slow burn."
             Jeremy developed a "macro," a small computer program, to insert his return address into all the letters he writes.
             The rabbit got out of its cage just as the neighbor's dog came over to visit, so for a few moments we had a rather "hare-raising" situation.

 NOTE Avoid using slang words in formal speaking and writing. When you use a technical term, be sure to explain its meaning. If you are not sure whether a word is appropriate or whether its meaning will be clear to your readers, check a recent dictionary. If necessary, replace the term with a more appropriate one.

 *QUICK CHECK 3* **Correcting Sentences by Adding Quotation Marks for Titles**

Correct the following sentences by adding quotation marks where they are needed.

1. Chapter 3 is titled Essays and Speeches.
2. A popular Old English riddle song is Scarborough Fair.
3. Have you read Jesse Stuart's story Split Cherry Tree?
4. Which Eve Merriam poem is your favorite, Cheers or How to Eat a Poem?
5. How I laughed when I read Fran Lebowitz's essay Tips for Teens!

 ## *Chapter Review*

A. Correcting Sentences by Adding Underlining (Italics) and Quotation Marks

For each of the following numbered items, add underlining (italics) and quotation marks where necessary.

EXAMPLE
1. Don't forget your umbrella, said Jody. I read in the Sun Times that it's going to rain today.

1. *"Don't forget your umbrella," said Jody. "I read in the <u>Sun Times</u> that it's going to rain today."*

1. My grandfather asked me which one I wanted for my birthday, Laura said, a subscription to Time or one to Popular Mechanics.
2. Welcome aboard the Elissa, said the skipper. The ship was built in the 1800s, but it has been restored and is still seaworthy.
3. Emerson once said, The only way to have a friend is to be one; I think he's right.
4. In the book The Complete Essays of Mark Twain, you'll find an essay titled Taming the Bicycle.
5. Jennifer said, I never can remember whether the word necessary has one s or two.

MECHANICS

6. Beth finally figured out that when Tranh used the Vietnamese phrase không biêt, he was telling her that he didn't understand.

7. The 18 on her uniform looks like a 13, Earl said.

8. Alexandra replied, I'm surprised you watched Gone with the Wind. Two days ago you said, I don't want to see the movie until I've read the book.

9. Every week the whole family gathers in front of the television to watch Star Trek: The Next Generation.

10. The Beatles' song Yesterday has been a favorite of several generations.

B. Correcting Paragraphs of Dialogue by Adding Underlining (Italics) and Quotation Marks

The following dialogue contains ten errors in the use of underlining (italics) and quotation marks. Correct these errors by adding the appropriate marks of punctuation. [Note: Each error in the use of quotation marks involves a *pair* of single or double quotation marks.]

EXAMPLE   [1] I thought the poetry unit in English class would be dull, Ella said, but it's not. We're studying Langston Hughes, and he's great!

   1. *"I thought the poetry unit in English class would be dull," Ella said, "but it's not. We're studying Langston Hughes, and he's great!"*

[11] Oh, I've heard of him, Sly said. Didn't he write a poem called The Dream Keeper?

[12] Yes, that's one of my favorites, Ella said. An entire book of his poems is called The Dream Keeper, too. And another one of his best-known poems is called Dreams.

[13] I guess he dreamed a lot, Sly replied.

[14] Ella said, He did a lot more than that! Mrs. Berry told us that Langston Hughes traveled a lot. For a time, he was on the crew of a steamer that sailed around Africa and Europe. In fact, one of his autobiographies is called The Big Sea.

MECHANICS

14 PUNCTUATION

Apostrophes, Hyphens, Dashes, Parentheses

✓ *Checking What You Know*

A. Correcting Sentences by Using Apostrophes Correctly

In the following sentences, apostrophes are either missing or incorrectly used. Write the correct form of each incorrect word. In some cases, an apostrophe must be added or deleted; in others, the spelling of the word must be changed.

EXAMPLE   **1.** The invention of written mark's to stand for spoken words is one of humanities greatest achievements.
          1. *marks; humanity's*

1. Many ancient peoples felt that writing had a magic power of it's own.
2. Writing was practiced by the elders' of a tribe to preserve the tribes lore as well as its laws.
3. Were not sure when or how writing began, but we do know that it existed several century's before 3000 B.C.

MECHANICS

4. Theres plenty of evidence that people communicated through they're drawings long before they had a system of writing.

5. Spain and France's wonderful cave drawings were painted more than thirty thousand year's ago.

6. The ancient Peruvians message system was a complicated arrangement of knots.

7. Someones research has shown that *W*'s and *J*'s werent used in English writing until the Middle Ages.

8. In China, ones mastery of basic reading depends on learning one thousand character's.

9. Hardwick Book Stores window display features early system's of writing.

10. Bess and Robert, who's reports were on the history of writing, asked one of Mr. Hardwicks clerks for permission to examine the stores display.

B. Using Hyphens, Dashes, and Parentheses Correctly

The following paragraph contains ten errors in the use of hyphens, dashes, and parentheses. Correct each error by inserting the appropriate punctuation. Don't add commas. [Note: A pair of dashes or a pair of parentheses may be needed to correct a single error.]

EXAMPLE   [1] Only one woman has served as prime minister of Israel an independent nation since 1948.

1. *Only one woman has served as prime minister of Israel (an independent nation since 1948).*

[11] You may be surprised to know I certainly was that an exschoolteacher from Milwaukee, Wisconsin, became prime minister of Israel. [12] Golda Meir pronounced may-EAR was prime minister from 1969 to 1974. [13] She was born in the Ukraine the city of Kiev, to be exact in 1898. [14] Eight years later, her family emigrated to the United States they settled in Milwaukee. [15] She grew up and married, and she and her husband emigrated to Palestine,

where she became active in pro Jewish affairs. **[16]** She was a signer one of only two women signers, in fact of Israel's Declaration of Independence. **[17]** In her twenty six years with the government, Meir also served as minister of labor, as the foreign minister, and as Israeli ambassador to the Soviet Union. **[18]** She died in 1978 just four years after she retired. ✓

Apostrophes

Possessive Case

The *possessive case* of a noun or pronoun shows ownership or relationship.

OWNERSHIP	She is a teacher in **Maria's** school.
	Can I count on **your** vote?
RELATIONSHIP	**Larry's** friend uses a wheelchair.
	You need a good **night's** sleep.
	I appreciate **your** waiting so long.

Nouns

14a. To form the possessive case of a singular noun, add an apostrophe and an *s*.

EXAMPLES   Yuki's problem   a bus's wheel
           the mayor's desk   this evening's paper
           Mrs. Ross's job   a dollar's worth

NOTE   For a proper name ending in *s*, add only an apostrophe if adding 's would make the name awkward to pronounce.

       EXAMPLES   **Ulysses'** plan
                  Mrs. Rawlings' car
                  Texas' capital

MECHANICS

For a singular common noun ending in *s*, add both an apostrophe and an *s* if the added *s* is pronounced as a separate syllable.

EXAMPLES   the actress's costumes
the class's teacher
the dress's sleeves

14b. To form the possessive case of a plural noun ending in *s*, add only the apostrophe.

EXAMPLES   birds' feathers   cousins' visit
watches' prices   witnesses' evidence

Although most plural nouns end in *s*, some are irregular. To form the possessive case of a plural noun that does not end in *s*, add an apostrophe and an *s*.

EXAMPLES   children's shoes   deer's food   mice's tails

 REFERENCE NOTE: For more examples of irregular plurals, see page 339.

NOTE   Do not use an apostrophe to form the *plural* of a noun. Remember that the apostrophe shows ownership or relationship.

INCORRECT   Two players' left their gym suits in the locker room.
CORRECT   Two **players** left their gym suits in the locker room. [simple plural]
CORRECT   Two **players'** gym suits were left in the locker room. [The apostrophe shows that the gym suits belong to the two players.]

Pronouns

14c. Possessive personal pronouns do not require an apostrophe.

> **Possessive Personal Pronouns**
> my, mine   our, ours
> your, yours   their, theirs
> his, her, hers, its

MECHANICS

My, your, her, its, our, and *their* are used before nouns. *Mine, yours, hers, ours,* and *theirs* are never used before nouns; they are used as subjects, complements, or objects in sentences. *His* may be used in either way.

EXAMPLES   Lee has **your** sweater. Lee has a sweater of **yours.**

That is **your** watch. That watch is **yours.**

Her idea was wonderful. **Hers** was the best idea.

This is **our** plant. This plant is **ours.**

There is **his** record. There is a record of **his.**

 The possessive form of *who* is *whose,* not *who's.* Similarly, do not write *it's* for *its,* or *they're* for *their.* For more discussion of these possessive pronouns, see pages 55 and 120.

14d. Indefinite pronouns in the possessive case require an apostrophe and an *s.*

EXAMPLES   nobody**'**s wish   another**'**s viewpoint
                 someone**'**s license   neither**'**s school

 For forms such as *everyone else* and *nobody else,* the correct possessives are *everyone else's* and *nobody else's.*

 REFERENCE NOTE: For a list of indefinite pronouns, see page 56.

Compounds

14e. In compound words, names of organizations and businesses, and word groups showing joint possession, only the last word is possessive in form.

COMPOUND WORDS   community **board'**s meeting
                         vice-**president'**s contract
                         brother-in-**law'**s gift
ORGANIZATIONS   United **Fund'**s drive
BUSINESSES   Berkeley Milk **Company'**s trucks
JOINT POSSESSION   Grandmother and **Grandfather'**s house

MECHANICS

NOTE   The possessive of an acronym is formed by adding an apostrophe and an *s*.

EXAMPLES   NASA's latest space probe
CBS's hit television program

When one of the words showing joint possession is a pronoun, all the words should be possessive in form.

EXAMPLE   **Peggy's, Lisa's** and **my** tent [not *Peggy, Lisa, and my tent*]

"Sorry, but I'm going to have to issue you a summons for reckless grammar and driving without an apostrophe."

Drawing by Maslin; ©1987 The New Yorker Magazine Inc.

STYLE NOTE   If a possessive sounds awkward to you, use a phrase beginning with *of* or *for* instead.

AWKWARD   the director of the play's son
BETTER   the son of the director of the play

AWKWARD   the Society for the Prevention of Cruelty to Animals' advertisement
BETTER   the advertisement for the Society for the Prevention of Cruelty to Animals

MECHANICS

14f. When two or more persons possess something individually, each of their names is possessive in form.

EXAMPLES **Ms. Martin's** and **Ms. Blair's** cars [the cars of two different women]
Asha's and **Daniella's** tennis rackets [individual, not joint, possession]
Jason's and **Eric's** haircuts [two different haircuts]

 QUICK CHECK 1 **Forming the Possessive Case**

Revise each of the following phrases by using the possessive case.

1. the car of Miss Williams
2. the cubs of the lionesses
3. the horns of the cattle
4. the dimensions of it
5. the business of her mother-in-law and the business of her cousin
6. the field trip of our class
7. the job of my brother-in-law
8. the project of Isabel and me
9. the pay of two weeks
10. the investigation by the FBI

Contractions

14g. Use an apostrophe to show where letters, words, or numerals have been omitted in a contraction.

A *contraction* is a shortened form of a word, a figure, or a group of words. The apostrophe in a contraction indicates where letters, words, or numerals have been left out.

EXAMPLES who is...............**who's**   I am ....**I'm**
1991 ....**'91**   you are ....**you're**
of the clock ....**o'clock**   we had...................**we'd**
let us....................**let's**   she has ....**she's**
she will ....**she'll**   I had ....**I'd**

MECHANICS

Bill is	...............**Bill's**	we have	...............**we've**
there is	...........**there's**	would have	...**would've**

Ordinarily, the word *not* can be shortened to *n't* and added to a verb without any change in the spelling of the verb.

EXAMPLES	is not	.................isn't	were not	...........weren't
	are not	...........aren't	has not	................hasn't
	does not	......doesn't	have not	...........haven't
	do not	.............don't	had not	...............hadn't
	did not	...........didn't	would not	......wouldn't
	was not	.........wasn't	should not	.....shouldn't
EXCEPTIONS	will not	..........won't	cannot	...................can't

Do not confuse contractions with possessive pronouns.

CONTRACTIONS	POSSESSIVE PRONOUNS
Who's [Who is] at bat?	**Whose** bat is that?
It's [It is] roaring.	Listen to **its** roar.
You're [You are] too busy.	**Your** friend is busy.
There's [There is] a kite.	That kite is **theirs.**
They're [They are] tall trees.	**Their** trees are tall.

NOTE Contractions are appropriate in informal speaking and writing situations. Avoid using them in formal writing, however.

Plurals

14h. Use an apostrophe and an *s* to form the plurals of all lowercase letters, some capital letters, and some words that are referred to as words.

EXAMPLES Grandma always tells me to mind my *p*'s and *q*'s.
Neither the *I*'s nor the *U*'s are readable on this printout. [Without the apostrophe, the plurals would spell *Is* and *Us.*]
His *hi*'s are always loud and cheerful.
[Without an apostrophe, the plural would spell the word *his.*]

MECHANICS

You may add only an *s* to form the plurals of such items (except lowercase letters) if the plural forms won't be misread.

EXAMPLE These **VCRs** are on sale today.

 NOTE Use apostrophes consistently.

EXAMPLE Those *U*'s look like *V*'s.

Without an apostrophe, the plural of *U* would spell the word *Us*. An apostrophe and an *s* are added to the plural of *V* to make the style consistent.

 REFERENCE NOTE: For more information on forming these kinds of plurals and plurals of numerals, see page 341.

☑ *QUICK CHECK 2* **Using Apostrophes with Contractions and Plurals**

For each of the following sentences, add apostrophes where they are needed.

1. "Youve changed," she said.
2. World War II ended in 45.
3. Whos coming to the party?
4. Did Amanda say that shell be there?
5. Well, she said shed try to make it by six oclock.
6. Were hoping to see you there.
7. Its too bad well be out of town that day.
8. Dont forget to cross your *t*s and dot your *i*s.
9. Youre making all As and Bs this year, aren't you?
10. Some of your *u*s look like *o*s.

 REFERENCE NOTE: See page 324 for a summary of rules of the apostrophe.

Hyphens

Word Division

14i. Use a hyphen to divide a word at the end of a line.

MECHANICS

EXAMPLE   The reelection celebration will be organ-
           ized by the governor's campaign committee.

When you divide a word at the end of a line, keep in mind
the following rules:

(1) Do not divide one-syllable words.

INCORRECT The line of people waiting for tickets stret-
           ched halfway down the block.
  CORRECT The line of people waiting for tickets
           stretched halfway down the block.
  CORRECT The line of people waiting for tickets stretched
           halfway down the block.

(2) Divide a word only between syllables.

NOTE   If you need to divide a word and are not sure about
       its syllables, look it up in a dictionary.

**(3) Words with double consonants may usually be
divided between those two consonants.**

EXAMPLES   **con-nect   drum-mer**

 REFERENCE NOTE: See rule (4) below for exceptions
such as *fall-ing* and *will-ing*.

**(4) Usually, a word with a prefix or a suffix may be
divided between the prefix and the base word (or the
root) or between the base word (or the root) and the
suffix.**

EXAMPLES   **pre-judge   post-pone**
            fall-ing   frag-ment

**(5) Divide an already hyphenated word only at a
hyphen.**

INCORRECT The speaker this morning is my moth-
           er-in-law.
  CORRECT The speaker this morning is my mother-
           in-law.

(6) Do not divide a word so that one letter stands alone.

INCORRECT The state built a dam to generate e-
           lectricity more cleanly.

CORRECT   The state built a dam to generate electricity more cleanly.

Compound Words

Some compound words are hyphenated (*red-hot*); some are written as one word (*redhead*); some are written as two or more words (*red tape, Red River Valley*).

Whenever you need to know whether a word is hyphenated, look it up in a recent dictionary.

14j. Use a hyphen with compound numbers from *twenty-one* to *ninety-nine* and with fractions used as adjectives.

EXAMPLES   twenty-four chairs
one-half cup [*One-half* is an adjective modifying *cup*.]
one half of the flour [*Half* is a noun modified by the adjective *one*.]

14k. Use a hyphen with the prefixes *ex-*, *self-*, and *all-*; with the suffix *-elect;* and with all prefixes before a proper noun or proper adjective.

EXAMPLES   ex-coach   mid-July
self-made   pro-American
all-star   anti-Communist
president-elect   pre-Revolutionary

14l. Hyphenate a compound adjective when it precedes the noun it modifies.

EXAMPLES   a well-written book
a book that is well written

a small-town boy
a boy from a small town

Do not use a hyphen if one of the modifiers is an adverb that ends in *-ly*.

EXAMPLE   a **bitterly cold** day

MECHANICS

NOTE Some compound adjectives are always hyphenated, whether they precede or follow the nouns they modify.

EXAMPLES   a brand-new shirt
a shirt that is brand-new

a down-to-earth person
a person who is down-to-earth

If you're not sure whether a compound adjective should be hyphenated, check a recent dictionary.

 QUICK CHECK 3   **Hyphenating Words Correctly**

For each of the following sentences, add hyphens where they are needed. If a sentence is correct, write *C*.

1. The exgovernor spoke at the banquet.
2. Who do you think will win the all American trophy this year?
3. In twenty five days my grandparents will celebrate their forty fifth wedding anniversary.
4. About three fourths of the family will attend the celebration.
5. Next, add one half teaspoon of vanilla to the mixture.

Dashes

14m. Use a dash to indicate an abrupt break in thought or speech or an unfinished statement or question.

Sometimes, words, phrases, and sentences are used *parenthetically;* that is, they break into the main thought of a sentence. Parenthetical words and expressions are usually set off by commas or by parentheses.

EXAMPLES   Anne, **however,** does not agree with him.
The decision **(which player should he choose?)** weighed on Coach Johnson's mind.

Sometimes, however, parenthetical elements are such an abrupt change that a stronger mark is needed to alert the reader. In such cases, dashes are used.

MECHANICS

EXAMPLES   Judy—Ms. Lane, I mean—will be your new
            supervisor.
            Our dog—he's a long-haired dachshund—is
            too affectionate to be a good watchdog.
            "Why—why can't I come, too?" Janet asked
            hesitatingly.
            "You're being—" Tina began and then
            stopped.

NOTE   When you type or input your writing on a word
            processor, indicate a dash with two hyphens. Do not
            leave a space before, between, or after the hyphens.
            When you write by hand, use an unbroken line about
            as long as two hyphens.

14n. Use a dash to mean *namely, that is, in other
words,* and similar expressions that introduce an
explanation.

EXAMPLES   I know what we could get Mom for her
            birthday—a new photo album. [namely]
            She could put all those loose pictures—the
            ones she's taken since Christmas—in it.
            [that is]

STYLE NOTE   Either a dash or a colon is acceptable in the
            first example above. In general, avoid using
            dashes in formal writing, and don't overuse
them in any case. When you evaluate your writing, check
to see that you haven't used dashes carelessly for commas,
semicolons, and end marks. Saving dashes for instances in
which they are most appropriate will make them more
effective.

Parentheses

14o. Use parentheses to enclose material that is not
considered of major importance in a sentence.

MECHANICS

EXAMPLES   During the Middle Ages (from about A.D. 500
            to A.D. 1500), Moors and Vikings invaded
            Central Europe.
            Aunt Constance (Mother's aunt and my
            great-aunt) will meet us at the airport.

Material enclosed in parentheses may range from a single word to a short sentence. A short sentence in parentheses may stand by itself or be contained within the main sentence.

Use punctuation marks within the parentheses when the punctuation belongs with the parenthetical matter. Do not use punctuation within the parentheses if it belongs to the sentence as a whole.

EXAMPLES   Fill in the application carefully. (Use a pen.)
            That old house (it was built at the turn of the
            century) may soon become a landmark.
            After we ate dinner (we had leftovers again),
            we went to the mall.

GUIDELINES FOR PUNCTUATING PARENTHETICAL MATERIAL

Use these guidelines to determine whether to use commas, dashes, or parentheses with parenthetical material.

1. Keep in mind that only material that can be left out without changing the basic meaning of the sentence is considered parenthetical.

2. To show that elements are closely related to the rest of the sentence, use commas.

   EXAMPLE   The dog, a stray, followed us home.

3. To indicate an abrupt change in thought, use dashes.

   EXAMPLE   The dog—the poor, homeless creature!— followed us home.

4. To indicate that the material is of minor importance, use parentheses.

   EXAMPLE   The dog (it must have been someone's pet once) followed us home.

5. Don't overuse parenthetical material, or you may confuse your readers.

With the search-and-replace function of a software program, you can check your writing for the incorrect or inappropriate use of apostrophes, hyphens, dashes, and parentheses. Take full advantage of such a function when you are proofreading your work. Keep in mind, however, that such a program may not catch all of your errors. Also, a particular program may be based on rules that differ slightly from the ones in this chapter.

 QUICK CHECK 4   **Using Dashes and Parentheses Correctly**

Insert dashes or parentheses where they are needed in each of the following sentences.

1. "I'd like to thank" Tom began and then blushed and sat down.
2. We were surprised no, make that amazed to learn that the game had been called off.
3. Edna St. Vincent Millay 1892–1950 began writing poetry when she was a child.
4. "I I just don't know," she murmured.
5. In 1850, California entered the Union as a Free State. You will read more about Free States in Chapter 5.
6. Killer whales they're the ones with the black and white markings often migrate more than one thousand miles annually.
7. My brother's engagement it's a secret, by the way will be announced Sunday.
8. The valedictorian that is, the student with the highest average will be given a special award at the commencement ceremony.
9. Gwendolyn Brooks a native of Topeka, Kansas has received high praise from critics.
10. A fly-specked bank calendar you know the type hung on the kitchen wall.

MECHANICS

✓ *Chapter Review*

A. Revising Sentences in a Letter by Using Apostrophes Correctly

In the following letter to his pen pal, Josh left out some apostrophes and used others incorrectly. Write the correct form of each incorrect word in his letter.

EXAMPLE [1] Im still working on todays assignment.
　　　　　　1. *I'm; today's*

[1] Ive just finished tonights homework. [2] Writing a composition is usually two hours hard work for me, but Im pleased with this one. [3] Ill read it over in the morning to make sure that my handwritings legible. [4] My teacher has trouble with my *d*s, *t*s, and *o*s. [5] He also objects to my overuse of *and*s and *so*s. [6] If theres an error, Ill have to revise my composition a little. [7] Thats one good reason for being careful, isnt it?

[8] My compositions title is "The Reign of Animals." [9] Moms friend suggested that I call it "Whose in Charge Here?" [10] My familys love for animals is well known in the neighborhood and among our friends'. [11] At the moment were owned by two inside cats, three outside cats, our resident dog Pepper, and a visiting dog we call Hugo.

[12] During Peppers walks, Im usually followed by at least one other dog. [13] Some owners care of their dogs never seems to go beyond feeding them. [14] The city councils decision to fine owners' who let they're dogs run loose makes sense. [15] Theres one huge dog who's always wandering loose in my neighborhood. [16] His names Hugo, and weve taken him in several times after hes narrowly escaped being hit by a car. [17] In fact, Hugos and Peppers feeding dishes sit side by side in our kitchen.

[18] Peter, our senior cat, who was once one of our neighborhoods strays, isnt about to run from anyones dog. [19] At times weve seen him safeguarding other cats of ours' by running in front of them and staring down an approaching dog and it's owner. [20] Our dogs and cats different personalities never cease to fascinate me.

B. Using Hyphens, Dashes, and Parentheses Correctly

Add hyphens, dashes, and parentheses where they are needed in the following sentences. (Don't add commas in these sentences.)

EXAMPLE **1.** Henry Viscardi he founded Abilities, Inc. dedicated his life to creating opportunities for people who have disabilities.

1. *Henry Viscardi—he founded Abilities, Inc.—dedicated his life to creating opportunities for people who have disabilities.*

21. The soup was three fourths water and one fourth vegetables.

22. Twenty six students most of them from the advanced math class represented our school at the all state chess match.

23. Even though they were forced to retreat, the Battle of Bunker Hill June 17, 1775 bolstered the American colonists' self confidence.

24. The toddler murmured, "Please turn out the" and then fell asleep.

25. My sister she lives in Boston now is studying pre Columbian art.

26. If you've ever dreamed of finding buried treasure and who hasn't? your search could begin on Padre Island.

27. George Grinnell, who was one of the founders of the National Audubon Society, was a self taught expert on the American West and helped negotiate treaties with three Native American peoples the Blackfoot, the Cheyenne, and the Pawnee.

28. The ex treasurer of our club he's an extremely self confident person is now running for class president.

29. Rachel Carson was working for the U.S. Fish and Wildlife Service created in 1940 when she first recognized how pesticides threaten plant and animal life.

30. Her book *Silent Spring* copyright 1962 alerted the public to the dangers of environmental pollution.

MECHANICS

SUMMARY OF RULES OF THE APOSTROPHE

Rules		Examples
14a	singular possessive nouns	**wife's** career **hostess's** idea **pony's** harness
14b	plural possessive nouns	**students'** papers **heroes'** medals **children's** toys
14c	possessive personal pronouns (apostrophe not used)	**his** bicycle **our** TV a friend of **theirs**
14d	possessive indefinite pronouns	**everyone's** wish **somebody's** jacket **no one's** concern
14e	possessive compound nouns, nouns that show joint possession	**great-uncle's** hat Sweeper Broom **Company's** ad Maya and **Theo's** project
14f	nouns that show individual possession	**Brad's** and **Nicole's** lunches **Mr. Molina's** and **Ms. Jackson's** jobs
14g	contractions	**Who's** there? **It's** ten **o'clock**. during the **'70s**
14h	plurals of lowercase letters, some uppercase letters, and some words referred to as words	*p***'s** and *q***'s** I got two **A's**. *ha ha***'s**

MECHANICS

15 SPELLING AND VOCABULARY

Improving Your Spelling and Building Your Vocabulary

Good Spelling Habits

The following techniques can help you spell words correctly.

1. **To learn the spelling of a word, pronounce it, study it, and write it.** Pronounce words carefully. Mispronunciation can cause misspelling. For instance, if you say *mis•chie•vi•ous* instead of *mis•chie•vous*, you will probably spell the word wrong.

   - First, make sure that you know how to pronounce the word correctly, and then practice saying it.
   - Second, study the word. Notice especially any parts that might be hard to remember.
   - Third, write the word from memory. Check your spelling.
   - If you missed the word, repeat the three steps of this process.

2. **Use a dictionary.** When you find that you have mis-spelled a word, look it up in a dictionary. Don't guess about correct spelling.

STYLE NOTE   Different dictionaries show variations in spelling in different ways. To understand your dictionary's arrangement of such variations, check the guide that explains how to use the book (usually found in the front). When you look up the spelling of a word, make sure that its use isn't limited by a label such as *British* or *chiefly British* (*honour* for *honor*), *obsolete* (*vail* for *veil*), or *archaic* (*innocency* for *innocence*). In general, optional spellings that are not labeled, such as *jeweler/jew-eller,* are equally correct.

3. **Spell by syllables.** A *syllable* is a word part that can be pronounced by itself.

EXAMPLES   **thor•ough** [two syllables]
             sep•a•rate [three syllables]
             ac•com•mo•date [four syllables]

   Instead of trying to learn how to spell a whole word, break the word into its syllables whenever possible. It's easier to learn a few letters at a time than to learn all of them at once.

 REFERENCE NOTE: For information on using a dictionary to determine the pronunciation of a word, see page 445.

4. **Proofread for careless spelling errors.** Reread your writing carefully, and correct any mistakes and unclear letters. For example, make sure that your *i*'s are dotted, your *t*'s are crossed, and your *g*'s don't look like *q*'s.

5. **Keep a spelling notebook.** Divide each page into four columns:

COLUMN 1   Correctly spell the word you missed. (Never enter a misspelled word.)
COLUMN 2   Write the word again, dividing it into sylla-bles and marking the stressed syllable(s). (Use a dictionary, if necessary.)

MECHANICS

COLUMN 3   Write the word once more and circle the
            spot(s) that give you trouble.

COLUMN 4   Jot down any comments that may help you
            remember the correct spelling.

A list of commonly misspelled words appears on pages
345–346.

Correct Spelling	Syllables and Accents	Trouble Spots	Comments
probably	prob'•a•bly	prob(ab)ly	Pronounce both b's
usually	u'•su•al•ly	usua(ll)y	usual + ly (Study Rule 15e)

COMPUTER NOTE   Spell-checking software programs can help
you proofread your writing. Even the best
spelling checkers aren't foolproof, however.
Some accept British spellings, obsolete words, archaic
spellings, and words that are spelled correctly but used incorrectly (such as *affect* for *effect*). Always double-check
your writing to make sure that your spelling is error-free.

DILBERT reprinted by permission of UFS, Inc.

MECHANICS

Understanding Word Structure

Many English words are made up of word parts from other languages or earlier forms of English. Learning how to spell some commonly used word parts and how to combine them with each other can help you spell thousands of words. Learning what these word parts mean can help you increase your vocabulary. See page 345.

Roots

The *root* is the part of the word that carries the word's core meaning. Other word parts can be added to a root to create many different words. For example, the root -*duc*- or -*duct*- comes from the Latin word *ducere,* meaning "to lead." The English words in which this root appears—such as *abduct, conductor, deductible, educate, induce,* and *production*—all have something to do with leading.

COMMONLY USED ROOTS		
ROOTS	**MEANINGS**	**EXAMPLES**
Latin		
-aud-, -audit-	hear	audible, auditorium
-bene-	well, good	benefit, benevolent
-cis-	cut	incision, concise
-cogn-	know	recognize, cognition
-cred-	belief, trust	incredible, credit
-dic-, -dict-	say, speak	dictator, predict
-duc-, -duct-	lead	educate, conductor
-fac-, -fact-, -fect-, -fic-	do, make	deface, manufacture, defective, efficient
-fid-	belief, faith	confident, fidelity
-frag-, -fract-	break	fragment, fracture
-gen-	birth, kind, origin	generate, generic, generous
-jac-, -ject-	lie, throw	adjacent, eject
-junct-	join	conjunction, juncture
-loqu-, -loc-	talk, speech	colloquial, eloquent, locution

(continued)

COMMONLY USED ROOTS *(continued)*		
ROOTS	**MEANINGS**	**EXAMPLES**
-magn-	large	magnitude, magnify
-mal-	bad	malady, dismal
-mit-, -miss-	send	remit, emissary
-ped-	foot	pedal, quadruped
-pend-, -pens-	hang, weigh	pendant, suspense
-pon-, -pos-	place, put	exponent, position
-port-	carry, bear	export, important
-scrib-, -script-	write	prescribe, manuscript
-solv-	loosen, accomplish	solvent, resolve
-tract-	pull, draw	tractor, extract
-ven-, -vent-	come	intervene, supervene
-verse-, -vert-	turn	reverse, convert
-vid-, -vis-	see	television, evident
-voc-, -vok-	call	vocal, provoke
-volv-	roll, turn around	revolve, evolve
Greek		
-anthrop-	human	anthropology, misanthrope
-biblio-	book	bibliography, bibliophile
-chron-	time	chronological, synchronize
-cycl-	circle, wheel	cyclone, bicycle
-dem-	people	democracy, epidemic
-graph-	write, writing	autograph, geography
-hydr-	water	hydrant, hydrate
-log-, -logue-	study, word	logic, mythology, dialogue
-micr-	small	microbe, microscope
-mon-	one, single	monogamy, monologue
-morph-	form	metamorphosis, polymorph
-neo-	new	neologism, neolithic
-phil-	like, love	philanthropic, philosophy
-phon-	sound	phonograph, euphony
-psych-	mind	psychology, psychosomatic
-sym-, -syn-	with, together	symphony, synchronize

MECHANICS

Prefixes

A *prefix* is a word part that is added before a root. When a prefix is added to a root, the new word combines the meanings of the prefix and the root.

COMMONLY USED PREFIXES		
PREFIXES	**MEANINGS**	**EXAMPLES**
Old English		
be-	around, about	beset, behind
mis-	badly, not, wrongly	misfire, misspell
over-	above, excessive	oversee, overdo
un-	not, reverse of	untrue, unfold
Latin and Latin-French		
bi-	two	bimonthly, bisect
co-, col-, com-, con-, cor-	with, together	coexist, collide, compare, convene, correspond
contra-	against	contradict, contrast
de-	away, from, off, down	defect, desert, decline
dif-, dis-	away, off, opposing	differ, dismount, dissent
ex-, e-, -ef-	away from, out	excise, emigrate, efface
in-, im-	in, into, within	induct, impose
il-, in-, im-, ir-	not	illegal, incapable, impious, irregular
inter-	between, among	intercede, international
non-	not	nonsense, noncommittal
post-	after, following	postpone, postscript
pre-	before	prevent, preposition
pro-	forward, in place of, favoring	proceed, pronoun, pro-American
re-	back, backward, again	revoke, reflect, reforest
sub-, suf-, sum-, sup-, sus-	under, beneath	subjugate, suffuse, summon, suppose, suspect
tra-, trans-	across, beyond	traffic, transport
Greek		
anti-	against, opposing	antipathy, antithesis
dia-	through, across, apart	diagonal, diameter, diagnose
hemi-	half	hemisphere, hemicycle

(continued)

COMMONLY USED PREFIXES *(continued)*		
PREFIXES	**MEANINGS**	**EXAMPLES**
hyper-	excessive, over	hyperactive, hypertension
para-	beside, beyond	parallel, paradox
syn-, sym-, syl-, sys-	together, with	synchronize, sympathy, syllable, system

Suffixes

A *suffix* is a word part that is added after a root. Often, adding a suffix changes both a word's part of speech and its meaning.

COMMONLY USED SUFFIXES		
NOUN SUFFIXES	**MEANINGS**	**EXAMPLES**
Old English		
-dom	state, rank, condition	freedom, wisdom
-hood	state, condition	childhood, falsehood
-ness	quality, state	softness, shortness
Latin, French, Greek		
-ance, -ancy	act, condition, quality	acceptance, vigilance, hesitancy
-cy	state, condition	accuracy, normalcy
-ence	act, condition, fact	conference, patience, evidence
-er	doer, native of	baker, westerner
-ion	action, result, state	union, fusion, dominion
-ism	act, manner, doctrine	baptism, barbarism, socialism
-ist	doer, believer	monopolist, capitalist
-ity	state, quality, condition	possibility, ability, civility
-ment	means, result, action	refreshment, disappointment, acknowledgment

(continued)

COMMONLY USED SUFFIXES *(continued)*		
NOUN SUFFIXES	**MEANINGS**	**EXAMPLES**
-or	doer, office, action	director, juror, error
-tion	action, condition	selection, relation
-tude	quality, state	fortitude, multitude
ADJECTIVE SUFFIXES	**MEANINGS**	**EXAMPLES**
Old English		
-en	made of, like	wooden, golden
-ful	full of, marked by	thankful, masterful
-ish	suggesting, like	smallish, childish
-ly	like, characteristic of	friendly, cowardly
-ward	in the direction of	backward, homeward
Latin, French, Greek		
-able	able, likely	capable, changeable
-ate	having, character-istic of	animate, collegiate
-ible	able, likely, fit	edible, flexible, possible, divisible
-ous	marked by, given to	religious, furious
-went	full of, character-ized by	succulent, virulent
ADJECTIVE OR NOUN SUFFIXES	**MEANINGS**	**EXAMPLES**
-al	doer, pertaining to	rival, animal, autumnal
-ant, -ent	actor, agent, showing	servant, confident, radiant
-ary	belonging to, one connected with	primary, adversary, auxiliary
-ese	of a place or style	Chinese, journalese
-ic	dealing with, caused by, person or thing showing	classic, choleric, workaholic
-ile	marked by, one marked by	juvenile, servile
-ite	formed, showing, one marked by	favorite, composite

(continued)

MECHANICS

COMMONLY USED SUFFIXES *(continued)*		
ADJECTIVE OR NOUN SUFFIXES	**MEANINGS**	**EXAMPLES**
-ive	belonging or tending to, one belonging to	detective, native
-ory	having the nature of	sensory, advisory
VERB SUFFIXES	**MEANINGS**	**EXAMPLES**
Old English -en	cause to be, become	deepen, darken
Latin, French, Greek -ate	become, cause, treat	populate, activate, vaccinate
-esce	become, grow, continue	convalesce, acquiesce
-fy	make, cause, cause to have	glorify, identify, fortify
-ize	make, cause to be	sterilize, motorize

Spelling Rules

ie and *ei*

15a. Write *ie* when the sound is long *e*, except after *c*.

EXAMPLES	achieve	ceiling	field	piece	shield
	believe	chief	grief	receive	thief
	brief	deceit	niece	relief	yield
EXCEPTIONS	either	leisure	neither	seize	weird

15b. Write *ei* when the sound is not long *e*.

EXAMPLES	counterfeit	height	reign
	foreign	heir	veil
	forfeit	neighbor	weigh

MECHANICS

EXCEPTIONS   ancient   friend   mischief
                 conscience   kerchief   view

NOTE Rules 15a and 15b apply only when the *i* and the *e* are in the same syllable.

Born Loser reprinted by permission of NEA, Inc.

-cede, -ceed, and -sede

15c. Only one English word ends in *-sede: supersede.* Only three words end in *-ceed: exceed, proceed,* and *succeed.* All other words with this sound end in *-cede.*

EXAMPLES   accede   intercede   recede
               concede   precede   secede

Adding Prefixes

15d. When a prefix is added to a word, the spelling of the original word remains the same.

EXAMPLES   im + mortal = **im**mortal
               mis + step = **mis**step
               un + certain = **un**certain
               over + rule = **over**rule

REFERENCE NOTE: For a list of common prefixes, see pages 330–331.

MECHANICS

Adding Suffixes

15e. When the suffix *-ness* or *-ly* is added to a word, the spelling of the original word remains the same.

EXAMPLES   sure + ly = sure**ly**   fair + ness = fair**ness**
real + ly = real**ly**   late + ness = late**ness**

EXCEPTIONS   Words ending in *y* usually change the *y* to *i* before *-ness* and *-ly*:
empty + ness = empt**iness**   easy + ly = eas**ily**

NOTE   Most one-syllable adjectives ending in *y* follow rule 15e.

EXAMPLES   dry + ness = dry**ness**   sly + ly = sly**ly**

However, *true, due,* and *whole* drop the final e before *-ly*.

EXAMPLES   due + ly = du**ly**
true + ly = tru**ly**
whole + ly = whol**ly**

☞ REFERENCE NOTE: For a list of common suffixes, see pages 331–332.

 ✔ *QUICK CHECK 1*   **Spelling Words with Prefixes and Suffixes**

Spell each of the following words, including the prefix or suffix that is given.

1. un + necessary
2. il + legal
3. mis + spell
4. over + rate
5. occasional + ly

6. dull + ly
7. whole + ly
8. cleanly + ness
9. mean + ness
10. lonely + ness

15f. Drop the final silent e before adding a suffix that begins with a vowel.

EXAMPLES   hope + ing = hop**ing**
strange + est = strang**est**
noble + er = nobl**er**
admire + ation = admir**ation**

MECHANICS

tickle + ish = tick**lish**
move + able = mov**able**

EXCEPTIONS   Keep the final silent *e*

- in words ending in *ce* or *ge* before a suffix that begins with *a* or *o:* peac**eable**; knowl-edg**eable**; courag**eous**; outrag**eous**
- in *dye* and, before -*ing,* in *singe:* dy**eing**, sing**eing** (compare *die* + -*ing* = *dying* *sing* + -*ing* = *singing*)
- in *mile* before -*age* = mil**eage**

15g.   Keep the final silent e before adding a suffix that begins with a consonant.

EXAMPLES   nine + ty = nin**ety**
entire + ly = entir**ely**
hope + ful = hop**eful**
awe + some = aw**esome**
care + less = car**eless**
pave + ment = pav**ement**

EXCEPTIONS   nine + th = nin**th**
awe + ful = aw**ful**
judge + ment = judg**ment**
argue + ment = argu**ment**

15h.   When a word ends in *y* preceded by a consonant, change the *y* to *i* before any suffix except one beginning with *i.*

EXAMPLES   fifty + eth = fift**ieth**
mystery + ous = myster**ious**
worry + ed = worr**ied**
terrify + ing = terrify**ing**

EXCEPTIONS   1. some one-syllable words:
shy + ness = shy**ness**
sky + ward = sky**ward**

2. *lady* and *baby* with suffixes:
lady**like**   lady**ship**   baby**hood**

15i.   When a word ends in y preceded by a vowel, simply add the suffix.

MECHANICS

EXAMPLES   joy + ful = joy**ful**
                    boy + hood = boy**hood**
                    array + ed = array**ed**
                    gray + est = gray**est**

EXCEPTIONS   day + ly = dai**ly**   pay + ed = pa**id**
                        say + ed = sa**id**   lay + ed = la**id**

Doubling Final Consonants

15j.   When a word ends in a consonant, double the
          final consonant before a suffix that begins with a
          vowel only if the word

■ has only one syllable or is accented on the last syllable

and

■ ends in a *single* consonant preceded by a *single* vowel.

EXAMPLES   drop + ing = dro**pping**
                    occur + ence = occu**rrence**
                    plan + ed = pla**nned**
                    propel + er = prope**ller**
                    sit + ing = si**tting**
                    refer + ed = refe**rred**

Otherwise, simply add the suffix.

EXAMPLES   jump + ed = jump**ed**
                    tunnel + ing = tunnel**ing**
                    sprint + er = sprint**er**
                    appear + ance = appear**ance**

NOTE   The final consonant in some words may or may not be
          doubled. Both spellings are equally correct.

          EXAMPLES   travel + er = trave**ler** *or* trave**ller**
                            shovel + ed = shove**led** *or* shove**lling**

✓ *QUICK CHECK 2*   **Spelling Words with Suffixes**

Add the suffix given for each word, and spell the new
word formed.

1. become + ing   **3.** care + ful
2. guide + ance   **4.** satisfy + ed

MECHANICS

5. deny + al   **8.** number + ing
6. swim + er   **9.** excel + ed
7. accept + ance   **10.** riot + ous

Forming Plurals of Nouns

15k. To form the plurals of most English nouns, simply add -*s*.

SINGULAR	boat	house	nickel	radio	teacher
PLURAL	boat**s**	house**s**	nickel**s**	radio**s**	teacher**s**

15l. To form the plurals of other nouns, follow these rules.

(1) If the noun ends in *s*, *x*, *z*, *ch*, or *sh*, add -*es*.

SINGULAR	glass	box	waltz	beach	dish
PLURAL	glass**es**	box**es**	waltz**es**	beach**es**	dish**es**

 NOTE   Proper nouns usually follow this rule, too:

EXAMPLES   the *Joneses*   the *Sánchezes*

(2) If the noun ends in *y* preceded by a consonant, change the *y* to *i* and add -*es*.

SINGULAR	army	baby	sky	story	mystery
PLURAL	arm**ies**	bab**ies**	sk**ies**	stor**ies**	myster**ies**
EXCEPTION	The plurals of proper nouns: the Hard**ys**, the Car**ys**				

(3) If the noun ends in *y* preceded by a vowel, add -*s*.

SINGULAR	joy	key	bay	valley	Momaday
PLURAL	joy**s**	key**s**	bay**s**	valley**s**	Momaday**s**

(4) For some nouns ending in *f* or *fe*, add -*s*. For other such nouns, change the *f* or *fe* to *v* and add -*es*.

EXAMPLES   belief → belief**s**   calf → cal**ves**
                giraffe → giraffe**s**   knife → kni**ves**
                roof → roof**s**   leaf → lea**ves**
                safe→ safe**s**   wife → wi**ves**

MECHANICS

NOTE Noticing how the plural is pronounced will help you remember whether to change the *f* or *fe* to *v*.

(5) If the noun ends in *o* preceded by a vowel, add *-s*.

SINGULAR	radio	patio	stereo
	kangaroo	Julio	
PLURAL	radios	patios	stereos
	kangaroos	Julios	

(6) If the noun ends in *o* preceded by a consonant, add *-es*.

SINGULAR	echo	hero	tomato	veto
PLURAL	echoes	heroes	tomatoes	vetoes

EXCEPTIONS Some common nouns ending in *o* preceded by a consonant, especially musical terms, and some proper nouns form the plural by adding only *-s*.

SINGULAR	peso	sombrero	photo	alto
	piano	solo	Sotho	Sakamoto
PLURAL	pesos	sombreros	photos	altos
	pianos	solos	Sothos	Sakamotos

NOTE A number of nouns that end in *o* preceded by a consonant have two plural forms.

SINGULAR	cargo	grotto	hobo
PLURAL	cargos	grottos	hobos
	or	*or*	*or*
	cargoes	grottoes	hoboes

If you are in doubt about how to spell the plural of a word ending in *o* preceded by a consonant, check the spelling in a current dictionary.

(7) The plurals of some nouns are formed in irregular ways.

SINGULAR	child	foot	goose	man	tooth
PLURAL	children	feet	geese	men	teeth

(8) Some nouns have the same form in both the singular and the plural.

EXAMPLES	deer	sheep	Chinese
	moose	species	Japanese
	series	trout	Navajo

Compound Nouns

(9) If a compound noun is written as one word, form the plural by adding *-s* or *-es* to the end of the compound.

SINGULAR   spoonful   smashup   icebox

PLURAL   spoonful**s**   smashup**s**   icebox**es**

(10) If a compound noun is hyphenated or written as two words, make the main noun plural. The *main noun* is the noun that is modified.

SINGULAR   sister-in-law   runner-up   attorney-at-law

PLURAL   sister**s**-in-law   runner**s**-up   attorney**s**-at-law

A few compound nouns form the plural in irregular ways.

EXAMPLES   go-between   mix-up   six-year-old

           go-between**s**   mix-up**s**   six-year-old**s**

NOTE   Whenever you're not sure about the plural form of a compound noun, check a recent dictionary.

Latin and Greek Loan Words

(11) Some nouns borrowed from Latin and Greek form the plural as they do in the original language.

SINGULAR	PLURAL
alumnus [male]	alumn**i**
alumna [female]	alumn**ae**
analysis	analys**es**
crisis	cris**es**
datum	dat**a**
phenomenon	phenomen**a**

NOTE   A few Latin and Greek loanwords have two plural forms.

SINGULAR   appendix   formula   radius

PLURAL   appendi**ces**   formula**s**   radi**i**

       or   *or*   *or*

       appendi**xes**   formul**ae**   radius**es**

To find the preferred spelling of a plural loanword, check a dictionary. The preferred spelling is the one listed first.

MECHANICS

Numerals, Letters, Symbols, and Words Used as Words

(12) To form the plurals of numerals, most capital letters, symbols, and words used as words, add either an *-s* or an apostrophe and an *-s*.

EXAMPLES   Put the **6s** [or **6's**] and the **Rs** [or **R's**] in the second column.
Change the **&s** [or **&'s**] to ***ands*** [or ***and's***].
My parents were teenagers during the **'60s** [or **'60's**].
Many immigrants came to this country during the **1800s** [or **1800's**].

 REFERENCE NOTE: See pages 464–466 for information on when to spell out numbers.

To prevent confusion, always use an apostrophe and an *-s* to form the plurals of lowercase letters, certain capital letters, and some words used as words.

EXAMPLES   Your ***i's*** look like ***e's***. [Without an apostrophe, the plural of *i* would look like *is.*]
Ramón got all **A's** last semester. [Without an apostrophe, the plural of *A* would look like *As.*]
Her ***and so's*** get tiresome after a while. [Without the apostrophe, the plural of *so* would look like *sos.*]

 NOTE   Using both an apostrophe and an *s* is never wrong. Therefore, if you have any doubt about whether or not to use the apostrophe, use it.

 REFERENCE NOTE: For more information on forming these kinds of plurals, see pages 314–315.

✓ *QUICK CHECK 3*   **Spelling the Plurals of Nouns**

Write the plural form of each of the following nouns.

1. guess
2. tongue
3. navy
4. cuff
5. theory
6. soprano
7. stereo
8. editor in chief
9. layoff
10. moose

MECHANICS

Learning New Words

One of the best ways to learn new words is to discover them when reading. You can increase your vocabulary by looking at how an unfamiliar term is used in a particular sentence or paragraph. Other ways of learning new words include knowing the meanings of frequently used word parts and learning how the parts are combined to form new words.

Adding to Your Word Bank

One good way to increase your vocabulary is to create a word bank. Start saving words. When you come across new words in your classes or in your reading, write these new vocabulary words in your notebook along with their definitions. Check your dictionary to see if you have understood the meaning of each word.

HOIST UP THE MAINSAIL!

TRIM THE UH...

THING.

I RUN OUT OF NAUTICAL TERMS REAL FAST.

Overboard copyright 1990 Universal Press Syndicate. Reprinted with permission. All rights reserved.

MECHANICS

Using Context Clues

Sometimes you can figure out the meaning of an unfamiliar word by examining the *context* in which it's used. The context of a word includes the words that surround the word and the circumstances in which the word is used. Sometimes clues that help define the word can be found in the sentence in which an unfamiliar word appears.

The following chart shows examples of some of the common types of context clues.

TYPES OF CONTEXT CLUES	
TYPE OF CLUE	**EXPLANATION**
Definitions and Restatements	Look for words that define the term or restate it in other words. ■ The judge seemed *impartial,* not favoring one side in the case over the other.
Examples	Look for examples that reveal the meaning of an unfamiliar word. ■ Many *sovereigns* attended the exhibit, including the Queen of England and the King of Denmark.
Synonyms	Look for clues that indicate that an unfamiliar word is similar in meaning to a familiar word or phrase. ■ Rico, like his overjoyed teammates, was *exultant* about the team's victory.
Comparisons	Look for clues that indicate that an unfamiliar word is compared with a familiar word. ■ The latest *submissions* are better than any entries previously received.
Contrast	Look for clues that indicate that an unfamiliar word is contrasted to a familiar word or phrase. ■ Instead of being stormy, the weather turned *balmy* in the afternoon.
Cause and Effect	Look for clues that indicate that an unfamiliar word is related to the cause of or is the result of an action, feeling, or idea. ■ Because his pet lizard was lost, Mark felt *dejected.*

MECHANICS

Determining Meanings from the General Context

Writers don't include obvious context clues in every sentence—or even in every paragraph. Sometimes you have to read an entire passage to understand the meaning of a word. However, you can draw on your own knowledge and experience of the topic to help you figure out the meanings of many unfamiliar terms.

Choosing the Right Word

Many English words have more than one meaning. Therefore, when you're looking for the meaning of a word, look at *all* the definitions given. Keep in mind the context in which you read or heard the word. Then try the various definitions in that context until you find the one that fits best.

If your dictionary provides sample contexts (words surrounding the defined word), use them to determine which meaning of the word best fits the context in which you encountered it.

English contains many *synonyms*—words that have the same general meaning but also have subtle shades of difference between them. Choosing the right synonym is very important when you are trying to write clearly and effectively. Make sure that you understand the exact context in which the word is being used in order to choose the right synonym to fit your purpose.

Keep in mind, too, that even words that have the same *denotation,* or dictionary definition, may have different *connotations,* or feelings associated with them. For example, the words *adequate* and *sufficient* both mean "enough." However, *sufficient,* which suggests exactly what is needed, has a more positive connotation than *adequate,* which suggests just barely enough. Similarly, the words *dispute* and *debate* both denote an argument. Yet a *debate* is a formal process in which speakers from both sides of the issue have time to present their points. A *dispute* is a much more heated or angrier argument than a debate is.

Using Word Parts

Most English words are of two kinds: those that can be divided into smaller parts (*ungracious, distrust*) and those that cannot (*truth, power*). Words that are complete by themselves are called **base words.** Words that can be subdivided are made up of two or more word parts. The three types of word parts are

- roots
- prefixes
- suffixes

Learning the meanings of some of the most commonly used word parts can help you figure out the meanings of unfamiliar words. Whenever you encounter a word that you don't know, refer to the lists of word parts on pages 328–333. First, determine the meaning of each part of the word. Then, use those meanings to make up a definition for the unfamiliar word as a whole. Check a recent dictionary to find the real definition of the word. You'll soon improve your ability to figure out the meanings of unfamiliar words.

75 Commonly Misspelled Words

The following list contains seventy-five words that are often misspelled. To find out which words give you difficulty, ask someone to read you the list in groups of twenty-five. Write down each word; then check your spelling. Make a list in your spelling notebook of any word you misspelled. Keep reviewing your list until you have mastered the correct spelling.

ache	always	busy
across	answer	buy
again	belief	can't
all right	built	color
almost	business	coming

MECHANICS

cough	know	tear
could	laid	though
country	likely	through
doctor	making	tired
doesn't	meant	together
don't	minute	tomorrow
eager	often	tonight
easy	once	tough
every	ready	trouble
February	really	truly
forty	safety	Tuesday
friend	said	until
grammar	says	wear
guess	shoes	Wednesday
half	since	where
having	speak	which
heard	speech	whole
hour	straight	women
instead	sugar	won't
knew	surely	write

300 Spelling Words

Learn to spell the following words if you don't already know how. They're grouped so that you can study them ten at a time.

absence	acquaintance	anticipate
absolutely	actually	apology
acceptance	administration	apparent
accidentally	affectionate	appearance
accommodate	agriculture	approach
accompany	amateur	approval
accomplish	ambassador	arguing
accurate	analysis	argument
accustomed	analyze	assurance
achievement	announcement	attendance

MECHANICS

authority
available
basically
beginning
believe
benefit
benefited
boundary
calendar
campaign

capital
category
certificate
characteristic
chief
circuit
circumstance
civilization
column
commissioner

committee
comparison
competent
competition
conceivable
conception
confidential
conscience
conscious
consistency

constitution
continuous
control
cooperate
corporation
correspondence
criticism
criticize
cylinder
debtor

decision
definite
definition
deny
description
despise
diameter
disappearance
disappointment
discipline

disgusted
distinction
distinguished
dominant
duplicate
economic
efficiency
eighth
elaborate
eligible

embarrass
emergency
employee
encouraging
environment
equipped
essential
evidently
exaggerate
exceedingly

excellent
excessive
excitable
exercise
existence
expense
extraordinary
fascinating
fatal
favorably

fictitious
financier
flourish
fraternity
frequent
further
glimpse
glorious
grabbed
gracious

graduating
grammar
gross
gymnasium
happiness
hasten
heavily
hindrance
humorous
hungrily

hypocrisy
hypocrite
icy
ignorance
imagination
immediately
immense
incidentally
indicate
indispensable

inevitable
innocence
inquiry
insurance
intelligence
interfere
interpretation
interrupt
investigation
judgment

MECHANICS

knowledge
leisure
lengthen
lieutenant
likelihood
liveliness
loneliness
magazine
maneuver
marriage

marvelous
mechanical
medieval
merchandise
minimum
mortgage
multitude
muscle
mutual
narrative

naturally
necessary
negligible
niece
noticeable
obligation
obstacle
occasionally
occurrence
offense

official
omit
operation
opportunity
oppose
optimism
orchestra
organization
originally
paid

paradise
parallel
particularly
peasant
peculiar
percentage
performance
personal
personality
perspiration

persuade
petition
philosopher
picnic
planning
pleasant
policies
politician
possess
possibility

practically
precede
precisely
preferred
prejudice
preparation
pressure
primitive
privilege
probably

procedure
proceed
professor
proportion
psychology
publicity
pursuit
qualities
quantities
readily

reasonably
receipt
recognize
recommendation
referring
regretting
reign
relieve
remembrance
removal

renewal
repetition
representative
requirement
residence
resistance
responsibility
restaurant
rhythm
ridiculous

sacrifice
satire
satisfied
scarcely
scheme
scholarship
scissors
senate
sensibility
separate

sergeant
several
shepherd
sheriff
similar
skis
solemn
sophomore
source
specific

sponsor
straighten
substantial
substitute
subtle
succeed
successful
sufficient
summary
superior

suppress
surprise
survey
suspense
suspicion
temperament
tendency
thorough
transferring
tremendous

truly
unanimous
unfortunately
unnecessary
urgent
useful
using
vacancies
vacuum
varies

MECHANICS

COMPOSITION

351

16 THE WRITING PROCESS

Writing involves more than sitting down with pen and paper and creating a polished piece of work on the first try. As the diagram below shows, writing is a process. At any point in the process, you can go back to an earlier stage or even start all over again.

Thinking is an important part of the writing process. In fact, in the first stage, prewriting, you do much more thinking than writing. Later in the process, you may focus more on writing than on thinking. In this chapter you will explore each stage of the process.

COMPOSITION

Prewriting

Finding Ideas for Writing

As long as people have been writing, they've been spending time thinking up ideas. The techniques in this section will help you think up ideas and will make writing an easier job.

Drawing by Booth; © 1976 The New Yorker Magazine, Inc.

"Write about dogs!"

Keeping a Writer's Journal

If you don't have one now, start keeping a **writer's journal.** Use your journal to record experiences and observations, feelings and opinions, ideas and questions. You can also use your journal to collect poems, songs, quotations, newspaper articles, cartoons—anything that pleases you. Here are some suggestions for getting started.

1. Use a blank book, a special notebook, or a file folder.
2. Get in the habit of writing daily, and date your entries. Some people like to write every day at a certain time—

maybe at night while listening to music. Others keep their journals handy and write whenever inspiration strikes.

3. Don't worry about grammar and punctuation.

4. Use your imagination. Write down dreams and day-dreams. Try creating songs, poems, story ideas. Decorate your journal with drawings or cartoons.

5. If you include something you like (a quotation, article, song lyric), tell why you like it or what it makes you think about.

Freewriting

When you **freewrite,** you write whatever pops into your head. If you have trouble getting started, look at the guidelines below for suggestions on approaches to freewriting.

1. Set a timer for three to five minutes, and keep writing until the timer goes off.

2. Start with a word or topic that's important to you. Write whatever the word or topic makes you think about or remember. Don't worry about complete sentences or proper punctuation.

3. If you can't think of anything new to write, copy the same word or phrase until something comes to mind.

4. You can also focus on one word or phrase from your original freewriting and use it to start freewriting again. This is called *focused freewriting* or *looping,* because you make a loop between freewritings.

HERE'S HOW

> Freedom. Freedom. Freedom—feeling free. Statue of Liberty
> I saw last year. Freedom. Feeling free on warm spring day when
> coats come off. Bell ringing at 3:15. Being outside in the sun and
> wind. Not everyone's so free. What about animals in cages at
> zoos? What about animals in cages? What about whales that
> swim around in small tanks? Do we have a right to do that to
> animals? IS FREEDOM ONLY FOR HUMANS?

COMPOSITION

A word processor can be a good tool for freewriting. But because it's so easy to edit on a word processor, you might be tempted to interrupt the flow of ideas in order to make corrections. When you're freewriting on a word processor, try turning the resolution of the monitor all the way down so that you don't *see* your words until you've put all of your thoughts down.

Brainstorming

Brainstorming is a way of coming up with ideas by using free association. You can brainstorm alone, with a partner, or in a group. Here's how it works.

1. Write any subject at the top of a sheet of paper (or on the chalkboard).
2. List every idea about the subject that comes to your mind. One person should record all of the ideas.
3. Don't stop to evaluate (judge) any of the ideas.
4. Keep going until you run out of ideas.

mummies	peat bog mummies
daddies	movie mummies
Egyptian mummies	Boris Karloff
famous mummies	horror movies—mummies trailing bandages
Pharaoh mummies	mummies—how preserved
King Tut	mummies—why
graves	religion
grave robberies	afterlife

Clustering

Clustering is sometimes called *webbing* or *making connections*. Like brainstorming, it is useful for thinking of topics or gathering information. When you use clustering, you break a large subject into its smaller parts, just as you do when you brainstorm. (You can also organize ideas with a *tree diagram,* showing your main subject as the trunk and supporting details as the branches and twigs.)

1. Begin by writing a subject in the center of your paper. Circle the subject.
2. In the space around the subject, write whatever related ideas occur to you. Circle each one, and draw a line from each to the original subject.
3. Let your mind wander. New ideas may make you think of other related ideas. Keep drawing circles and lines to show the connections.

Asking Questions

Reporters often collect information for their news stories by using the **5W-How? questions:** *Who? What? Where? When? Why? How?* Not every question applies to every topic, and sometimes you can think of more than one good question for a question word.

COMPOSITION

CUBAN REVOLUTION

HERE'S HOW

WHO? Who were the major political figures in the Cuban Revolution?

WHAT? What were the causes of the Cuban Revolution? What were some results?

WHERE? Where did political refugees go?

WHEN? When did the Cuban Revolution take place?

WHY? Why did some Cubans flee to the United States?

HOW? How did the revolution affect life in Cuba?

Using Your Five Senses

Every second you're awake, your brain is taking in information through all five senses: sight, hearing, smell, taste, and touch. If you stop to focus on all the sensory details around you, you'll have an endless supply of specific details for your writing. Suppose you spent a day at a Chinese New Year's festival. You might make notes like these:

HERE'S HOW

TOUCH: damp, chilly morning; cool breeze; warmth of sun when it comes out about 11 o'clock; crisp, crunchy, fried won tons

HEARING: cymbals and drums as parade goes by; cheering of spectators; chatter of street vendors and their customers; gong of passing streetcar

SMELL: garlic and ginger cooking in hot oil; egg rolls frying; dumplings cooking in bamboo steamers

TASTE: tangy hot tea; salty soy sauce on steamed dumpling; spicy hot mustard and sweet plum sauce on egg roll

SIGHT: dazzling light; many colors of merchandise in street vendors' carts; red-and-gold decorations on dragon in parade; hanging above the streets, banners with Chinese characters

Reading with a Focus

Reading to find specific information is very different from reading for pleasure. When you read to find information, you look for main ideas and supporting details. Keep these suggestions in mind.

1. Don't read everything. Use the index, check the table of contents, and look for chapter headings and subheadings. Skim, or glance through, the material, searching only for information about your topic.
2. When you find relevant information, slow down. Read carefully for main ideas. Take notes on specific details as well as main ideas.

Listening with a Focus

You can also gather ideas for writing by listening to radio and television programs, to audio tapes, and to experts during personal or telephone interviews. Use these suggestions to prepare in advance.

1. Write down your topic.
2. Brainstorm what you already know about the topic, or refer to your notes if you've already done some research.
3. Write down what you want to know. This list of questions should help guide and focus your listening.
4. With your questions in front of you, listen carefully. Take careful notes, and don't let your mind wander.

Asking "What if?" Questions

Asking *"What if?" questions* is a creative thinking technique that can help you gather ideas for writing. It's really an exercise in cause-and-effect thinking. If one thing changes (cause), what will happen (effect)? Asking questions like these can help you discover topics and details.

1. *What if I could change one thing in the past?* (What if there had never been wars between countries? What if schools had never been invented?)

2. *What if something we take for granted were totally different?* (What if the sun never shone and it was always night on earth? What if there were no gravity on earth?)
3. *What if I could make one change in the way an object or situation is now?* (What if cars weren't allowed in cities? What if there were no such thing as television?)

You can also ask "What if?" questions about a specific topic.

HERE'S HOW

How to Get More Americans to Vote

- <u>What if</u> everyone who didn't vote had to pay a fine?

- <u>What if</u> people who did vote in every election were rewarded in some way—say, with a credit on their income tax?

- <u>What if</u> everybody over eighteen were mailed a ballot and a stamped envelope, and the only way you could vote was by mail?

Visualizing

Visualizing means making images of something in your "mind's eye." With visualizing, you can use all your senses, not just sight, to think of details for your writing. For example, visualizing yourself driving a snappy red sports car down a country road at sunset on a hot summer day calls up more details than just thinking about cars in general.

You can also visualize the answer to a "What if?" question, as in the example below.

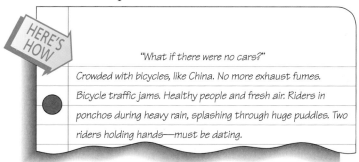

HERE'S HOW

"What if there were no cars?"

Crowded with bicycles, like China. No more exhaust fumes.

Bicycle traffic jams. Healthy people and fresh air. Riders in

ponchos during heavy rain, splashing through huge puddles. Two

riders holding hands—must be dating.

⊖ *Prewriting*

Considering Purpose, Audience, and Tone

Thinking About Your Purpose

When you write, you always have some *purpose* in mind. You write in many different forms, but you have one or more of these basic purposes. (A single piece of writing may combine two or more purposes.)

MAIN PURPOSE	FORMS OF WRITING
To express yourself	Journal, letter, personal essay
To be creative	Short story, poem, play, novel
To explain, inform or explore	Science and history writing, newspaper or magazine article, biography, autobiography, travel essay
To persuade	Persuasive essay, letter to the editor, advertisement, political speech

Analyzing Your Audience

As you consider your purpose, think about your *audience* (your readers) at the same time. You may not realize it, but you often write for many different audiences. In a journal or in prewriting notes, you write for yourself. You may write letters to friends or relatives or even to school or local newspapers. As you practice writing in school, you often write for your teachers and classmates. Good writers—ones who get their ideas across—always tailor what they say and how they say it to fit their audiences.

Unless you're writing for yourself, audiences always expect certain things from you. For example, they expect writing that is clear and easy to understand. They also expect writing that shows that you're knowledgeable about your topic. Before you write, consider these questions about your audience.

- Why is my audience reading my writing? Do they expect to be informed, amused, or persuaded?
- What does my audience already know about my topic? (Is there a way to take advantage of what they already know?)
- What does the audience want or need to know about the topic? What will interest them?
- What type of language suits my readers? Should vocabulary be simple or somewhat complex? Should sentences be long, short, or a combination of both?

Creating Tone

When you speak, your tone of voice lets your audience know how you feel about your subject—and about your listeners. In writing, too, you can sound formal or informal, personally involved or detached, sincere or sarcastic, serious or playful. The *tone* you create comes from your word choice, your choice of details, and your sentence structure.

To create a tone that conveys your attitude, be aware of

- **Word Choice.** Contractions, colloquialisms, and first-person pronouns help create a conversational, informal tone. Precise, objective words, technical or scientific terms, and third-person pronouns tend to create a more formal, serious tone.
- **Choice of Details.** Impersonal facts and statistics contribute to a serious, detached tone. Anecdotes and personal examples help create a relaxed, informal tone.
- **Sentence Length and Structure.** In general, short, simple sentences result in an informal tone. Longer, more complex sentences can produce a more formal tone.

Whatever your audience or purpose, try to write in a genuine, natural *voice*. Even in a formal essay, you don't want to sound stuffy or stilted. Using a natural voice in your writing doesn't mean being careless with language. But it does mean sounding like yourself.

Prewriting

Arranging Ideas

COMPOSITION

Before you start writing, you need to spend some time arranging your prewriting ideas. The following chart shows four of the most common ways of ordering, or arranging, information.

ARRANGING IDEAS		
TYPE OF ORDER	**DEFINITION**	**EXAMPLES**
Chronological	Narration: Order in which events happen in time	Story, narrative poem, explanation of a process, history, biography, drama
Spatial	Description: Order in which objects are described according to location	Descriptions (near to far, left to right, top to bottom, and so forth)
Importance	Evaluation: Order in which details are given, from least to most important or the reverse	Persuasive writing, description, explanations (main idea and supporting details), evaluative writing
Logical	Classification: Order in which items and groups are related	Definitions and classifications

REFERENCE NOTE: For more information on arranging ideas, see pages 388–394.

How you arrange ideas depends on your purpose, audience, and topic. Sometimes, information is arranged to be helpful to the people who will use it. Names in a telephone book, for example, are arranged in alphabetical order. Television schedules are arranged in the order the shows are broadcast. Sometimes, the subject itself suggests an order. For example, the events involved in the surrender of General Robert E. Lee to General Ulysses S. Grant at Appomattox took place over time. Thus, the natural order for a paper about the surrender is chronological. If you were to discuss the *reasons* for Lee's surrender, however, order of importance would probably be a good way to present the information.

Using Charts

Making a chart is a good way to arrange your prewriting notes, because a chart is actually a graphic aid for ordering information. The most important step in creating a chart is to decide on the headings that will cover the information. Here is a chart about scientific research that can be conducted in space. The writer wants to organize information according to two categories: the branch of science and the type of experiment, or study.

SCIENTIFIC RESEARCH IN SPACE	
BRANCH OF SCIENCE	**TYPE OF EXPERIMENT**
Biology	Experiments on how zero gravity affects the biological clocks of living things such as fish and plants
Physics	Experiments on how zero gravity affects the development or manufacture of crystals
Astronomy	Studies of the universe, using X-ray astronomy, without the distorting effects of the earth's atmosphere

To organize information for a chart, read through your notes and ask yourself these two questions:

- Which items seem closely related to one another? List each group of related items together on a separate paper.
- What do all of the items on each new list have in common? In other words, what makes them go together? Answering this question will give you the headings for your chart.

 REFERENCE NOTE: See pages 398–400 and 418–423 for information on creating prewriting plans and formal outlines.

COMPOSITION

COMPUTER NOTE

A computer lets you group and regroup information from your notes until you're satisfied that related items appear together. It also lets you create charts and graphics.

A time line is a way to arrange information chronologically. The following example traces civil rights events.

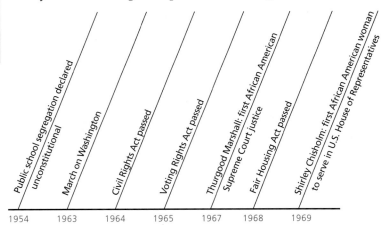

Public school segregation declared unconstitutional
March on Washington
Civil Rights Act passed
Voting Rights Act passed
Thurgood Marshall: first African American Supreme Court justice
Fair Housing Act passed
Shirley Chisholm: first African American woman to serve in U.S. House of Representatives

1954   1963   1964   1965   1967   1968   1969

Writing a First Draft

There's no single approach to turning prewriting notes into a first draft. Some writers work from very rough prewriting notes, while others work from a detailed outline. Some write quickly to get their ideas down on paper in sentences. Others shape each sentence slowly and connect ideas carefully. As you write your first draft, try these suggestions.

- Use your prewriting plans to guide your draft.
- Write freely, focusing on expressing your ideas clearly.
- Include new ideas that you discover about your topic.
- Don't worry about correcting errors in grammar, usage, and mechanics at this stage—you can do that later.

COMPOSITION

Here is the first draft of a paragraph about being an active listener. As you read, notice how the writer makes some changes even in the first draft. Also notice how the writer indicates a return to prewriting by inserting notes to be checked later. You can do the same things as you develop your own first draft.

HERE'S HOW

I read somewhere the other day that it's not enough to just listen to people, you should be a listener. That means that you <u>really</u> listen to what another person is saying. In case you're interested, here are some of the things that an active listener is supposed to do. First, you should make eye contact. Eye contact means the listener is looking at you—he or she's not reading a newspaper or watching television or looking around at other people in the room. An active listener says things like [NOTE: check brainstorming list for what listener says.] That shows he's still awake and paying attention. My sister Sara really listens, and I think that might be why she's so popular and people like her so much. Sara gives off the feeling that she really cares about you. ~~There are~~ *An active listener uses* nonverbal clues too. [NOTE: Find out exactly what these clues are—can't remember.]

Getting those first ideas down on paper isn't easy, and they're usually far from perfect—but that's okay. If you have a hard time beginning your first draft, try these tips.

- Force yourself to write. Get a piece of paper, sit down, and don't get up until you fill one side of it.
- Make an appointment with yourself. Set aside a definite time and place, and don't get up or do anything else until you've finished the first draft (or at least a big chunk of it).
- When you've finished, reward yourself! Call a friend, listen to your favorite tape, or go outside to shoot some baskets.

Hagar the Horrible reprinted with special permission of King Features Syndicate, Inc.

Evaluating and Revising

Evaluating means deciding on the strengths or weaknesses of a paper. *Revising* is making needed improvements.

Evaluating

You may not realize it, but you evaluate all the time: the movies and television programs you see, the music you hear. And you use those evaluations to decide whether to watch the show again or buy the tape. It's much harder to evaluate your own work, though, especially your writing.

Self-Evaluation

These techniques can help you evaluate your own writing.

> ## TIPS FOR SELF-EVALUATION
>
> 1. **Reading Carefully.** Read your paper at least three times. First read for *content* (what you say), then for *organization* (how you've arranged your ideas), and then for *style* (how you've used words and sentences).
> 2. **Listening Carefully.** Read your draft aloud and try to "hear" what you've written. Sometimes you notice things you wouldn't pick up during a silent reading.
> 3. **Taking Time.** Set your draft aside for a while and come back to it later. Taking time away from your work can help you become objective about it.

Peer Evaluation

Professional writers almost always have someone else read what they've written. They know that another person always has a more objective eye. You can use this technique yourself by working in peer-evaluation groups with your classmates. A group may be as small as just you and a partner, or it may include four or five students. In a peer-evaluation group, you will have two roles—part of the time you'll be the writer whose work is being evaluated, and part of the time you'll be the evaluator of someone else's work. Here are some guidelines for filling both of these roles.

> ## PEER-EVALUATION GUIDELINES
>
> ### Guidelines for the Writer
> 1. Make a list of questions or concerns for your classmate. What part of your paper are you worried about?
> 2. Keep a positive attitude. Try to make use of the evaluator's comments rather than being defensive about them.
>
> ### Guidelines for the Peer Evaluator
> 1. Remember that people like to know what they've done well. Tell your classmate what you think is particularly effective. Point out strengths as well as weaknesses.
> 2. Provide some encouragement—suggest something your classmate can do to improve the paper.
> 3. Look at content and organization. Don't comment on mechanical errors such as spelling or punctuation.
> 4. Be sensitive to the writer's feelings. When you spot a weakness, try asking a question about it rather than pointing it out as a problem.

COMPOSITION

Shoe, by Jeff MacNelly, reprinted by permission: Tribune Media Services.

Revising

Now it's time to think about the evaluations. Which comments from your classmates do you think are most helpful, given your purpose and audience? Which suggested changes do you want to make? Once you've decided, you can begin revising—making the actual changes in your paper's content, organization, and style.

The important thing is not to take a shortcut and skip the revising stage. If you write in longhand or use a typewriter, write or type your paper over again. Make handwritten corrections on your paper, perhaps using a different color ink, and then write or type a new copy. You can indicate any changes by using the revising and proofreading symbols on pages 374–375.

COMPUTER NOTE

If you have a word processor, you'll find revising easier. Be sure to mark your revisions on a *hard copy,* or printout. Otherwise, you can't see your paper as a whole, from beginning to end. When you're satisfied with your paper, input the changes and print out a new copy.

When you revise, use the following techniques to make changes.

COMPOSITION

REVISING	
TECHNIQUE	**EXAMPLE**
1. Add. Add new information and details to help your audience understand your main idea. Add words, phrases, sentences, whole paragraphs.	The Mayas *↑a Native American people↑* wrote in hieroglyphics and used extremely accurate calendars.
2. Cut. Take out information, details, examples, or words that will distract your audience. Cut repetition, wordiness, and details unrelated to your main idea.	The Mayas' civilization flourished until it fell to Spanish conquistadors about ~~the year~~ A.D. 1600.
3. Replace. Take out weak words, clichés, awkward-sounding sentences, unnecessary information or details. Replace with more precise words, more relevant details, and more vivid comparisons.	The Living Maya is a book by Jeffrey Foxx with *detailed* ~~really very~~ beautiful color photographs of Mayas today in *Central America and Mexico.* ~~various parts of the world.~~
4. Reorder. Move information, details, examples, or paragraphs for variety and an order that makes sense.	If you are at all interested in photography, you will enjoy reading this book, or in Native American traditions, about the Mayas.

COMPOSITION

Here's the paragraph on active listening (page 365), revised by using the four revision techniques. To understand the changes, refer to the chart of Symbols for Revising and Proofreading on pages 374–375. Notice how the writer has answered the notes in the first draft.

HERE'S HOW

I read ~~somewhere the other day~~ that it's not enough (to just) listen to people, you should be a listener. That means that you really listen to what another person is saying. ~~In case you're interested,~~ here are some of the things that an active listener ^should^ ~~is supposed to~~ do. First, you should make eye contact. ~~Eye~~ ^This^ means that you should look into the speaker's ~~contact means the listener is looking at~~ eyes as you listen. You don't read ~~you he or she's not reading~~ a newspaper or watching television or looking around at other people in the room. An active listener ^also responds with^ ~~says things like~~ "Yes," "Uh-huh," or "Really?" every once in a while. ^Do this to show^ ~~That shows~~ that ^you are^ ~~he or she's~~ interested, ~~she's~~ still awake and paying attention. My sister Sara really listens, and I think that might be why she's so popular. Sara gives ^people^ ~~off~~ the feeling that she really cares about ^them^ ~~you.~~ ^Finally,^ an active listener uses ~~There are~~ nonverbal clues, too. ~~Nonverbal means body language, an active listener~~ ^You^ might nod, ^and^ lean~~s~~ forward, ~~as if what they're~~ ^to show that what the speaker's saying^ ~~listening to~~ is really important ^to you.^

Following are some general guidelines that apply to all types of writing.

GUIDELINES FOR EVALUATING AND REVISING

EVALUATION GUIDE	REVISION TECHNIQUE
CONTENT	
1 Is the writing interesting?	**Add** examples, an anecdote (brief story), dialogue, or additional details. **Cut** repetitious or boring details.
2 Does the writing do what the writer wanted it to do?	**Add** details that inform or explain, express feelings, create pictures, or persuade.
3 Are there enough details?	**Add** more details, facts, or examples to support ideas about the topic.
4 Are there unrelated ideas or details that distract the reader?	**Cut** irrelevant or distracting information.
5 Are unfamiliar terms defined?	**Add** definitions or other explanations of unfamiliar terms. **Replace** unknown or hard terms with familiar ones.
ORGANIZATION	
6 Are ideas and details arranged in the best possible order?	**Reorder** ideas and details to make the meaning clear.
7 Are the connections between ideas and sentences clear?	**Add** transitional words to link ideas: *first, since,* or *then.*
STYLE	
8 Is the meaning clear?	**Replace** vague or unclear wording. Use words and phrases that are precise and easy to understand.
9 Does the writing contain clichés or tired phrases?	**Cut** or **replace** with specific details and fresh comparisons.
10 Does the language fit the audience and purpose?	**Replace** formal words with less formal ones to create an informal tone, or feeling. To create a more formal tone, **replace** slang and contractions.
11 Do sentences read smoothly?	**Reorder** to vary sentence beginnings and sentence structure.

Proofreading and Publishing

COMPOSITION

Proofreading

When you *proofread,* you carefully reread your revised draft to correct mistakes in grammar, usage, and mechanics (spelling, capitalization, and punctuation). Allow enough time to put your writing away for a while. A little distance will help you see mistakes. The following techniques can help make proofreading easier.

1. Focus on one line at a time. Use a sheet of paper to cover all the lines below the one you are proofreading. Some writers proofread backward—beginning with the bottom line and moving to the top. Some writers also proofread by reading from right to left.
2. Try peer proofreading. Exchange papers with a classmate or two and check each other's papers for errors.
3. When you're not sure if something's right, look it up. Use a college dictionary for spelling and the appropriate pages of a handbook like this one for grammar, usage, and mechanics.
4. Indicate any changes by using the revising and proofreading symbols on pages 374–375.

The guidelines on the facing page will help you find and correct some of the most common errors.

COMPUTER NOTE

Spell-checking software can help you proofread your writing, but it isn't foolproof. For example, if you use the possessive pronoun *its* where you should have used the contraction *it's* (for *it is* or *it has*), the spell checker won't catch the error. It simply determines misspelled words, not whether those words are used correctly in a particular sentence. The computer's "Search/Replace" function makes it easy to find and correct every instance in which you did make a particular error.

GUIDELINES FOR PROOFREADING

1. Is every sentence a complete sentence, not a fragment or run-on? (See pages 214–222.)
2. Does every sentence end with the appropriate end punctuation mark? Are other punctuation marks used correctly? (See pages 268–321.)
3. Does every sentence begin with a capital letter? Are all proper nouns and appropriate proper adjectives capitalized? (See pages 248–265.)
4. Does every verb agree in number with its subject? (See pages 77–87.)
5. Are verb forms and tenses used correctly? (See pages 95–115.)
6. Are subject and object forms of personal pronouns used correctly? (See pages 119–130.)
7. Does every pronoun agree with its antecedent in number and in gender? Are pronoun references clear? (See pages 88–90 and 130–132.)
8. Are frequently confused words (such as *lie* and *lay*) used correctly? (See pages 113–116 and **Writer's Quick Reference**.)
9. Are all words spelled correctly? Are the plural forms of nouns correct? (See pages 338–341.)
10. Is the paper neat and in correct manuscript style? (See pages 451–465.)

COMPOSITION

Publishing

Deciding on an audience early in the writing process means that you plan to share your paper with others. Now is the time to do that. Here are some ways to share your writing.

- Enter a writing contest. Some contests have prizes or certificates. Ask your teacher or counselor for information about writing contests throughout the year.
- Send your writing to a newspaper or a magazine. Try the school newspaper, yearbook, or magazine. Your local newspaper may be interested in publishing a letter to the editor or a feature article. Find out which national magazines publish student stories, poems, and essays.
- Make a class anthology. Each student might contribute one piece of writing, a drawing, or a favorite cartoon.

COMPOSITION

Exchange anthologies with other classes. Donate your class anthology to your school library or to the children's ward in a hospital.

■ Make an anthology of your best writing. Keep your writing in a separate folder or notebook, and add to it throughout your high school years. Share it with your family and friends.

■ Post book and movie reviews written by students on a school bulletin board or in the library.

The guidelines for manuscript style on pages 451–465 will help improve the appearance of your paper.

SYMBOLS FOR REVISING AND PROOFREADING		
SYMBOL	**EXAMPLE**	**MEANING OF SYMBOL**
☰	Fifty-first street	Capitalize a lowercase letter.
/	Jerry's Aunt	Lowercase a capital letter.
∧	differ*e*ant	Change a letter.
∧	the capital *of* Ohio	Insert a missing word, letter, or punctuation mark.
⟋—	beside the *lake* river	Replace a word.
℘	Where's the the key?	Take out a word, letter, or punctuation mark.
℘	an invisib̂le guest	Take out and close up.
⌒	a close friend ship	Close up space.
∩	thier	Change the order of letters.
(tr)	Avoid having too many corrections of your paper on the final version.	Transfer the circled words. (Write (tr) in the nearby margin.)
¶	¶ "Hi," he smiled.	Begin a new paragraph.

(continued)

SYMBOLS FOR REVISING AND PROOFREADING *(continued)*

SYMBOL	EXAMPLE	MEANING OF SYMBOL
⊙	Stay well⊙	Add a period.
⋏	Of course⋏you may be wrong.	Add a comma.
#	ice#hockey	Add a space.
⌃	one of the following⌃	Add a colon.
⋏	Maria Simmons, M.D.⋏Jim Fiorello, Ph.D.	Add a semicolon.
=	A great=grandmother	Add a hyphen.
⌄	Paul⌄s car	Add an apostrophe.
⬭stet⬭	On the fifteenth of ~~July~~	Keep the crossed-out material. (Write ⬭stet⬭ in nearby margin.)

COMPOSITION

17 PARAGRAPH AND COMPOSITION STRUCTURE

Usually, a *paragraph* is defined as a group of sentences that develops a main idea. Similarly, a *composition* can be thought of as a group of paragraphs that develops a main idea. As these definitions suggest, paragraphs and compositions have a great deal in common. By learning how a paragraph is put together, you will be well on your way to understanding how a composition is built.

The Elements of a Paragraph

Writers don't always use a paragraph of many sentences to develop a main idea. Sometimes a writer will use a one-sentence paragraph to bridge two other paragraphs or to emphasize a particular point. The models in this chapter, though, show how writers use longer paragraphs to develop their main ideas. Most of the models have a topic sentence and several supporting sentences.

 NOTE All of the model paragraphs in this chapter were written as parts of longer works. They are presented out of context here so that you can focus on their form and structure.

The Topic Sentence

You will often express the main idea of a paragraph in a single sentence, called the *topic sentence.*

Location of a Topic Sentence

The topic sentence often appears as the first or second sentence of a paragraph. A topic sentence at the beginning of a paragraph helps a reader know what to expect in the rest of the paragraph. However, a topic sentence can occur at any place in a paragraph. In fact, you'll sometimes find a topic sentence at or near the end of a paragraph. Writers sometimes place topic sentences there to create surprise or to summarize ideas.

As you read the following paragraph, look to see how the writer draws all the details together with a topic sentence at the very end.

> In the summer, hosts of big red-and-yellow grasshoppers, with heads shaped like horses, will descend and eat holes in all the softer leaves. Walking sticks fly like boomerangs. Shining brown leaf-shaped palmetto bugs scurry like cockroaches. Spiders like tiny crabs hang in stout webs. The birds snap at small moths and butterflies of every kind. A blue racer, the snake that moves across the cleared sand like a whiplash, will with one flick destroy the smooth, careful cup of the ant lion in the hot sand. The whole world of the pines and of the rocks hums and glistens and stings with life.
>
> Marjory Stoneman Douglas,
> *The Everglades: River of Grass*

Importance of a Topic Sentence

Many paragraphs you read won't have topic sentences. In fact, some of them, especially those that relate sequences of events or actions, won't even seem to have a single main idea. But that doesn't mean topic sentences aren't useful. Topic sentences at the beginning of a paragraph help you when you're reading. They let you know what to expect in the rest of the paragraph, and they often let you know what the author's attitude is toward the topic. In your own writing, they help you focus your ideas for your paragraph.

Supporting Sentences

With or without a topic sentence, a paragraph needs details—specific bits of information—to make the main idea clear. *Supporting sentences* give those details. The kinds of details you'll use depends upon your subject. You might support your main idea with sensory details, facts or statistics, examples, or an anecdote.

Sensory Details

Sensory details are precise bits of information that you observe, or collect, through any of your five senses—sight, hearing, smell, touch, taste. In the following paragraph, the writer uses details of sight, sound, and smell to create images of her childhood home in the morning.

Sight	In the summer my mother got up just after sunrise, so that when she called Matthew and me for breakfast, the house was filled with sounds and smells
Smell	of her industrious mornings. Odors of frying scrapple or codfish cakes drifted up the back stairs, mingling sometimes
Smell	with the sharp scent of mustard greens she was cooking for dinner that night.
Smell/Sight Sound	Up the laundry chute from the cellar floated whiffs of steamy air and the churning sound of the washing machine. From the dining room, where she liked to sit ironing and chatting on the telephone, came the fragrance of hot
Smell Sound Sight	clean clothes and the sound of her voice: cheerful, resonant, reverberating a little weirdly through the high-ceilinged
Sound	rooms, as if she were sitting happily at the bottom of a well.

Andrea Lee, "Mother"

Facts and Statistics

You can also support a main idea with *facts* and *statistics*. A *fact* is something that can be proven true by concrete information: *General Lee surrendered to General Grant in the front parlor of the Wilmer McLean house.* A ***statistic*** is a fact that is based on numbers: *During the Civil War, the South lost about 260,000 soldiers, and the North lost about 360,000.*

In the following paragraph about movie theaters, facts and statistics support the main idea that concession sales are big moneymakers. (*Rialto* is a name for a theater district. The writer uses it to represent a typical theater.)

COMPOSITION

	Let's look at how concession sales affect the bottom line of the Rialto. In
Statistic	large cities, about 15–20 percent of all customers will stop at the concession
Fact	stand (in smaller towns, even more customers eat), and the theater owner fig-
Statistic	ures to gross about 75 cents for every customer who walks through the turn-
Statistic	stile, meaning that the average purchase is over $3. The key to making money in
Fact	the concession area is maintaining a high profit margin, and the items sold do a terrific job. The average profit mar-
Statistics	gin on candy—77 percent; on popcorn—86 percent; on soft drinks—a whopping 90 percent. For every dollar spent at the concession counter, the theater operator nets over 85 cents.

David Feldman, *Imponderables*

Examples

Examples are specific instances, or illustrations, of general ideas. A cow is an example of an animal; a test score of 67 is an example of what can happen if you don't study. The following paragraph uses specific examples to show how bathing varies among birds.

COMPOSITION

Main idea	Bathing behavior varies from species
Example 1	to species. Many birds stand in shallow water and, through a complex series of movements—rolling their head and body and fluttering their wings—get water trapped in featherless areas next to their body and then press the water
Example 2	out through their feathers. Some aerial birds, like swallows, may dive into
Example 3	water and immediately fly up. Still others may jump into water and be briefly
Example 4	submerged before getting out. Some birds bathe in rain or drizzle, in dew on grass, or among wet leaves. Take time to watch bathing behavior; it is fascinating.

> Donald and Lillian Stokes,
> *The Bird Feeder Book*

Anecdotes

An *anecdote* is a brief story, usually one that is biographical or autobiographical. The following paragraph uses an anecdote to support the writer's main idea: that Olympic boxer Mark Breland is capable of performing well outside the ring as well as within it.

A little more than two years ago Breland proved that his ability to learn and adapt extends outside the ring. A casting director from Paramount saw his photograph in the newspaper and was struck by his stark good looks. She offered him a role in *The Lords of Discipline,* and he accepted with the alacrity of any eighteen-year-old discovered by Hollywood. In the film Breland plays Pearce, the first black cadet at a southern military academy that is unofficially bent on continuing as an all-white institution. Pearce is subjected to brutal hazing and then torture at the hands of his fellow cadets. The role of a strong, silent man-child who resolutely takes what the world dishes out and still triumphs was a familiar one to Breland after his youth in Bedford-Stuyvesant. Although the film role did not demand a broad range of emotion, he performed with dignity and little self-consciousness.

> G. A. Taubes, "Boxer with a Future"

The Clincher Sentence

A *clincher sentence* restates or summarizes the main idea of a paragraph. It pulls all the details together. The following paragraph uses a clincher to restate the idea that basketball legend Magic Johnson is "truly great."

Greatness is one of the most overused words in sports these days. But Magic Johnson is a *truly great* basketball player, one of only three or four in the entire league. There are a lot of guys who are very good, and some are even special, but only a handful of players like Magic—guys like Larry Bird and Michael Jordan—have that special ability to make those around them better. That's one way to define basketball greatness—to be able to use your skills to benefit your teammates. When the Lakers chose Earvin (Magic) Johnson with the first pick of the 1979 college draft, he became the foundation that allowed the team to dominate the next entire decade. The Lakers won five championships—including two straight in the 1987 and 1988 seasons—and reached the NBA finals eight times during the 1980s, Magic's first ten years as a pro and the leader of our team. So our success was no coincidence. <u>I once told a friend that when Earvin Johnson, Jr., was born, he was sprinkled with Magic dust.</u>

> Foreword by Jerry West
> in *Magic's Touch*

Unity

When something has *unity,* all of its parts work together as a unit—that is, as one. A paragraph has unity when all the sentences work together as a unit to express or support one main idea. Sentences can work as a unit in one of three ways: (1) by supporting a main idea that is stated in a topic sentence, (2) by supporting a main idea that is implied (suggested without being directly expressed), or (3) by expressing a related series of actions.

All Sentences Relate to the Stated Main Idea

In the following paragraph, the topic sentence gives the main idea—that whales are physical wonders. Each of the supporting sentences includes a detail that helps explain why whales are physical wonders.

Topic sentence	Whales not only have fascinating behavior but are physical wonders as well.
Detail	The Blue Whale is the largest animal that has ever graced our planet.
Detail	Such giant herbivorous dinosaurs as the brontosaurus weighed up to fifty tons. A
Detail	Blue Whale weighs that much long before it reaches puberty; full grown they weigh a hundred and fifty tons, as much as three brontosauri! Blue Whales grow
Detail	to more than a hundred feet—longer
Detail	than any other animals. When such a whale is vertical in the water with its tail at the surface, its nose is deep enough to be subjected to the weight of three at-
Detail	mospheres. It is possible that they dive deep enough, more than a mile, to be subjected to more than two hundred times the atmospheric pressure experienced by people on land at sea level.

Paul and Anne Ehrlich,
Extinction

All Sentences Relate to an Implied Main Idea

The following paragraph doesn't have a topic sentence. But each sentence helps support an implied main idea—that when he opens his eyes, the man sees the results of the birds' attack.

> He took the blanket from his head and stared about him. The cold gray morning light exposed the room. Dawn and the open window had called the living birds; the dead lay on the floor. Nat gazed at the little corpses, shocked and horrified. They were all small birds, none of any size; there must have been fifty of them lying there upon the floor. There were robins, finches, sparrows, blue tits, larks, and bramblings, birds that by nature's law kept to their own flock and their own territory, and now, joining one with another in their urge for battle, had destroyed themselves against the bedroom walls or in the strife had been destroyed by him. Some had lost feathers in the fight; others had blood, his blood, upon their beaks.
>
> Daphne du Maurier, "The Birds"

All Sentences Relate to a Sequence of Events

In the following paragraph, the narrator is trying to save Harry, who fears that a deadly snake called a krait has slithered into his bed. The paragraph doesn't actually have a main idea. But each action detail is part of a sequence of events. In this paragraph, the sequence begins when the narrator leaves the room and ends as he stands beside Harry's bed wondering what to do.

> I went softly out of the room in my stocking feet and fetched a small sharp knife from the kitchen. I put it in my trouser pocket, ready to use instantly in case something went wrong while we were still thinking out a plan. If Harry coughed or moved or did something to frighten the krait and got bitten, I was going to be ready to cut the bitten place and

try to suck the venom out. I came back to the bedroom and Harry was still lying there very quiet and sweating all over his face. His eyes followed me as I moved across the room to his bed, and I could see he was wondering what I'd been up to. I stood beside him, trying to think of the best thing to do.

Roald Dahl, "Poison"

Coherence

A *coherent* paragraph is one in which the ideas are arranged and connected so that they fit together well. You can create coherence by paying attention to two things: (1) the order in which you arrange your ideas, and (2) the connections you make between ideas.

Order of Ideas

This chart shows four basic ways of arranging ideas.

WAYS OF ORDERING IDEAS	
Chronological Order	Arrange events in the order they occur.
Spatial Order	Arrange details according to how they are perceived in space.
Order of Importance	Arrange details or ideas according to how important they are.
Logical Order	Arrange details or ideas according to their relation to each other.

REFERENCE NOTE: For more information on arranging ideas, see the section **Strategies of Development** on pages 388–395.

Connections Between Ideas

Besides putting ideas in an order that makes sense, you need to show how the ideas are connected. You can show connections by

1. making *direct references* to something else in the paragraph, or
2. using words that make a *transition,* or bridge, from one idea to another

☞ REFERENCE NOTE: Unity and coherence are as important to compositions as they are to paragraphs. See page 405.

See page 405.

Direct References.   A direct reference links ideas by referring to a word or an idea that you've used earlier. You can make that reference in several ways:

1. Use a noun or pronoun that refers to a word or an idea used earlier.
2. Repeat a word used earlier.
3. Use a word or phrase that means the same thing as one used earlier.

The following paragraph uses several direct references to make connections between ideas. Each reference is coded with the number of the type of reference in the numbered list above.

> That same evening, however, Leiningen assembled *his*[1] workers. *He*[1] had no intention of waiting till the news reached *their*[1] ears from other sources. *Most*[1] of *them*[1] had been born in the district; the cry "The ants are coming!" was to *them*[1] an imperative signal for instant, panic-stricken flight, a spring for life itself. But so great was the *Indians'*[1] trust in *Leiningen,*[2] in *Leiningen's*[2] word, and in *Leiningen's*[2] wisdom, that *they*[1] received *his*[1] curt *tidings*[3] and *his*[1] orders for the imminent struggle, with the calmness with which *they*[1] were given. *They*[1] waited, unafraid, alert, as if for the beginning of a new game or hunt which *he*[1] had just described to *them.*[1] The *ants*[2] were indeed mighty, but not so mighty as the *boss.*[1] Let *them*[1] come!
>
> Carl Stephenson,
> "Leiningen Versus the Ants"

COMPOSITION

COMPOSITION

Transitional Words and Phrases. *Trans-* means "across" or "over." A transition in writing—whether it's a word, a phrase, or even a sentence—reaches *across* or *over*, connecting one idea to another. When you use transitions, you not only connect ideas, but you also show *how* the ideas are connected. As you refer to the chart on the next page, notice that certain transitions are also related to certain types of writing.

The following paragraph uses transitional words and phrases, which are underlined, to make connections in time and place.

> With nervous hands he lowered the piece of canvas which served as his door, <u>and</u> pegged it at the bottom. <u>Then</u> quickly <u>and</u> quietly, looking at the piece of canvas frequently, he slipped the records into the case, snapped the lid shut, <u>and</u> carried the phonograph to his couch. <u>There</u>, pausing often to stare at the canvas <u>and</u> listen, he dug earth from the wall <u>and</u> disclosed a piece of board. <u>Behind</u> this there was a deep hole in the wall, <u>into</u> which he put the phonograph. <u>After</u> a moment's consideration, he went <u>over and</u> reached <u>down</u> for his bundle of books and inserted it <u>also</u>. <u>Then</u>, guardedly, he once more sealed up the hole with the board <u>and</u> the earth. He <u>also</u> changed his blankets, and the grass-stuffed sack which served as a pillow, <u>so that</u> he could lie facing the entrance. <u>After</u> carefully placing two more blocks of peat on the fire, he stood for a long time watching the stretched canvas, <u>but</u> it seemed to billow naturally with the first gusts of a lowering wind. <u>At last</u> he prayed, <u>and</u> got in <u>under</u> his blankets, <u>and</u> closed his smoke-smarting eyes. On the <u>inside</u> of the bed, <u>next</u> to the wall, he could feel with his hand, the comfortable piece of lead pipe.
>
> Walter Van Tilburg Clark,
> "The Portable Phonograph"

TRANSITIONAL WORDS AND PHRASES

Comparing Ideas/Classification and Definition

also	besides	other
and	in addition to	similarly
another	moreover	too

Contrasting Ideas/Classification and Definition

although	instead	otherwise
but	nevertheless	still
however	on the other hand	yet
in spite of		

Showing Cause and Effect/Narration

as a result	for	so that
because	since	therefore
consequently	so	thus

Showing Time/Narration

after	finally	next
at last	first	then
at once	for a time	thereafter
before	meanwhile	when
eventually		

Showing Place/Description

above	from	next
across	here	on
around	in	over
before	inside	there
behind	into	to
beyond	nearby	under

Showing Importance/Evaluation

first	mainly	then
last	more important	to begin with

Strategies of Development

Description, narration, classification, and evaluation are four strategies for developing a main idea. The strategy, or method, you choose to develop a paragraph depends upon your specific purpose for writing and your audience. The strategy determines what kinds of supporting details you will use, such as facts or examples, and affects the order of your ideas. The four strategies of development shown in the chart below are basically four different ways of looking at a topic or subject.

STRATEGIES OF DEVELOPMENT	
Description	Looking at individual features of a particular subject
Narration	Looking at changes in a subject over a period of time
Classification	Looking at a subject in relation to other subjects
Evaluation	Looking at the value of a subject (judging)

Each paragraph or each piece of longer writing you create should have both a purpose and a strategy that develops that purpose. In some paragraphs, you may use more than one strategy of development. In relating an experience, for example, you may want to describe the setting as well as to narrate the events. Thus, you would combine description and narration in writing the paragraph.

Description

When you want to tell what something is like or what it looks like, you need to consider its particular features. You need to use the strategy of *description.* In a description, you will use sensory details (details of sight, sound, taste, touch, and smell). Your purpose in using description may be to create literature, to inform, or simply to express your-self. Often, you will use *spatial order* (see page 362). Notice how the writer of the following paragraph uses details and spatial order to describe a town.

I can see the town now on some hot, still weekday afternoon in midsummer: ten thousand souls and nothing doing. Even the red water truck was a diversion, coming slowly up Grand Avenue with its sprinkler on full force, the water making sizzling steam-clouds on the pavement while half-naked black children followed the truck up the street and played in the torrent until they got soaking wet. Over on Broadway, where the old men sat drowsily in straw chairs on the pavement near the Bon-Ton Café, whittling to make the time pass, you could laze around on the sidewalks—barefoot, if your feet were tough enough to stand the scalding concrete—watching the big cars with out-of-state plates whip by, the driver hardly knowing and certainly not caring what place this was. Way up that fantastic hill, Broadway seemed to end in a seething mist—little heat mirages that shimmered off the asphalt; on the main street itself there would be only a handful of cars parked here and there, and the merchants and the lawyers sat in the shade under their broad awnings, talking slowly, aimlessly, in the cryptic summer way. The one o'clock whistle at the sawmill would send out its loud bellow, reverberating up the streets to the bend in the Yazoo River, hardly making a ripple in the heavy somnolence.

Willie Morris,
"The Phantom of Yazoo"

Funky Winkerbean reprinted with special
permission of North America Syndicate, Inc.

Narration

Narration describes changes over a period of time. Usually, you will arrange your ideas and information in *chronological order.* You may use the strategy of narration *to tell a story, to explain a process,* or *to explain causes and effects.*

Telling a Story. A story may be true or it may be imaginary (fictional). In the following paragraph, the writer tells a story to explain how a place came to be called Ape Canyon.

> Near Mount Saint Helens in the state of Washington there is a place known locally as "ape canyon." There, so the story goes, a group of miners was attacked by a party of seven-foot apes. Earlier in the day, a miner had shot one of the "giant apes," and in the evening a gang of them bombarded the miners' windowless cabin with rocks and boulders. The miners crouched inside the cabin for hours while rocks rained down on them. When the attack was over, the miners fled down the mountain and back to town. They returned to the canyon with a bunch of well-armed friends, but the apes had departed, leaving behind only their giant footprints and a badly battered cabin. The giant apes of Mount Saint Helens, if they were ever more than a tall tale, are doubtless extinct today because of the eruption of the Mount Saint Helens volcano. In 1982 a retired logger named Rant Mullens claimed he and a friend started the Mount Saint Helens story by rolling rocks down on the miners' cabin, as a joke.
>
> Daniel Cohen,
> *The Encyclopedia of Monsters*

Explaining a Process. When you tell how something works or how to do something, you're explaining a process. In explaining a process, you also use narration. In the following paragraph, the writer explains how to find the source of honey.

To find a honey tree, first catch a bee. Catch a bee when its legs are heavy with pollen; then it is ready for home. It is simple enough to catch a bee on a flower: hold a cup or glass above the bee, and when it flies up, cap the cup with a piece of cardboard. Carry the bee to a nearby open spot—best an elevated one—release it, and watch where it goes. Keep your eyes on it as long as you can see it, and hie you to that last known place. Wait there until you see another bee; catch it, release it, and watch. Bee after bee will lead toward the honey tree, until you see the final bee enter the tree.

Annie Dillard, *The Writing Life*

COMPOSITION

Explaining Cause and Effect.   When you explain what caused something or the effects of something, you again use narration. The following paragraph looks at a likely cause and the violent effects of the collapse of a dam.

At one minute before 8:00, the dam simply collapsed. There is little evidence that water came over the top of the dam, although that remains one of the obvious possibilities. It is a good deal more likely that the whole structure became saturated with moisture, dissolved into something resembling wet paste, and just slumped over on its foundation of silt and sludge. In any event, the entire lake of black water, all 132 million gallons of it, roared through the breach in a matter of seconds. It was already more than water, full of coal dust and other solids, and as it broke through the dam and landed on the banks of refuse below, it scraped up thousands of tons of other materials, the whole being fused into a liquid substance that one engineer simply called a "mud wave" and one witness described as "rolling lava." The wave set off a series of explosions as it drove a channel through the smoldering trough of slag, raising mushroom-shaped clouds high into the air and throwing great spatters of mud three hundred feet up to the haul road where a few men were returning from the mines. The rock and debris dislodged by those explosions were absorbed into the mass too. By now, there were something like a million tons of solid waste caught up in the flow.

Kai Erikson, *Everything in Its Path*

Classification

Classification looks at a subject as it relates to other subjects in a group. Sometimes, your purpose in using classification might be to inform. At other times you might use it to express your feelings, "pro" and "con," about a subject. When you classify, you may divide a subject into its parts, define it, or compare and contrast it with something else. Usually, writers use *logical order*—grouping related ideas together—in paragraphs that classify.

Dividing. Sometimes you need to look at the parts of a subject in order to explain the subject as a whole. For example, the following paragraph uses the strategy of dividing in order to explain the human muscular system. The paragraph divides the system into the three types of muscles.

Our muscles represent about 40 percent of the weight of our bodies, but they are not all alike. We actually have three different types of muscles. One type of muscle, the cardiac muscle, is present only in the heart. The cells of the cardiac muscle form long rows of fibers. Unlike other muscle tissue, cardiac muscles contract independently. Another type of muscle, the smooth muscle, is present in the walls of internal organs, our arteries, and our veins. Since we can't control our smooth muscles, they are called involuntary muscles. The third type of muscle, the striated muscle, is called a voluntary muscle. Striated muscles are voluntary because we can control them, and they are attached to our legs, arms, back, and torso.

Defining.   When you *define* a subject, you first identify the large class or group it belongs to. Then you tell what makes the subject unique, or different, from other members of that group. In the following paragraph, the first sentence defines the word *mummy*, and the other sentences give examples that more fully explain what a mummy is.

Definition

    A mummy is the preserved body of a human being or an animal, by any means, either deliberate or accidental.

Example

Mummies survive from many ancient cultures, some preserved in a wet state, others dry. The bog bodies of northern Europe, such as the 2,000-year-old Lindow Man, found in Cheshire, England, in 1984, belonged to people who had either fallen, or been thrown, into wet, marshy places. The exclusion of oxygen and acidity in the peat of the bog effectively preserved their bodies.

Example

Most mummies, though, were preserved by being dried, or desiccated. Many civilizations, including the Egyptian, Chinese and some South American cul-

Example

tures, tried to achieve this artificially.

Christine El Mahdy,
Mummies, Myth and Magic

Comparing and Contrasting.   You can look at subjects by *comparing* them (telling how they are alike), *contrasting* them (telling how they are different), or by both comparing and contrasting them. The following paragraph contrasts places used to film a nature series.

Contrast 1

    The fascinating thing about shooting this series was the contrast. One minute you would be filming in snow and the next minute sweating in the heat of a

Contrast 2

tropical forest. One minute paddling a canoe down an English river, the next

COMPOSITION

COMPOSITION

Contrast 3

minute paddling a canoe over a tropical reef. So in this case we had a contrast, for we left the giant cactus forests of Arizona and flew down to the rolling grasslands of southern Africa. . . .

Gerald Durrell,
How to Shoot an Amateur Naturalist

Evaluation

Evaluation means determining the value of something. Sometimes your purpose in evaluating a subject may be to inform or to persuade. An evaluation should provide reasons to support your judgment. A good way to arrange your reasons is by *order of importance.* You can emphasize one reason by putting it first in the paragraph, as in the excerpt from the movie review below, or last.

Evaluation

Support

Support

Support

Support

A supernatural romantic comedy thriller? Sounds like a high concept run amok. But somehow "Ghost" pulls it off. It's a sleeper, a charmer, a real disarmer, the kind of stardust you almost thought Hollywood forgot how to make. What makes it work is that you're willing to believe that Demi Moore and Patrick Swayze really go for each other, that something is really lost when he's shot to death on a dark street in SoHo. Actually, "Ghost" is a triple comeback film. Swayze recaptures the sincerity and vulnerability he projected so winningly in "Dirty Dancing." Moore, pared down to gamine winsomeness, is at her most appealing since "About Last Night." And Whoopi Goldberg breaks her long losing streak, too, playing a phony medium who becomes the real thing when she finds to her surprise that she can pick up on Swayze's vibes.

Jay Carr, *Boston Globe*

STYLE NOTE From your reading, you know that professional writers use paragraphs ranging in length from a single word to a page or more. In general, the length of a paragraph depends on the writer's purpose and audience. For example, to inform readers about the events of a flood, the writer of a news story would probably use a series of brief and to-the-point paragraphs. That approach would enable readers to grasp the situation quickly. To persuade readers to contribute to flood relief efforts, the writer of an editorial would probably use longer, more detailed paragraphs. That treatment would enable the writer to provide a carefully constructed argument that would gain wide support from readers.

The Composition

You will use the composition form both in and out of school. In school, you will use it to write compositions, or essays, both for assigned papers and for tests. Outside of school, you will use the same principles of form in other kinds of writing, such as business reports and letters of application. In this section, you will learn some basic principles of composition form. You will learn that

- most compositions have thesis statements
- most have good, attention-grabbing introductions
- each paragraph in the composition's body is unified and clearly connected to the surrounding paragraphs
- most compositions have strong conclusions

The Thesis Statement

A **thesis statement** gives the composition's main idea about a topic. It's a sentence or two in the introduction that announces your limited topic and expresses your main idea about it. A thesis statement in a composition works in the same way that a topic sentence works in a paragraph.

Some thesis statements simply identify what the writer is going to write about: "There are several qualifications for the Young American Medal for Bravery." Other thesis statements identify an idea that the writer is actually trying to prove to the reader. For example, later in this chapter, you will read this thesis statement: "While it's true that the brain's two sides have different functions, they work together, not in conflict." Most of the thesis statements in this section are of this type: They identify a point the writer wants to prove or discuss.

Location, Length, and Aim

Often, the thesis statement appears in the introduction. In that position, it introduces or summarizes the composition's main idea. Whether the thesis statement is long or short depends on your topic, your purpose, and your writing style.

Preliminary and Revised Thesis Statements

With practice, you can learn to write lively thesis statements that have punch and zing. When you're planning your composition, you will probably want to work with a preliminary (or working) thesis statement that is direct and straightforward. When you begin to draft your introduction, however, you may find that you need to revise the thesis statement. Once you have fleshed out the text of your introduction, you may find that your thesis statement can be less blunt, smoother, and more intriguing.

Here's an example of how a final thesis statement can be different from one used in prewriting or planning.

In an article about the sense of smell, the poet Diane Ackerman might have had something like this in mind as a preliminary thesis statement: "Smell is a powerful, emotional sense for two reasons: (1) humans' sense of smell is very precise and (2) odor molecules go directly to the brain." But in her finished essay, Ackerman used this short, attention-getting thesis statement instead. Notice that while this statement announces the topic, it only hints at what the main idea is:

"Nothing is more memorable than a smell."

HINTS FOR WRITING AND USING A THESIS STATEMENT

1. **Develop your thesis statement from the information you've gathered.** A thesis statement comes out of your prewriting material. Review your facts and details, and begin thinking about how they fit together. *What main, or unifying, idea do you see?*

2. **Check your thesis statement for both a limited topic and your main idea about it.** Remember the two parts. The question your thesis statement must answer is not just *What's my topic?* but also *What about the topic?* For example, examine this thesis statement: "While it's true that the brain's two sides have different functions, they work together, not in conflict." The writer's limited topic is the two sides of the brain. The main idea is that the two sides work together, not in conflict.

3. **Be clear and specific.** Suppose the writer had written, "The brain has two sides that work in a very interesting way." This thesis statement is not only boring—it's fuzzy. Check your thesis statements for vague words like *interesting* and *important.* Then sharpen your language and present a definite, focused idea.

4. **Rewrite your thesis statement if necessary.** Try out more than one version of your thesis statement to find the one that works best. Remember, it isn't carved in stone. You can revise it as you go along.

5. **Use your thesis statement as you outline, draft, and revise.** In every stage of your writing, your thesis statement is a good checkpoint. You can test ideas and details against your main idea. You can then cut the ones that don't support, illustrate, or explain your main point.

MY ESSAY IS ENTITLED, "AFTER SCHOOL AT MY HOUSE." ...AHEM...

"IT'S NOT THAT I *MIND* BEING CHAINED IN THE BASEMENT, IT'S JUST THAT WHEN THE MEAT IS THROWN DOWN, THE RATS HAVE THE ADVANTAGE OF NUMBERS, AND THEY..."

WHAT, MISS WORMWOOD?

ANOTHER PARENT-TEACHER CONFERENCE?!

I TOLD HER TO EXPECT YOU TO DENY EVERYTHING.

Calvin & Hobbes copyright 1991 Watterson. Reprinted with permission of Universal Press Syndicate. All rights reserved.

COMPOSITION

Development and Organization

During the prewriting stage (see pages 353–364), you gather information and determine your unifying idea, or thesis. Then you choose a strategy of development and order your material to create a prewriting plan.

Like a paragraph, a composition uses the four strategies of development—*narration, description, classification, evaluation* (page 388). It also uses the four basic orders—*chronological, spatial, logical, order of importance* (page 384). In the larger structure of the composition, though, you order several ideas and paragraphs and the details and sentences within each paragraph.

 NOTE You will often use more than one strategy of development in a composition. For a composition *evaluating* your school's sports program for girls, for example, you might also use *narration* by recounting the history of the program's development. You might instead *classify* the girls' program by comparing and contrasting it with the boys' program and also *describe* the facilities and equipment available to each group.

The Early Plan

An **early plan,** sometimes called an *informal,* or *rough, outline,* doesn't have a set form. You simply sort your ideas or facts into groups and arrange the groups in order.

Grouping. Begin by grouping together related ideas. The following steps will help you decide how to group your notes.

STEPS FOR GROUPING INFORMATION

■ Ask yourself: *Which items belong together?* Sort the related ideas and details into separate groups.
■ Ask yourself: *Which items don't fit anywhere?* Make a separate list of details that don't fit into any of your groups. You may find a place for some of these items as you draft your paper.

■ Ask yourself: *What do the items in each group have in common?* Give each group of details a label that shows what the items have in common.

Ordering.   Next, order, or arrange, your information in a way that will make sense to your readers. The purpose of your composition may clearly suggest a particular order. But at other times, you just have to decide what makes sense for your material. More than one order may be possible. The test is whether readers can follow your thoughts and facts easily. Ask this question: *Is the purpose and the order of each grouping of details understandable?*

Here's the early plan the writer of the composition on pages 400–402 came up with.

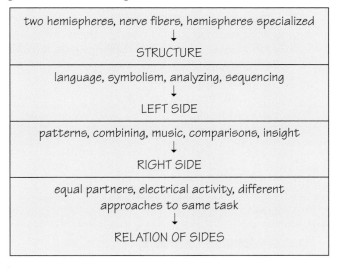

two hemispheres, nerve fibers, hemispheres specialized
↓
STRUCTURE

language, symbolism, analyzing, sequencing
↓
LEFT SIDE

patterns, combining, music, comparisons, insight
↓
RIGHT SIDE

equal partners, electrical activity, different approaches to same task
↓
RELATION OF SIDES

REFERENCE NOTE: See pages 363–364 for information on using charts as early plans. For more help in arranging ideas, see pages 384 and 388–394.

The Formal Outline

A *formal outline* is a highly structured, clearly labeled writing plan. It has a set pattern, using Roman numerals and letters to show main headings and subheadings. An outline may use either *topics* (words and phrases) *or* complete *sentences* for each item. For the sake of consistency, do not mix topics and sentences in one outline.

 REFERENCE NOTE: For more information on formal outlines, see pages 422–423.

Here is a portion of a topic outline that goes with the essay "Two Brains or One?" below. Notice that the introduction and the conclusion are not included in the outline.

<u>Title:</u> Two Brains or One?
<u>Thesis Statement:</u> While it's true that the brain's two sides have different functions, they work together, not in conflict.
  I. Structure of brain
      A. Cerebrum: two hemispheres
      B. Nerve connection <u>(corpus callosum)</u>
      C. Specialization
 II. Left hemisphere
      A. Language (symbols)
      B. Analysis
      C. Sequence
          1. Counting
          2. Marking time
          3. Steps
          4. Logical statement

A COMPOSITION MODEL

Two Brains or One?

INTRODUCTION   If you're right-brained, you're creative and emotional. If you're left-brained, you're logical and steady. Perhaps you've heard this popular explanation of the "two-sided" human brain—and haven't liked it. Are there only two kinds of people in the world? Are we really ruled by one side of our gray matter? No.

Thesis statement While it's true that the brain's two sides have different functions, they work together, not in conflict.

BODY
Main topic:
brain structure It's a fact that the human brain is split in two. The cerebrum, the brain's large upper part, has two separate sides, called hemispheres. A band of nerve fibers (the <u>corpus callosum</u>) connects them and is constantly passing information back and forth. What scientists have learned is that the brain's two hemispheres are specialized, with each side being better at different mental work.

Main topic:
left hemisphere The left hemisphere, for example, allows us to speak and is better at all language skills. It is good with anything symbolic, like words and numbers. Also, when you are analyzing something—breaking it into parts to understand it—you are mostly using your left brain. Counting, marking time, planning step by step, and making logical statements are typical functions. The left brain likes to go in sequence.

Main topic: right
hemisphere The right hemisphere, on the other hand, is more visual and is good at taking in patterns. Combining is its strength. Typical functions are recognizing musical melodies, seeing relationships, and thinking in metaphors (comparisons). The right brain can work like the "flash" of intuition: It sees things whole, all at once.

Main topic: rela-
tion of sides The two sides of the brain, however, are not in conflict. Through research, psychologists know that no one uses

(Note: This topic is covered in three paragraphs, because the writer has several examples.)

only a single side of the brain. People may strongly favor one side, but one hemisphere doesn't "dominate"—control—the other. Painters and musicians are not necessarily illogical and scatterbrained. People good at math and grammar don't automatically have dull imaginations.

Instead, both hemispheres are needed for most mental acts. For example, people do have sudden creative breakthroughs, but first they lay some groundwork of step-by-step thinking. And logical analysis is a dead end until people draw conclusions—organize the details into a meaning. Besides this, scientists explain that language isn't "in" the left brain and music or shapes "in" the right.

When people read poetry or stories, both sides show electrical activity because literature involves images, feelings, and metaphors. When people listen to music, they hear melody with the right brain, but they use the left brain to focus on arrangement, instruments, and so on.

CONCLUSION

The two hemispheres of the brain have different styles of thinking, but they are partners. And while your brain may seem to be more talented at one style, it uses the other one too. Just because you can't carry a tune doesn't mean you can't be creative in other ways. Just because you struggle with algebra doesn't mean you can't be logical about decisions. If you want to apply the split-brain theory to yourself, use it to expand your mental power. Don't let it pigeonhole your personality!

The Introduction

The *introduction* should accomplish three things:

- catch the reader's attention
- set the tone
- present the thesis statement

There's no set length for an introduction. Professional writers may use one, two, or even more paragraphs, depending on their opening techniques and content. But a single paragraph is usually enough for a brief composition.

Techniques for Writing Introductions

The following techniques illustrate some of the ways you can get your readers' attention.

1. **Begin with a question.** The writer of the composition about the brain (pages 400–402) tries to get your attention by beginning with a question that seems to contradict his thesis.

2. **Begin with an anecdote.** An anecdote (a brief story) draws readers into your essay with concrete, vivid details. These details not only spark interest but can introduce important aspects of your topic.

> It's five o'clock and you're hungry. A bag of chips sits on the counter. There's nothing in the refrigerator but a few wilted carrot sticks and limp stalks of celery. Temptation strikes.
>
> The problem with snacking is not when you snack or even that you snack in the first place—but what you choose to eat.
>
> "Guiltless Snacks,"
> *The Saturday Evening Post*

3. **Begin by stating a startling fact or by adopting an unusual position.** Surprising facts or an unexpected opinion can give readers a jolt and make them curious.

> Those prone to nightmares or panic attacks may not want to read this. It's the ultimate cosmic hor-

COMPOSITION

> ror story: Somewhere out there is an asteroid or comet that's on a collision course with planet Earth. Someday it will fulfill its destiny, careening through our atmosphere and dealing a devastating blow. We may never even know what hit us.
>
> Jane Bosveld, "Apocalypse, How?"

4. **Use an appropriate quotation.** Don't hesitate to use someone else's words if those words are interesting and make a point important to your topic. You can quote experts, authors, or someone mentioned in your composition.

> George Orwell's novel *1984* opens with "It was a bright cold day in April and the clocks were striking thirteen," implying that something is terribly wrong with the world.
>
> Far too many Americans believe that the censorship described in *1984* could not exist under the vigilant eye of the First Amendment. But it does happen. Our right to free speech was assaulted in two highly publicized cases this year.
>
> Howard Wornom,
> "For Goodness Sake?"

5. **Start with background information.** Sometimes setting the scene is a good way to begin. Background details may help readers understand your thesis, or remind them what they know about your topic, or simply build interest.

> Arising spontaneously from the people, folktales are little windows into the collective human psyche. Most people think of them as stories concerning the long ago and the faraway. In fact, all times and places have produced them, and modern times are no exception. Instead of dealing with dragons, wolves, and other menaces to the medieval world order, however, present-day folktales often revolve

> around modern technology and the attempts of human beings to come to terms with it.
>
> John Steele Gordon,
> "Financial Folklore"

6. **Begin with a simple statement of your thesis.** Not every introduction has to be surprising or unusual. You can just state your thesis plainly—a technique which immediately focuses attention on your main idea.

> If you have a monster or a villain, you must also have a victim. The victim in the horror film is almost always a woman. It isn't that the monsters don't kill men. They wipe out scores of males. A really good monster can stomp out a whole village. But in the end, it always comes down to the scene where the monster or villain menaces the girl.
>
> Daniel Cohen, "The Victims"

The Body

The *body* develops the main idea in your thesis. Each body paragraph expresses one of your main points and supports that point with details. Together, the body paragraphs—the parts—form a whole. As you write the body, your focus shifts to *unity* and *coherence* (connections).

Unity

In an essay, *unity* means that all the paragraphs work together to support *one* main idea—the thesis. Each body paragraph has its own main idea that must relate to or support the essay's thesis. In turn, each detail in a paragraph should support that paragraph's main idea.

Coherence

In an essay that has *coherence,* the ideas are connected in a way that makes them easy to follow. You can achieve coherence by arranging your ideas in an order that makes sense to readers and by using *direct references* (see page 385) and *transitional expressions* (see pages 386–387).

COMPOSITION

The Conclusion

A composition needs a *conclusion* that gives it a sense of completeness, of "being over." Here are some ways you can bring your composition to a definite close.

Techniques for Writing Conclusions

1. **Restate your main idea in different words.** The following conclusion ends the essay whose introduction you read on pages 403–404.

> In the end, the vastness of space, which seems so peaceful by earthly standards, may be so only for what amounts to a cosmic moment. Sooner or later, the moment will end and we may see a faint light coming toward us, casting a shadow on the face of civilization.
>
> Jane Bosveld, "Apocalypse, How?"

2. **Summarize your major points.** You can emphasize the major points you've made by summarizing them for your reader.

> Trust your material—it's stronger than you think. But it's only as strong as the structure you build for it and the control you maintain over it from the first sentence to the last.
>
> William Zinsser, "Trust Your Material"

3. **Close with a final idea or example.** Sometimes a final example allows you to reinforce or pull together your main points.

> Nothing illustrates the difference between the old, passive female victim of the horrors, and the new, more active ones, than the fine 1978 sci-fi hor-

COMPOSITION

ror film *Alien*. In this film, the heroine, played by Sigourney Weaver, not only fights back against a really horrifying monster—she wins. All the men are killed, but she manages to blast the thing out into space.

Monsters of the future, watch out!

Daniel Cohen, "The Victims"

4. **End with a comment on the topic.** A final comment can take several forms: a thoughtful observation, a personal reaction, a look to the future or to larger issues. Here the writer tells what he thinks about the possibility that road bikes are disappearing.

It's intriguing to speculate, of course, but in a way it doesn't matter which bikes thrive and which fade, as long as people keep riding something. Only if they stop will we really have cause to mourn.

Scott Martin, "Are Road Bikes Dead?"

5. **Call on your readers to take action.** Especially in persuasive essays, you may want to urge readers to do something or to accept a belief. A direct appeal to your audience, though, can work in other kinds of compositions—as it does in the conclusion of the model essay, page 402.

The two hemispheres of the brain have different styles of thinking, but they are partners. And while your brain may seem to be more talented at one style, it uses the other one too. Just because you can't carry a tune doesn't mean you can't be creative in other ways. Just because you struggle with algebra doesn't mean you can't be logical about decisions. If you want to apply the split-brain theory to yourself, use it to expand your mental power. Don't let it pigeonhole your personality!

6. **Close with a quotation.** A surprising or thought-provoking quotation can help your ideas linger in your reader's mind. Here the writer quotes one of the people who created a community garden in an inner-city neighborhood.

> The gardeners still have nagging worries they could lose El Jardin to developers. "I don't think there is another place where our neighborhood people could go," said Ms. Kirkpatrick. "You need a ray of hope and you find it seeing what can grow out of rubble."
>
> Kathleen Teltsch, "For Young and Old, a Pocket Paradise"

The Title

The title of your composition should catch the reader's attention and suggest your main idea. You may think of a working title as you're writing, but be sure to reevaluate when your paper is finished. Try writing several versions, using key words from your introduction and your conclusion. In choosing the title you'll use, keep in mind your purpose and tone. For example, a slangy title or one based on a pun could work well for an informal composition, but it would be out of place for a formal research paper.

FRAMEWORK FOR A COMPOSITION	
Introduction	■ Arouses the reader's interest
	■ Sets the tone
	■ Presents the thesis statement
Body	■ States the main points
	■ Provides support for the main points
Conclusion	■ Reinforces the main idea
	■ Leaves reader with a final impression and a sense of completeness

18 THE RESEARCH PAPER

You use some form of research in much of the factual writing you do: listening, observing, reading, or experimenting. Often, you present your findings in an *informal report,* one without a detailed list of your information sources. A research paper is a *formal report;* it tells readers exactly where your information comes from. A research paper

- draws together information from several sources
- presents factual information about the topic
- tells readers the sources of the information

Prewriting

Finding a Topic for Your Report

Ideas for research subjects are all around you. You can find them by being curious about what you read, what you see, and what you hear.

Identifying a General Subject for Your Research

You may find ideas for research from books, from your own interests, or even from a casual conversation with

COMPOSITION

your next-door neighbor. Here's a list of sources and some examples of subjects they might suggest to you.

SOURCES FOR RESEARCH SUBJECTS		
SOURCES	**EXAMPLES**	**SUBJECTS**
Hobbies and interests	an interest in computer games; a collection of baseball cards	computer color graphics; baseball records
Family and neighbors	a parent who is a nurse; a neighbor from Lithuania	nursing careers; life in Lithuania
Neighborhood and community	local jazz festival; an interesting building	jazz musicians; Victorian architecture
Books, magazines, and newspapers	*Danger—Shark!;* "Landfill Lodes" (*Natural History,* May 1990)	sharks; problems with garbage
Movies, television programs, videotapes, audiotapes	the *Star Wars* movies; "A History of U.S. 'Spy Machines'" (*NOVA,* PBS).	special effects in movies; spies and spying

Limiting Your Subject to a Specific Topic

Broad subjects such as "movies" or "sharks" cover so many subtopics that even a long report couldn't discuss them in enough detail to be informative. You need to limit your subject to a specific topic, one you can explore in detail in the time and space you have available. For example, within the broad subject "sharks," you could identify specific topics such as these: feeding patterns of sharks, sharks in captivity, sharks in literature, and the economic importance of sharks.

Here are some ways you can identify specific topics within a subject.

■ Look up your subject in your library's card catalog or on-line catalog (a computerized version of the card catalog) or in the *Readers' Guide to Periodical Literature.* Notice the topics that are listed there.

- Find some books on your subject. Look through their tables of contents and indexes.
- Read an encyclopedia article about your subject. Many encyclopedias list related topics at the end of articles.
- Talk with someone who has expert knowledge about your subject—for example, a relative, a neighbor, or a teacher.

Selecting a Suitable Topic

Not all topics are suitable for a research report. To select the best possible topic from all your ideas, choose one that

- *will inform your audience*—Your audience will want to learn something new or unusual.
- *will interest your audience*—You don't want to lose your readers halfway through because they're bored.
- *you can find information about*—If a topic is very recent or very technical—for instance, a newly announced medical breakthrough—you may not be able to find much information about it.
- *will allow you to use outside sources*—A good research topic is developed from a *variety* of sources. A personal topic such as "My experiences with Hurricane Zelda" is unsuitable because it has only one source: you.

Thinking About Purpose, Audience, and Tone

The basic *purpose* of your research report is to inform your readers—to share the facts and details you've learned through your research and to share any insights or conclusions that you've reached. If you've accomplished your purpose, your *audience* will come away from your report with a better understanding of your topic. As you research and write your report, ask yourself these questions about your audience.

1. Who will read my report?
2. What do my readers already know about my topic?

COMPOSITION

3. What information can I give my audience that will be surprising or new to them?
4. How can I be sure to give my audience complete information, not leaving out any important area my readers want to hear about?

A research report usually has a serious, formal *tone.* Such a tone shows that you've given serious thought to your topic, and it inclines your audience to take your ideas seriously. Remember that a formal tone calls for the use of

- *third-person point of view*—Avoid using the pronoun *I.*
- *fairly formal language*—Formal language usually does not contain slang, colloquialisms, or contractions.

Developing Research Questions

To give yourself a sense of direction as you begin your research, start with a list of questions. Begin with your natural curiosity. What do *you* want to know about your topic? For example, for a report on "combining live action with cartoon animation," you might ask the following questions.

GENERAL QUESTIONS	SPECIFIC QUESTIONS
1. What is the topic? (How can you define it?)	1. What exactly is cartoon animation?
2. What groups, or classes, make up the topic?	2. What movies have combined live action with cartoon animation?
3. What are the topic's parts, and how do they work together?	3. How do filmmakers combine cartoon characters and live actors?
4. How has the topic changed over time?	4. How have the methods for combining live action and cartoon characters changed over the years?
5. How is the topic similar to or different from related topics?	5. How does a live-action cartoon differ from an animated cartoon?
6. What are the topic's advantages or disadvantages?	6. What are the advantages of live-action cartoons?

Calvin & Hobbes copyright 1989 Watterson. Reprinted with
permission of Universal Press Syndicate. All rights reserved.

COMPOSITION

Finding and Evaluating Sources of Information

Locating Sources of Information

Your search for information may begin in the library, but
many other sources are available in your community.

SOURCES OF INFORMATION	
LIBRARY	
RESOURCES	**INFORMATION**
Card catalog or on-line catalog	Books listed by title, author, and subject; in some libraries this catalog also lists audiovisual materials—videotapes, records, CDs, audiotapes, filmstrips, and films
Readers' Guide to Periodical Literature or an on-line index	Articles in magazines and journals, indexed by subject and by author (InfoTrac® is one computerized index.)
Microfilm or microfiche	Indexes to major newspapers such as *The New York Times,* back issues of some newspapers and magazines
Vertical file	Pamphlets and news clippings arranged by subject
General reference books	Encyclopedias (electronic or print)
Specialized reference books	Biographical references, atlases, almanacs

(continued)

SOURCES OF INFORMATION *(continued)*	
LIBRARY	
RESOURCES	**INFORMATION**
Videotapes and audiotapes	Movies, documentaries, instructional tapes, audiotapes of books
Librarian	Help in using reference materials and finding sources, including audiovisual materials
COMMUNITY	
RESOURCES	**INFORMATION**
Local government agencies	Facts and statistics on various subjects, information on local government policies, experts on local government
Local offices of state and federal government officials	Voting records, recent or pending legislation, experts on state and federal government
Local newspaper offices	Accounts of events of local interest, historical information on city or area
Museums and historical societies	Historical events; scientific achievements; art and artists; special exhibits; experts on history, science, art
Schools and colleges	Print and nonprint sources in libraries, experts on various subjects
Video stores	Documentary and instructional video-tapes and audiotapes

 REFERENCE NOTE: For more information on using the library, see pages 436–438. For more on using reference materials, see pages 439–441.

Evaluating Sources

Not all information is equally helpful. Evaluate, or judge, the usefulness of a source by checking it against the following "4 R" test.

1. *Relevant.* Does the information relate directly to your topic? Check a book's table of contents and index. Skim

a magazine or newspaper article. Read a review or summary of a nonprint source.

2. *Reliable.* Does the information seem objective and accurate? If information in a source is inconsistent with your knowledge or with material from other sources, the information may be inaccurate.

3. *Recent.* Does the information seem outdated? Even historical topics, such as the drafting of the Declaration of Independence or the causes of the Civil War, continue to be researched. Be sure that at least some of your sources are as up-to-date as possible.

4. *Representative.* For a controversial topic, be sure to find sources that present more than one point of view. For example, balance information from the Organization of Believers in Unidentified Flying Objects with information from scientists who dispute the existence of UFOs.

Preparing Source Cards

Keeping track of your sources from the moment you begin your research is essential. Otherwise, when you start shaping your notes into a report, you will be unable to identify the source of quotations and other information. Giving credit to your sources is essential in a research paper. You will also need accurate and complete information on each source in order to prepare your **Works Cited list,** the list of sources at the end of your paper.

You may record your sources on a piece of paper, but most people find it easier to use source cards. Write each source on a separate 3" x 5" index card (sometimes called a *bibliography card*). For each source, list the author, title, and publication information, and give each source card a number. Use the guidelines on the following page to record information for your sources. The guidelines tell how to record the necessary information for different types of sources. As you fill out your cards, refer to these guidelines. Note the special uses of punctuation and abbreviations, as shown in the examples for items 3, 5, 6, 8, and 9 of the guidelines. For sample source cards, see page 417.

COMPOSITION

GUIDELINES FOR SOURCE CARDS

1. **Book with One Author.** Write the author's name, last name first; the title of the book; the place of publication; the publishing company's name; and the year of publication.

2. **Book with More Than One Author.** For the first author listed, write the last name first. For all other authors, write the first name first.

3. **Anthology or Compilation.** Write the name of the editor, last name first; the abbreviation *ed.;* the title of the book; the place of publication; the publishing company's name; and the year of publication.

4. **Magazine Article.** Write the author's name, last name first; the title of the article; the name of the magazine; the day (if given), month, and year of publication; and the page numbers on which the article begins and ends. If there is no author given, start with the name of the article.

5. **Newspaper Article.** Write the author's name, last name first; the title of the article; the name of the newspaper; the day, month, and year of publication; and the page number (and section number if there is one). If the newspaper has different editions (morning, afternoon), write the edition and *ed.* (for *edition*) before the page number. If there is no author given, start with the title of the article. (Example: *New York Times* 1 Aug. 1991, early ed.: A2.)

6. **Encyclopedia Article.** Write the author's name, last name first; the title of the article; the name of the encyclopedia; and the year of publication, followed by the abbreviation *ed.* (for *edition*). If the article doesn't have an author credited, write the title first.

7. **Radio or Television Program.** Write the title of the program; the local station's call letters; the city of broadcast; and the day, month, and year of the broadcast.

8. **Movie.** Write the title of the work; the director's name preceded by the abbreviation *Dir.* (for *director*); the distributor's name; and the year of release.

9. **Filmstrip, Slide Program, or Videotape.** Write the title of the work; the medium; the producer, director, or developer's name; the distributor's name; the year of release; and the running time or number of slides. (For *director* and *producer,* use *Dir.* or *Prod.* before the individual's name.)

10. **Interview.** Write the interviewee's name; the type of interview (personal or telephone); and the day, month, and year of the interview.

The following sample source cards show how the writer of the model research paper in this chapter recorded her sources. Notice that she has numbered each source card for easy identification.

HERE'S HOW

Bailey, Adrian. *Walt Disney's World of Fantasy.*　　1
　　New York: Everest, 1982.

Travers, Peter. "Summer Sizzlers or Fizzlers?"　　2
　　People Weekly 27 June 1988:11.

Canemaker, John. "Animation." *The World Book*　　3
　　Encyclopedia. 1990 ed.

NBC Nightly News. WNBC, New York.　　4
　　22 June 1990.

Mary Poppins. Dir. Robert Stevenson.　　5
　　Walt Disney, 1964.

Washington, John. Personal interview. 4 July 1991.　　6

COMPOSITION

STYLE NOTE

The style for documenting sources used in this chapter is the one used by the Modern Language Association of America (MLA). Your teacher may ask you to use a different style. Whichever style you use, remember to include all of the required information.

REFERENCE NOTE: For information on capitalizing and punctuating titles, see pages 258–259, 296–297 and 303–304.

COMPUTER NOTE

With access to a computer, you can create a working reference list, add to it (or delete sources that aren't useful) as you go along, and easily keep the list in alphabetical order. You can then use a printout of the list as the first draft of your Works Cited list.

Planning, Recording, and Organizing Information

Preparing an Early Plan

You'll save time in the long run if you take a little time to prepare an **early plan,** a rough list of headings and sub-headings for your report. For example, after some preliminary reading about the combination of animation and live-action film, one writer developed this early plan.

HERE'S HOW

> Combining Animation with Live Action
>
> An early example of animation and live action
> > Methods
> > Problems
>
> Later examples of animation and live action
> > <u>Mary Poppins</u>
> > <u>Who Framed Roger Rabbit</u>
>
> The future of animation and live-action films

This kind of plan will help you decide what information to include in your notes. Keep in mind that you can always change your early plan if you come across new information on your topic.

Taking Notes

If you take good notes, you'll have a record of the information you need when you draft your report.

GUIDELINES FOR TAKING NOTES

1. Use 4" x 6" note cards or half sheets of 8 1/2" x 11" paper.
2. Use a separate note card or sheet of paper for each item of information and for each source.
3. Put a heading of two or three key words in the upper left-hand corner of the card.
4. Write the source card number (see page 417) in the upper right-hand corner and the page numbers at the bottom of the card.

When you take notes, you can *quote directly, summarize,* or *paraphrase.* In some cases, you may have two or three of these different kinds of notes from the same source.

Direct Quotation

Use a **direct quotation** only when the author's *exact words or ideas* are an especially precise or interesting way of saying something. Be sure to copy the author's exact words, using the same capitalization, punctuation, and spelling. Put quotation marks at the beginning and end of any quoted passage.

 NOTE   Taking careful notes and keeping track of your sources will help you avoid *plagiarism.* **Plagiarism** is using someone else's words or ideas as though they were your own. No matter how you use your sources (direct quotation, paraphrase, or summary), be sure to give credit for other people's ideas as well as their words.

Direct Quotation

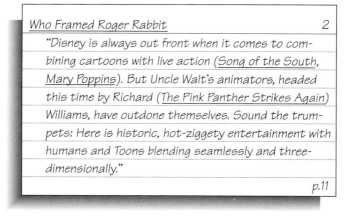

Who Framed Roger Rabbit   2

"Disney is always out front when it comes to combining cartoons with live action (Song of the South,
Mary Poppins). But Uncle Walt's animators, headed
this time by Richard (The Pink Panther Strikes Again)
Williams, have outdone themselves. Sound the trumpets: Here is historic, hot-ziggety entertainment with
humans and Toons blending seamlessly and three-
dimensionally."

                                                        p.11

Summary

A **summary note** includes only the main ideas and the most important supporting ideas. Shorter than the original material, it allows you to save space. Write the note in your own words and sentence structure. (Most of your notes will probably be summary notes.)

Summary Note

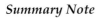

> <u>Who Framed Roger Rabbit</u>   2
>
>   Disney has led the field in combining animation and
> live action. <u>Who Framed Roger Rabbit</u> does so even
> better than before.
>
>
>
>
>
>
>
>   *p.11*

Paraphrase

A **paraphrase note** includes most of the author's ideas, not just the main ones. Like a summary note, it's written in your own words and sentence structure. Begin by identifying the writer whose words you're paraphrasing.

Paraphrase Note

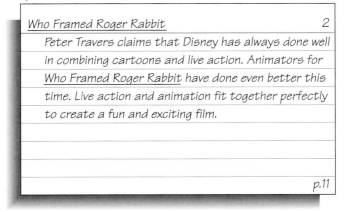

> <u>Who Framed Roger Rabbit</u>   2
>
>   Peter Travers claims that Disney has always done well
> in combining cartoons and live action. Animators for
> <u>Who Framed Roger Rabbit</u> have done even better this
> time. Live action and animation fit together perfectly
> to create a fun and exciting film.
>
>
>
>
>
>   *p.11*

Developing a Thesis Statement

During the planning stage of your research, you should be able to identify a preliminary **thesis statement,** or main

COMPOSITION

COMPOSITION

idea, of your report. Eventually, as you develop your paper, the thesis will become a sentence or two in your paper. For example, here's how one writer began to identify the thesis for a research report on film animation: *Joining animation and live action in one film changes the definition of "cartoon."*

 REFERENCE NOTE: For more information on writing thesis statements, see pages 395–397.

Preparing an Outline

To begin organizing the information you've collected, sort your note cards into groups according to the headings in your early plan. (If you have some information that won't fit under those headings, you may have to create new headings for your final outline.) Then examine each stack, looking for items that if grouped together can create subheadings. Once you've sorted your note cards, think about how best to order the ideas and which supporting details to use, in which sequence.

After you've finished your outline, put your note cards in the same order as your headings. When you begin to write, you will be able to follow your outline and to refer to your cards for facts and information.

NOTE A stack with only a few cards may indicate that the idea should be left out because it isn't very important. Or the stack may instead indicate that you should look for more information on the idea. Think about how important the idea is to the thesis of your paper.

At this stage, your working outline can be in rough form, as long as it contains enough information to guide you as you draft your paper. For your completed paper, however, your teacher may ask for a *formal outline* like the one below.

This is the formal outline the writer created after completing research on the combination of animation and live action. Based on the early plan on page 418, this **formal outline** uses Roman numerals and capital letters. A formal outline is usually composed after the report is written. Included with the research paper, it serves as a table of contents for the reader.

Humans and "Toons": Together Again
 I. Appeal of cartoon characters
 II. Walt Disney's Alice cartoons
    A. Methods
    B. Problems
 III. <u>Mary Poppins</u>
    A. Description of scenes
    B. Problems
 IV. <u>Who Framed Roger Rabbit</u>
    A. Place in film history
    B. Basic method
    C. New methods
       1. Large cameras
       2. Tall movie sets
       3. "Multi-dimensional" characters
 V. Future of animation and live action
    A. New interest in cartoons
    B. Financial success of <u>Roger Rabbit</u>

☞ REFERENCE NOTE: For help in preparing a formal out-line, see pages 399–400.

Writing a First Draft

Combining the Basic Elements of a Research Report

When you write your first draft, you don't just copy down a series of notes from your note cards. Instead, you **synthesize** information and ideas. To *synthesize* means to pull together from various sources and then draw your own conclusions. It's important that your report be more than a string of someone else's ideas. It's also important that you pull information from a variety of sources together in a way that will interest your readers and help them understand the topic. To do that, you begin with the basic form of a composition and add to it several other important elements. The chart on page 424 provides descriptions of the elements of a research report.

COMPOSITION

ELEMENTS OF A RESEARCH REPORT	
Formal outline (optional)	Your teacher may ask you to include a formal outline of your report's content.
Title	Often on a separate page, the title should be both informative and attention-catching. Ask your teacher what format to use.
Introduction	The introduction should catch the reader's attention with interesting details or a striking quotation.
Thesis statement	The thesis statement should be included in the introduction. It may be more than one sentence.
Body	A series of paragraphs in the body should develop the main ideas that support the thesis statement.
Conclusion	The conclusion should briefly restate your thesis in different words, summarize your main points, or do both.
Citations	Sources of specific information should be credited throughout the paper in brief parenthetical references (or in footnotes, if your teacher prefers them).
Works Cited list	All the sources you have cited should be listed at the end of the report, usually on a separate piece of paper.

You can use your outline as a guide for developing your draft. Each heading of your outline may become a separate paragraph, or even two paragraphs, in your paper.

 REFERENCE NOTE: For more information on thesis statements and composition form, see pages 395–397 and 403–408.

Using Quotations

Working a few direct quotations into your report helps make your paper livelier and more believable. Use a direct quotation if you particularly like the author's wording, or if you are afraid that rewording the quotation will introduce an error.

GUIDELINES FOR USING QUOTATIONS

1. Use a phrase or a clause from quoted material as part of one of your own sentences.

    In a process called "multi-dimensional interactive character generation" (Reese 54), lights and shadows were added to the "Toon" drawings.

2. Incorporate a longer quotation by identifying the writer, and follow the writer's name with the quotation itself.

    Peter Travers, for example, writes, "Sound the trumpets: Here is historic, hot-ziggety entertainment with humans and Toons blending seamlessly and three-dimensionally" (11).

3. For a quotation longer than four lines, indent each line ten spaces from the left margin. Lead into the quotation with a few of your own words (usually followed by a colon), but do not use quotation marks—the indentation takes their place.

    In People Weekly, for example, Peter Travers gave the movie this glowing review:

    Disney is always out front when it comes to combining cartoons with live action (Song of the South, Mary Poppins). But Uncle Walt's animators, headed this time by Richard (The Pink Panther Strikes Again) Williams, have outdone themselves. Sound the trumpets: Here is historic, hot-ziggety entertainment with humans and Toons blending seamlessly and three-dimensionally.

Giving Credit to Your Sources

In a research report you borrow the ideas of other people, but you have to acknowledge that you borrowed the ideas. You need to *document*, or give credit to, your sources in the body of your report and in a list at the end of your report.

Giving Credit in the Body of Your Report

As you're writing the body of your report, you must decide *what* to credit and *how* to credit it.

1. *How do you know what to give credit for?* If the same information can be found in several sources, it is considered

common knowledge. You don't have to give credit. For example, it's common knowledge that Martin Luther King, Jr., gave his "I Have a Dream" speech in Washington, D.C., in 1963. You wouldn't have to document that fact.

2. *How do you show the credit?* There are several different ways to give credit. The model research paper in this chapter (pages 427–430) uses examples of the ***parenthetical citation*** format recommended by the Modern Language Association of America (MLA). Some teachers prefer that students use footnotes at the bottom of the page, keyed to numerals in the text, as in this example:

> [1]Finch, Christopher, <u>The Art of Walt Disney: From Mickey Mouse to the Magic Kingdom</u> (New York: Abrams, 1975) 21.

GUIDELINES FOR GIVING CREDIT WITHIN THE REPORT

Place the information in parentheses at the end of the sentence in which you've used someone else's words or ideas.

1. **Print Source with One Author.** Last name of the author followed by the page number(s): (Travers 11)

2. **Print Source with Two or More Authors.** All authors' last names, followed by the page number(s): (Johnson and Smith 64) (Smithers, Jones, and Nye 88)

3. **Print Sources by Authors with the Same Last Name.** First and last name of the particular author, followed by the page number(s): (Marie Muñoz 46) (Ramon Muñoz 19)

4. **Print Source with No Author Given.** Title or a shortened form of it followed by the page number(s): ("New Wave Animation" 22)

5. **One-Page Print Source.** Author's name or the title if no author is listed: (Travers)

6. **Nonprint Source.** The title or a shortened form: (<u>NBC Nightly News</u>)

7. **More Than One Print Source by the Same Author.** Author's last name, followed by the title or a shortened version of it, followed by page number(s): (Cohen, <u>Mysterious Places</u> 3)

8. **Author's Name Included in Paragraph.** Page number only: (11)

Preparing the List of Sources

Anyone who wants to read more about your topic will turn to the list of sources at the end of your report. This list, usually called *Works Cited,* includes all the sources you've used in your report. Another name for this listing, when it includes print sources only, is *Bibliography.*

GUIDELINES FOR PREPARING THE LIST OF WORKS CITED

1. Center the heading *Works Cited* (or *Bibliography*) on a separate sheet of paper, one inch from the top of the page.
2. Begin each listing at the left margin. If the listing is longer than one line, indent the remaining lines five spaces. (See the list of Works Cited on page 430.)
3. For each entry, follow the format you used for your source cards. (See pages 416–417.)
4. List your sources in alphabetical order by the authors' last names (or if no author is listed, by the first important word in the title of the work).
5. If you use more than one source by the same author, include the author's name in only the first entry. For the same author's other entries, use three hyphens followed by a period (- - -.) in place of the name. List the author's works alphabetically by title.

Now read the following research report on animation/live-action films. Notice how the report combines basic composition form with parenthetical documentation and a list of Works Cited.

A MODEL RESEARCH PAPER

Humans and "Toons": Together Again

INTRODUCTION
Specific details
about cartoon
characters

For more than sixty years, movie theater audiences have laughed at cartoon characters like Mickey and Minnie Mouse, Daffy and Donald Duck, Pluto, Wile E. Coyote, and the Road Runner. For the most part, these animated characters lived in

COMPOSITION

their own world. The cartoon usually came first. Then, with Porky Pig's "That's all folks" or the Road Runner's final "Beep! Beep!" the cartoon ended and the real live-action film began. A few creative film-makers, however, have tried to erase the line between "cartoon" and "real" by joining animation and live action in the same film.

Thesis statement

Walt Disney led the way in the 1920s with a series of cartoons about a real girl named Alice. In these cartoons, Alice seems to step into a fantasy world of animated animals. Neither Alice nor the animated figures, however, are very convincing. To make the cartoons, technicians first filmed the little actress against a white back-ground. Then they combined that print with the film of the animated figures. After filming sixty episodes of the Alice comedies, Disney discarded the idea and was eager to return to animation with no human characters (Finch 21).

BODY
First example of animation/live-action film

Explanation of method

Print source—author's name

Not much happened to change animation for forty years. Then cartoon and "real" actors met again in one scene of Walt Disney's 1964 movie <u>Mary Poppins</u>. In this scene, Mary Poppins, the chimneysweep Bert, and the two children step into a cartoon world of animals and people. The live actors sing and dance with the animals and ride horses with the cartoon people. In a few shots, the actors and animated figures actually seem to be touching. In one scene, for example, Mary Poppins and Bert stand on the backs of animated turtles to cross a pond. Like the earlier Alice cartoons, however, the animated figures appear flat, and the scene seems artificial (<u>Mary Poppins</u>).

Second exam-ple—details arranged in chronological order

Nonprint source—title

COMPOSITION

For more than twenty years, there were no other major attempts to join animation and live action. In fact, Americans seemed to lose interest in cartoons entirely; cartoons became an "endangered species" (NBC Nightly News). Then, in 1988, a film titled Who Framed Roger Rabbit made movie history. In this film, live actors star with cartoon characters known as "Toons." Critics agree that Roger Rabbit is a technical success. Peter Travers, for example, writes, "Sound the trumpets: Here is historic, hot-ziggety entertainment with humans and Toons blending seamlessly and three-dimensionally" (11).

To combine animation and live action, the Roger Rabbit filmmakers used the same basic method that was used in Mary Poppins. That is, live action scenes were first shot with the actors pretending that the cartoon characters were present. Later, the animated figures were drawn onto the film, frame by frame (Reese 56).

Roger Rabbit works so well, however, because of several new methods. First, filmmakers used very large, specially made cameras that produced large frames of film. Artists then had plenty of room to draw in the animation, including sophisticated special effects. Also, the movie sets were built ten feet off the ground. Underneath the sets, puppeteers used wires and other devices to make glasses, handkerchiefs, and other objects seem to float through the air. Later, when the cartoon figures were added, they seemed to be carrying the glasses or using the handkerchiefs. As a result, the "Toons" seem actually to be sharing the sets with the real actors (Reese 58).

Margin annotations:

Nonprint sources—titles

Direct quotation— expert opinion

Print source— page number

Explanation of method

Print source— author's name

Explanation of method

Print source— author's name

COMPOSITION

Print source—
author's name

Nonprint
source—title

CONCLUSION
Direct quotation

Print source—
author's name

Print source—
author's name

Another important new method solved the problem of the flat cartoon characters. In a process called "multi-dimensional interactive character generation" (Reese 54), lights and shadows were added to the "Toon" drawings. For the first time, the cartoon characters seem as three-dimensional as the live actors—they even cast shadows (Roger Rabbit).

Roger Rabbit apparently sparked a new interest among Americans in cartoons, a rediscovery of "this world of exaggeration, where good always triumphed, evil was vanquished and funny stuff happened along the way" (Maltin). The financial success of the movie, which earned $153 million during its first year out, means that movie audiences are likely to see more animation/live-action combinations (Wilson 23). Humans and "Toons" are together again, and it looks like a long run.

Works Cited

Finch, Christopher. The Art of Walt Disney: From Mickey Mouse to the Magic Kingdoms. New York: Abrams, 1975.

Maltin, Leonard. "Why We Love Our Cartoon Characters." TV Guide 9 June 1990: 27.

Mary Poppins. Dir. Robert Stevenson. Walt Disney, 1964.

NBC Nightly News. WNBC, New York. 22 June 1990.

Reese, Michael. "The Making of Roger Rabbit." Newsweek 27 June 1988: 54-59.

Travers, Peter. "Summer Sizzlers or Fizzlers?" People Weekly 27 June 1988: 11.

Who Framed Roger Rabbit. Dir. Robert Zemeckis. Touchstone Home Video, 1988.

Wilson, David S. "Tooned On!" TV Guide 9 June 1990: 22+.

COMPOSITION

Evaluating and Revising

To evaluate your report, ask yourself the questions in the left-hand column of the following chart. If you uncover weaknesses, use the revision techniques in the right-hand column to correct them.

EVALUATING AND REVISING RESEARCH REPORTS	
EVALUATION GUIDE	**REVISION TECHNIQUE**
1 Does the introduction grab the reader's attention and present a clear thesis statement?	Start with an interesting fact or quotation. **Add** a sentence that presents your conclusions about your research.
2 Are ideas and information pulled together (synthesized) and stated in the writer's own words?	Be sure that the topic sentence of each paragraph in your report is in your own words and expresses your own ideas. **Add** or **replace** topic sentences as necessary.
3 Are ideas supported with enough information? Will readers find the information complete?	**Add** information such as facts and statistics, expert opinions, examples, and explanations. **Add** surprising details.
4 Are enough print and non-print sources used? Are they relevant, recent, reliable, and representative?	Use your library's on-line or card catalog and the *Readers' Guide* to find more sources. **Interview** someone. **Add** information from these sources to your report.
5 Does all the information relate directly to the topic?	**Cut** information not directly related to your topic
6 Is proper credit given for each source of information used?	**Add** documentation for any information that isn't common knowledge.
7 Are the formats for giving credit to sources within a report and at the end of a report carefully followed?	**Replace** incorrect items in your documentation so that it follows the MLA format or another format recommended by your teacher.

COMPOSITION

The following paragraph from the sample report on pages 427–430 illustrates how the writer used the revision techniques.

so well, however, because of several new methods,
Roger Rabbit works ~~well.~~ First, filmmakers   **replace**

used very large, specially made cameras that

produced large frames of film. ~~I wonder who~~   **cut**

~~invented those.~~ Artists then had plenty of
                    ∧*including sophisticated special effects,*
room to draw in the animation. Also, the   **add**

movie sets were built ten feet off the ground.

Underneath the sets, puppeteers used wires
                glasses, handkerchiefs, and other objects,
and other devices to make ~~things~~ seem to   **replace**

float through the air. Later, when the cartoon

figures were added, they seemed to be
        the glasses   *the handkerchiefs*
carrying or using ~~these things.~~ As a result,   **add/replace**

the "Toons" seem actually to be sharing the
                        (Reese 58)
sets with the real actors.   **add**

Calvin & Hobbes copyright 1989 Watterson. Reprinted with permission of Universal Press Syndicate. All rights reserved.

Proofreading and Publishing

Proofread your report to clean up any careless errors, and then try one of these suggestions for publishing your research findings.

- Prepare a copy of your report to present to an elementary school library for reference.
- If you wrote about a science or history topic, volunteer to make an oral report about your research to your science or history class.

RESOURCES

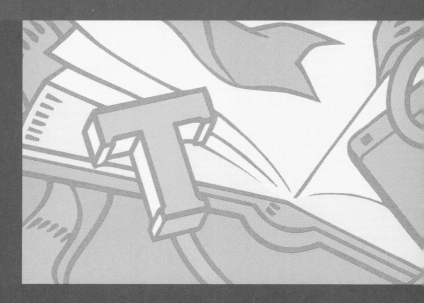

RESOURCES

RESOURCES

Exploring the Library; Using Dictionaries; Preparing Letters, Forms, and Manuscripts

The Library/Media Center

Finding Books in the Library

Libraries classify and arrange books by one of two classification systems: *the Dewey decimal system* or *the Library of Congress system.* By using one of these systems, a library can give a number and letter code—a **call number**—to each book. This number tells you how the book has been classified and where it has been placed on the shelves.

The Dewey Decimal System

Nonfiction. In the Dewey decimal system, which most school libraries use, works of nonfiction are assigned numbers according to their subjects.

Collective biographies (biographies about several people) are classified separately. They may be given a special number or placed in a separate section. Biographies are arranged in alphabetical order according to the subjects' last names. If there are multiple volumes about the same person, the biographies are then arranged according to the last names of their authors.

DEWEY CLASSIFICATION OF NONFICTION		
NUMBERS	**SUBJECT AREAS**	**EXAMPLES OF SUBDIVISIONS**
000–099	General Works	encyclopedias, handbooks
100–199	Philosophy	psychology, ethics, personality
200–299	Religion	bibles, mythology, theology
300–399	Social Science	government, law, economics, education
400–499	Languages	dictionaries, grammar, foreign languages
500–599	Science	general science, biology, chemistry, geology, mathematics
600–699	Technology	engineering, business, health, medical science, environment
700–799	The Arts	music, painting, theater, recreation
800–899	Literature	poetry, drama, essays
900–999	History	biography, geography, travel

NOTE Some libraries use the letter *R* before the call numbers of reference books in any of these categories.

Fiction. The Dewey decimal system groups works of fiction in alphabetical order according to the authors' last names. When a library has several novels by the same author, they are arranged alphabetically by the first word of the title (not counting *A, An,* or *The*). Sometimes, collections of short stories are grouped separately.

The Card Catalog

The *card catalog* is a cabinet of small drawers containing cards. These cards list books by title, author, and subject. For each book in the library, there are at least two cards—a *title card* and an *author card.* If the book is nonfiction, there is a third card—a *subject card.* Occasionally, you may find "see" or "see also" cards. These are cross-reference cards that direct you to another section of the card catalog where additional information on a particular subject may be found.

An *on-line catalog* is a computerized version of the card catalog. It contains the same information found on the title, author, subject, and "see also" cards.

RESOURCES

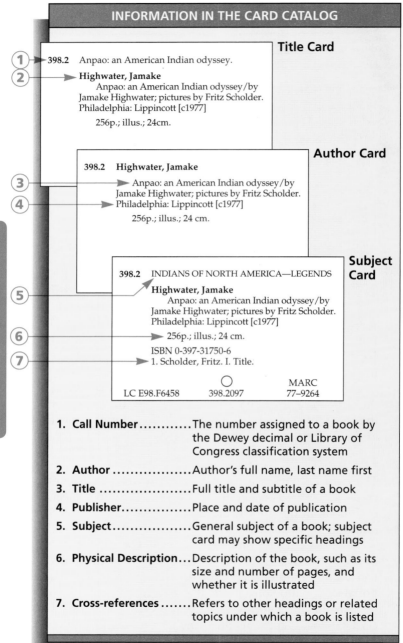

INFORMATION IN THE CARD CATALOG

Title Card

1 ► 398.2 Anpao: an American Indian odyssey.

2 ► **Highwater, Jamake**
Anpao: an American Indian odyssey/by Jamake Highwater; pictures by Fritz Scholder. Philadelphia: Lippincott [c1977]

256p.; illus.; 24cm.

Author Card

398.2 **Highwater, Jamake**

3 ► Anpao: an American Indian odyssey/by Jamake Highwater; pictures by Fritz Scholder.

4 ► Philadelphia: Lippincott [c1977]

256p.; illus.; 24 cm.

Subject Card

398.2 INDIANS OF NORTH AMERICA—LEGENDS

Highwater, Jamake
Anpao: an American Indian odyssey/by Jamake Highwater; pictures by Fritz Scholder. Philadelphia: Lippincott [c1977]

5 ►
6 ► 256p.; illus.; 24 cm.

ISBN 0-397-31750-6

7 ► 1. Scholder, Fritz. I. Title.

LC E98.F6458   398.2097   MARC 77–9264

RESOURCES

1. **Call Number** .... The number assigned to a book by the Dewey decimal or Library of Congress classification system

2. **Author** .... Author's full name, last name first

3. **Title** .... Full title and subtitle of a book

4. **Publisher** .... Place and date of publication

5. **Subject** .... General subject of a book; subject card may show specific headings

6. **Physical Description** ... Description of the book, such as its size and number of pages, and whether it is illustrated

7. **Cross-references** .... Refers to other headings or related topics under which a book is listed

Using Reference Materials

The *Readers' Guide to Periodical Literature*

To find a magazine article, use the *Readers' Guide to Periodical Literature.* The *Readers' Guide* indexes all the articles, poems, and stories from more than one hundred magazines. Paperback editions of the *Readers' Guide* are printed throughout the year. Bound volumes are published annually.

In the *Readers' Guide,* magazine articles are listed alphabetically by author and by subject. These headings are printed in boldfaced capital letters.

Entries may contain abbreviations. Use the key at the front of the *Readers' Guide* to find the meanings of these abbreviations.

The *Readers' Guide* gives a great deal of information in a very compact space. You can see how *Readers' Guide* entries are arranged by looking at the following excerpt.

RESOURCES

(1) **Subject entry**

(2) **Title of article**

(3) **Name of magazine**

(4) **Volume number of magazine**

(5) **Author entry**

(6) **Page reference**

(7) **Author of article**

(8) **Date of magazine**

(9) **Subject cross-reference**

Special Information Sources

The *vertical file* is a set of file drawers containing up-to-date materials such as pamphlets, newspaper clippings, and pictures. The pamphlets may include government, business, and educational information.

Microforms are photographically reduced articles from newspapers and magazines. The two most common kinds of microforms are *microfilm* (a roll or reel of film) and *microfiche* (a sheet of film). A special machine enlarges the images and projects them onto a screen.

Libraries can store many reference sources on a computer in a *database.* A *database* is a body of information that is stored on a computer for easy retrieval.

Many libraries also have *audiovisual materials* such as audiocassettes and videotapes. The librarian can tell you what information sources are available in these forms.

Reference Books

You can use many types of reference books to find specific kinds of information.

REFERENCE WORKS	
TYPE	**DESCRIPTION**
ENCYCLOPEDIAS *Collier's Encyclopedia* *Compton's Encyclopedia* *The Encyclopedia Americana* *The New Encyclopaedia Britannica* *The World Book Encyclopedia*	■ multiple volumes ■ articles arranged alphabetically by subject ■ best source for general information ■ may have index or annuals
GENERAL BIOGRAPHICAL REFERENCES *Current Biography Yearbook* *Dictionary of American Biography* *The International Who's Who* *Webster's New Biographical Dictionary*	■ information about birth, nationality, and major accomplishments of prominent people

(continued)

RESOURCES

REFERENCE WORKS *(continued)*	
TYPE	**DESCRIPTION**
SPECIAL BIOGRAPHICAL REFERENCES *American Men and Women of Science* *Biographical Dictionary of American Sports* *A Biographical Dictionary of Film* *Mexican American Biographies*	■ information about people noted for accomplishments in a specific field or for membership in a specific group
ATLASES *Atlas of World Cultures* *Hammond World Atlas* *National Geographic Atlas of the World*	■ maps and geographical information
ALMANACS *Information Please Almanac, Atlas and Yearbook* *The World Almanac and Book of Facts*	■ up-to-date information about current events, facts, statistics, and dates
BOOKS OF QUOTATIONS Bartlett's *Familiar Quotations* *The New Book of Unusual Quotations* *The Oxford Dictionary of Quotations*	■ famous quotations indexed or grouped by subject ■ often tell author, source, and date
BOOKS OF SYNONYMS *The New Roget's Thesaurus in Dictionary Form* *Roget's International Thesaurus* *Webster's New Dictionary of Synonyms*	■ lists of exact or more interesting words to express ideas
LITERARY REFERENCES *Essay and General Literature Index* *Granger's Index to Poetry* *Play Index* *Short Story Index* *Subject Index to Poetry*	■ information about various works of literature

RESOURCES

The Dictionary

Types of Dictionaries

Many different versions of dictionaries are available for the English language. Different versions contain different kinds and amounts of information.

TYPES OF DICTIONARIES		
EXAMPLE	**NUMBER OF ENTRIES**	**NUMBER OF PAGES**
Unabridged *Webster's Third New International Dictionary, Unabridged*	460,000	2,662
Abridged or College *Random House College Dictionary*	173,000	1,565
Paperback *Funk and Wagnalls Standard Dictionary*	82,000	1,014

The key on page 443 explains the parts of the sample entry below.

① ② ③ ④ ⑤

⑥ ⑦ ⑧ ⑨ ⑩

in·dulge (in dulj′) *vt.* **-dulged′, -dulg′ing** [L *indulgere*, to be kind to, yield to < *in-* + base prob. akin to Gr *dolichos*, long & Goth *tulgus*, firm] **1** to yield to or satisfy (a desire); give oneself up to [to *indulge* a craving for sweets] **2** to gratify the wishes of; be very lenient with; humor **3** [Archaic] to grant as a kindness, favor, or privilege —*vi.* to give way to one's own desires; indulge oneself (*in* something) —**in·dulg′er** *n.*

SYN.—indulge implies a yielding to the wishes or desires of oneself or another, as because of a weak will or an amiable nature; **humor** suggests compliance with the mood or whim of another [they *humored* the dying man]; **pamper** implies overindulgence or excessive gratification; **spoil** emphasizes the harm done to the personality or character by overindulgence or excessive attention [grandparents often *spoil* children]; **baby** suggests the sort of pampering and devoted care lavished on infants and connotes a potential loss of self-reliance [because he was sickly, his mother continued to *baby* him] —**ANT.** discipline, restrain

From *Webster's New World Dictionary,* Third College Edition. Copyright © 1988 by Simon and Schuster, Inc. Reprinted by permission of Webster's New World Dictionaries, a division of Simon & Schuster, New York.

Information Found in Dictionaries

1. **Entry word.** The entry word shows how the word is spelled and how it is divided into syllables. The entry word may also show capitalization and alternate spellings.

2. **Pronunciation.** The pronunciation is shown by the use of accent marks and either phonetic respellings or diacritical marks. A pronunciation key (often at the bottom of every page or two) explains the sounds represented by these symbols.

3. **Part-of-speech label.** This label (usually in abbreviated form) indicates how the entry word should be used in a sentence. Some words may be used as more than one part of speech. In this case, a part-of-speech label is given in front of each numbered (or lettered) series of definitions.

4. **Other forms.** These spellings may show plural forms of nouns, tenses of verbs, or the comparison forms of adjectives and adverbs.

5. **Etymology.** The etymology is the origin and history of a word. It tells how the word (or its parts) came into English.

6. **Examples.** Phrases or sentences may demonstrate how the defined word is used.

7. **Definitions.** If a word has more than one meaning, its definitions are numbered or lettered. Most dictionaries arrange definitions in order of the frequency of their current use.

8. **Special usage labels.** These labels identify words that have special meaning or are used in special ways in certain fields. These labels are usually abbreviated. The dictionary contains a key to explain the abbreviations used.

9. **Related word forms.** These various forms of the entry word are usually created by adding suffixes or prefixes.

10. **Synonyms and antonyms.** Sometimes synonyms or antonyms appear at the end of a word entry.

RESOURCES

Letters and Forms

Business Letters

The Appearance of a Business Letter

Follow these standards for the style and format of business letters.

- Use plain, unlined $8\frac{1}{2}"$ x $11"$ paper.
- Type your letter if possible (single-spaced, leaving an extra line between paragraphs). Otherwise, neatly write the letter by hand, using black or blue ink.
- Center your letter on the page with equal margins (usually one inch) on the sides and at the top and bottom.
- Use only one side of the paper. If your letter won't fit on one page, leave a one-inch margin at the bottom of the first page and carry over at least two lines onto the second page.
- Avoid cross-outs, smudges, erasures, and inkblots. Check for typing errors and misspellings.

The Parts of a Business Letter

The six parts of a business letter are

(1) the heading   (4) the body
(2) the inside address   (5) the closing
(3) the salutation   (6) the signature

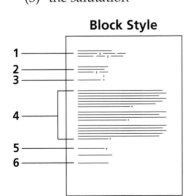

Block Style   **Modified Block Style**

RESOURCES

These six parts are usually arranged on the page in one of two styles. When you use the *block form,* begin every part of the letter at the left margin and do not indent the paragraphs. However, if you use the *modified block form,* place the heading, the closing, and your signature just to the right of the center of the page. Put all the other parts of the letter at the left margin, and indent each paragraph.

The Heading. The heading usually has three lines:
- your street address (or post office box number)
- your city, state, and ZIP Code
- the date the letter was written

The Inside Address. The inside address gives the name and address of the person or organization to whom you are writing. If you're directing your letter to someone by name, use a courtesy title (such as *Mr., Ms., Mrs.,* or *Miss*) or a professional title (such as *Dr.* or *Professor*) in front of the person's name. After the person's name, include the person's business title, if you know what it is. Follow that line with the name of the company or organization and the address.

The Salutation. The salutation is your greeting. If you are writing to a specific person, begin with *Dear,* followed by a courtesy title or a professional title and the person's name. End that line with a colon.

If you don't have the name of a specific person, use a general salutation, such as *Dear Sir or Madam* or *Ladies and Gentlemen.* Or you can use a department or a position title, with or without the word *Dear.*

The Body. The body, or main part, of your letter contains your message. If the body of your letter contains more than one paragraph, leave a space between paragraphs.

The Closing. The closing should end your letter courteously. Among the closings often used in business letters are *Yours truly, Sincerely,* and *Sincerely yours.* Capitalize only the first word of the closing.

The Signature. Your signature should be handwritten in ink, directly below the closing. Always sign your full name, and do not use a title (such as *Mr., Ms., Dr.,* and so on). If your letter is typed, type your name neatly just below your signature (four lines below the closing).

GUIDELINES FOR THE CONTENTS OF A BUSINESS LETTER

Business letters follow a few simple guidelines.

- *Use a polite, respectful, professional tone.* A courteous letter is more effective than a rude or angry one.

- *Use formal, standard English.* Avoid slang, contractions, and most abbreviations. Informal language that might be acceptable in a telephone conversation or personal letter is often inappropriate in a business letter.

- *Explain the purpose of your letter quickly and clearly.* Be polite, but get to the point.

- *Include all necessary information.* Be sure your reader can understand why you wrote and what you are asking.

Types of Business Letters

Request or Order Letters. In a *request letter,* you're asking for something. Perhaps you want information about a product you're thinking about buying or a place you're planning to visit. Or maybe you want someone to do something for you—speak to your class, sponsor a charity walkathon, or provide space for a school event.

An *order letter* is a special kind of request letter that asks for something specific, such as a free brochure advertised in a magazine. An order letter may be used to order an item in a catalog or magazine when you don't have a printed order form.

When you are writing a request or order letter, remember the following points.

1. Clearly state your request.
2. If you're asking someone to send you information, enclose a self-addressed, stamped envelope.
3. If you're asking someone to do something for you, make your request well in advance.
4. If you're ordering something, include all important information. Give the size, color, brand name, or any other specific information. If there are costs involved, add the amount correctly.

Here is a sample request letter.

Bethlehem High School
700 Delaware Avenue
Delmar, NY 12054
October 12, 1995

Ms. Ellen Phillips, Staff Writer
The Albany Times Mirror
News Plaza, Box 1000
Albany, NY 12212

Dear Ms. Phillips:

I would like to invite you to be one of our speakers at the Bethlehem High School Career Day. This year's event will be held on December 16, from 9:00 A.M. to 4:00 P.M.

Please let me know if you would be interested in speaking to an audience of about fifty students for a fifteen-minute talk about your career in journalism. We can schedule your talk at your convenience.

I look forward to hearing from you soon.

Yours truly,

Jennifer Savage

Jennifer Savage,
Student Coordinator
Career Day '95

Complaint or Adjustment Letters. The purpose of a *complaint* or *adjustment letter* is to report an error or to state that you have not received services or products that you have reason to expect.

When you are writing a complaint or an adjustment letter, remember these points.

1. Be prompt about registering your complaint.
2. Be sure to mention specifics. Necessary details might include
  ■ why you are unhappy with the product or service
  ■ how you were affected (lost time, money, or convenience)
  ■ what solution you want to correct the problem

3. Keep the tone of your letter calm and courteous.
Here is the body of a sample adjustment letter.

> On January 2, 1995, I ordered a plaid shirt from
> your catalog: Item #3121HH, size 38 medium,
> described as "a washable wool/polyester blend."
> The shirt cost $27, plus $1.50 shipping and
> handling, for a total of $28.50.
>
> However, the first time I washed the shirt, the
> side seam split apart. I followed the washing
> directions on the label carefully.
>
> I am returning the shirt. Please send a replacement
> shirt or a refund. Thank you for your attention to
> this matter.

Appreciation or Commendation Letters. In an *appreciation* or *commendation letter,* you express your appreciation for a person, a group, an organization, or a product or service. Be specific about why you are pleased. For example, you may have appreciated the fine service you received at a restaurant or the excellent performance of a local theater company.

Here is the body of a sample appreciation letter.

> I am writing to let you know how much I enjoyed
> your museum's recent exhibition on contemporary
> African American artists. My high school's art
> class was impressed and inspired by what we saw.
> I particularly enjoyed the paintings by Jacob
> Lawrence.
>
> I hope you will continue to present such
> exceptional shows. I plan to revisit your gallery
> whenever I can.

RESOURCES

Letters of Application. In a *letter of application,* you provide a selection committee or a potential employer with information so that a decision can be made about whether you are qualified for a position. That position may be a scholarship, membership in an organization, or a job.

Here is a sample application letter.

> 5231 Meadowbrook Ave.
> Spokane, WA 99210
> February 7, 1995
>
> Ms. Regina Lewis, Coordinator
> French Student Exchange Program
> P.O. Box 2711
> New Haven, CT 06510
>
> Dear Ms. Lewis:
>
> Please consider me a candidate for the exchange program in Lyon, France, advertised in the January 24 <u>New York Times</u>. I am a freshman at McAuliffe High School in Spokane, Washington. I have been taking French courses since the sixth grade, and last year I won my middle school's French medal for my work in that subject. My overall grade-point average this year is 3.8.
>
> Being selected to participate in this program would be an honor for me. I understand that representing the United States in such a program is a great responsibility, and I would welcome the opportunity to bring a better understanding of the French language and culture to my school and my community.
>
> My parents actively support my interest in the program. Several other adults who know me well have agreed to provide you with references of my qualifications for the program.
>
> If you need more information, please let me know. I look forward to hearing from you.
>
> Sincerely,
>
> *Angela Dowling*
> Angela Dowling

RESOURCES

Keep the following points in mind when you write a letter of application.

1. Identify the position you are applying for. Mention how you heard about the position.
2. Tell something about yourself. Depending on the position, you might include information about
   - your age, grade in school, and grade-point average
   - your activities, awards, and honors
   - personal attributes or character traits that make you a good choice for the position
   - the date or times you are available
3. Offer to provide references. Suitable references are usually two or three responsible adults (other than relatives) who know your character or qualifications and who have agreed to recommend you. Be prepared to supply the names and addresses of your references.

Writing Personal Letters

There are times when a letter is the most appropriate form of communication for personal messages. You might write letters of this type for thank-you letters, invitations, or regret letters.

Personal letters are much less formal than business letters. Use the modified block form, but do not include an inside address. Often, personal letters are neatly handwritten rather than typed. You can use the stationery or writing paper of your choice.

Thank-you letters. These informal letters of appreciation tell someone that you appreciate his or her taking time, trouble, or expense on your behalf. Try to think of something about the person's effort or gift that made it special to you.

Invitations. An informal invitation should contain specific information about the occasion, the time and place, and any other special details your guests might need to know (such as that everyone is expected to bring a gift, wear a costume, or bring food for a potluck meal).

Letters of Regret. Send a letter of regret if you have been invited somewhere and are unable to go. A written reply is especially appropriate if you were sent a written invitation with the letters *R.S.V.P.* (in French, an abbreviation for "please reply").

Addressing an Envelope

Place your complete return address in the top left-hand corner of the envelope. Center the name and address of the person or organization to whom you are writing on the envelope. For a business letter, the addressee's name and address should exactly match the inside address. Use the two-letter postal service abbreviation on the envelope rather than writing out the state name. Be sure to include the correct ZIP Code.

☞ REFERENCE NOTE: See pages 457–458 for a list of abbreviations for state names and other political units.

Completing Printed Forms

Printed forms vary, but there are certain standard techniques that will help you fill out any form accurately and completely.

Read all of the instructions carefully. Be sure you know what to do before you begin writing.

Type or write neatly, using a pen or pencil as directed. Unless you are specifically instructed to use pencil, type or print your information on the form in blue or black ballpoint pen.

Proofread your completed form. Make sure you have given all the information that has been requested on the form. Check for errors and correct them neatly.

Manuscript Style

A carefully prepared manuscript gives your readers a good first impression of your ideas. Present your ideas in a favorable light by setting up your paper correctly, by using abbreviations and numbers correctly, and by avoiding sexist language.

Materials and Arrangement

Use the following guidelines as you make a final copy of your paper.

Handwritten Papers

■ Use regular 8 $^1/_2$" x 11" lined paper. Do not use ragged-edged paper torn from a spiral-bound notebook.
■ Use blue or black ink.
■ Write legibly: Dot your *i*'s, cross your *t*'s, and distinguish among *o*'s, *a*'s, and *e*'s.
■ Use only one side of a sheet of paper.
■ Do not skip lines unless your teacher tells you to do so.

Typewritten Papers

■ Use regular 8 $^1/_2$" x 11" typing paper. Avoid very thin (onionskin) paper and erasable paper.
■ Use a fresh black ribbon.
■ Double-space between lines.

Word-Processed Papers

■ Use letter-sized sheets or continuous-feed paper that separates cleanly along the edges.
■ Make sure that the printer you use can produce clear, dark, letter-quality type.
■ Check with your teacher to be sure that the typeface you plan to use is acceptable.
■ Double-space between lines.

General Guidelines

Set up your pages to make them clear and readable. Whether your paper is handwritten, typed, or word-processed, use the following format.

■ Leave one-inch margins at the top, sides, and bottom of each page.
■ Indent the first line of each paragraph five spaces from the left margin.

- Number all pages (except the first page) in the upper right-hand corner, one-half inch from the top.
- Follow your teacher's instructions for placement of your name, the date, your class, and the title of your paper.
- Make corrections neatly. You may make a few corrections with correction fluid, but they should be barely noticeable. To insert a word or a short phrase, use a caret mark (∧) and add the word(s) immediately above it.
- Use charts, graphs, tables, and illustrations effectively. Place such materials close to the text they illustrate. Label and number each one. The standard labels are *Table* (for tables) and *Figure* or *Fig.* (for photographs, drawings, maps, graphs, charts, and the like). Give each table or figure a number and title. Whenever necessary, give the source of the material.

EXAMPLE

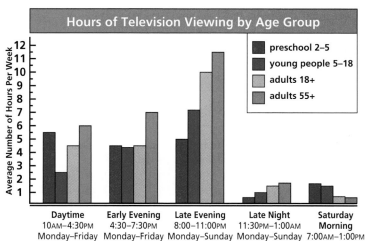

RESOURCES

Word-processing software and printers can help you format your paper in some or all of these ways:

- producing *italic* and **bold** type
- centering heads
- numbering pages

- generating black-and-white or color graphics
- setting up tables, charts, and graphs
- formatting Works Cited list with hanging indent

NOTE Keep a copy of any paper you submit, either by photocopying it or by storing it on a computer disk. Also, keep your notes and any rough drafts until after your teacher returns your paper to you. These steps will make life a lot easier should anything happen to the original copy of your paper.

Abbreviations

An **abbreviation** is a shortened form of a word or phrase. Only a few abbreviations are appropriate in the text of a formal paper written for a general (nontechnical) audience. In tables, notes, and bibliographies, abbreviations can be used more freely in order to save space.

Personal Names

Abbreviate given names only if the person is most commonly known that way.

EXAMPLES   Ida **B.** Wells   **T. H.** White   **M.F.K.** Fisher

NOTE Leave a space between two such initials, but not between three or more.

Titles

(1) Abbreviate social titles whether used before the full name or before the last name alone.

EXAMPLES   **Mr.**   **Mrs.**   **Ms.**
            Sr. (Señor)   **Sra.** (Señora) **Dr.**

(2) Civil and military titles may be abbreviated when used before full names or before initials and last names. Spell them out before last names alone.

EXAMPLES   **Brig. Gen.** Norman   **Brigadier General**
                    Schwartzkopf   Schwartzkopf

Sen. Carol Moseley Braun	**Senator** Moseley Braun
Prof. S. I. Hayakawa	**Professor** Hayakawa

COMMON CIVIL AND MILITARY TITLES	
CIVIL	**MILITARY**
Amb., Ambassador	Adm., Admiral
Gov., Governor	Brig. Gen., Brigadier General
Lt. Gov., Lieutenant Governor	Capt., Captain
Pres., President	Col., Colonel
Prof., Professor	Gen., General
Rep., Representative	Lt., Lieutenant
Sen., Senator	Maj., Major
Supt., Superintendent	Sgt., Sergeant

(3) Abbreviate titles and academic degrees that follow proper names.

EXAMPLES   Hank Williams, **Jr.**   Joycelyn Elders, **M.D.**

NOTE   Do not include the titles *Mr., Mrs., Ms.,* or *Dr.* when you use a title or degree after a name.

EXAMPLE   **Dr.** Joan West *or* Joan West, **M.D.** [*not* Dr. Joan West, M.D.]

Company Names

Spell out most company names in text. They may be abbreviated in tables, notes, and bibliographies.

TEXT	Novak Brothers Shipping Company
TABLES, NOTES, ETC.	Novak Bros.

COMMON PARTS OF COMPANY NAMES	
Bro., Bros., Brothers	Inc., Incorporated
Co., Company	Ltd., Limited
Corp., Corporation	& (ampersand), and

RESOURCES

Agencies and Organizations

After spelling out the first use, abbreviate the names of agencies, organizations, and other things commonly known by their initials.

EXAMPLE	My older sister encouraged me to sign up for the **Preliminary Scholastic Aptitude Test (PSAT).** She said that taking the **PSAT** is a good practice for the standardized tests I'll face in the next few years.
EXAMPLES	AMA, American Medical Association
	CPU, Central Processing Unit
	HUD, (Department of) Housing and Urban Development
	RAM, random-access memory

A few acronyms (abbreviations pronounced as words) such as *radar, laser,* and *sonar,* are now considered common nouns and thus are no longer capitalized. Such acronyms do not need to be spelled out on first use. When you're not sure whether an acronym should be capitalized, check a recent dictionary.

☞ REFERENCE NOTE: See rule 14h, pages 314–315, for information on forming the plurals of abbreviations.

Geographical Terms

States.   In text, spell out the names of states and of other political units whether they stand alone or follow any other geographical term. Abbreviate them in tables, notes, and bibliographies.

EXAMPLES	Sandra Cisneros spent her early years in **Chicago, Illinois,** and **Mexico City, Mexico.** On our vacation to **Canada,** we visited **Victoria,** the capital of **British Columbia.**
EXCEPTION	Always include the traditional abbreviation for the District of Columbia, *D.C.,* with the city name, *Washington,* to distinguish it from the state of Washington.

In tables, notes, and bibliographies, use the first of the two forms shown in the following table. Use the second form only in addresses that include the ZIP Code.

ABBREVIATIONS FOR POLITICAL UNITS		
POLITICAL UNIT	**TRADITIONAL**	**POSTAL SERVICE**
Alabama	Ala.	AL
Alaska	Alaska	AK
Arizona	Ariz.	AZ
Arkansas	Ark.	AR
California	Calif.	CA
Colorado	Colo.	CO
Connecticut	Conn.	CT
Delaware	Del.	DE
District of Columbia	D.C.	DC
Florida	Fla.	FL
Georgia	Ga.	GA
Guam	Guam	GU
Hawaii	Hawaii	HI
Idaho	Idaho	ID
Illinois	Ill.	IL
Indiana	Ind.	IN
Iowa	Iowa	IA
Kansas	Kans.	KS
Kentucky	Ky.	KY
Louisiana	La.	LA
Maine	Maine	ME
Maryland	Md.	MD
Massachusetts	Mass.	MA
Michigan	Mich.	MI
Minnesota	Minn.	MN
Mississippi	Miss.	MS
Missouri	Mo.	MO
Montana	Mont.	MT
Nebraska	Nebr.	NB
Nevada	Nev.	NV
New Hampshire	N.H.	NH
New Jersey	N.J.	NJ
New Mexico	N.Mex.	NM
New York	N.Y.	NY
North Carolina	N.C.	NC
North Dakota	N.Dak.	ND
Ohio	Ohio	OH
Oklahoma	Okla.	OK
Oregon	Oreg.	OR
Pennsylvania	Pa.	PA
Puerto Rico	P.R.	PR
Rhode Island	R.I.	RI

RESOURCES

(continued)

ABBREVIATIONS FOR POLITICAL UNITS *(continued)*		
POLITICAL UNIT	**TRADITIONAL**	**POSTAL SERVICE**
South Carolina	S.C.	SC
South Dakota	S.Dak.	SD
Tennessee	Tenn.	TN
Texas	Tex.	TX
Utah	Utah	UT
Vermont	Vt.	VT
Virgin Islands	V.I.	VI
Virginia	Va.	VA
Washington	Wash.	WA
West Virginia	W.Va.	WV
Wisconsin	Wis.	WI
Wyoming	Wyo.	WY

Countries. In text, spell out the names of countries. Such names may be abbreviated in tables, notes, bibliographies, and so on.

TEXT	**TABLES, NOTES, ETC.**
Brazil	Braz.
Canada	Can.
France	Fr.
Germany	Ger.
Great Britain	G.B.
Jamaica	Jam.
Mexico	Mex.
New Zealand	N.Z.
People's Republic of China	P.R.O.C.
United Kingdom	U.K.
United States	U.S.

Addresses. In text, spell out every word in an address. Such words should be abbreviated in letter and envelope addresses and may be abbreviated in tables, notes, bibliographies, and so on.

TEXT	TABLES, NOTES, ETC.
Avenue	Ave.
Boulevard	Blvd.
Drive	Dr.
North, South, East, West (before street names)	N., S., E., W.
Road	Rd.
Route	Rte.
Street	St.

Time

Eras. Abbreviate the two most frequently used era designations, *A.D.* and *B.C.*

The abbreviation *A.D.* stands for the Latin phrase *anno Domini,* meaning "in the year of the Lord." It is used with dates in the Christian era. When used with a specific year number, *A.D.* precedes the number. When used with the name of a century, it follows the name.

EXAMPLES In **A.D.** 476, the last Roman emperor, Augustulus, was overthrown by Germanic tribes.
The legends of King Arthur may be based on the life of a real British leader of the fourth century **A.D.**

The abbreviation *B.C.,* which stands for "before Christ," is used for dates before the Christian era. It follows either a specific year number or the name of a century.

EXAMPLES Homer's epic poem the *Iliad* was probably composed between 900 and 700 **B.C.**
The poem describes battles that probably occurred around the twelfth century **B.C.**

Months and Days. In text, spell out the names of months and days whether they appear alone or in dates. Both types of names may be abbreviated in tables, notes, and bibliographies.

RESOURCES

TEXT		TABLES, NOTES, ETC.	
MONTHS	**DAYS**	**MONTHS**	**DAYS**
January	Sunday	Jan.	Sun.
February	Monday	Feb.	Mon.
March	Tuesday	Mar.	Tues.
April	Wednesday	Apr.	Wed.
May	Thursday	May	Thurs.
June	Friday	June	Fri.
July	Saturday	July	Sat.
August		Aug.	
September		Sept.	
October		Oct.	
November		Nov.	
December		Dec.	

Time of Day.   Abbreviate the designations for the two halves of the day measured by clock time.

The abbreviation *A.M.* stands for the Latin phrase *ante meridiem,* meaning "before noon." The abbreviation *P.M.* stands for *post meridiem,* meaning "after noon." Both abbreviations follow the numerals designating the specific time.

EXAMPLE   My mom works four days a week, from 8:00 **A.M.** until 6:00 **P.M.**

STYLE NOTE

Do not use *A.M.* or *P.M.* with numbers spelled out as words or as substitutes for the words *morning, afternoon,* or *evening.*

INCORRECT   The walkathon will begin at eight A.M. Saturday.

CORRECT   The walkathon will begin at **8:00 A.M.** (or **eight o'clock in the morning**) Saturday.

INCORRECT   In "The Love Song of J. Alfred Prufrock," T. S. Eliot describes the catlike movements of fog on a P.M. in London.

CORRECT   In "The Love Song of J. Alfred Prufrock," T. S. Eliot describes the catlike movements of fog on an **evening** in London.

Also, do not use the words *morning, afternoon,* or *evening* with numerals followed by *A.M.* or *P.M.*

INCORRECT	The next bus for Roanoke leaves at 1:30 P.M. in the afternoon.
CORRECT	The next bus for Roanoke leaves at **1:30 P.M.** (*or* **one-thirty in the afternoon**).

Other Abbreviations

Parts of Books.   In text, spell out the words *volume, part, unit, chapter,* and *page.*

EXAMPLE   The graph in **Volume 1, Chapter 6, page 178,** shows the percentage of school-age children in the United States from 1900 to 1980.

NOTE   With the exception of *page,* the names of parts of books identified by a number are usually capitalized.

School Subjects.   In text, spell out the names of school subjects.

EXAMPLE   Mrs. Colón teaches **Algebra I** [*not* Alg. I] and coaches the girls' soccer team.

☞ REFERENCE NOTE: See **Chapter 11: Capitalization** for information on capitalizing the names of school subjects.

Units of Measurement.   In text, spell out the names of units of measurement whether they stand alone or follow a spelled-out number or a numeral. Such names may be abbreviated in tables and notes when they follow a numeral.

TEXT	TABLES, NOTES, ETC.
Traditional	
Fahrenheit	F
foot, feet	ft
gallon(s)	gal
inch(es)	in.
mile(s)	mi
ounce(s)	oz
pint(s)	pt
pound(s)	lb
quart(s)	qt
tablespoon(s)	tbsp *or* T
teaspoon(s)	tsp *or* t
yard(s)	yd

(continued)

RESOURCES

TEXT	TABLES, NOTES, ETC.
Metric	
Celsius	C
centimeter(s)	cm
gram(s)	g
kilogram(s)	kg
liter(s)	l *or* L
milliliter(s)	ml
meter(s)	m
millimeter(s)	mm

Symbols

In text, spell out the words for the symbols % (percent), + (plus), – (minus), = (equals), and ¢ (cents).

EXAMPLE   The local newspaper just raised its price to fifty **cents** (*not* ¢) for the Monday through Saturday editions.

STYLE NOTE   The dollar sign ($) may be used whenever it precedes numerals. Do not substitute the symbol for the words *money* or *dollars.*

EXAMPLES   In Juan A. A. Sedillo's story "Gentleman of Río en Medio," Don Anselmo agrees to sell his house and land for **$1,200** [*not* $ one thousand two hundred].
Felicia makes extra money [*not* $] baby-sitting. What would you do with a million dollars [*not* a million $]?

☞ REFERENCE NOTE: See below through page 464 for information on using figures or words for numbers.

Numbers

(1) Spell out a *cardinal number*—a number that states how many—if it can be expressed in one or two words. Otherwise, use numerals.

EXAMPLES   **eleven** acres   **720** acres
             twenty-two students   **180** students

RESOURCES

three thousand cattle   **3,210** cattle
three fourths of them   **1 1/2** (*or* **1.5**) inches

NOTE   Cardinal numbers in compounds from twenty-one to ninety-nine are hyphenated.

Do not spell out some numbers and use numerals for others in the same context. If any of the numbers require numerals, use numerals for all of them.

INCONSISTENT   The 250-mile flight took only thirty-five minutes.

CONSISTENT   The **250**-mile flight took only **35** minutes.

However, to distinguish between numbers appearing beside each other, spell out one number and use numerals for the other.

EXAMPLE   The recipe calls for **two 8-ounce** containers of plain yogurt.

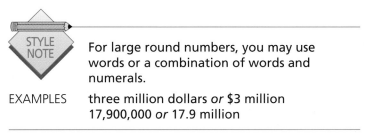

STYLE NOTE   For large round numbers, you may use words or a combination of words and numerals.

EXAMPLES   three million dollars *or* $3 million
17,900,000 *or* 17.9 million

(2) Spell out any number that begins a sentence.

EXAMPLE   **One hundred thirty-two** viewers called the TV station to protest the scheduling change.

If a number appears awkward when spelled out, revise the sentence so that it does not begin with the number.

AWKWARD   One hundred thirty-one thousand seven hundred forty-two people were counted in the last census of our city.

IMPROVED   In the last census of our city, **131,742** people were counted.

(3) Spell out an *ordinal number*—a number that expresses order.

EXAMPLES   Mae Jemison, the **first** [*not* 1st] African American woman astronaut, joined NASA in 1987.

RESOURCES

> Of the four main islands of Japan, Shikoku
> ranks **fourth** [*not* 4th] in geographic area.

(4) Use numerals to express numbers in conventional situations such as those in the following chart.

TYPE OF NUMBER	EXAMPLES	
Names	Margaret II	Arturo Méndez III
Identification	Room 16 Model S–27	pages 109–207
Numbers	Channel 6 lines 1–5	County Road 59
Measurements and Statistics	72 degrees 41.2 ounces 12 feet by 6 feet	7 1/2 yards 74 percent ratio of 4 to 1
Dates	July 29, 1994 *or* 29 July 1994 [*not* July 29th, 1994] the 1990's *or* the 1990s in 1700 in 1993–1994 *or* in 1993–94 from 1990 to 1995 *or* 1990–1995 *or* 1990–95 [*not* from 1990–1995 *or* from 1990–95]	
Addresses	1271 Oleander Way Sacramento, CA 95813-6124	
Times of Day	6:10 P.M. (*or* p.m.) 11:20 A.M. (*or* a.m.)	

NOTE Spell out a number used with *o'clock.*

EXAMPLE   four o'clock

Nonsexist Language

Nonsexist language is language that applies to people in general, both male and female. For example, the nonsexist terms *humanity, human beings,* and *people* can substitute for the gender-specific term *mankind.*

In the past, many skills and occupations were closed to either men or women. Expressions like *seamstress, stewardess,* and *mailman* reflect those limitations. Since most jobs are now held by both men and women, language is adjusting to reflect this change.

When you are referring to humanity as a whole, use nonsexist expressions rather than gender-specific ones. Following are some widely used nonsexist terms that you can use to replace the older, gender-specific ones.

GENDER-SPECIFIC	NONSEXIST
businessman	executive, businessperson
chairman	chairperson, chair
deliveryman	delivery person
fireman	firefighter
foreman	supervisor
housewife	homemaker
mailman	mail carrier
man-made	synthetic, manufactured
manpower	workers, human resources
may the best man win	may the best person win
policeman	police officer
salesman	salesperson, salesclerk
steward, stewardess	flight attendant
watchman	security guard

If the antecedent of a pronoun may be either masculine or feminine, use both masculine and feminine pronouns to refer to it.

EXAMPLES **Anyone** who wants to enter the poster contest should bring **his or her** entry to Room 21 by Friday.
Any **student** may enter **his or her** poster in the contest.

Often, you can often avoid the awkward *his or her* construction (or the alternative *his/her*) by substituting an article (*a, an,* or *the*) for the construction. Or you can rephrase the sentence, using the plural forms of both the pronoun and its antecedent.

EXAMPLES Any interested **student** may submit **a** poster.
All interested **students** may submit **their** posters.

☞ REFERENCE NOTE: See page 89 for more information on alternatives to the *his/her* construction.

RESOURCES

DIAGRAMING SENTENCES

A *sentence diagram* is a picture of how the parts of a sentence fit together and how the words in a sentence are related.

Subjects and Verbs (pages 193–197)

The sentence diagram begins with a horizontal line intersected by a short vertical line, which divides the complete subject from the complete predicate.

EXAMPLE   **Fish swim.**

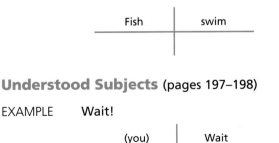

Understood Subjects (pages 197–198)

EXAMPLE   **Wait!**

| (you) | Wait |

Nouns of Direct Address (page 280)

EXAMPLE   **Sit, Fido.**

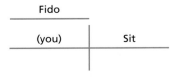

Sentences Beginning with *There* (page 197)

EXAMPLE **There** is a fly in my soup.

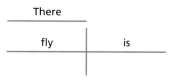

 REFERENCE NOTE: For more information on diagraming *there* in a sentence, see page 470.

Compound Subjects (page 198)

EXAMPLE **Carmen** and **Basil** were fishing.

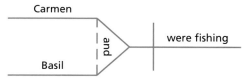

Compound Verbs (page 199)

EXAMPLE They **stopped** and **ate**.

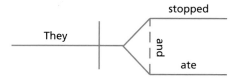

This is how a compound verb is diagramed when the helping verb is not repeated.

EXAMPLE They **are sitting** and **reading**.

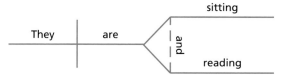

Compound Subjects and Compound Verbs (page 208)

EXAMPLE   **Coaches** and **players jumped** and **cheered.**

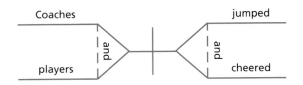

Sometimes parts of a compound subject or a compound verb will be joined by correlative conjunctions. Correlatives are diagramed like this:

EXAMPLE   **Both** Bob **and** Teri can **not only** draw **but also** paint.

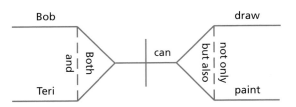

Modifiers (pages 57–60, 65–67, and 136–139)

Adjectives and Adverbs (pages 57–60 and 65–67)

Both adjectives and adverbs are written on slanted lines connected to the words they modify.

EXAMPLE   **That old** clock has **never** worked.

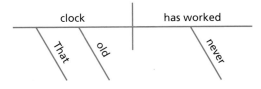

When an adverb modifies an adjective or an adverb, it is placed on a line connected to the word it modifies.

EXAMPLE   This **specially** designed glass **very** seldom breaks.

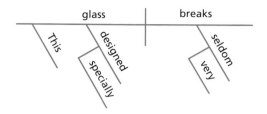

Notice the position of the modifiers in the next example:

EXAMPLE   **Soon** Anne and **her** sister will graduate and will move.

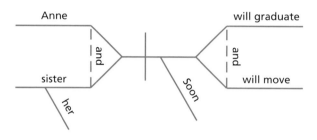

Her modifies only one part of the compound subject: *sister*. *Soon* modifies both parts of the compound verb: *will graduate* and *will move*.

When a conjunction joins two modifiers, it is diagramed like this:

EXAMPLE   The **English** and **Australian** athletes worked **long** and **very hard**.

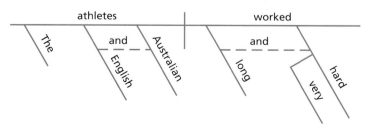

Here and *There* as **Modifiers** (page 197)

EXAMPLES   **Here** comes the parade!

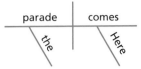

There is my old yearbook.

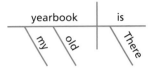

NOTE   Sometimes *there* begins a sentence without modifying a verb. When used in this way, *there* is called an **expletive.** It is diagramed on a line by itself. See page 467.

EXAMPLE   **There** is a foul plot afoot.

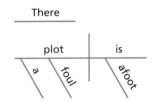

Subject Complements (pages 201–202)

The subject complement is placed on the horizontal line with the subject and verb. It comes after the verb. A line slanting toward the subject separates the subject complement from the verb.

Predicate Nominatives (page 202)

EXAMPLE   Cathedrals are **large churches.**

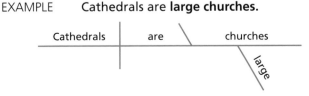

Predicate Adjectives (page 202)

EXAMPLE   Cathedrals are **large**.

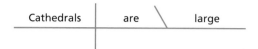

Compound Subject Complements (page 202)

EXAMPLE   My cat is **small** and **quiet**.

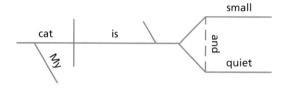

Objects (pages 202–204)

Direct Objects (page 203)

EXAMPLE   We like **music**.

Notice that a vertical line separates the direct object from the verb.

Compound Direct Objects (page 204)

EXAMPLE   We like **plays** and **movies**.

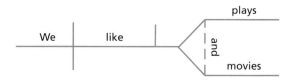

Indirect Objects (page 204)

The indirect object is diagramed on a horizontal line beneath the verb.

EXAMPLE   Pete bought **Mario** a sandwich.

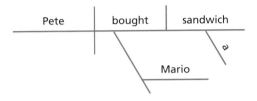

Compound Indirect Objects (page 204)

EXAMPLE   LaTonya gave her **family** and **friends** free
            tickets.

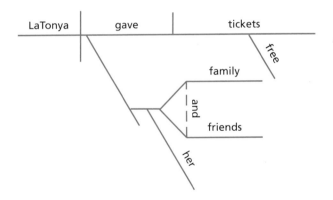

Phrases (pages 155–171)

Prepositional Phrases (pages 156–160)

The preposition is placed on a slanting line leading down
from the word that the phrase modifies. The object of the
preposition is placed on a horizontal line connected to the
slanting line.

EXAMPLES **By chance,** a peasant uncovered a wall **of ancient Pompeii.** [adverb phrase modifying the verb; adjective phrase modifying the direct object]

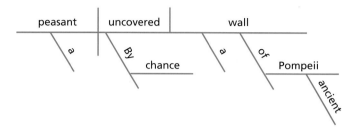

Our team practices late **in the afternoon.** [adverb phrase modifying an adverb]

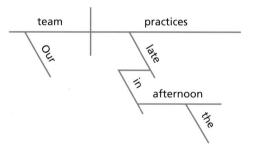

They drove **through the Maine woods** and **into southern Canada.** [two phrases modifying the same word]

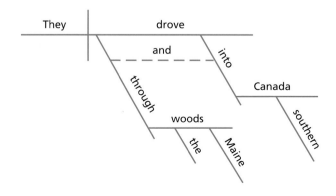

Mom taught the computer game **to my father, my uncles, and me.** [compound object of preposition]

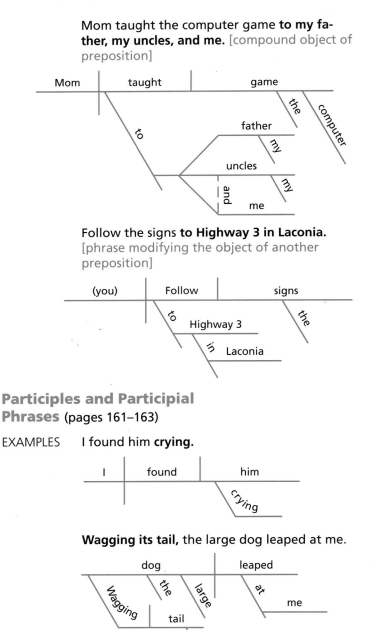

Follow the signs **to Highway 3 in Laconia.**
[phrase modifying the object of another preposition]

Participles and Participial Phrases (pages 161–163)

EXAMPLES I found him **crying.**

Wagging its tail, the large dog leaped at me.

Gerunds and Gerund Phrases (pages 164–166)

EXAMPLES **Walking** is healthful exercise. [gerund used as subject]

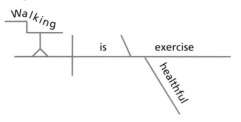

Being tired of the constant cold is a good reason for **taking a vacation in the winter.**
[gerund phrases used as subject and as object of preposition]

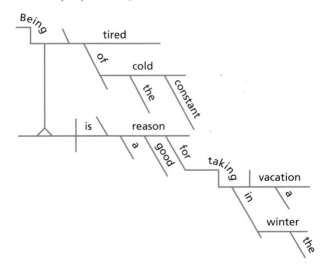

Infinitives, Infinitive Phrases, and Infinitive Clauses (pages 166–169)

EXAMPLES **To leave** would be rude. [infinitive as subject]

To join the Air Force is her longtime ambition.
[infinitive phrase used as subject]

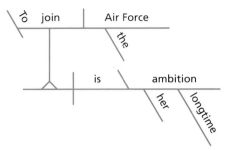

Infinitive phrases and infinitive clauses used as modifiers
are diagramed like prepositional phrases.

I am leaving early **to get the tickets.** [infini-
tive phrase used as adverb]

Our brother helped **us play the game.** [infini-
tive clause with subject, *us; to* omitted]

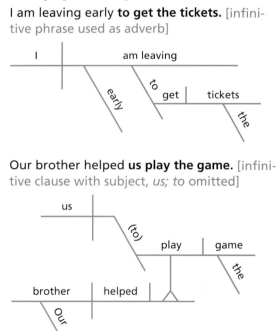

Appositives and Appositive
Phrases (pages 170–171)

Place the appositive in parentheses after the word it identifies or explains.

EXAMPLES   My brother **Josh** is a drummer in the band.

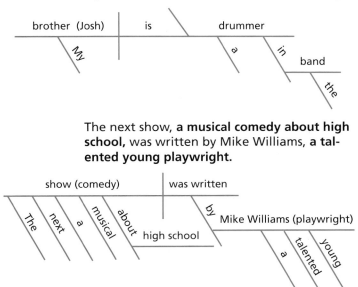

The next show, **a musical comedy about high school,** was written by Mike Williams, **a talented young playwright.**

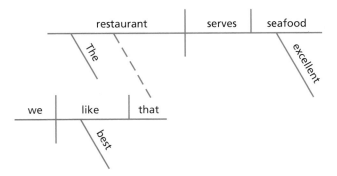

Subordinate Clauses (pages 178–186)

Adjective Clauses (pages 179–181)

An adjective clause is joined to the word it modifies by a broken line leading from the relative pronoun to the modified word.

EXAMPLES   The restaurant **that we like best** serves excellent seafood.

He is the teacher **from whom I take lessons.**

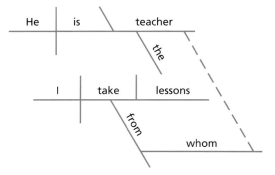

Adverb Clauses (pages 182–184)

Place the subordinating conjunction that introduces the adverb clause on a broken line leading from the verb in the adverb clause to the word the clause modifies.

EXAMPLE   **If you visit Texas,** you should see the Alamo.

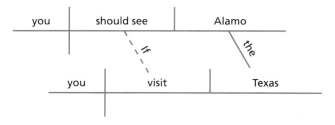

Noun Clauses (pages 185–186)

Noun clauses often begin with introductory words such as *that, what, who,* or *which.* These introductory words may have a function within the dependent clause, or they may simply connect the clause to the rest of the sentence. How a noun clause is diagramed depends on its use in the sentence. It also depends on whether or not the introductory word has a specific function in the noun clause.

EXAMPLES   **What you eat** affects your health. [The noun clause is used as the subject of the independent clause. The introductory word *what* functions as the direct object of the noun clause.]

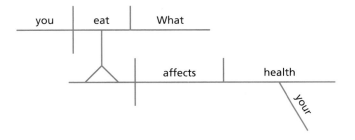

We strongly suspected **that the cat was the thief.** [The noun clause is the direct object of the independent clause. The introductory word *that* does not have a specific function within the noun clause.]

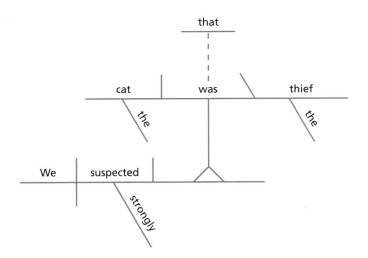

Sometimes the introductory word in a subordinate clause may be omitted. In the example above, the word *that* can be left out: *We strongly suspected the cat was the thief.* To diagram this new sentence, simply omit the word *that* and the solid and broken lines under it from the diagram above. The rest of the diagram stays the same.

Sentences Classified According to Structure (pages 207–209)

Simple Sentences (page 207)

EXAMPLE George Vancouver was exploring the Northwest.

Compound Sentences (pages 207–208)

EXAMPLE James Baldwin wrote many articles for magazines, but he is probably more famous for his novels.

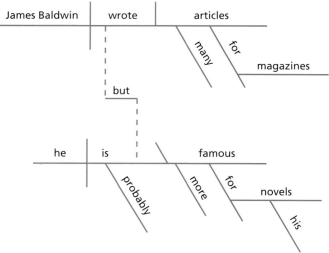

NOTE If the compound sentence has a semicolon and no conjunction, place a straight broken line between the two verbs.

EXAMPLE   Baldwin was a distinguished essayist; his nonfiction works include *Notes of a Native Son.*

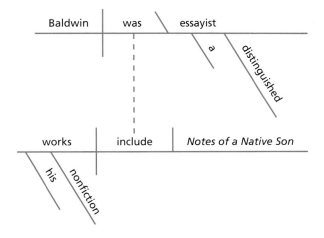

Complex Sentences (page 208)

EXAMPLE   Jaime Escalante always believed that his students could make high scores on the math achievement test.

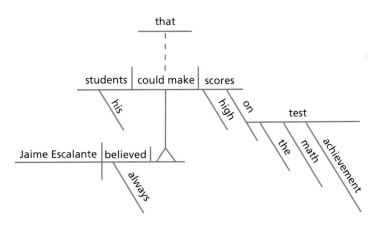

Compound-Complex Sentences (pages 208–209)

EXAMPLE   Before her plane mysteriously disappeared in 1937, Amelia Earhart had already forged the way for women in aviation, and she was later recognized for her achievements.

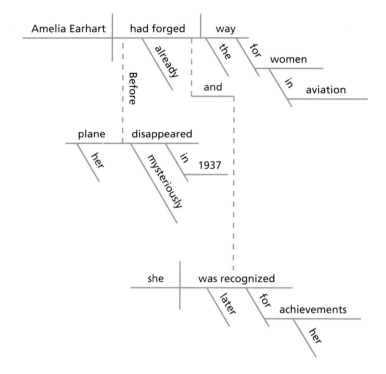

✓ *Quick Check Answer Key*

Chapter 1
Parts of Speech

p. 52 *QUICK CHECK* 1

1. proper noun—author
2. proper noun—country
3. common noun
4. proper noun—mountain
5. common noun
6. common noun
7. common noun
8. proper noun—library
9. common noun
10. proper noun—explorer

p. 57 *QUICK CHECK* 2

1. I—personal; myself—intensive
2. Few—indefinite; much—indefinite
3. What—interrogative; you—personal; that—demonstrative
4. whom—relative; she—personal
5. We—personal; ourselves—reflexive

p. 60 *QUICK CHECK* 3

Adjectives	Word Modified
1. marble	towers
autumn	sky
2. Most	libraries
public	libraries
classic	videotapes
library	card
3. that	store
those	shoes
basketball	shoes
4. late	seventies
Dorothy Hamill	haircut
popular	hairstyle
5. That	cat
Siamese	cat
peculiar	look

p. 64 *QUICK CHECK* 4

1. felt—linking; arrived—intransitive
2. study—transitive; will be—linking
3. could have danced—intransitive; was—linking
4. should charge—transitive
5. made—transitive; ate—intransitive

p. 67 *QUICK CHECK* 5

Adverbs	Words Modified
1. downstairs	are waiting
2. almost	always
always	right
3. quite	recently
recently	visited
4. immediately	exited
5. tonight	are seeing
tomorrow	are seeing

p. 69 *QUICK CHECK* 6

1. aboard, at
2. besides, to
3. Without
4. Prior to
5. in, as, about

p. 70 *QUICK CHECK* 7

1. and—coordinating
2. both . . . and—correlative
3. Whether . . . or—correlative
4. so—coordinating
5. Not only . . . but also—correlative; and—coordinating; and—coordinating

p. 72 *QUICK CHECK* 8

1. verb
2. adjective
3. noun
4. adverb
5. preposition
6. noun
7. verb
8. adjective
9. preposition
10. conjunction

Chapter 2
Agreement

p. 80 *QUICK CHECK* 1

1. eat	4. serves
2. are	5. order
3. makes	

p. 82 *QUICK CHECK* 2

1. look	4. hear
2. was	5. has
3. is	

p. 85 *QUICK CHECK* 3

Subject	Verb
1. class	have
2. prize	was
3. Two thirds	were
4. paragraphs	are
5. Four weeks	is

p. 87 *QUICK CHECK* 4

Subject	Verb
1. *Wild Swans*	tells
2. Philippines	Is
3. freshman, sophomore	is
4. Women in Communication, Inc.	hosts
5. economics	Is

p. 90 *QUICK CHECK* 5

1. his or her—our
2. their—his
3. C
4. their—his
5. they—he or she

Chapter 3
Using Verbs

p. 96   *QUICK CHECK* 1

1. used	4. supposed
2. happened	5. asked
3. frowned	

p. 100 *QUICK CHECK* 2

1. told	4. drunk
2. fallen	5. took
3. saw	

p. 106 *QUICK CHECK* 3

1. a. At a precise moment in the future you will put down your pencils (*future*).
   b. By a precise time you will already have put down your pencils (*future perfect*).

2. a. He worked at the gas station at a definite point in the past (*past*).
   b. He has worked at the gas station at some indefinite time in the past (*present perfect*).

3. a. What caused the computer to crash at a specific point in the past (*past*)?
   b. What has been causing the computer to crash for an indefinite and ongoing period starting in the past

and still continuing
(*present perfect progressive*)?
4. a. Morton was the current
champion last year (*past*).
   b. Morton was a former
champion by last year
(*past perfect*).
5. a. For an ongoing period
starting and ending in the
past, Shelley worked on
her bicycle (*past
progressive*).
   b. For an ongoing period in
the past, which ended
before some other past
action or event, Shelley
worked on her bicycle
(*past perfect progressive*).

p. 107 *QUICK CHECK* 4

Paragraphs should be in past
tense. The verbs that changed
tenses are shown in italics.

[1] To my surprise, Nancy
Chang *decided* to drop by about
five o'clock last Friday.
[2] What she wanted *was* a
fishing companion. She *had
been thinking* about going
fishing all week. [3] As I was
getting my gear together, I
became excited and in my
imagination *saw* the fish on my
line. [4] On our way out to the
lake, clouds *began* to form, and
we knew we *were* in for trouble.
[5] It *rained* all right, for the
whole weekend; the fish were
safe for another week.

p. 113 *QUICK CHECK* 5

1. passive   4. passive
2. passive   5. active
3. active

p. 116 *QUICK CHECK* 6

1. set   4. raised
2. lying   5. laid
3. sat

Chapter 4
Using Pronouns

p. 122 *QUICK CHECK* 1

1. She; we   4. he
2. We; she   5. she; I
3. they

p. 124 *QUICK CHECK* 2

1. me   4. me
2. me   5. her, him
3. them

p. 127 *QUICK CHECK* 3

1. who   4. whom
2. who   5. whom
3. who

p. 129 *QUICK CHECK* 4

1. she   4. We
2. me   5. they
3. us

p. 130 *QUICK CHECK* 5

1. I was surprised
2. it mystified us *or* we
mystified him
3. he is old
4. she has known him *or* we
have known her
5. we read

p. 133 *QUICK CHECK* 6
(*Answers will vary.*)
1. Mavis is absent today
because she has a bad cold.
2. The Glee Club's concert
next Friday should be
enjoyable.

3. I became interested in stamp collecting when I got a stamp from Fiji.
4. This article discusses how teenagers spend their allowances.
5. My mother told my sister to be home early.

Chapter 5
Using Modifiers

p. 140 *QUICK CHECK* 1

Part of Speech	Word Modified
1. adverb	wanted
2. adjective	person
3. adjective	chair
4. adverb	becoming
5. adjective	stew

p. 142 *QUICK CHECK* 2

Comparative	Superlative
1. worse	worst
2. looser	loosest
3. better	best
4. noisier	noisiest
5. more patiently	most patiently

p. 145 *QUICK CHECK* 3

1. . . . the most interesting . . .
2. . . . more than any other sport . . .
3. Today is colder . . .
4. . . . than our next-door neighbor's.
5. . . . more than I call Joe. *or* . . . more than Joe does.

p. 149 *QUICK CHECK* 4

(Answers may vary.)
1. When I was a child, my grandfather taught me how to make corn tortillas.
2. Birds, which like to eat seeds, are kept away from crops by scarecrows.
3. While we were standing on the beach, a school of dolphins suddenly appeared.
4. Chuck went outside with our dog Snickers to trim the hedge and weed the garden.
5. She crossed the river, which was more than a mile wide, on a ferry.

Chapter 6
Phrases

p. 160 *QUICK CHECK* 1

1. about the universe—adj.—modifies *Theories*
   over the years—adv.—modifies *have changed*
2. In the 1920s—adv.—modifies *discovered*
   of galaxies outside the Milky Way—adj.—modifies *existence*
   outside the Milky Way—adj.—modifies *galaxies*
3. inside the bowl of the Big Dipper—adv.—modifies *are*
   of the Big Dipper—adj.—modifies *bowl*
4. among billions throughout the universe—adj.—modifies *one*
   throughout the universe—adj.—modifies *billions*
5. about outer space—adv.—modifies *curious*
   at the extent of space exploration in the modern world—adv.—modifies *amazed*

of space exploration in the modern world—adj.— modifies *extent* in the modern world—adj.— modifies *exploration*

p. 164 *QUICK CHECK* 2

1. standing—them
2. reinforced with steel— concrete
3. spread across the bottom of a deep basement—pad
4. supporting the walls and floors—skeleton
5. Covered with a "skin" of glass and metal—skeleton working—space living—space

p. 166 *QUICK CHECK* 3

1. hunting with a gun—object of a preposition
2. knowing the animals' habits and habitats—subject
3. being quiet—predicate nominative keeping your aim steady— predicate nominative
4. lighting the prey—direct object choosing the correct film— direct object
5. killing it—object of a preposition

p. 169 *QUICK CHECK* 4

1. To dance gracefully—noun
2. to study—noun
3. to fish—adverb
4. to get there—adjective to take the bus—noun
5. [to] open that present—noun

p. 171 *QUICK CHECK* 5

1. a writers' club called Writers,

Inc.—organization
2. fiction or poetry—drafts
3. People from all walks of life—members
4. Alnaba—friend the Navajo—culture
5. a verse form invented by the Japanese—haiku

Chapter 7
Clauses

p. 179 *QUICK CHECK* 1

1. subordinate
2. independent
3. subordinate
4. subordinate
5. independent

p. 182 *QUICK CHECK* 2

1. who were furious about the recent tax increase—modifies *citizens*—used as subject
2. that she entered—modifies *campaign*—used as direct object
3. that surprised everyone in the audience—modifies *announcement*—used as subject
4. which were yellow and tattered from many years of use—modifies *books*—used as subject
5. to whom we took the injured cat—modifies *veterinarian*— used as object of a preposition

p. 184 *QUICK CHECK* 3

1. Although he used only nonviolent methods—under what condition
2. until the government met his requests—when *or* to what extent

3. As India's Congress and people increasingly supported Gandhi's nonviolent program—when *or* how
4. After India's independence was assured—when
5. Because he was loved throughout India and the world—why

p. 186 *QUICK CHECK* 4

1. what time it is—direct object
2. Where I left my keys—subject
3. where the concert will be held—predicate nominative
4. whoever completes the race—indirect object
5. whether we should have a car wash or a bake sale—object of a preposition

Chapter 8
Sentence Structure

p. 193 *QUICK CHECK* 1

1. sentence
2. fragment
3. sentence
4. fragment
5. fragment

p. 199 *QUICK CHECK* 2

1. <u>Did</u> <u>you</u> and your <u>brother</u> <u>watch</u> the Super Bowl?
2. A female <u>vocalist</u> with a throaty voice <u>charmed</u> the audience with her singing.
3. Down the street from our house, there <u>are</u> two <u>bakeries</u>.
4. Please <u>clear</u> the table and <u>load</u> the dishwasher. (you)
5. On the bulletin board located outside the principal's office <u>have been posted</u> the winners' <u>names</u>.

p. 205 *QUICK CHECK* 3

1. eager—predicate adjective
   quiet—predicate adjective
2. Charlene, LaReina—predicate nominative
3. quiet—predicate adjective
   throat—direct object
   speech—direct object
4. Todd, me—indirect object
   instructions—direct object
   scene—direct object
5. Soft, cool—predicate adjective

p. 207 *QUICK CHECK* 4

1. declarative—period
2. declarative—period
3. imperative—period
4. interrogative—question mark
5. exclamatory—exclamation point

p. 209 *QUICK CHECK* 5

1. simple
2. complex
3. compound-complex
4. complex
5. simple

Chapter 9
Writing Complete Sentences

p. 216 *QUICK CHECK* 1

1. C
2. S
3. I
4. V
5. S

p. 218 *QUICK CHECK* 2
(Answers will vary.)

1. She carefully adjusted her helmet before setting foot on the planet.

2. She knew she wanted to explore the craters.
3. Hera saw before her a planet without any signs of life.
4. She was one of three astronauts on their first mission into outer space.
5. After they completed their exploration, they planned to return to Earth.

p. 220 *QUICK CHECK* 3

(Answers will vary.)

1. As we watched the spaceship land, I got a queasy feeling in my stomach.
2. From the spaceship emerged a creature who approached the house in long leaps.
3. The creature greeted us with a shrill cry which startled the dog.
4. Now we always feel a subtle vibration in the ground if we go outside the house.
5. I'll always remember that moment when they handed me a glowing sphere that I held briefly before it disappeared.

p. 223 *QUICK CHECK* 4

(Answers may vary.)

1. The first movie theaters opened in the early 1900s. They were called *nickelodeons*.
2. Thomas Edison was a pioneer in early movie making; he invented the first commercial motion-picture machine.
3. Early movies were silent, but sometimes offscreen actors would fill in the dialogue for the audience.

4. The first sound films were shown in the late 1920s; they marked a milestone in movie-making history.
5. Movies are great entertainment; furthermore, they are also an art form.

Chapter 10
Writing Effective Sentences

p. 230 *QUICK CHECK* 1

(Answers will vary.)

1. Auguste Piccard of Switzerland created an important invention, an airtight gondola.
2. Attached to a balloon, the gondola took Piccard ten miles into the air.
3. Studying electricity, Piccard then made numerous balloon trips.
4. Piccard turned his interest to the ocean depths, designing a deep-sea-diving ship.
5. In 1953, Piccard and his son Jacques went two miles below the surface of the Adriatic Sea.

p. 232 *QUICK CHECK* 2

(Answers will vary.)

1. The Hopi people live in Arizona; they occupy villages called pueblos.
2. Some Hopi carve wooden dolls and dress the dolls in elaborate costumes.
3. The dolls are called kachina dolls, and they have a special meaning for the Hopi.

4. Kachina dolls represent spirits and play an important part in Hopi religious ceremonies.
5. Peace and religion are important to the Hopi people.

p. 234 *QUICK CHECK* 3
(Answers will vary.)
1. The shark is a member of the fish family that includes the largest and fiercest fish.
2. Sharks have long bodies, wedge-shaped heads, and pointed back fins, which sometimes stick out of the water.
3. Although sharks live mostly in warm seas, some sharks have been found in bodies of cold water.
4. The whale shark, which feeds on plankton, is harmless to people.
5. However, many sharks are ruthless killers that feed on flesh.

p. 236 *QUICK CHECK* 4
(Answers will vary.)
1. Paris, the capital of France, is famous for its history, its culture, and its excellent restaurants.
2. C
3. Visiting Notre Dame Cathedral, walking through the Louvre Museum, and seeing the Eiffel Tower are all favorite pastimes of tourists.
4. It is interesting that Paris has always both attracted artists and welcomed refugees.

5. Many famous Americans, including Ernest Hemingway, lived and wrote in Paris during the 1920s.

p. 238 *QUICK CHECK* 5
(Answers will vary.)
1. Alexandre Gustave Eiffel was a famous Frenchman who was born in 1832 and died in 1923.
2. Eiffel, an engineer, designed the Eiffel Tower, which was built for the 1889 World's Fair.
3. Eiffel's chief interest was bridges; the Eiffel Tower displays his bridge-designing skills, as does another familiar historical monument.
4. C
5. Toward the end of his life, Eiffel studied the effects of air on airplanes. In 1912, he built a wind tunnel and an aerodynamics laboratory. Later he conducted experiments from the Eiffel Tower, now a favorite tourist attraction.

p. 241 *QUICK CHECK* 6
(Answers will vary.)
    [1–2] Because of oil pollution and commercial fishing, many penguin species in oceans of the Southern Hemisphere are at risk. [3] Because they are slaughtered for food and their shells, turtles are also endangered. [4] And when people overfish, lobsters, too, become threatened. [5] Increased land development and tourism also

threaten Mediterranean monk seals.

Chapter 11
Capitalization

p. 252 *QUICK CHECK* 1

1. b
2. b
3. a
4. b
5. a

p. 257 *QUICK CHECK* 2

1. Earth, Mars, Jupiter
2. Golden Gate Bridge
3. Lafayette Park, Tallahassee, Florida
4. Wheaties
5. Junior Prom, Jefferson Racquet Club
6. Harvard University
7. Supreme Court
8. Memorial Day, Democratic
9. African American, Newbery Medal
10. *Lusitania*, Ireland

p. 261 *QUICK CHECK* 3

1. Mayor Feinstein
2. "Home on the Range"
3. *C*
4. *C*
5. President Clinton
6. the Roman god Mars
7. my mom and Grandma Higgins
8. my cousin's parents
9. *C*
10. *C*

Chapter 12
Punctuation

p. 271 *QUICK CHECK* 1

1. What a car!

2. We asked who owns that car.
3. Roman troops invaded Britain in 54 B.C.
4. Why do children enjoy using computers?
5. Please explain why so many children enjoy using computers.
6. Did you know paper was invented in 105 B.C.?
7. Watch out for sharks!
8. I was surprised to hear the news.
9. Tell me why you are so upset. *or* . . . upset!
10. Will you please say goodbye to your aunt. *or* . . . aunt?

p. 276 *QUICK CHECK* 2

(Optional commas are underlined.)

1. crafts, books‚
2. *A Raisin in the Sun,* Lorraine Hansberry,
3. airy,
4. hours,
5. *C*

p. 278 *QUICK CHECK* 3

(Optional commas are underlined.)

1. road, large, spider, tarantula, Steve, Alice‚
2. dogs, Labrador retrievers, golden retrievers‚
3. certificate, 7, 1976, Juneau,
4. Yes, fact,
5. above,

p. 282 *QUICK CHECK* 4

1. Whitney, Don,
2. Jennifer,

3. Contest, Drive, City,
4. seeds, course, season, hot,
5. neighbor, Allen,

p. 286 *QUICK CHECK* 5

1. families;
2. toothless whale; bottlenose whale; Arctic whale;
3. breaths; ocean;
4. C
5. whales;

p. 289 *QUICK CHECK* 6

1. novels:
2. C
3. words:
4. 1:16   follows:
5. 8:00   6:00

Chapter 13
Punctuation

p. 297 *QUICK CHECK* 1

1. <u>Argo</u>
2. <u>semper fidelis</u>
3. <u>Dragonsong</u>
4. <u>occurrence</u>
5. <u>The Mikado</u>, <u>Madame Butterfly</u>

p. 303 *QUICK CHECK* 2

1. C
2.   "Race-car driver Janet Guthrie," said Chet, reading from his notes, "is a trained physicist who has spent many years working for an aircraft corporation."
3.   "Who shot that ball?" Coach Larsen wanted to know.
    "I did," came the reply from the small, frail-looking player.

"Good shot," observed the coach, "but always remember to follow your shot to the basket."
    "I tried, but I was screened," the player explained.
4.   "The *Brownsville Beacon,*" the editorial began, "will never support a candidate who tells the taxpayers, 'Vote for me, and I will cut taxes.'
    "The reason is simple: Taxes, just like everything else in this inflationary society, must increase. Any candidate who claims otherwise is either a fool or a liar."
5.   In the interview the candidate said, "I am a very hospitable person."
    "Yes," her husband agreed, "Ralph Waldo Emerson must have been thinking of you when he said, 'Happy is the house that shelters a friend.'"

p. 305 *QUICK CHECK* 3

1. "Essays and Speeches."
2. "Scarborough Fair."
3. "Split Cherry Tree"?
4. "Cheers" or "How to Eat a Poem"?
5. "Tips for Teens"!

Chapter 14
Punctuation

p. 313 *QUICK CHECK* 1

1. Miss Williams' car
2. the lionesses' cubs
3. the cattle's horns
4. its dimensions
5. her mother-in-law's and her cousin's businesses

6. our class's field trip
7. my brother-in-law's job
8. Isabel's and my project
9. two weeks' pay
10. the FBI's investigation

p. 315 *QUICK CHECK* 2

1. "You've changed," she said.
2. World War II ended in '45.
3. Who's coming to the party?
4. Did Amanda say that she'll be there?
5. Well, she said she'd try to make it by six o'clock.
6. We're hoping to see you there.
7. It's too bad we'll be out of town that day.
8. Don't forget to cross your *t*'s and dot your *i*'s.
9. You're making all A's and B's this year, aren't you?
10. Some of your *u*'s look like *o*'s.

p. 318 *QUICK CHECK* 3

1. ex-governor
2. all-American
3. twenty-five; forty-fifth
4. C
5. one-half

p. 321 *QUICK CHECK* 4

1. . . . thank—"
2. . . . surprised—no, make that amazed—to . . .
3. . . . (1892–1950) . . .
4. "I—I just . . .
5. . . . (You will read more about Free States in Chapter 5.)
6. Killer whales (they're the ones with the black and white markings) . . .

7. . . . engagement—it's a secret, by the way—will . . .
8. . . . valedictorian—that is, the student with the highest average—will . . .
9. . . . Brooks (a native of Topeka, Kansas) has . . .
10. . . . calendar—you know the type—hung . . .

Chapter 15
Spelling and Vocabulary

p. 335 *QUICK CHECK* 1

1. unnecessary
2. illegal
3. misspell
4. overrate
5. occasionally
6. dully
7. wholly
8. cleanliness
9. meanness
10. loneliness

p. 337 *QUICK CHECK* 2

1. becoming
2. guidance
3. careful
4. satisfied
5. denial
6. swimmer
7. acceptance
8. numbering
9. excelled
10. riotous

p. 341 *QUICK CHECK* 3

1. guesses
2. tongues
3. navies
4. cuffs
5. theories
6. sopranos
7. stereos
8. editors in chief
9. layoffs
10. moose

Index

INDEX

INDEX

INDEX

D

INDEX

INDEX

Q

INDEX

INDEX

W

INDEX

Acknowledgments

For permission to reprint copyrighted material, grateful acknowledgment is made to the following sources:

Addison-Wesley Publishing Company, Inc.: From *Magic's Touch* by Earvin "Magic" Johnson, Jr. and Roy S. Johnson. Copyright © 1989 by Earvin "Magic" Johnson and Roy S. Johnson.

American Heritage Magazine, a division of Forbes Inc.: From "The Business of America: Financial Folklore" by John Steele Gordon from *American Heritage,* vol. 42, no. 1, Feb/March 1991. Copyright © 1991 by Forbes Inc.

Ronald F. Arias: From "El Mago" by Ron Arias from *El Grito: A Journal of Contemporary Mexican-American Thought,* Spring 1970.

The Boston Globe: From "A romantic 'Ghost' to believe in" by Jay Carr from the *Living Arts Section* of *The Boston Globe,* July 13, 1990. Copyright © 1990 by The Boston Globe.

Carol Brissie on behalf of William K. Zinsser: From "Trust Your Material" from *On Writing Well,* Third Edition, by William K. Zinsser. Copyright © 1976, 1980, 1985, 1988 by William K. Zinsser.

Clarion Books, a division of Houghton Mifflin Co.: From *The Masters of Horror* by Daniel Cohen. Copyright © 1984 by Daniel Cohen. All rights reserved.

Daniel Cohen and Henry Morrison, Inc.: From *The Encyclopedia of Monsters* by Daniel Cohen. Copyright © 1982 by Daniel Cohen.

Doubleday, a division of Bantam Doubleday Dell Publishing Group, Inc.: From "The Birds" from *Kiss Me Again Stranger* by Daphne du Maurier. Copyright 1952 by Daphne du Maurier.

Marjory Stoneman Douglas: From *The Everglades: River of Grass* by Marjory Stoneman Douglas. Copyright © 1947 by Marjory Stoneman Douglas.

Ann Elmo Agency, Inc.: From *Leiningen Versus the Ants* by Carl Stephenson.

HarperCollins Publishers, Inc.: From *The Writing Life* by Annie Dillard. Copyright © 1989 by Annie Dillard.

International Creative Management: From "The

Portable Phonograph" from *The Watchful Gods and Other Stories* by W. Van Tilburg Clark. Copyright © 1941, 1969 by Walter Van Tilburg Clark.

Alfred A. Knopf, Inc.: From "Poison" from *Someone Like You* by Roald Dahl. Copyright © 1950 by Roald Dahl.

Los Angeles Times Syndicate: From "Why we love our cartoon characters" by Leonard Maltin from *TV Guide*, June 9, 1990. Copyright © 1990 by Los Angeles Times Syndicate.

William Morrow and Company, Inc.: From *Imponderables: The Solution to the Mysteries of Everyday Life* by David Feldman. Copyright © 1986 by David Feldman.

The New York Times Company: From "For Young and Old, a Pocket Paradise" by Kathleen Teltsch from *The New York Times*, April 30, 1989. Copyright © 1989 by The New York Times Company.

Newsweek, Inc.: From "A Hot Time in Toontown Tonight" by Michael Reese from *Newsweek*, June 27, 1988. Copyright © 1988 by Newsweek, Inc. All rights reserved.

Omni Publications International, Ltd.: From "Apocalypse, How?" by Jane Bosveld and from "For

Goodness Sake?" by Howard Wornom from *Omni*, vol. 12, no. 3, December 1989. Copyright © 1989 by Omni Publications International, Ltd.

People Weekly: From "Who Framed Roger Rabbit" from "Picks & Pans" from *People Weekly*, June 27, 1988. Copyright © 1988 by Time Inc.

Random House, Inc.: From "Woman Work" from *And Still I Rise* by Maya Angelou. Copyright © 1978 by Maya Angelou. From *Extinction: The Causes and Consequences of the Disappearance of Species* by Paul and Anne Ehrlich. Copyright © 1981 by Paul R. Ehrlich and Anne H. Ehrlich.

Rodale Press, Inc.: From "Are Road Bikes Dead?" by Scott Martin from *Bicycling*, vol. 31, no. 5, June 1990. Copyright © 1990 by Rodale Press, Inc.

The Saturday Evening Post: From "Guiltless Snacks" from "Heart Beat" from *The Saturday Evening Post*, vol. 262, no. 3, April 1990. Copyright © 1990 by The Saturday Evening Post.

Simon & Schuster, Inc.: From *Everything In Its Path* by Kai T. Erikson. Copyright © 1976 by Kai T. Erikson.

Sterling Lord Literistic, Inc.: From "The Phantom of Yazoo" from *North Toward Home* by

Willie Morris. Copyright © 1967 by Willie Morris.

Gary A. Taubes: From "Boxer with a Future" by Gary A. Taubes from *The Atlantic,* vol. 254, no. 2, August 1984. Copyright © 1984 by Gary A. Taubes.

Mrs. Edwin Way Teale: From "The Death of a Tree" from *Dune Boy* by Edwin Way Teale. Copyright 1943, © 1971 by Edwin Way Teale.

Thames and Hudson Ltd.: From *Mummies, Myth and Magic in Ancient Egypt* by Christine El Mahdy. Copyright © 1989 by Christine El Mahdy.

Webster's New World Dictionaries, a Division of Simon & Schuster, New York: Entry, "indulge," from *Webster's New World Dictionary of American English,* Third College Edition. Copyright © 1988 by Webster's New World Dictionaries, a Division of Simon & Schuster.

The H. W. Wilson Company: Entries, "Pop Art"–"Popular Culture," from *Readers' Guide to Periodical Literature,* May 1990, Vol. 90, No. 5, p. 494. Copyright © 1990 by the H. W. Wilson Company.

The following excerpts also appear in *Holt High School Handbook 1.*

From "The Mute Sense" from *A Natural History of the Senses* by Diane Ackerman. Copyright © 1990 by Diane Ackerman. Published by Random House, Inc.

From "Work Without Hope" by Samuel Taylor Coleridge.

From *The Sayings of Confucius* by Confucius.

From *How to Shoot an Amateur Naturalist* by Gerald Durrell. Copyright © 1984 by Gerald Durrell. Published by Little, Brown and Company.

From "The Interesting Narrative of the Life of Olaudah Equiano," 1791.

From *Among My People* by Jovita González, as it appeared in "Shelling Corn by Moonlight" from *Tone the Bell Easy,* edited by J. Frank Dobie from *Publications of the Texas Folklore Society,* Number X, 1932. Copyright 1932 by Texas Folklore Society.

Quote from the 1961 Inaugural Address by John F. Kennedy.

From "Mother" from *Sarah Phillips* by Andrea Lee. Copyright © 1984 by Andrea Lee. Published by Random House, Inc.

From "NBC Nightly News," June 22, 1990. Copyright 1990 by National Broadcast Company, Inc.

From "Drinking and Bathing" from *The Bird Feeder Book: An Easy Guide to Attracting, Identifying, and Understanding Your Feeder Birds* by Donald and Lillian Stokes. Copyright © 1987 by Donald W. Stokes and Lillian Q. Stokes. Published by Little, Brown and Company.

From "O Captain! My Captain!" by Walt Whitman, 1865.

ILLUSTRATION CREDITS

Ram Garza—cover

Tom Gianni—28, 112, 127, 147, 237, 295, 327

Linda Kelen—106, 261, 342

Martin Kornick—62, 142, 143, 413

Rich Lo—269, 366, 397

Executive Editor: Mescal Evler

Managing Editor: Robert R. Hoyt

Project Editor: Amy Strong

Editorial Staff: Laura Britton, Max Farr, Karen Forrester, Connie Giles, Guy Holland, Eileen Joyce, Christy McBride, Kathleen Magor, Michael Neibergall, Amy Simpson, Elizabeth Smith, Atietie Tonwe

Editorial Support Staff: Carla Beer, Margaret Guerrero, Stella Galvan, Ruth Hooker, Pat Stover

Editorial Permissions: Catherine Paré, Janet Harrington

Design, Photo Research, and Production: Pun Nio, *Senior Art Director;* Diane Motz, *Senior Designer;* Cassandra Lien, *Cover Design;* Beth Prevelige, *Production Manager;* Joan Eberhardt, *Production Assistant;* Debra Saleny, *Photo Research Manager;* Angi Cartwright, *Photo Coordinator;* Carol Martin, *Electronic Publishing Manager;* Maria Homic, Mercedes Newman, *Electronic Publishing Staff*

PE Design and Production: Preface, Inc.